ROAD ATLAS BRITAIN

ROAD ATLAS BRITAIN

John Bartholomew & Son Ltd.

Printed and Published in Scotland by John Bartholomew & Son Ltd.

New Edition Revised 1981
Reprinted 1982
ISBN 0 7028 0419 3
8711X

John Bartholomew & Son Ltd
Duncan Street
Edinburgh
EH9 1TA

FOREWORD

Britain is a land of contrasts, small in physical extent - at least in world terms -yet great in diversity. Physically it is a country of mountains and plains, hills and valleys, of rugged bleakness and gentle fertility. Economically diverse, in agriculture and industry: cottage industries and multi-national corporations, crofting and high technology farming exist virtually side by side in this small land. Here is a nation rich in history and varied in culture even in this age of encroaching homogeneity. How best to explore and discover this diversity of land and nation is a tantalising problem. The Road Atlas Britain captures and interprets this diversity in maps and diagrams. It's scope is wide, it's range of interest extending from the student to the tourist, from the school pupil to the motorist. It's easily distinguishable sections include detailed maps of Britain with up-to-date road coverage, a section of plans of major towns and cities, an easy reference index and sections on London and on the economy and industry in Britain. This and much more make the Road Atlas Britain a reference work which is a useful as well as accurate guide to the diversity of Britain.

John C. Bartholomew

CONTENTS

TOURING MAPS

x

KEY TO MAPS

Outer Hebrides, Orkney and
Shetland at 1:600 000

Scale 1:3 000 000

Motorways
Main Roads

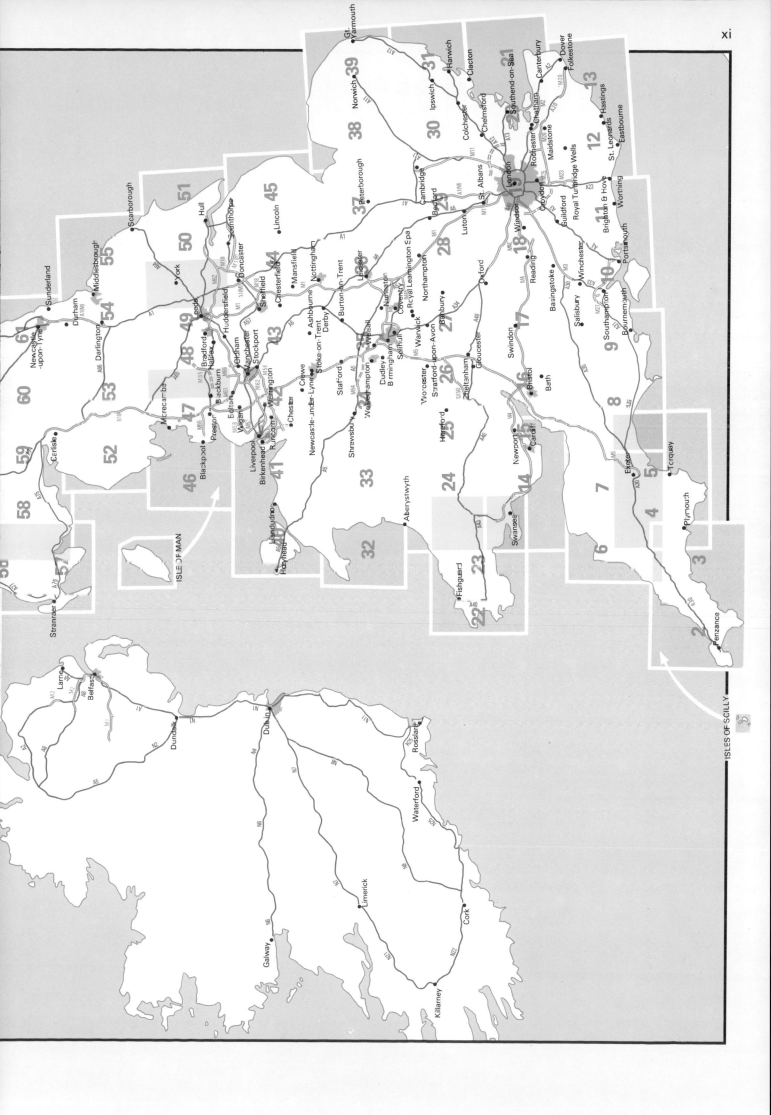

ISLE OF MAN

ISLES OF SCILLY

Stranraer
Larne
Belfast
M2
A6
M1
A1
Dundalk
N2
A5
M3
Dublin
N4
N7
N6
Rosslare
N8
Limerick
N6
N25
Waterford
N24
N21
Galway
N20
Cork
N22
Killarney

Penzance
Plymouth
Torquay
Exeter
Swansea
Fishguard
Aberystwyth
Newport
Cardiff
Bristol
Bath
Hereford
Gloucester
Cheltenham
Worcester
Stratford-upon-Avon
Warwick
Birmingham
Dudley
Wolverhampton
Walsall
Solihull
Coventry
Royal Leamington Spa
Banbury
Northampton
Oxford
Swindon
Reading
Basingstoke
Salisbury
Winchester
Southampton
Bournemouth
Portsmouth
Brighton & Hove
Worthing
Eastbourne
St. Leonards
Hastings
Royal Tunbridge Wells
Guildford
Windsor
London
Croydon
Maidstone
Rochester
Chatham
Canterbury
Dover
Folkestone
St. Albans
Luton
Bedford
Cambridge
Peterborough
Chelmsford
Southend-on-Sea
Colchester
Clacton
Harwich
Ipswich
Norwich
Gt. Yarmouth
Leicester
Nuneaton
Burton-on-Trent
Derby
Stoke-on-Trent
Stafford
Crewe
Newcastle-under-Lyme
Shrewsbury
Chester
Runcorn
Warrington
Wigan
Bolton
Liverpool
Birkenhead
Llandudno
Holyhead
Preston
Blackburn
Blackpool
Morecambe
Carlisle
Lancaster
Burnley
Halifax
Bradford
Leeds
Huddersfield
Manchester
Stockport
Oldham
Sheffield
Chesterfield
Mansfield
Nottingham
Lincoln
Doncaster
Southport
Hull
York
Scarborough
Middlesbrough
Darlington
Durham
Sunderland
Newcastle-upon-Tyne

Explanation to Symbols

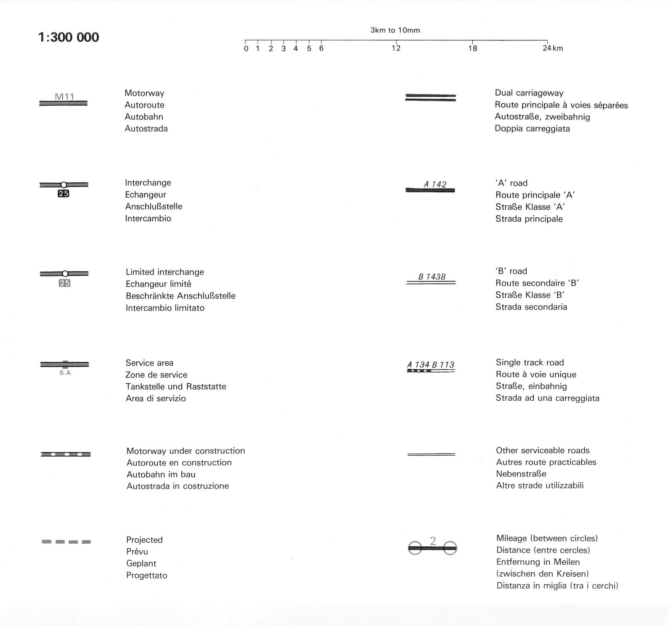

1:300 000

3km to 10mm

0 1 2 3 4 5 6   12   18   24 km

Motorway
Autoroute
Autobahn
Autostrada

Dual carriageway
Route principale à voies séparées
Autostraße, zweibahnig
Doppia carreggiata

Interchange
Echangeur
Anschlußstelle
Intercambio

A 142 'A' road
Route principale 'A'
Straße Klasse 'A'
Strada principale

Limited interchange
Echangeur limité
Beschränkte Anschlußstelle
Intercambio limitato

B 1438 'B' road
Route secondaire 'B'
Straße Klasse 'B'
Strada secondaria

S.A. Service area
Zone de service
Tankstelle und Raststatte
Area di servizio

A 134 B 113 Single track road
Route à voie unique
Straße, einbahnig
Strada ad una carreggiata

Motorway under construction
Autoroute en construction
Autobahn im bau
Autostrada in costruzione

Other serviceable roads
Autres route practicables
Nebenstraße
Altre strade utilizzabili

Projected
Prévu
Geplant
Progettato

2 Mileage (between circles)
Distance (entre cercles)
Entfernung in Meilen
(zwischen den Kreisen)
Distanza in miglia (tra i cerchi)

10 miles to 2.1 inches

0 1 2 3 4 5   10   15 miles

Feet

Track
Piste
Fahrweg
Strada non pavimentata

Canal
Canal
Kanal
Canale

3000

Path
Sentier
Pfad
Sentiero

Church
Eglise
Kirche
Chiesa

2000

1000

Car ferry
Bac pour autos
Autofähre
Autotraghetto

County boundary
Limite de comté
Grafschaftsgrenze
Confine di contea

500

Passenger ferries
Bac pour piétons
Personenfähre
Traghetto per passenggeri

△ 2450 ·167

Height (in feet)
Altitude
Höhe
Altitudine

100

Principal civil airport
Aérodrome civil principal
Verkehrsflughafen
Aeroporto civile principale

75

Page continuation
Continuation à la page
Anschlußseite
Pagina di continuazione

Sea
level

Below
Sea
Level

Railway (passenger)
Chemin de fer (voyageurs)
Eisenbahn (Personenverkehr)
Ferrovie (passeggeri)

Certain built-up areas
Terrain bâti
bebaute Fläche
Agglomerati urbani

Making More of Maps

A map is a handy aid or tool and, like other instruments, its usefulness will be greatly improved by understanding how it works. It is not difficult to find out how to gain greater enjoyment and benefit from maps into which the maker has stowed an amazing variety of interesting information.

Try looking at maps this way. Maps are really pictures of the world about us. Just as pictures use conventions, so do maps. It would be surprising to find a landscape painting the same size as the real landscape and equally surprising to find a map drawn at the same size as the ground it described. Both maps and pictures are drawn much smaller than reality. By this means a map can show huge areas on a small piece of paper. The whole world can be seen at once on one small page. Such a view is impossible in reality.

Again, just like a painter, the mapmaker will select those items of the landscape he wishes to emphasise. He may choose roads, for instance, and deliberately leave out fences, walls and hedges. He may choose to show political boundaries which, though present, cannot actually be seen on the ground. In this way he makes his map so that it will be most helpful to the user who reads it. The map reader's job is to build up, in his mind's eye, a picture of the landscape from the details the mapmaker has provided as clues. This making up of a sort of 'identikit' picture of the landscape from the map can be an exciting process - and one which will become

more fascinating every time you try it. Take a map and try it out on a journey.

Before starting out it is a good idea to get to know how the mapmaker helps to make map reading easier.

Scale: Scale is simple to understand. It is the means by which the mapmaker tells the user how much smaller than reality the map is. Some idea of the scale can be gauged by simply looking carefully at the map itself. If towns, for instance, are shown by small dots or rings and not by their true shape, then we must be dealing with a map at quite a small scale. If, on the other hand, buildings are shown in great detail, then the scale must be quite large. To help us be more exact, a scale line is provided by the mapmaker in the margin or on the map itself. This is drawn as a straight line with divisions representing miles or kilometres at the size they would be if drawn on the map. By means of these scale lines we can make measurements of distance on the map. If the scale line shows a mile drawn as small as one inch, then we can say that one mile on the ground is shown by one inch on the map. If a kilometre is drawn at the length of one centimetre, then the map scale is one centimetre (on the map) equal to one kilometre (on the ground). In shorter form this might be written 1cm:1km, or because there are 100 000 centimetres in one kilometre, 1cm:100 000cm. This is in fact written on maps as 1:100 000 as the relationship between one unit on the map

and 100 000 of the same units on the ground is all that is required. In the same way the scale of 1 inch to 1 mile is shown as 1:63 360, because there are 63 360 inches in one mile. Symbols: Symbols are part of the language of maps. They enable the mapmaker to simplify his map and make it clearer to read. Towns, on small scale maps, are often shown by symbols such as dots or rings to pinpoint their actual position. Churches are frequently shown by small crosses. Railway lines and even roads are shown symbolically for otherwise they would be too small to show up. Understanding the symbols is easy. The mapmaker supplies an Explanation or Key (sometimes called a Legend) which explains all the symbols he has used on the map. This summary of what the map shows is a great help in map reading. Get into the habit of using it.

There are many other aspects of map using which can be obtained from books about map reading, and from actual experience. The most important thing is to go out and try using maps. A simple car journey can be made much more interesting by planning it out beforehand with small scale maps which cover the whole route in a small page. An overall picture of what you can expect to find on the way can be quickly obtained. When making the journey maps at the scale

of, say, 1:300 000 will be helpful. On such a map you can readily see the road on which you will be travelling. You can build up a picture of the road which lies ahead and the countryside round about you. You can see the point on your route where you will pass under a railway bridge, or where you will cross a county boundary. You can keep your driver informed about road numbers and whether or not roads he will be following will be main roads or minor roads. What sort of situations he is likely to experience at road junctions on the route ahead, can be described by using the map.

By adding your own background knowledge, you can increase the pleasure obtained from your maps. Place names take on a new significance and often describe the origins of the place. Ironbridge, for example is the site of the first ever iron bridge - which is still there! Maps show where the places are but they often help to show why these places are there too. In a country like Britain, history as well as geography can be seen on maps. Roman roads can still be seen and followed on maps. Just as history and geography mingle on the map, many other subjects do too. By using maps more frequently, you can go on finding out more and more about the landscape round about you - or the whole world itself.

A decorative panel from Edward Wright's world map of 1599 - helping the user to make more of his map.

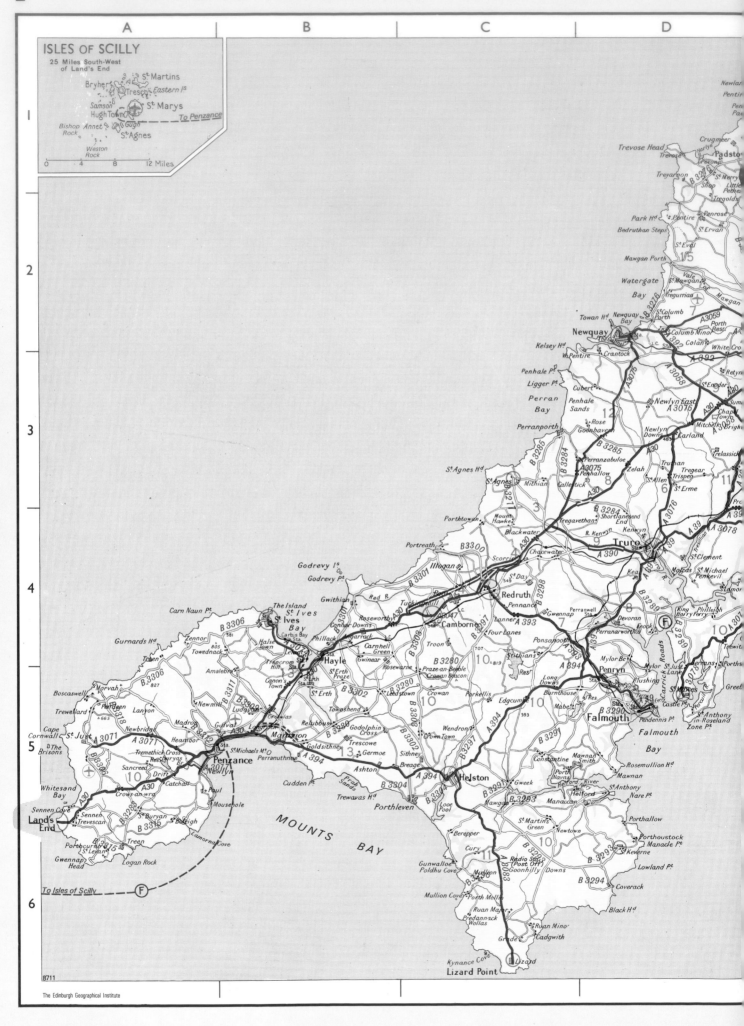

2

ISLES OF SCILLY
25 Miles South-West
of Land's End

St Martins
Bryher Tresco Eastern Is
Samson St Marys
Hugh Town To Penzance
Bishop Annet Gugh
Rock St Agnes
Weston
Rock

0   4   8   12 Miles

A   B   C   D

MOUNTS BAY

Land's End

To Isles of Scilly (F)

Penzance
Newlyn
Mousehole

St Just
Sennen
Sennen Cove

Whitesand
Bay

Cape
Cornwall

St Ives
Bay
St Ives
Carbis Bay

Hayle

Camborne

Redruth

Truro

Newquay

Perran
Bay

Perranporth

St Agnes

Falmouth
Bay

Falmouth

Penryn

Helston

Lizard Point
Lizard

Trevose Head

Padstow

8711

The Edinburgh Geographical Institute

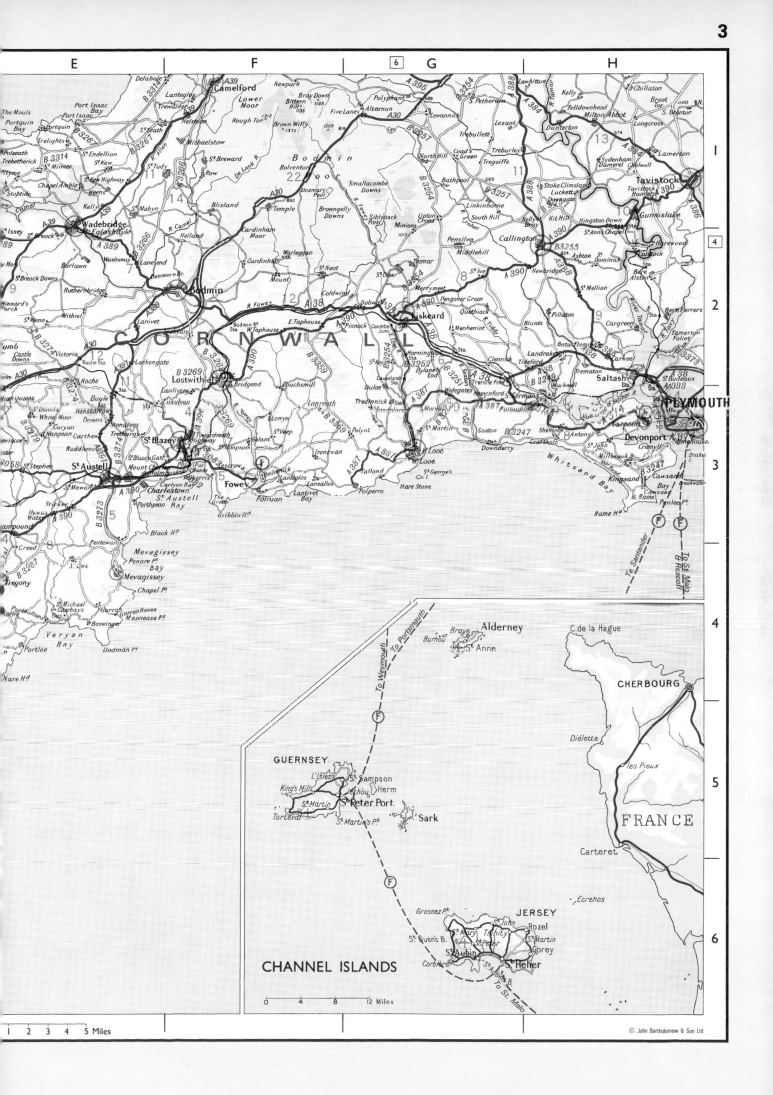

E F 6 G H

1

4

2

3

4

5

6

CORNWALL

Camelford

Wadebridge
Egloshayle

Bodmin

Lostwithiel

St Blazey

St Austell
Charlestown

Fowey

Mevagissey
Mevagissey Bay

Liskeard

Callington

Saltash

PLYMOUTH

Devonport

Tavistock

Gunnislake

Whitsand Bay

To Santander

To St Malo & Roscoff

To Weymouth

To Portsmouth

Alderney
St Anne
Braye
Burhou

C. de la Hague

CHERBOURG

Diélette

Iles Pieux

FRANCE

Carteret

GUERNSEY
L'Islet
St Sampson
Herm
King's Mills
Jethou
St Martin
St Peter Port
Torteval
St Martin's Pt
Sark

Ecrehos

Grosnez Pt
St John
Rozel
JERSEY
St Mary
Trinity
St Peter
St Ouen's B.
St Aubin
St Martin
Gorey
Corbière
St Helier
St Aubin's B.
To St Malo

CHANNEL ISLANDS

0 4 8 12 Miles

1 2 3 4 5 Miles

© John Bartholomew & Son Ltd

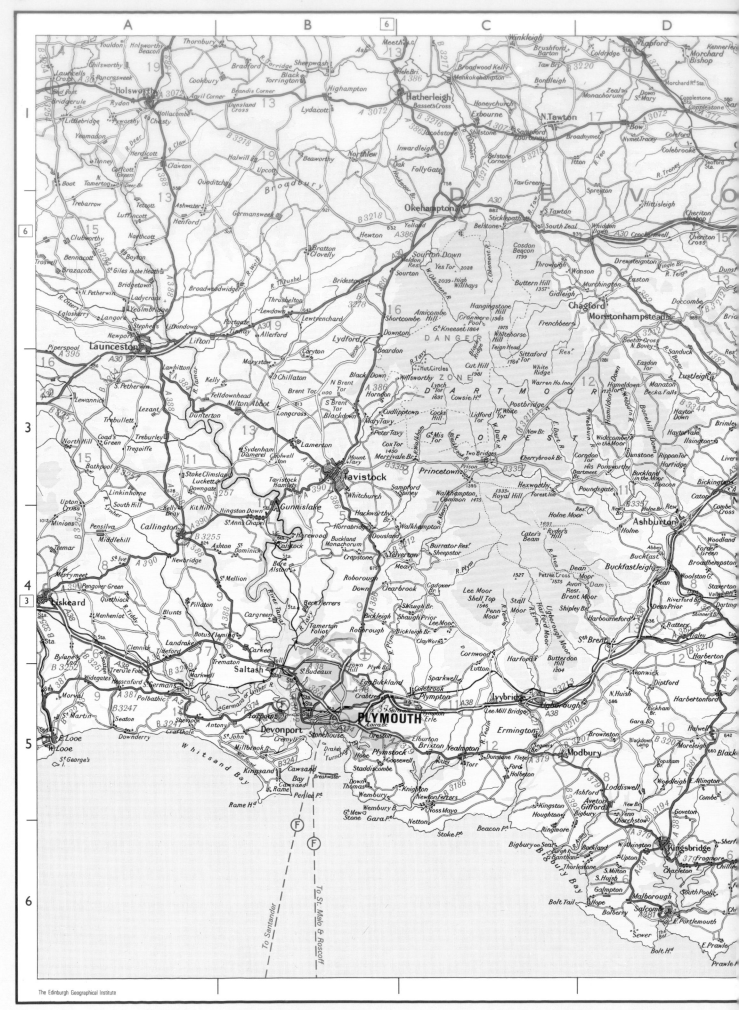

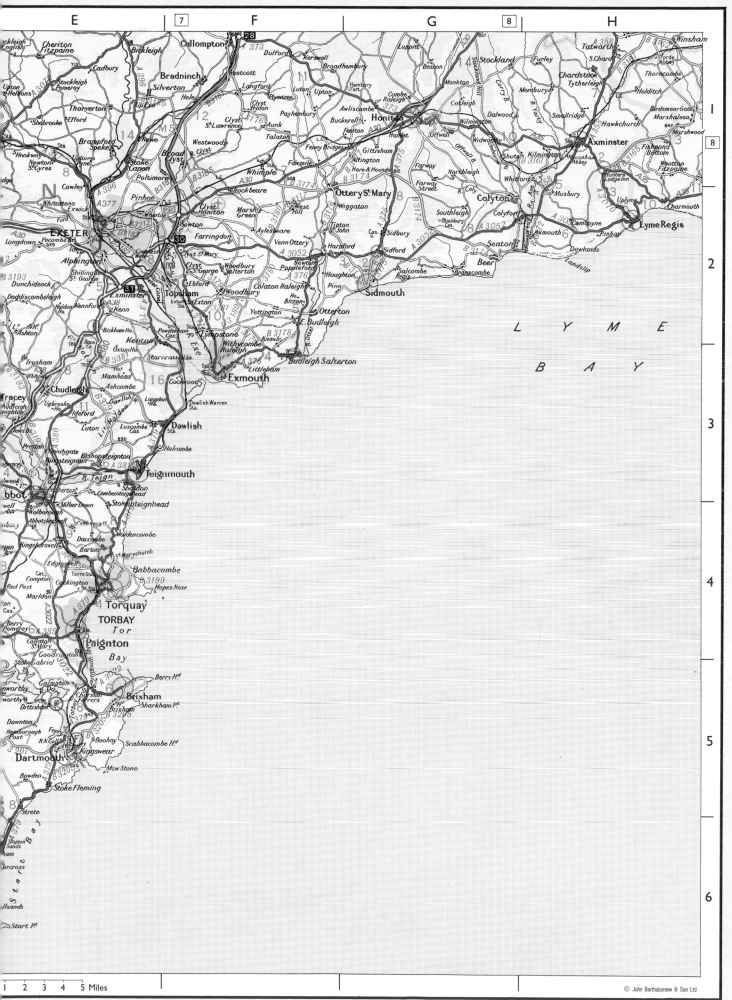

5

E 7 F G 8 H

Scale: 1 2 3 4 5 Miles

© John Bartholomew & Son Ltd

6

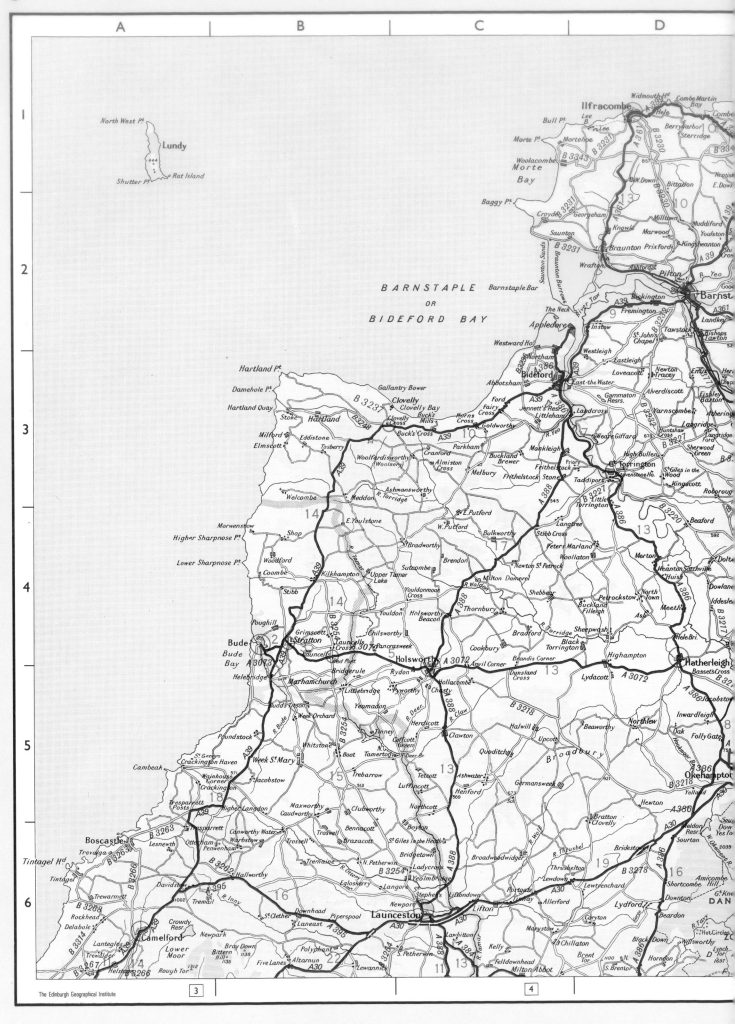

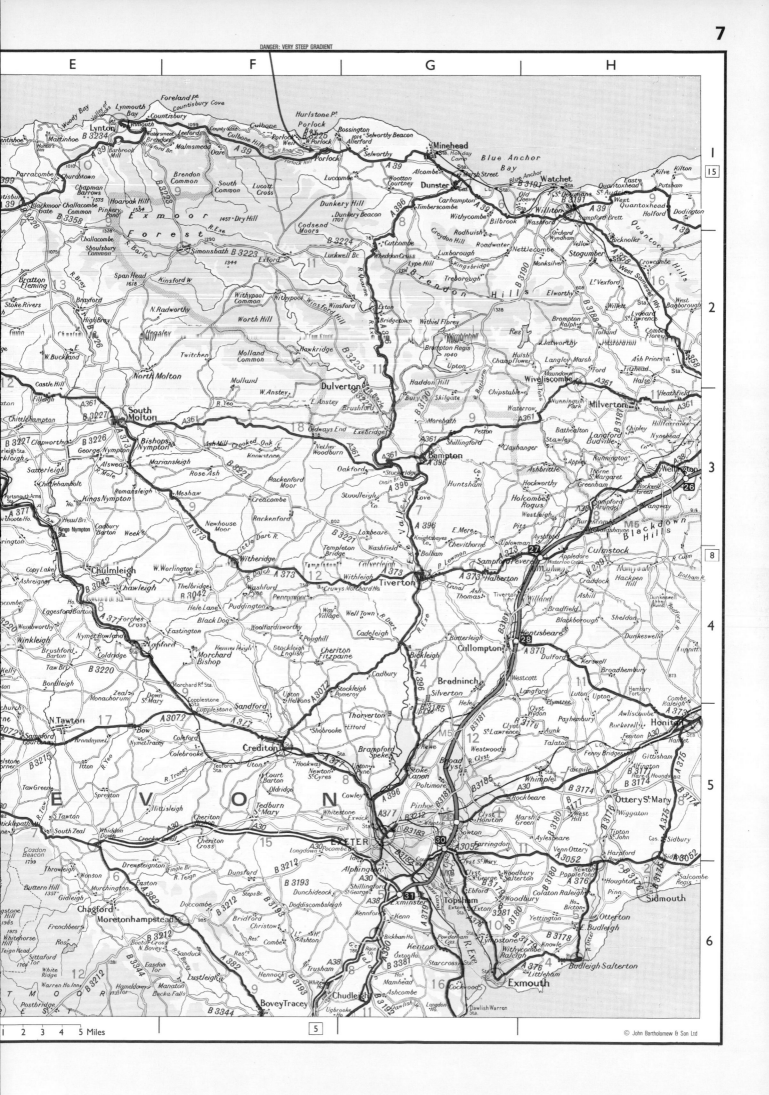

DANGER: VERY STEEP GRADIENT

E   F   G   H

© John Bartholomew & Son Ltd

1 2 3 4 5 Miles

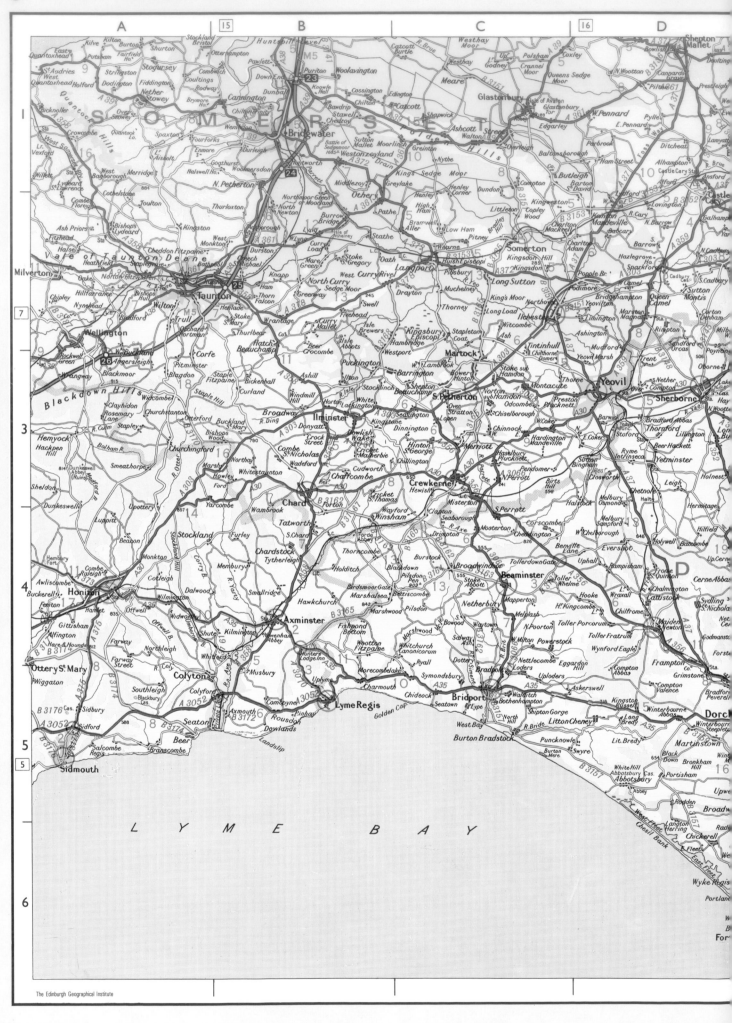

A 15 B C 16 D

L Y M E B A Y

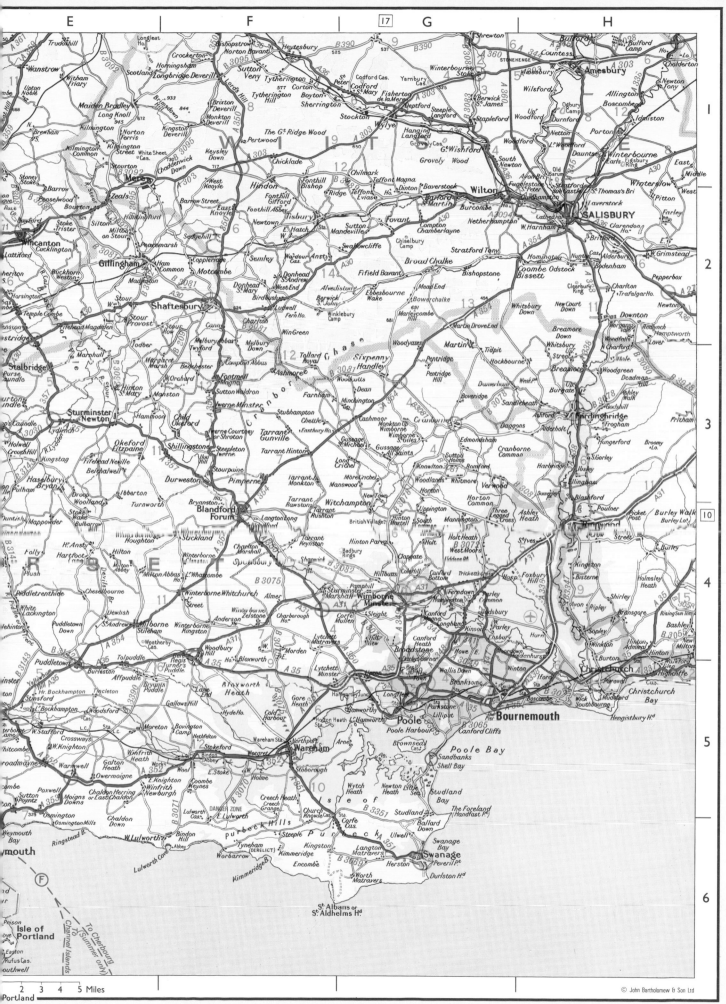

E   F   17   G   H

1

2

3

10

4

5

6

SALISBURY

Amesbury

Wilton

Shaftesbury

Blandford Forum

Wimborne Minster

Poole

BOURNEMOUTH

Christchurch

Wareham

Swanage

Isle of Portland

2   3   4   5 Miles
Portland

© John Bartholomew & Son Ltd

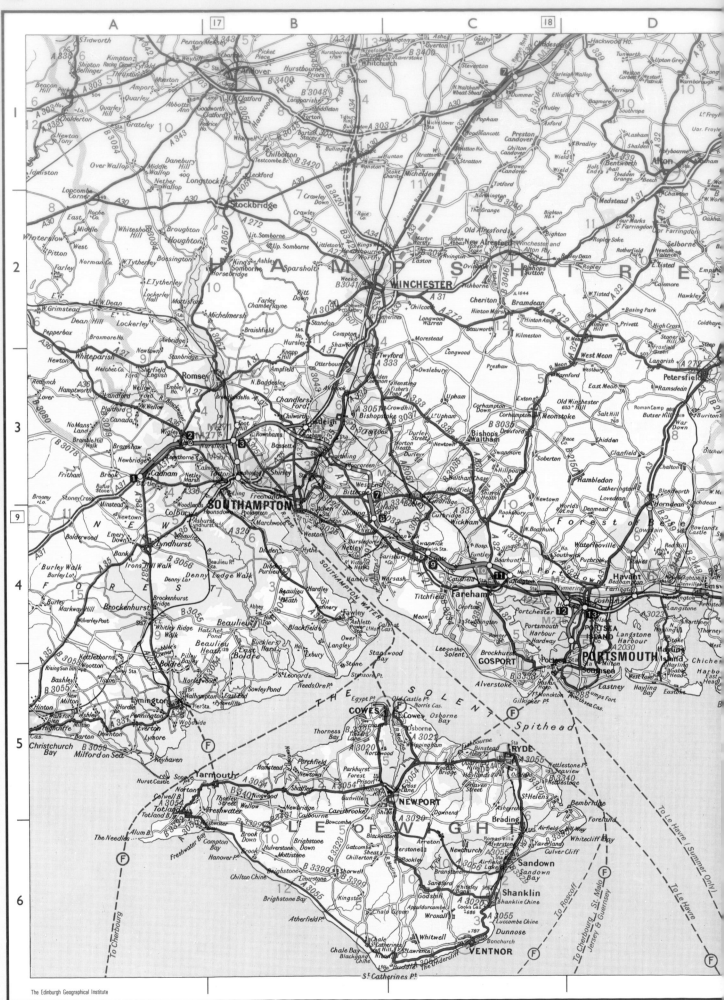

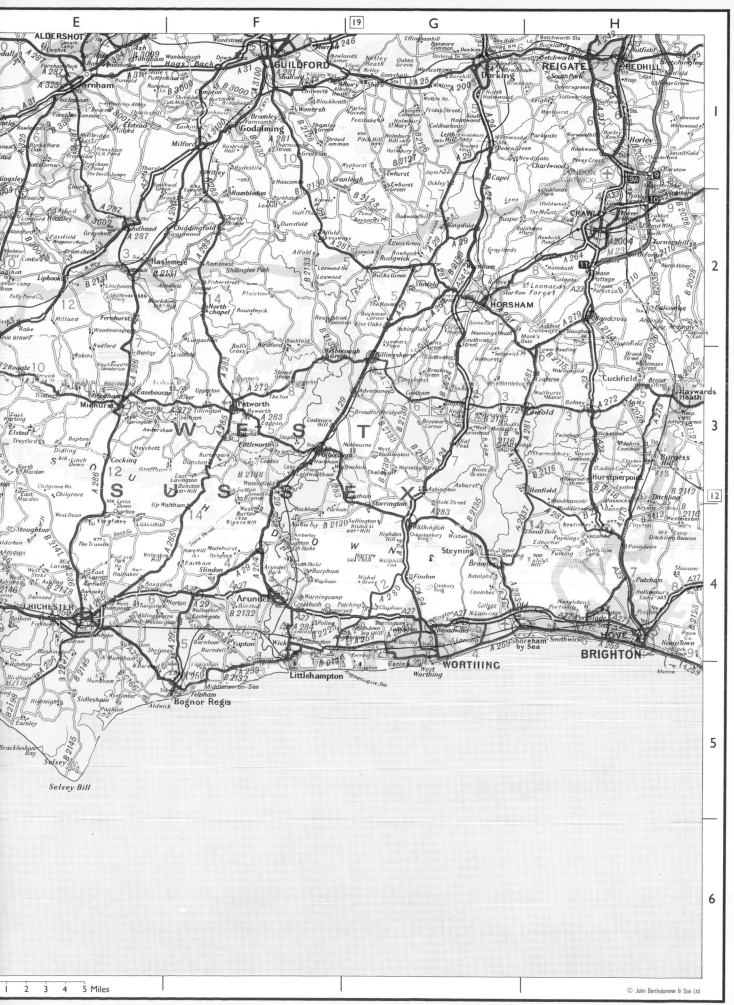

1 2 3 4 5 Miles

© John Bartholomew & Son Ltd

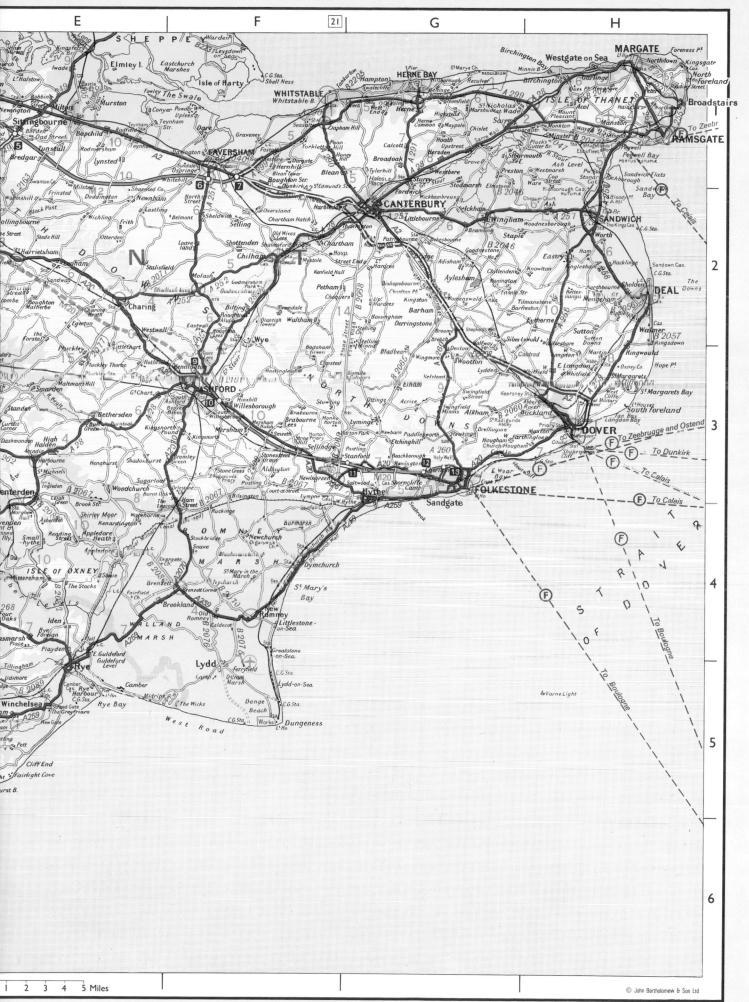

I 1 2 3 4 5 Miles

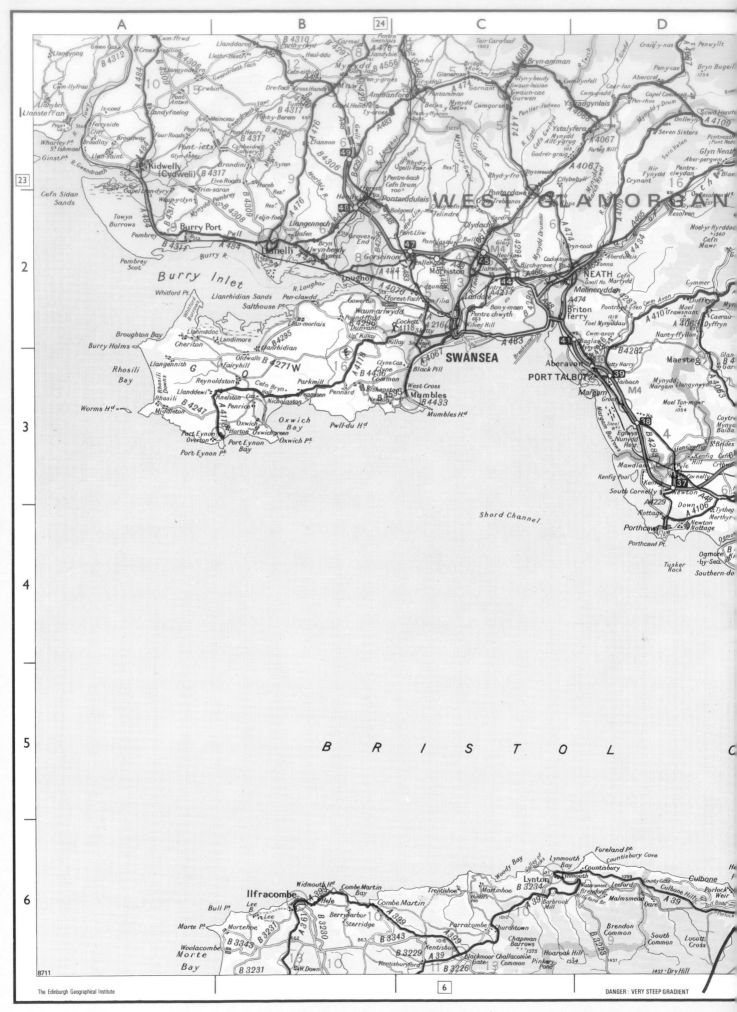

DANGER : VERY STEEP GRADIENT

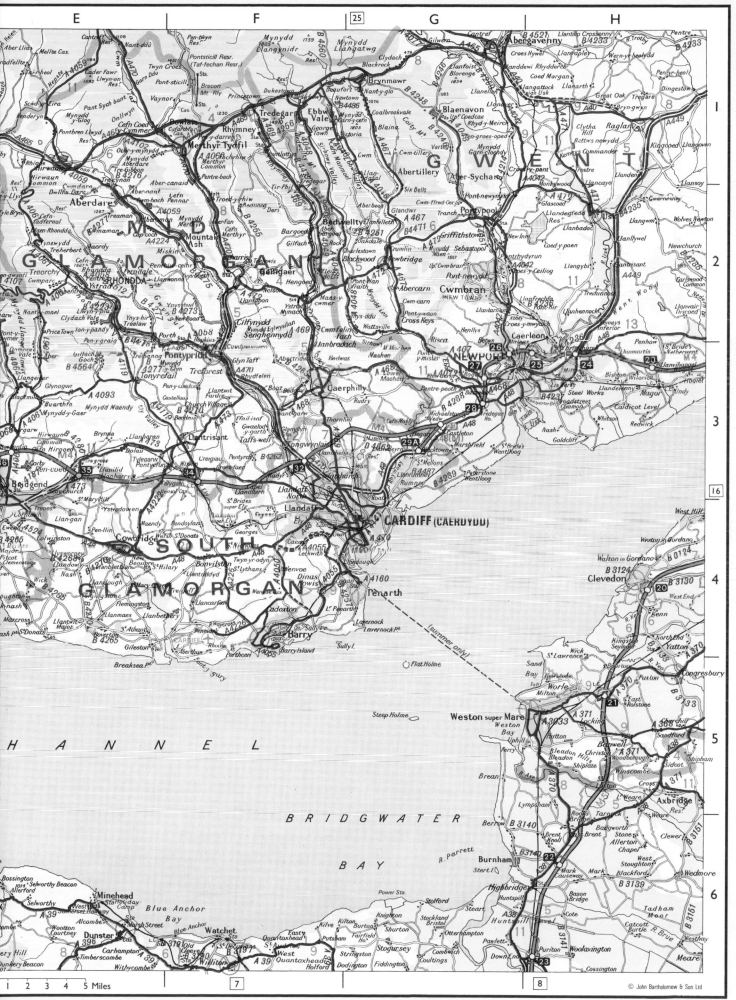

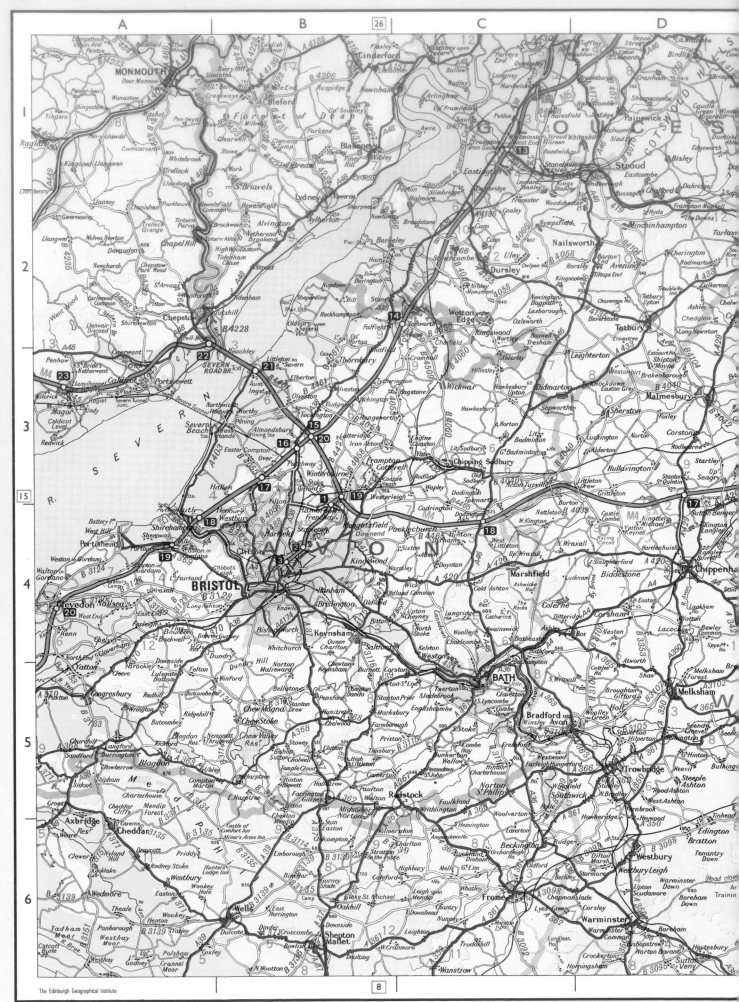

The Edinburgh Geographical Institute

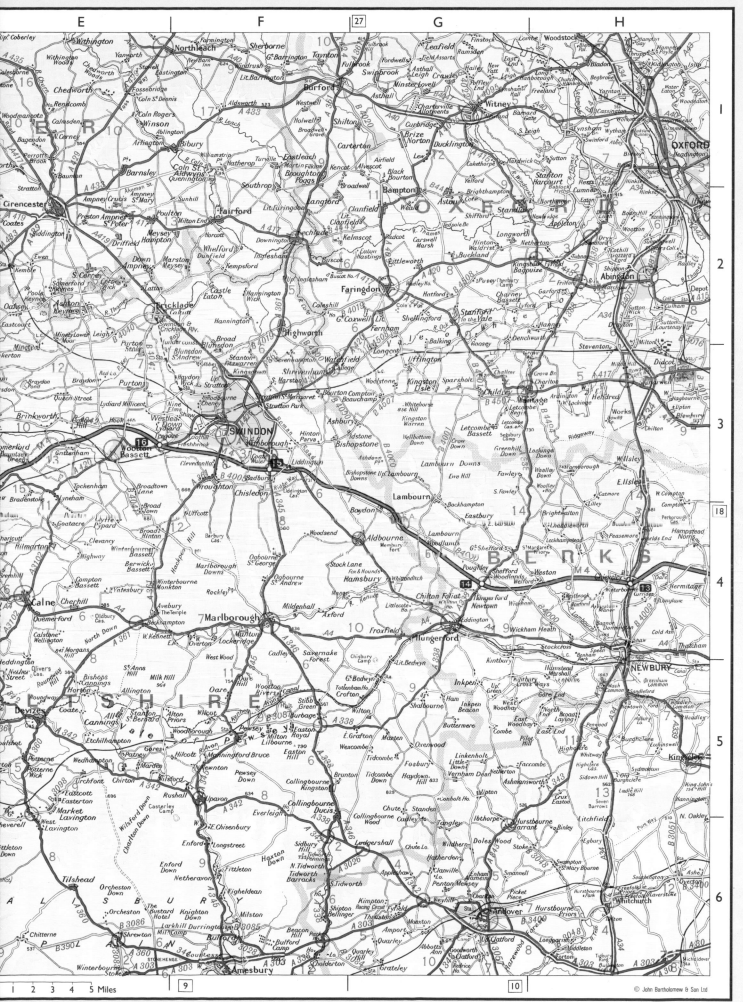

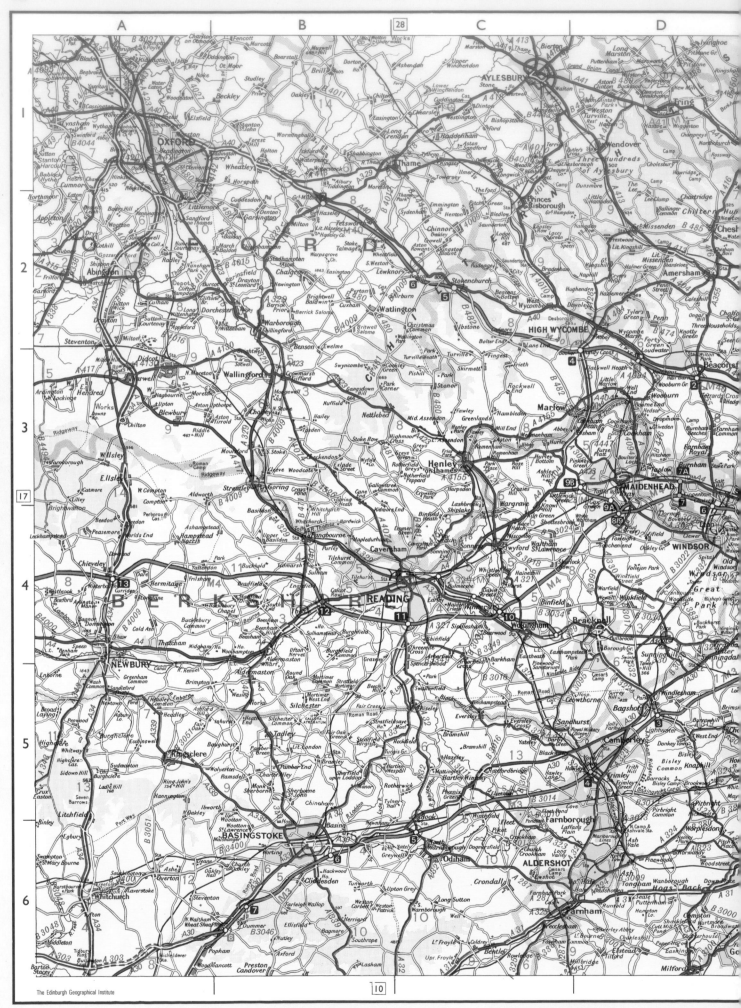

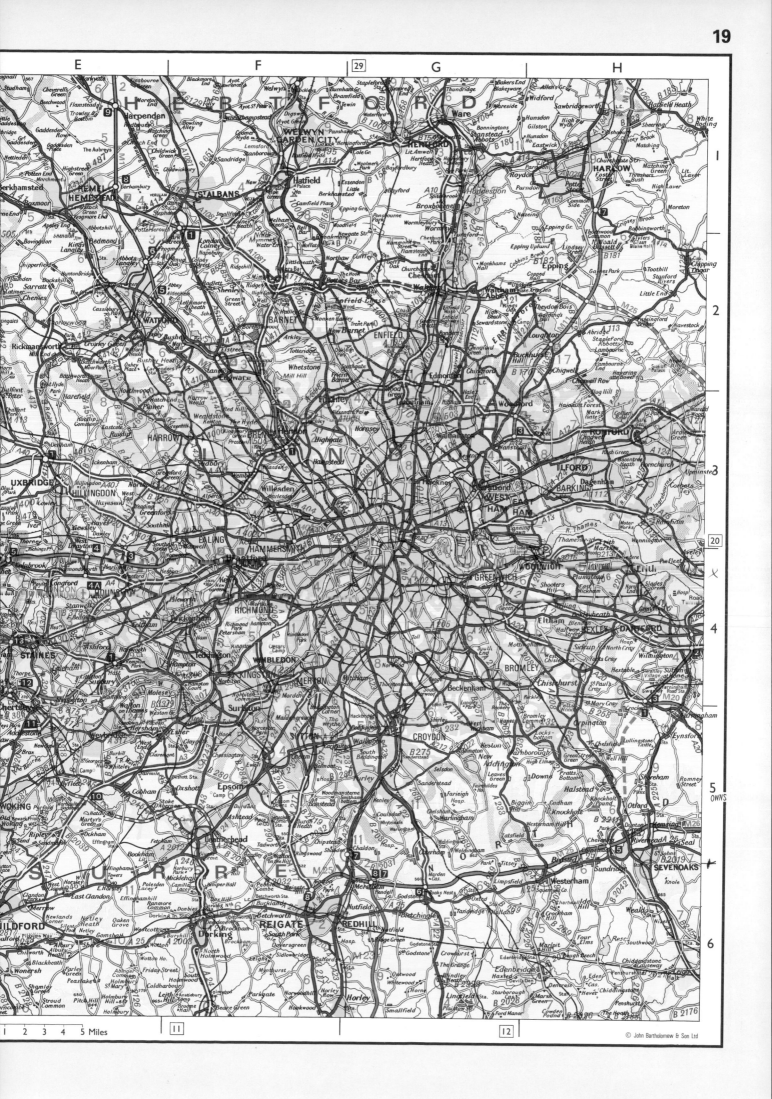

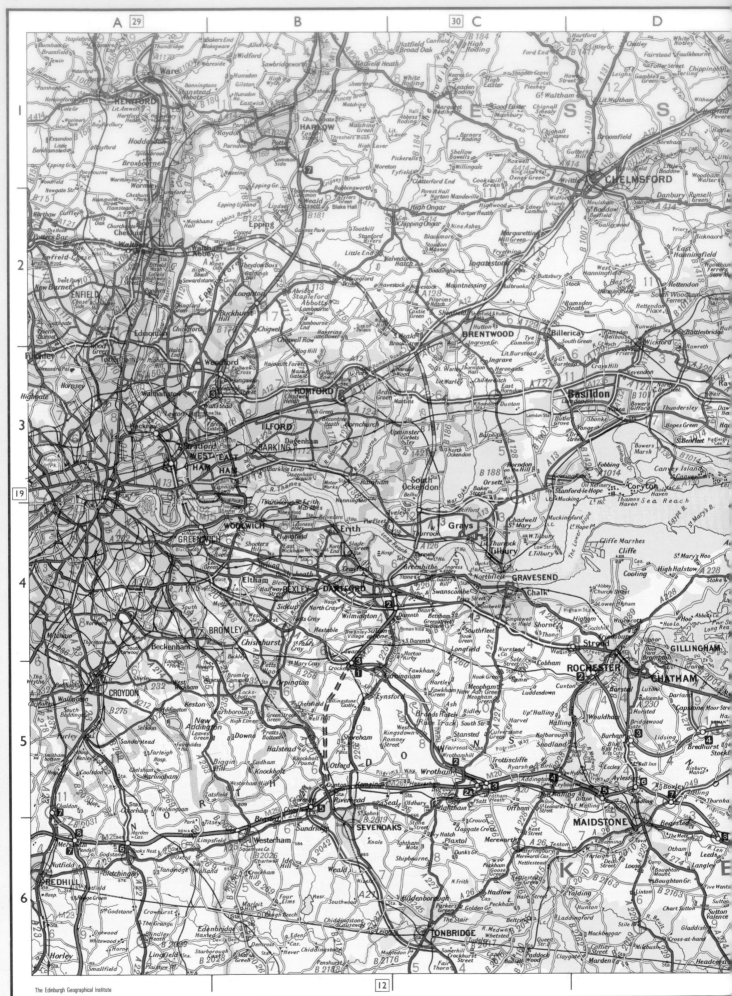

The Edinburgh Geographical Institute

I

2

3

4

5

6

1 2 3 4 5 Miles

13

© John Bartholomew & Son Ltd

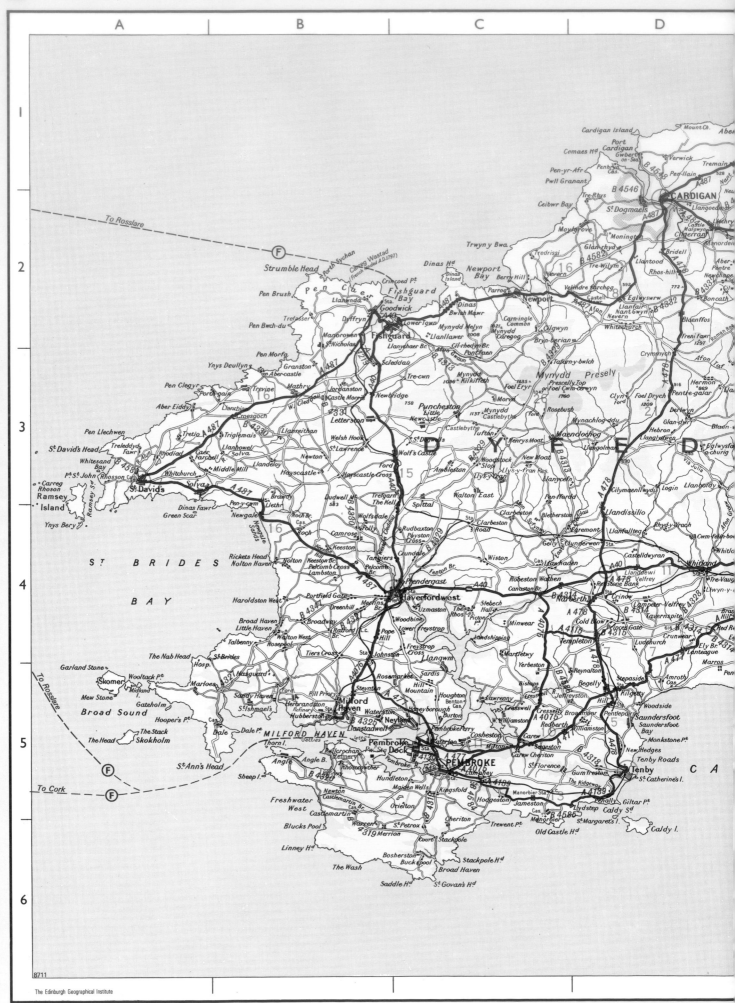

A B C D

1

2

3

4

5

6

To Rosslare

Cardigan Island
Mount Ch.
Cemaes Hd
Port Cardigan
Gwbert on-Sea
Pen-yr-Afr
Penrhiw
Verwick
Tremain
Pwll Granant
B 4546
CARDIGAN
Ceibwr Bay
Tre-Rhys
St Dogmaels
A 487
Llangoedmor
Moylgrove
Castle Malgwyn
Cilgerran
Manordeilo
Trwyn y Bwa
Glan-rhyd
Llantood
Bridell
Aber
Pentre
Newchapel
Trefdissi
Newport
B 4582
Nevern
Tre-wilym
Rhos-hill
16
Newport
Bay
Berry Hill
Velindre farchog
Eglwyswrw
Bldenffos
Strumble Head
Dinas Hd
Parrog
Newport
Castell
Bryn-berian
Whitechurch
Freni Fawr
Carreg Wastad
Dinas
Island
Nevern
Mynydd
Carn-ingle
Common
Mynydd
Caregog
Crymmych
Porth Sychan
Dinas Hd
A 487
Bwlch Mawr
Olgwyn
Roman Rd
Pen Caer
Crincoed Pt
Fishguard
Bay
Mynydd Melyn
Tafarn-y-bwlch
Afon Taf
Pen Brush
Llanwnda
Sta.
Goodwick
Lower Town
Llanllawer
1008
Mynydd Presely
Hermon
Pen Bwch-du
Dyffryn
A40
Cil-rhedyn Br.
Presely Top
or Foel Cwm cerwyn
916
Foel Drych
Pentre-galar
Trefasser
Fishguard
Llanychaer Br.
Pontfaen
1760
Clyn
Ford
Derllys
Pen Morfa
St Nicholas
Scleddau
1096 Kilkiffeth
Foel Eryr
Rosebush
Glan-dwr
Blaen
Ynys Deullyn
Granston
A 487
Tre-cwn
Moryil
Mynydd
Castlebythe
Maenclochog
Hebron
Llanglydwen
Aber-castle
B 4313
Pen Clegyr
Mathry
Jordanston
Newbridge
758
Little
Newcastle
Rosebush
Llangolman
Eglwys
fa-churig
Porth-gain
16
Castle Morris
1137
Mynydd
Llanycefn
Whitlo
Aber Eiddy
Llanrhian
Tretio
Triglemais
Llanhowel
Solva
B 4330
Welsh Hook
St Dogwells
Henrys Moat
Rhyd-y-Wrach
Cwm-felin-boeth
Pen Llechwen
Treleddyd
Fawr
Rhodiad
Cae
Farchell
Llanreithan
Ford
DYFED
890
A 478
Llandissilio
St David's Head
Whitchurch
Middle Mill
Newton
St Lawrence
15
Walton
East
Pen-ffordd
Cilymaenllwyd
Llanboidy
Whitesand
Bay
Pt St John
Rhoson
St David's
Llandeloy
Hayscastle
Trefgarn
The Kell
583
Ambleston
Ullys-yr-fran Res.
Gelly
Clynderwen
Llanfallteg
Login
Carreg
Rhoson
Ramsey
Island
Solva
A 487
Brawdy
Hayscastle Cross
Ullys-y-fran
Clarbeston
Sta.
Egremont
Castelldwyran
Pen-y-cwm
Llethr
Wolfsdale
Spittal
Walton
West
Clarbeston
Road
Cas.
Llawhaden
Llandewi
Velfrey
Ynys Bery
Newgale
Folly
Rudbaxton
Wiston
A40
Crinow
Newgale
Sands
Roch Br.
Cas.
Poyston
Cross
A 40
Robeston
Wathen
Redstone Bank
Tre-Vaug
16
Roch
Camrose
Crundale
Fenton Br.
Cas.
Canaston Br.
Narberth
B 4314
Llwyn-y
St BRIDES
Rickets Head
Nolton Haven
Hill
Keeston
Tanglers
Pelcomb
Br.
Robeston
Wathen
A 478
B 4314
A 4328
BAY
Nolton
Keeston Br.
Pelcomb Cross
Lambston
Prendergast
A40
Slebech
Hall
Cold Blow
Tavernspite
Red Ro
Haroldston West
Merlins
Br.
Haverfordwest
Uzmaston
Picton
Cas.
Minwear
A 4115
Templeton
Princes
Gate
B 4316
A 4314
Broad Haven
Little Haven
B 4341
Dreenhill
Woodbine
Landshipping
Mantletwy
Yerbeston
Crunwear
Lanteague
Talbenny
Broadway
Ratford
Br.
Pope
Hill
Lower Freystrop
A 4075
Bishops
B 4314
Red Re
The Nab Head
St Brides
Walton West
Rosepool
Tiers Cross
Johnston
Freystrop
Cross
Llangwm
Reynalton
Marros
Garland Stone
Hosp.
Sta.
Houghton
Begelly
Amroth
Cas.
Skomer
Wooltack Pt
B 4327
Hasguard
Marloes
Steynton
Langwm
Rosemarket
Sardis
Hill
Mountain
Benton
Cas.
Cresselly
Jeffreyston
Stepaside
Mew Stone
Midland
I.
Sandy Haven
Ford
Pill Priory
Houghton
Lawrenny
Broadmoor
Saundersfoot
Gateholm
St Ishmael's
Herbrandston
Milford
Haven
Waterston
Burton
W. Williamston
A 4075
Pentlepoir
Woodside
Broad Sound
Hooper's Pt
Refinery
Hubberston
B 4325
Neyland
Coshesto
Carew
Williamston
Kilgetty
5
Saundersfoot
Bay
The Stack
Skokholm
The Head
Cas.
Dale Pt
Llanstadwell
Pembroke
Ferry
Williamston
Monkstone Pt
Thorn I.
MILFORD HAVEN
Jetties
Waterloo
A 477
Milton
Sageston
B 4318
New Hedges
St Ann's Head
Angle
Angle B.
Pembroke
Dock
Sta.
Pw.
Sta.
A 477
Carew Cheriton
A 478
Tenby Roads
C A
To Cork
Sheep I.
B 4320
Microchan
Refinery
Pembroke
A 4139
PEMBROKE
St Florence
13
Gumfreston
Tenby
St Catherine's I.
Rhoscrowther
Hundleton
Lamphey
A 4139
Freshwater
West
Newton
Castlemartin Br.
Maiden Wells
Kingsfold
Hodgeston
Manorbier Sta.
The Ridgeway
Jameston
Penally
Giltar Pt
Castlemartin
Orielton
B 4584
Hoyles
Manorbier
Lydstep
Caldy Sd
Blucks Pool
Warren
St Petrox
Cheriton
B 4585
St Margaret's I.
Caldy I.
B 4319
Merrion
Trewent Pt
Old Castle Hd
Linney Hd
Court
Stackpole
The Wash
Bosherston
Buckspool
Stackpole Hd
Broad Haven
Saddle Hd
St Govan's Hd

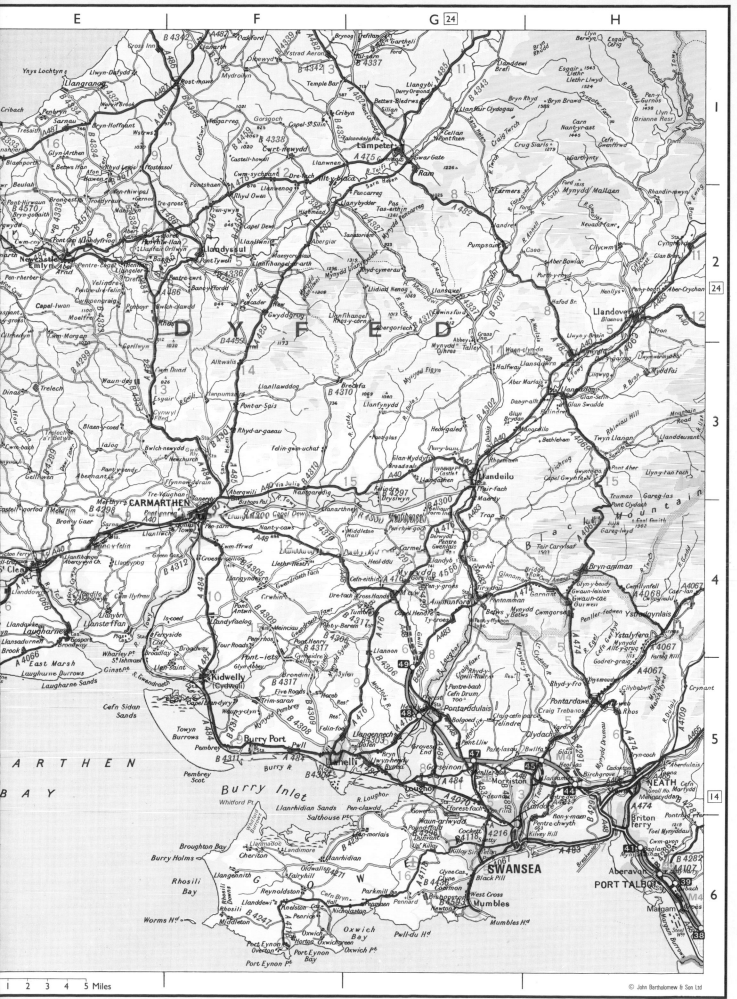

1 2 3 4 5 Miles

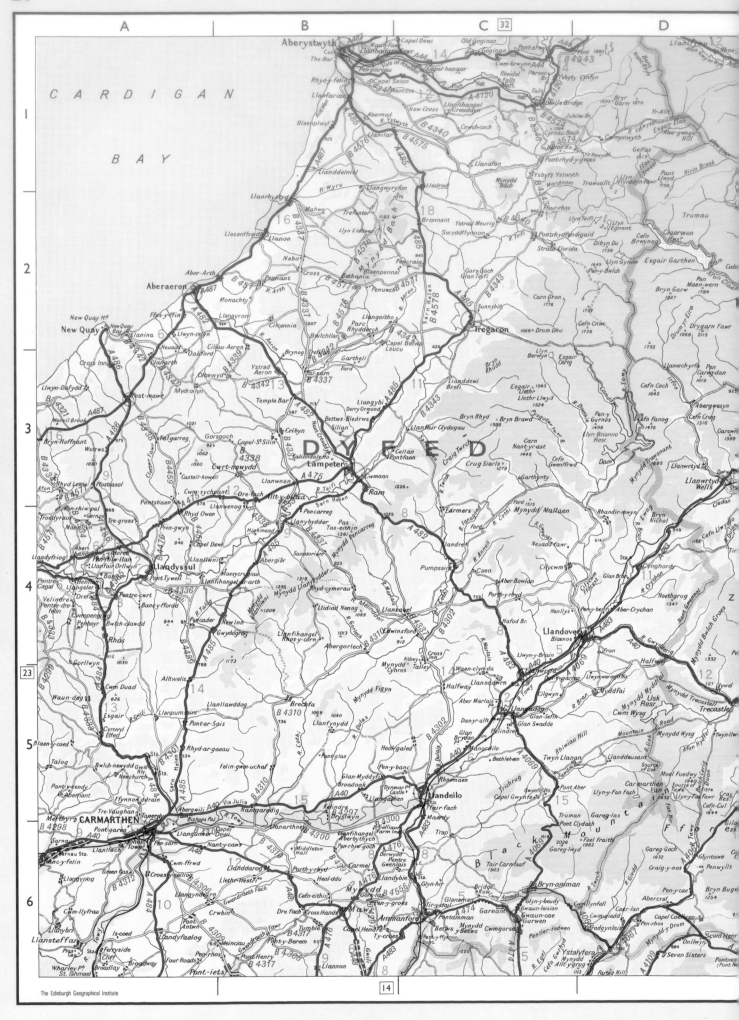

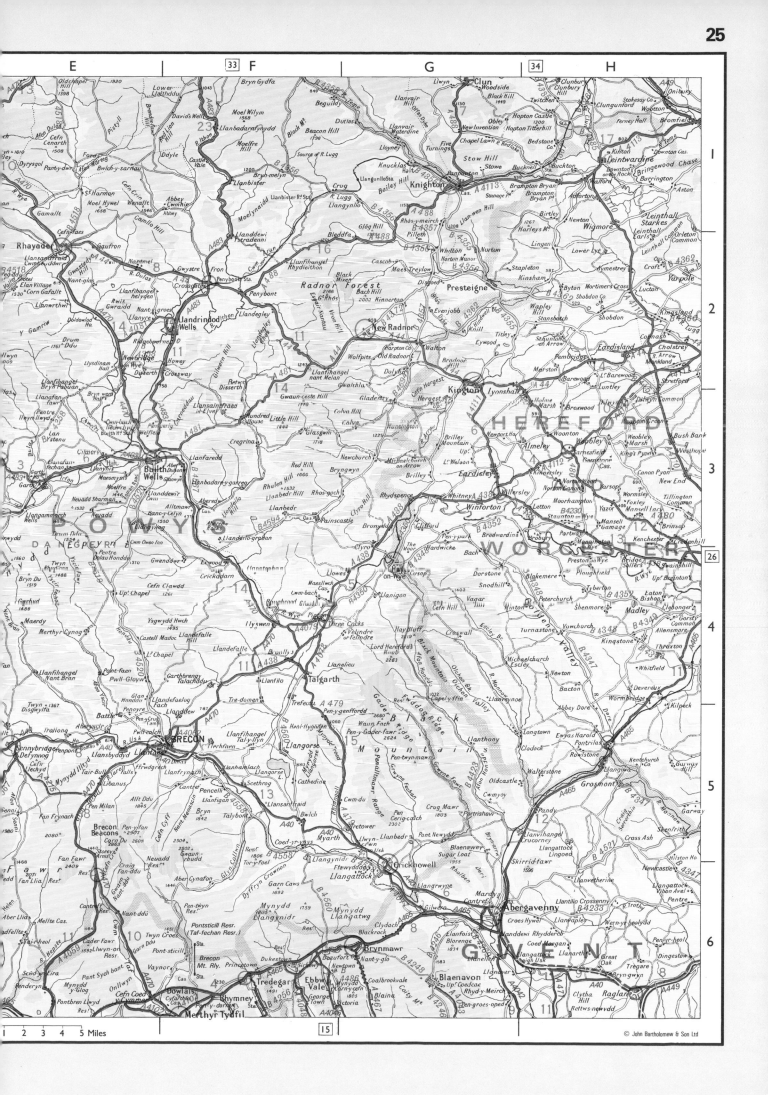

E · 33 · F · G · 34 · H

St Harmon

Rhayader

POWYS

Builth Wells

BRECON

Brecon Beacons

Merthyr Tydfil

Knighton

Presteigne

New Radnor

Radnor Forest

Kington

HEREFORD

WORCESTER

Hay-on-Wye

Talgarth

Crickhowell

Abergavenny

Blaenavon

Brynmawr

Ebbw Vale

Tredegar

GWENT

Clun

Leintwardine

Wigmore

Eardisland

Weobley

Eardisley

Madley

Grosmont

Raglan

1 · 2 · 3 · 4 · 5 Miles

© John Bartholomew & Son Ltd

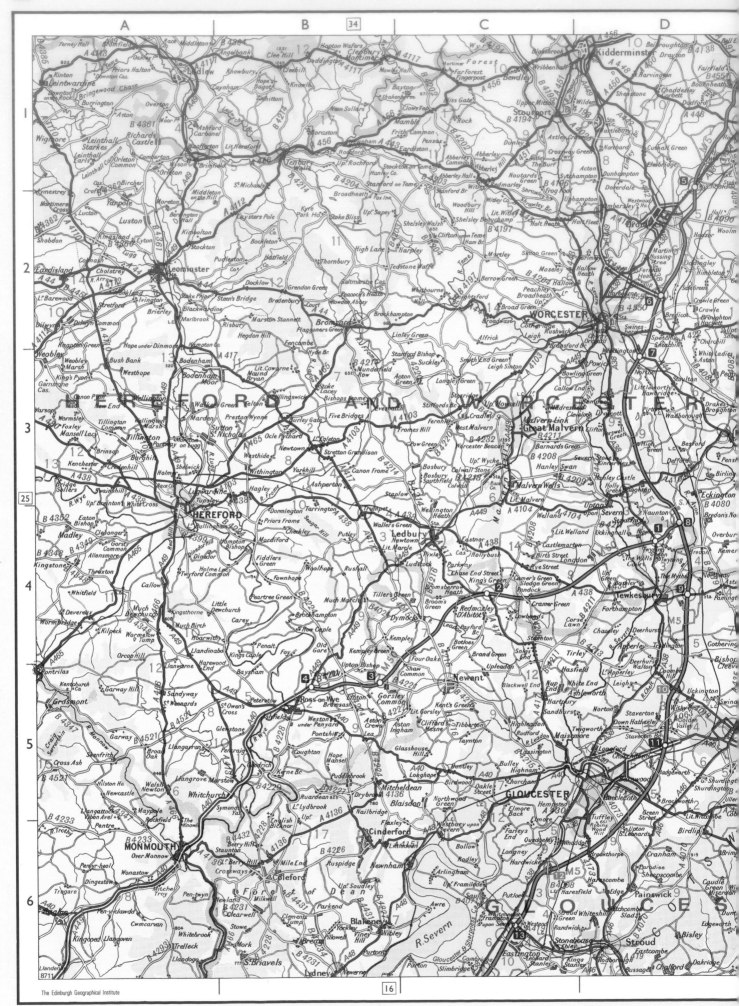

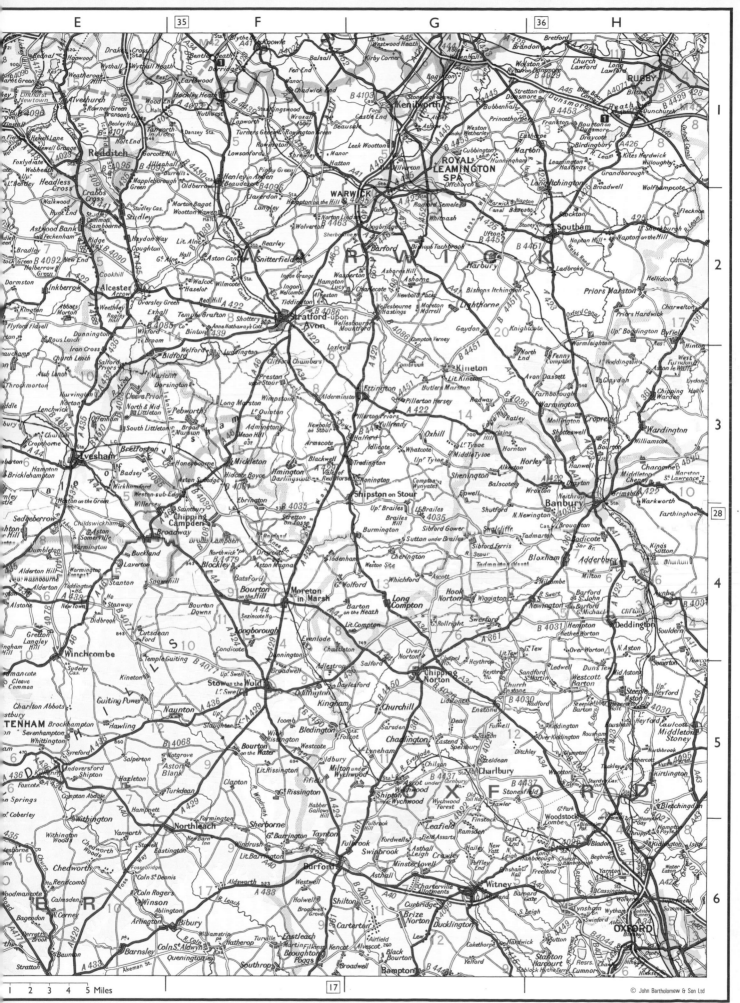

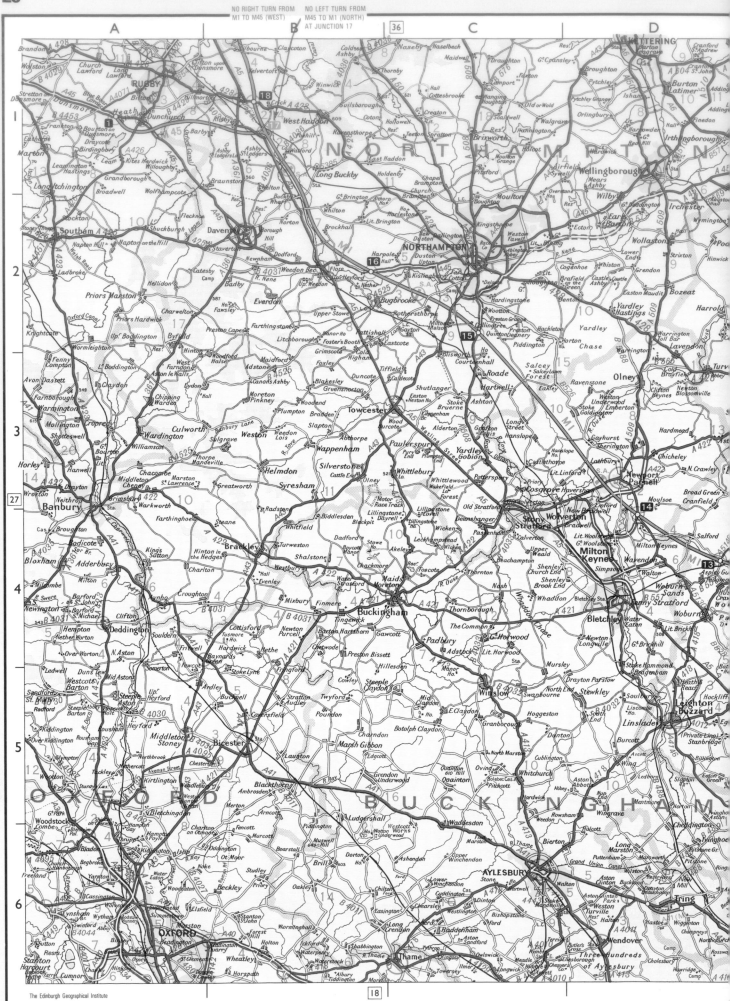

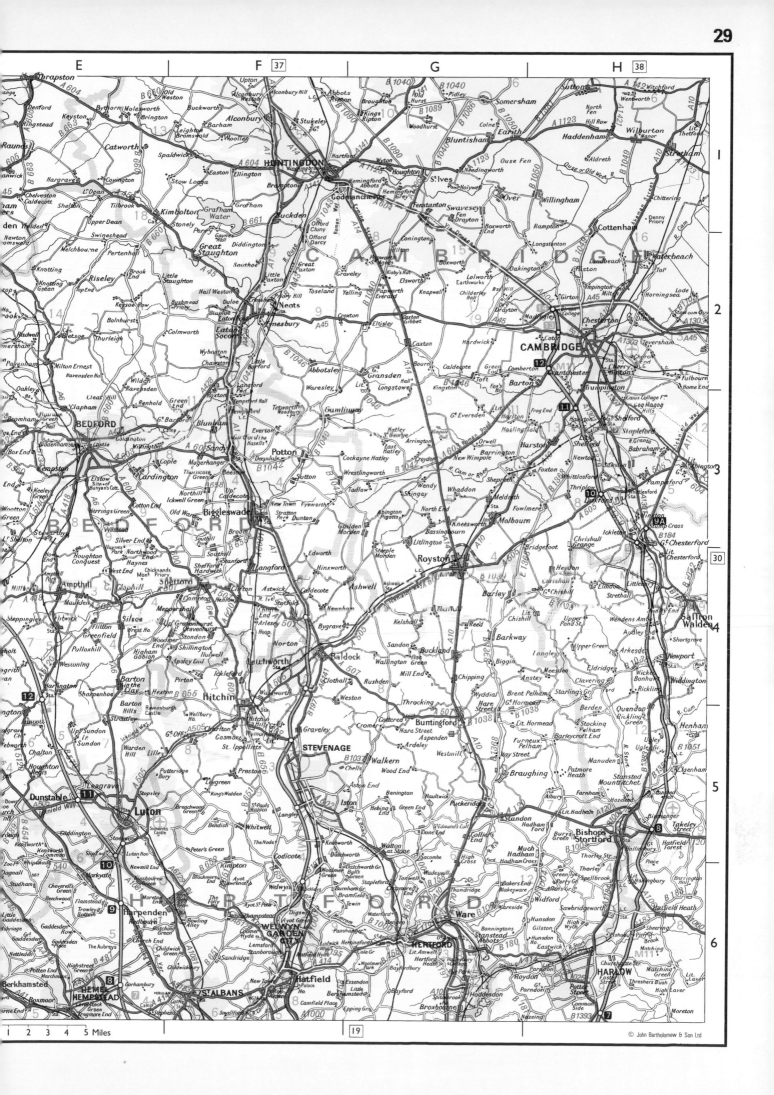

E F 37 G H 38

Thrapston
A 604
Denford
Ringstead
Keyston
A 603
Old
Weston
Molesworth
Brington
Barham
Alconbury
Upton
Alconbury Hill
Abbots
Ripton
Kings
Ripton
Broughton
Old
Hurst
Pidley
Somersham
Sutton
Witchford
Wentworth
A 142
Catworth
Spaldwick
Ellington
Easton
Stow Longa
Woolley
Stukeley Gt
Hartford
Wyton
Houghton
St Ives
Needingworth
Holywell
Over
Willingham
North
Fen
Hill Row
Wilburton
Manor
Little
Thetford
Bythorn
Leighton
Bromswold
Buckworth
Grafham
HUNTINGDON
A 604
A 141
A 1123
Strethan
Shelton
Tilbrook
Kimbolton
Grafham
Water
Godmanchester
Hemingford
Abbots
Fenstanton
Swavesey
Fen
Drayton
Earith
Haddenham
Aldreth
Chittering
Stow cum Quy
Upper Dean
Cas
Stonely
Per
Buckden
Offord
Cluny
Offord
Darcy
Conington
Boxworth
End
Rampton
Landbeach
Oakington
Waterbeach
Sta.
Horningsea
Lode
Melchbourne
Pertenhall
Great
Staughton
Southoe
Graveley
Elsworth
Lolworth
Earthworks
Childerley
Hall
Girton
College F
Chesterton
Impington
Milton
Cottenham
Denny
Priory
R. Cam
Knotting
Riseley
Little
Staughton
Hail Weston
Toseland
Yelling
Papworth
Everard
Knapwell
Bar Hill
Madingley
CAMBRIDGE
Fen Ditton
A 1303
Keysoe
Row
Bushmead
Priory
Priory Hill
Tristian
St Neots
Croxton
Caxton
Gibbet
Hardwick
Cobb
CAMBRIDGE
12
M 11
Sta.
Teversham
Fulbourn
Knotting
Green
Top End
Keysoe
Bolnhurst
Duloe
Eaton
Eynesbury
A 45
Eltisley
Caxton
Comberton
Barton
Grantchester
Trumpington
Cherry
Hinton
Homeend
Radwell
Thurleigh
Colmworth
Wyboston
Little
Barford
Abbotsley
Gransden
Lit
Gransden
Longstowe
B 1046
Toft
Kingston
Fox's
Gt Eversden
Haslingfield
Harston
Shelford
Babraham
Oakley
Milton Ernest
Ravensden Hal
Roxton
Tempsford
Hall
Waresley
Hatley
St George
East
Hatley
Arrington
Orwell
New Wimpole
Barrington
Newton
R. Granta
Lit. Shelford
Clapham
Green
End
Renhold
Gt Barford
Tempsford
Croydon
Wendy
Whaddon
R. Cam or Rhee
Shepreth
Foxton
Whittlesford
Pampisford
BEDFORD
Blunham
A 1
Everton
The Hasells
Cockayne Hatley
Shingay
Meldreth
Sta.
Fowlmere
Thriplow
10
Duxford
Lit.
Abington
Sandy
Potton
Deepdale
Sutton
Wrestlingworth
B 1042
Tadlow
Abington
Pigotts
North
End
Aneesworth
Melbourn
Chrishall
Grange
9A
Duxford
Stump Cross
Cardington
Northill
Ickwell Green
Old Warden
Beeston
New Town
Fyeworth
Stratton
Park
Dunton
Golden
Morden
Litlington
Bassingbourn
Bridgefoot
Ickleton
Gt Chesterford
Lit.
Chesterford
30
Herrings Green
Silver End
Southill
Shefford
Hardwick
Langford
Edworth
Hinxworth
Royston
B 1039
Heydon
Chrishall
Elmdon
Strethall
Littlebury
Saffron
Walden
Houghton
Conquest
Haynes
Clifton
Astwick
Caldecote
Ashwell
Barley
Gt Chishill
Shortgrove
Ampthill
Maulden
Shefford
Henlow
Stotfold
Newnham
Kelshall
Sandon
Reed
Barkway
Lit. Chishill
Upper
Pond St.
Wendens Ambo
Sta.
Newport
Steppingley
Flitwick
Silsoe
Wrest Ho.
Arlesey
Hosp.
Bygrave
Buckland
Biggin
Langley
Anstey
Wyddial
Hare
Street
Eldridge
Clavering
Ricklin
Widdington
Flitton
Greenfield
Pulloxhill
Woodmer
End
Shillington
Holwell
Norton
Baldock
Wallington
Green
Rushden
Mill End
Chipping
Gt Hormead
Berden
Quendon
Rickling
Green
Henham
Westoning
Barton
in the Clay
Hexton
Pirton
Ickleford
Clothall
Weston
Throcking
Hare
Street
Aspenden
Buntingford
Lit. Hormead
Stocking
Pelham
Furneux
Pelham
Barleycroft End
Manuden
Elsenham
Harlington
Sharpenhoe
Barton
Hills
Ravensburgh
Castle
Wellbury
Ho.
Charlton
HITCHIN
Hitchin
Hills
Graveley
Cromer
Ardeley
Westmill
Hay Street
Braughing
Patmore
Heath
Farnham
Stansted
Mountfitchet
Chalton
Houghton
Regis
Gt Offley
Gosmore
St. Ippollitts
STEVENAGE
Walkern
Wood End
Albury
Lit. Hadham
Hazelend
Birchanger
Leagrave
Stopsley
Kings Walden
Preston
Chells
Aston End
Benington
Haultwick
Puckeridge
Standon
Hadham
Ford
Bury
Green
8
Takeley
Street
Dunstable
11
Luton
Breachwood
Green
St Pauls
Walden
Langley
Iston
Hebing
End
Green End
Much
Hadham
Hadham Cross
Thorley Str.
Hatfield
Forest
Caddington
Stockwood
Slip End
Peter's Green
Bendish
Whitwell
The Node
Codicote
Knebworth
Datchworth
Watton
at Stone
Sacombe
High
Cross
Collier's
End
Bakers End
Green Tye
Perry Gr
Spellbrook
Place
10
Markyate
Luton Hoo
Newmill End
Kimpton
Ayot
St Lawrence
Welwyn
Digswell
Woolmer
Green
Burnham
Green
Bramfield
Tewin
Stapleford
Tonwell
Thundridge
Wareside
Widford
Sawbridgeworth
Lit. Hallingbury
Hatfield Heath
9
Harpenden
Redbourn
Hatching
Green
Church
End
The
Folly
Ayot St Peter
Welham
Green
WELWYN
GARDEN
CITY
Lemsford
Stanborough
Hertingfordbury
Hertford
Bayfordbury
Hertford
Heath
Hunsdon
Gilston
High
Wych
Pinso
Brook
Matching
Gaddesden
Row
Gaddesden
Place
The Aubreys
Sandridge
Childwick
Green
Hatfield
Hyde
A 414
Panshanger
St Andrews
Woolmers
Park
Ware
Bennington
Bonningtons
Stanstead
Abbots
Roydon
HARLOW
Matching
Green
Threshers Bush
High Laver
Hemel
Hempstead
8
St Albans
Verulam
Camfield Place
Essendon
Little
Berkhamsted
Hatfield
Epping Grn
Hoddesdon
Broxbourne
Parndon
Potter
Street
Common
Side
7
Moreton
Boxmoor
A 41
Bovingdon
Potten End
Frogmore End
Gorhambury
New Town
Hatfield
Palace
Bayford
A 1000
Broxbourn
Nazeing
B 1393

37 19 38

© John Bartholomew & Son Ltd

I 2 3 4 5 6

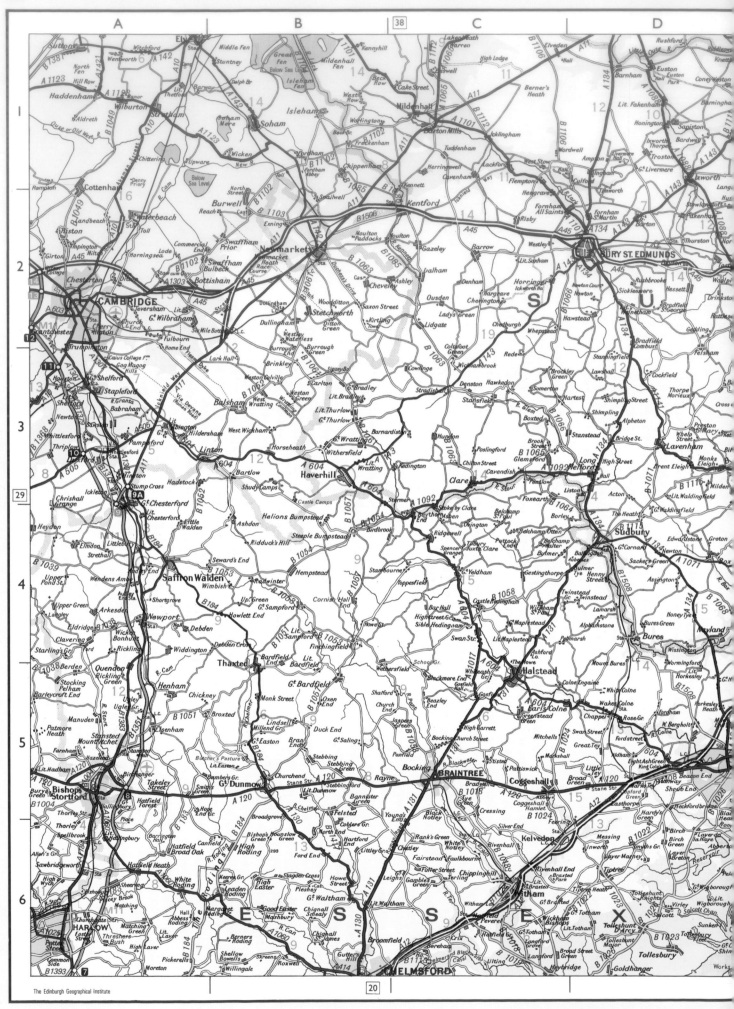

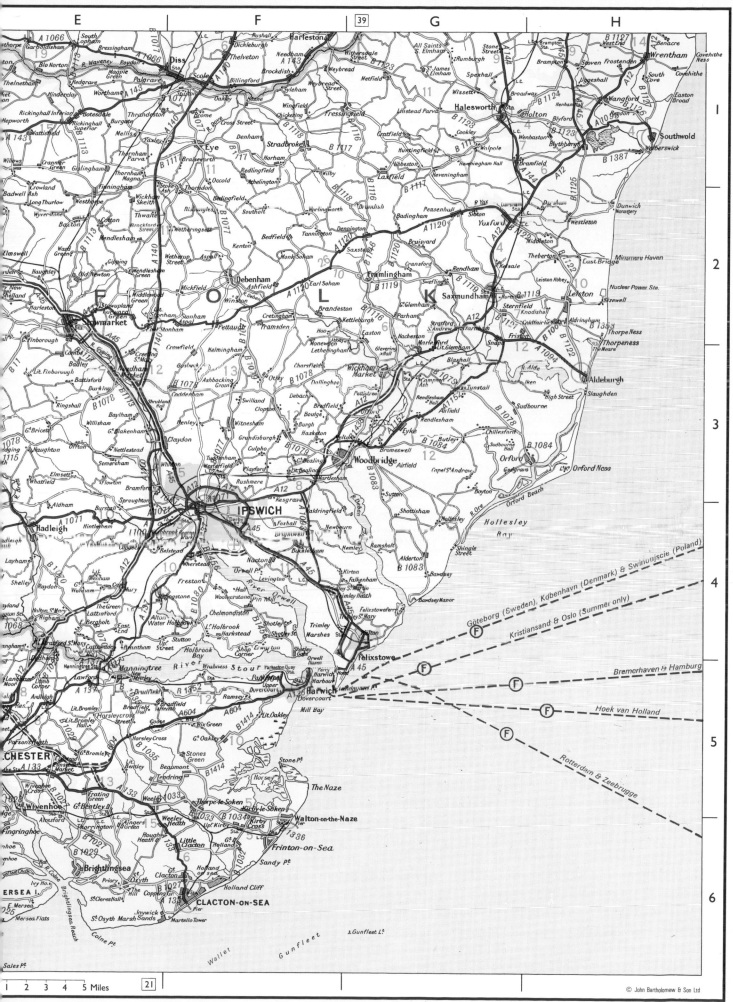

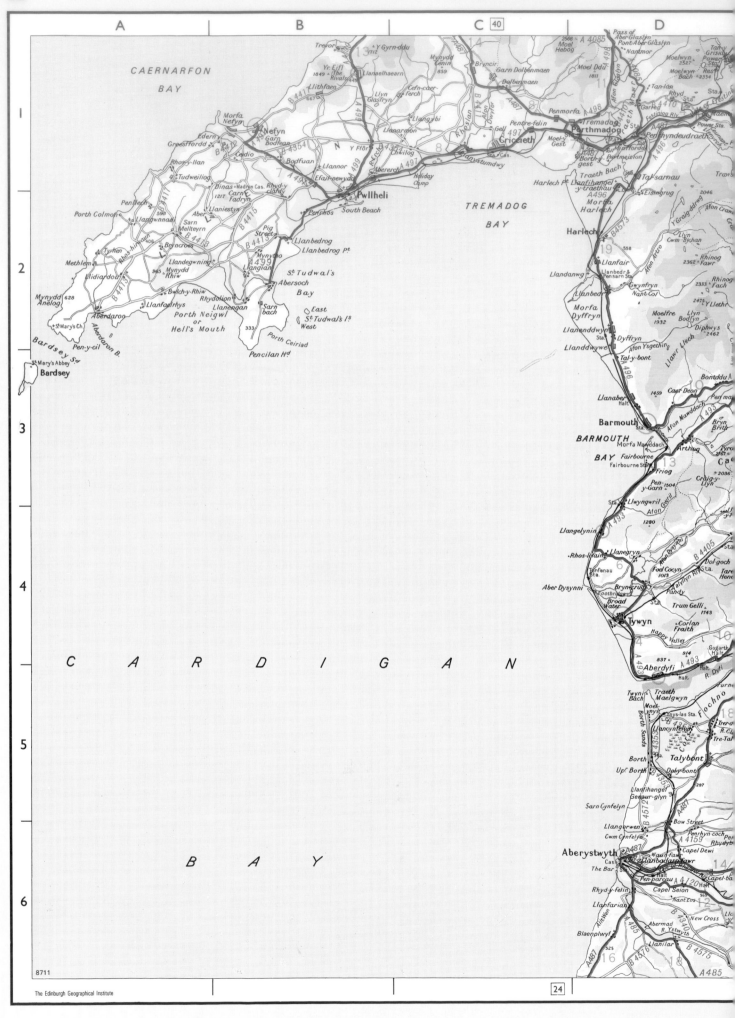

A B C 40 D

CAERNARFON BAY

Trevor
Y Gyrn-ddu
Yr Eifl 1849 The Rivals
Mynydd Cenin 859
Moel Hebog
Pass of Aber-Glaslyn
Pont-Aber-Glaslyn
Nantmor
Tan-y-Grisiau Power Sta.
Moelwyn 2527
Moel Ddu 1811
Moelwyn Bach 2334

Morfa Nefyn
Nefyn
Garn Bodfean
Llithfaen
Llanaelhaearn
Cefn-caer-ferch
Bryncir
Garn Dolbenmaen
Dolbenmaen
Penmorfa
A 498
Tremadog
Power Sta.
Ffestiniog Rly

GreesfTordd
Edern
Ceidio
Bodfuan
Llannor
Llangybi
Llanarmon
Llyn Glasfryn
Chwilog
Gell
Pentre-felin
Porthmadog
Penrhyndeudraeth
Power Sta.

Rhosy-llan
Tudweiliog
Madryn Cas.
Rhyd-y-clafdy
Efail-newydd
Abererch
Criccieth
Moel-y-Gest
Borth-y-gest
Portmeirion
Harlech Pt
Llanfihangel-y-traethau
Traws

Penllech
Porth Colmon
Llangwnnadl
Binas
Carn Fadryn 1217
Pig Street
Pwllheli
South Beach
TREMADOG BAY
Traeth Bach
Talsarnau
Eisingrug
Llanfihangel

Methlem
Aber
Llaniestyn
Llandegwning
Bryncroes
Mynytho
Llanbedrog
Llanbedrog Pt
Harlech
Llanfair
Morfa Harlech
Llandanwg

Mynydd Rhiw 945
Rhydolion
Langian
Abersoch
St Tudwal's Bay
Llanbedr & Pensarn Sta.
Gwynfryn
Nant Col
Rhinog Fawr 2362
Rhinog Fach 2333

Mynydd Anelog 628
Bwlch-y-Rhiw
Llanfaelrhys
Llanengan
Sarn bach
East St Tudwal's I. West
Llanbed
Moelfre 1932
Y Llethr 2475
Diphwys 2462

St Mary's Ch.
Aberdaron
Aberdaron B.
Porth Neigwl or Hell's Mouth
333
Porth Ceiriad
Pencilan Hd
Morfa Dyffryn
Llanenddwyn
Dyffryn
Afon Ysgethin
Llawr Llech
Llanddwywe
Tal-y-bont
Bontddu

Bardsey Sd
Pen-y-cil
St Mary's Abbey
Bardsey
Llanaber Halt
Caer Deon 1459
Per-y-man

Barmouth
BARMOUTH BAY
Sta.
Afon Mawddach
Bryn Brith

Morfa Mawddach
Arthog
Fairbourne
Fairbourne Sta.
Friog
Pen-y-Garn 1504
Craig-y-Llyn
2036

Llwyngwril
Afon
Sta.
1280

Llangelynin
Rhos-lefain
Llanegryn
Afon Dysynni
Foel Cocyn 1013
Dol-goch
Tal-y-llyn Rly

Tanfanau Sta.
Bryncrug
Talyllyn Sta.
Tare Hen

Aber Dysynni
Footbridge
Pandy
Trum Gelli 1743

Broad Water
Tywyn
Corlan Fraith
Happy Valley

C A R D I G A N
Aberdyfi
A 493
R. Dyfi

Twynir Bach
Traeth Maelgwyn
Moel ynys
Ynys-las Sta.
Cors Fochno

Borth Sands
Llancynfelyn
Tre-Tal

Borth
Talybont
Upr Borth
Dolybont
297

Llanfihangel Genaur-glyn
Sarn Cynfelyn

Llangorwen
Cwm Cynfelyn
Bow Street
Penrhyn-coch
Rhydyb

Aberystwyth
Llanbadarn-fawr
Waun-fawr
Capel Dewi
14

The Bar Sta.
Pen-parcau Halt
Capel-ba

Rhyd-y-felin
Capel Seion
Nant Eos
12

Llanfarian
Alltwen
New Cross

Blaenplwyf
525
Abermad R. Ystwyth
Llanilar
B 4575

16
A 4120
A 485

B A Y

The Edinburgh Geographical Institute

24

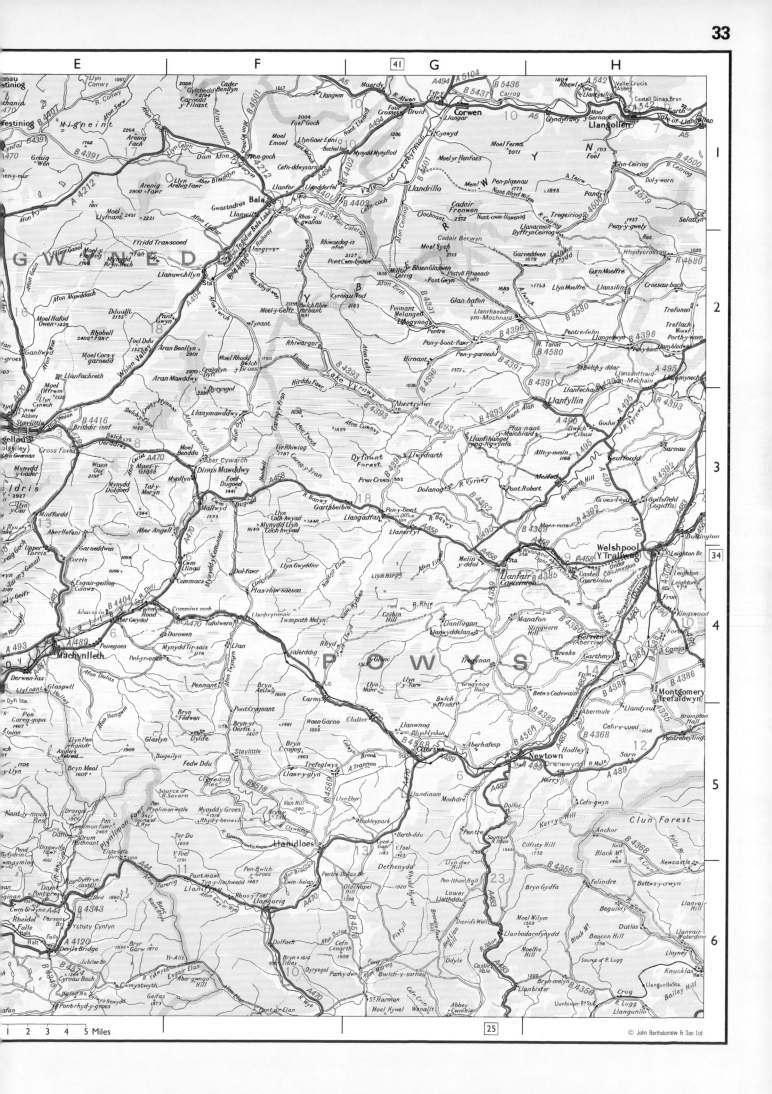

E   F   41   G   H

© John Bartholomew & Son Ltd

1 2 3 4 5 Miles

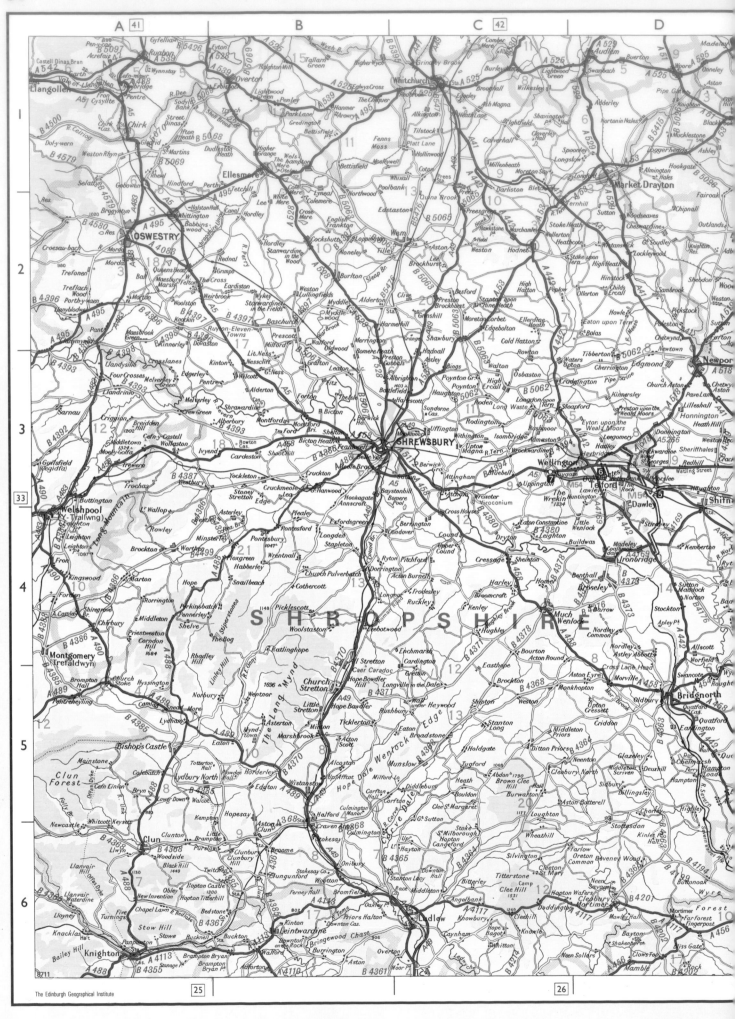

A [41] B C [42] D

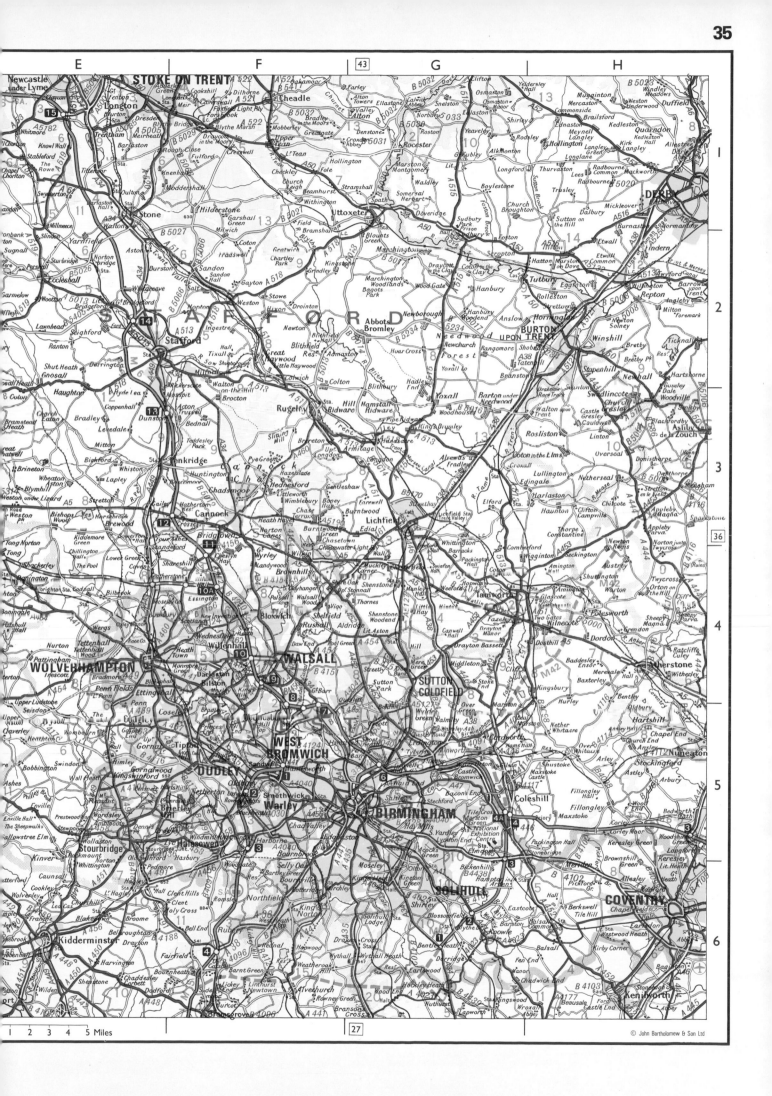

© John Bartholomew & Son Ltd

| 1 | 2 | 3 | 4 | 5 Miles |

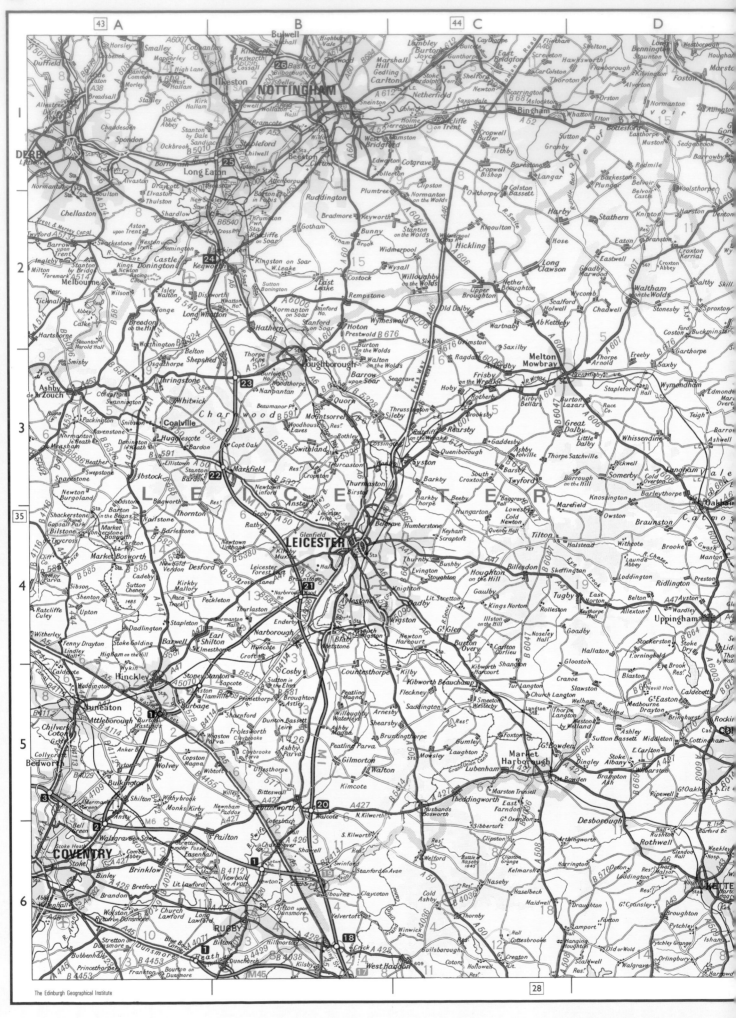

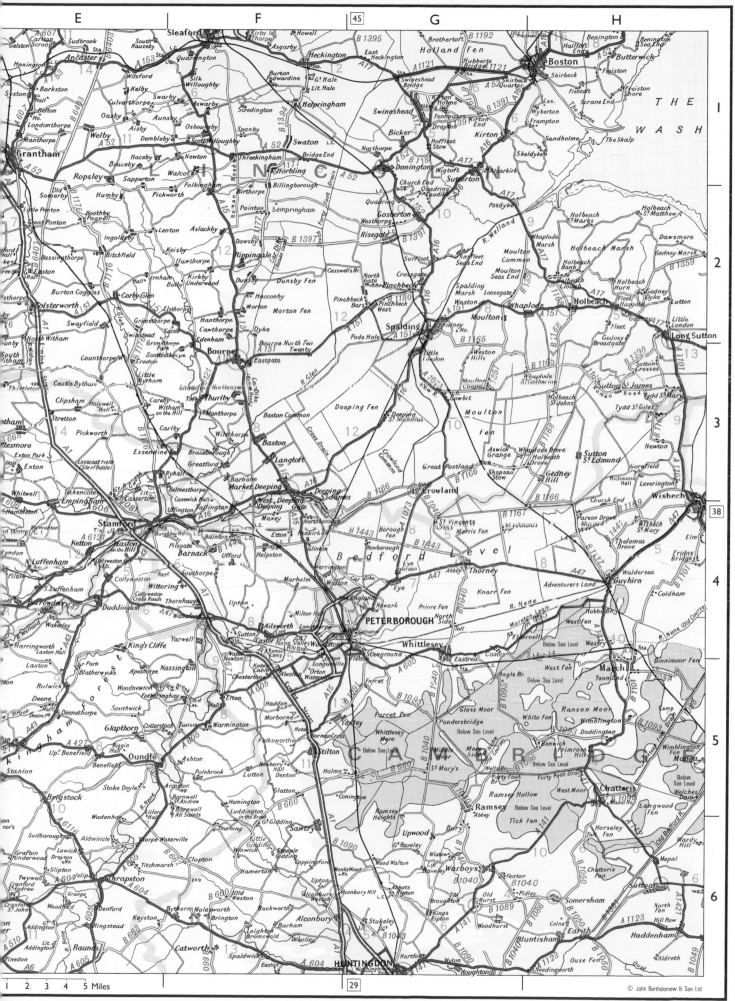

1 2 3 4 5 Miles

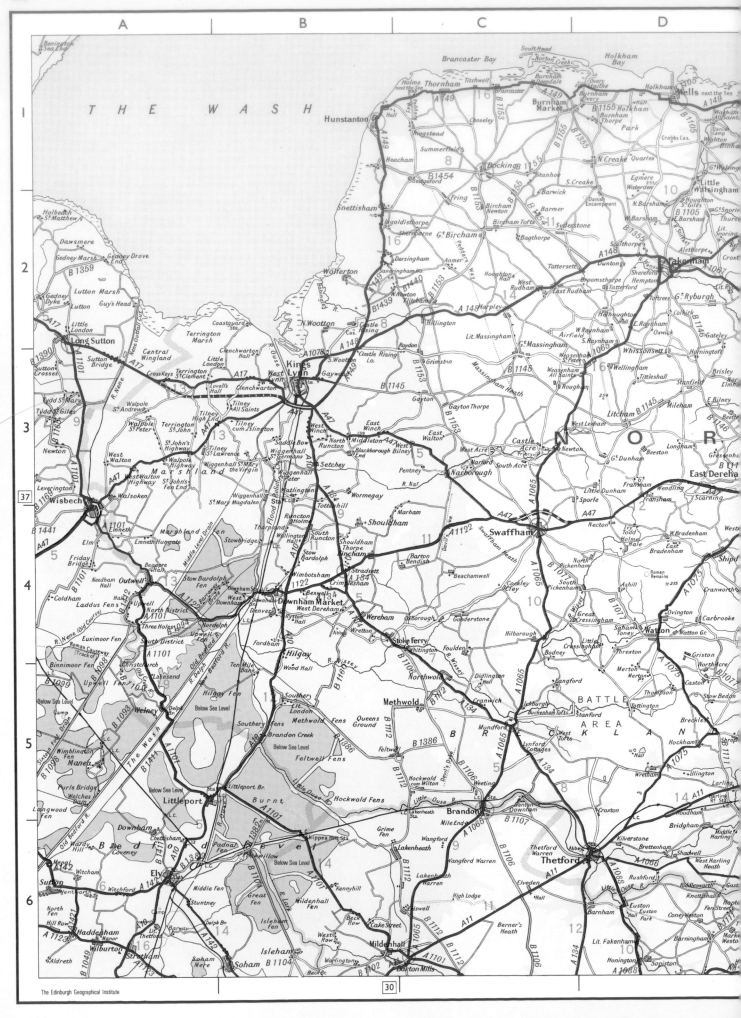

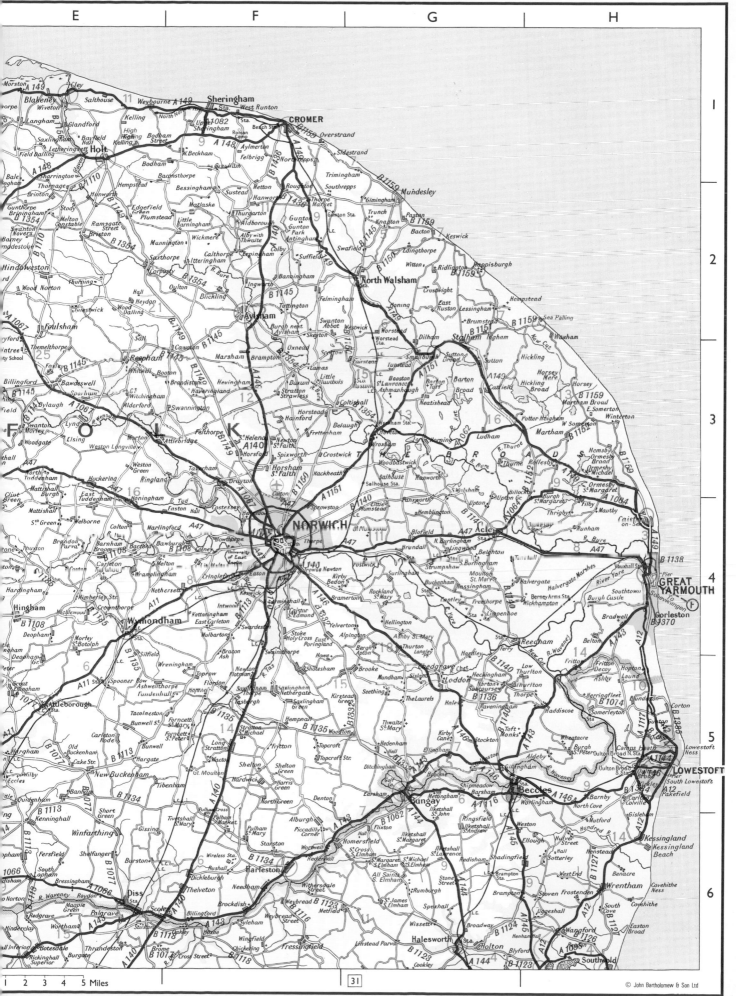

E · F · G · H

I

2

3

4

5

6

Morston A 149 · Cley · Blakeney · Salthouse · Weybourne A 149 · Sheringham · West Runton · CROMER · Overstrand

Wiveton · Kelling · High Kelling · Upr 1082 Sheringham Sta. · Beeston Regis · Roman Camp · Beach Sta.

Langham · Glandford · Bayfield Hall · Bodham Street · 9 · A 148 · Aylmerton · Felbrigg · North Repps · Sidestrand

Holt · Saxlingham · Field Dalling · Letheringsett · Baconsthorpe · W. Beckham · Gresham · Trimingham

Bale · A 148 · Sharrington · Thornage · Hempstead · Hanworth · Southrepps

Brinton · B 1110 · Edgefield Green · Plumstead · Little Barningham · Thorpe Market · Gimingham · Mundesley

Gunthorpe · Briningham · Melton Constable · Ramsgate Street · Matlaske · Sustead · Metton · Gunton Sta. · Trunch · Paston · B 1159

Swanton Novers · Briston · Thurgarton · Aldborough · Alby with Thwaite · Gunton Park Antingham · Knapton · Bacton · Keswick

Wood Norton · Thurning · Corpusty · Saxthorpe · Calthorpe · Itteringham · Colby · Suffield 149 · Swafield · Witton · Edingthorpe · Happisburgh

Hindolveston · Hall · Heydon · R. Bure · Ingworth · Banningham · North Walsham · Ridlington · B 1159

Foulsham · Wood Dalling · Blickling · Felmingham · Honing · East Ruston · Lessingham · Hempstead · Sea Palling

Guestwick · A 1067 · Reepham · B 1145 · Tuttington · Swanton Abbot · Westwick · Worstead · Dilham · Stalham · Ham · B 1151 · Ingham · Waxham

Themelthorpe · Whitwell · Booton · Marsham · Burgh next Aylsham · Skeyton · Worstead Sta. · Smallburgh · Sutton · Hickling · New Cut

Billingford · Foxley · B 1145 · Brandiston · Hevingham · Brampton · Lamas · Buxton · Lamas · Tupstead · Beeston St. Lawrence · Barton Turf · Hickling · Horsey Mere · Horsey

Bawdeswell · Sparham · Witchingham · Haveringland · Oxnead · Stratton Strawless · Coltishall · Ashmanhaugh · Barton Broad · Potter Heigham · Martham Broad · Winterton

Bylaugh · A 1067 · Alderford · Swannington · Horstead · Hainford · Belaugh · Wroxham Sta. · Neatishead · Catfield · Martham · B 1152 · Hemsby

Swanton Morley · Lyng · Attlebridge · Felthorpe · St. Helena A 140 · Newton St. Faith · Frettenham · Horning · Ludham · Thurne · Rollesby · Ormesby · St. Michael · B 1159

Elsing · Weston Longville · Morton · Taverham · Horsford · Spixworth · Crostwick · Woodbastwick · Salhouse · R. Thurne · Runham · Ormesby St. Margaret · Caister-on-Sea

North Tuddenham · Ringland · Weston Green · Drayton · Horsham St. Faith · Hackheath · Ranworth · Upton · Burgh St. Margaret · Filby · Mautby

A 47 · Honingham · Costessey · Catton · Sprowston · Blofield · Acle · A 47 Sta. · Thrigby · Caister

Welborne · Colton · Marlingford · Bowthorpe · NORWICH · Thorpe · Postwick · Brundall · Lingwood · Beighton · Runham · R. Bure

Mattishall · East Tuddenham · Barford · Bawburgh · University of East Anglia · Surlingham · Strumpshaw · N. Burlingham · Moulton St. Mary · Vauxhall Sta. · GREAT YARMOUTH

Hingham · Wramplingham · Colney · Eaton · A 140 · Trowse Newton · Kirby Bedon · Rockland St. Mary · Cantley · Freethorpe · Wickhampton · Halvergate · Southtown · Gorleston

Kimberley Str. · Hethersett · Cringleford · Keswick · Intwood · Framingham · A 146 · Bramerton · Hassingham · Berney Arms Sta. · Burgh Castle · Bradwell

Deopham · Crownthorpe · Wymondham · Kettering ham · East Carleton · Caistor St. Edmund · Yelverton · Hellington · Ashby St. Mary · Freethorpe · Reedham · Belton

Morley St. Botolph · Mulbartons · Swardeston · Stoke Holy Cross · Alpington · Thurton · Langley · Ferry · R. Waveney · Fritton Decoy · Ashby · Hopton

Attleborough · Spooner Row · Ashwellthorpe · Flordon · Bracon Ash · Newton Flotman · R. Tas · Shotesham · Bergh Apton · Brooke · Mundham · Seething · The Laurels · Hales · Chedgrave · Heckingham · Loddon · Norton Subcourse · Thorpe · Ravingham · Haddiscoe · Somerleyton · Herringfleet · Blundeston · Corton

Great Ellingham · Tacolneston · Fundenhall · Hapton · Tasburgh · Saxlingham Nethergate · Saxlingham Green · Kirstead Green · Thwaite St. Mary · Ellingham · Thurlton · B 1136 · Wheatacre · Burgh St. Peter · Oulton Broad N. Sta. · Lowestoft Ness

Old Buckenham · Carleton Rode · Bunwell St. Mary · Forncett St. Peter · Long Stratton · Wacton · Hempnall · Woodton · Hedenham · Ditchingham · Broome · Shipmeadow · Barsham · Gillingham · Aldeby · Barnby · North Cove · Carlton Colville · LOWESTOFT

New Buckenham · Bunwell · Hargate · Gt. Moulton · Shelton · Shelton Green · Hardwick · Harris Green · Topcroft · Topcroft Str. · Hall · Earsham · Bungay · Mettingham · Worlingham · Beccles A 146 · Weston · Mutford · Gisleham · Kessingland · Kessingland Beach

Banham · Tibenham · Pulham Market · Denton · Alburgh · Flixton · Ilketshall St. John · Ringsfield · Ilketshall St. Andrew · A 145 · Ellough · Hulver Street · Henstead · South Cove

Quidenham · Winfarthing · Tivetshall St. Mary · Pulham St. Mary · Piccadilly Corner · Homersfield · St. Cross S. Elmham · Ilketshall St. Margaret · Ilketshall St. Lawrence · Redisham · Shadingfield · Sotterley · West End · Benacre

Kenninghall · Gissing · Starston · Rushall · Harleston · Redenhall · St. Margaret S. Elmham · St. Michael S. Elmham · Brampton · Sloven · Covehithe Ness

Shelfanger · Burston · Wireless Sta. · B 1134 · Needham · Withersdale Street · All Saints S. Elmham · Stone Street · A 145 · Frostenden · Wrentham · Covehithe

Fersfield · South Lopham · Bressingham · Roydon · Dickleburgh · Thelveton · Brockdish · Weybread · Metfield · St. James S. Elmham · Spexhall · Rumburgh · Uggeshall · Wangford · Easton Broad · South Cove

Diss · Scole · Billingford · Syleham · Hoxne · Weybread Street · Wingfield · Wissett · Broadway · B 1124 · Henham · A 12 · B 1127 · Southwold

Botesdale · Rickinghall Superior · Burgate · Thrandeston · Brome · Cross Street · Chickering · Fressingfield · Linstead Parva · Halesworth · Holton · Cookley · Blyford · A 144 · B 1123

1 2 3 4 5 Miles

© John Bartholomew & Son Ltd

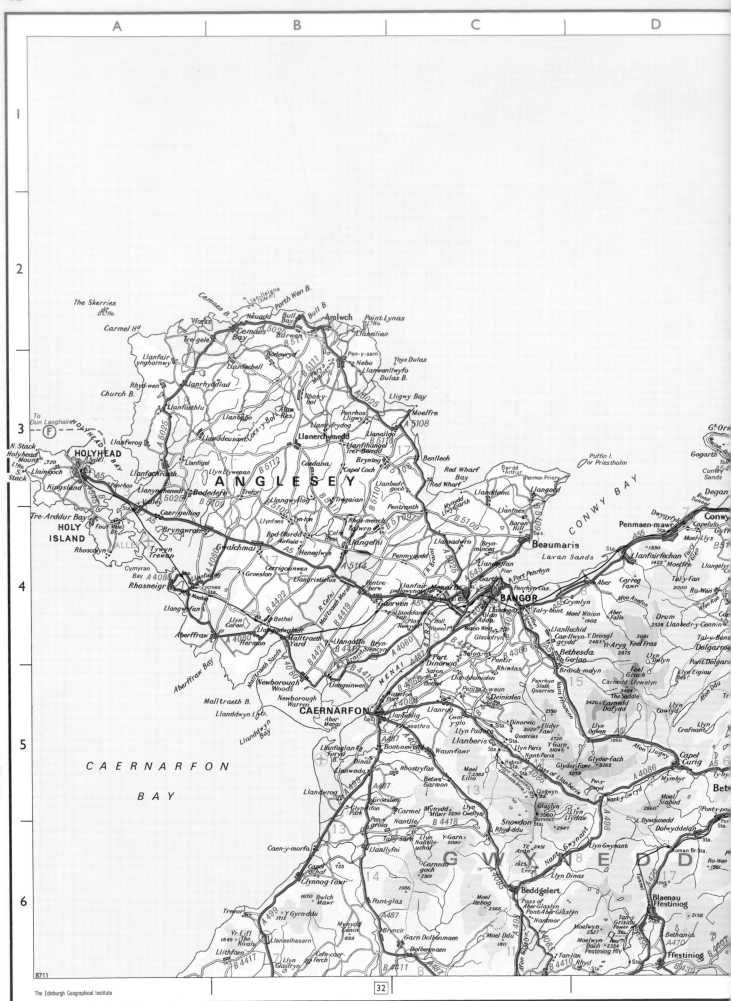

The Edinburgh Geographical Institute

2 3 4 5 Miles

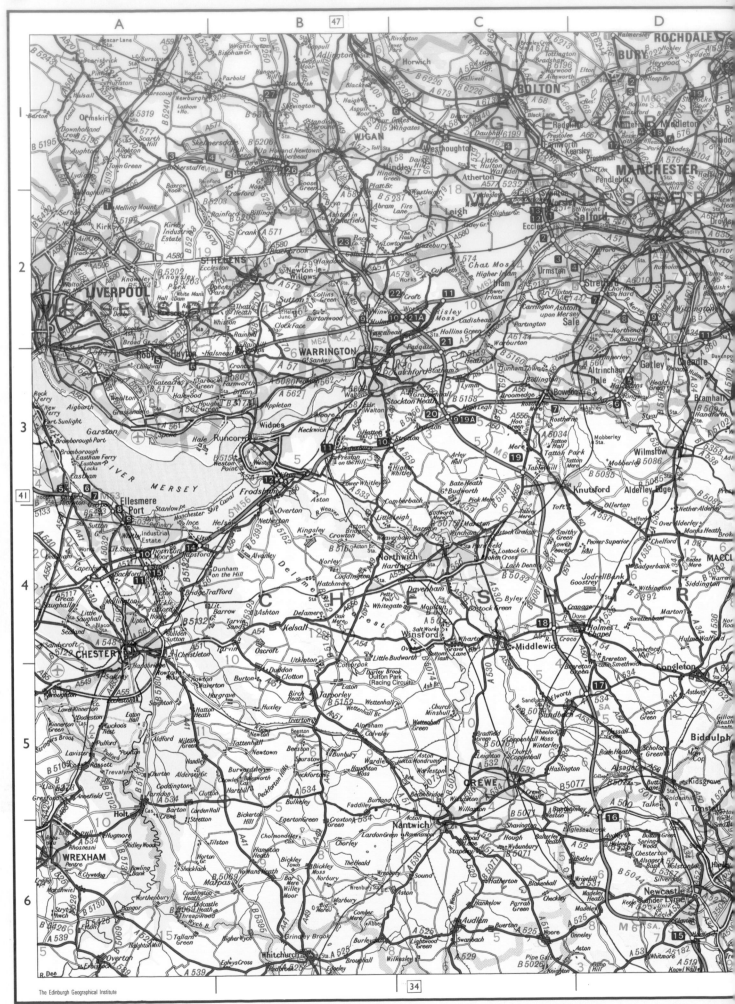

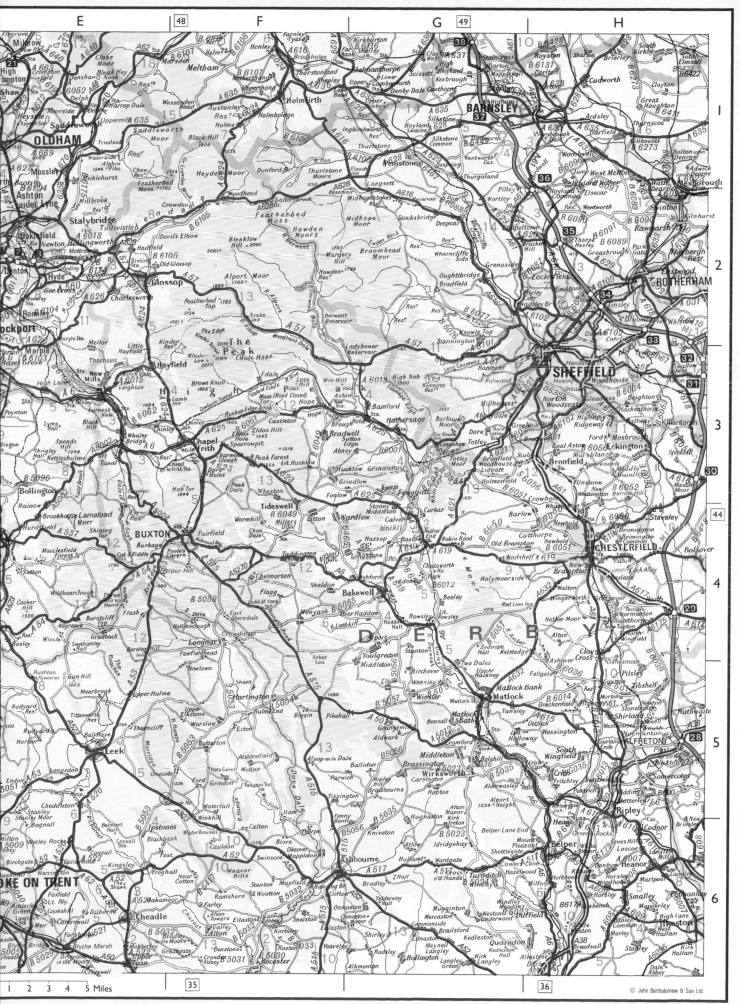

1 2 3 4 5 Miles

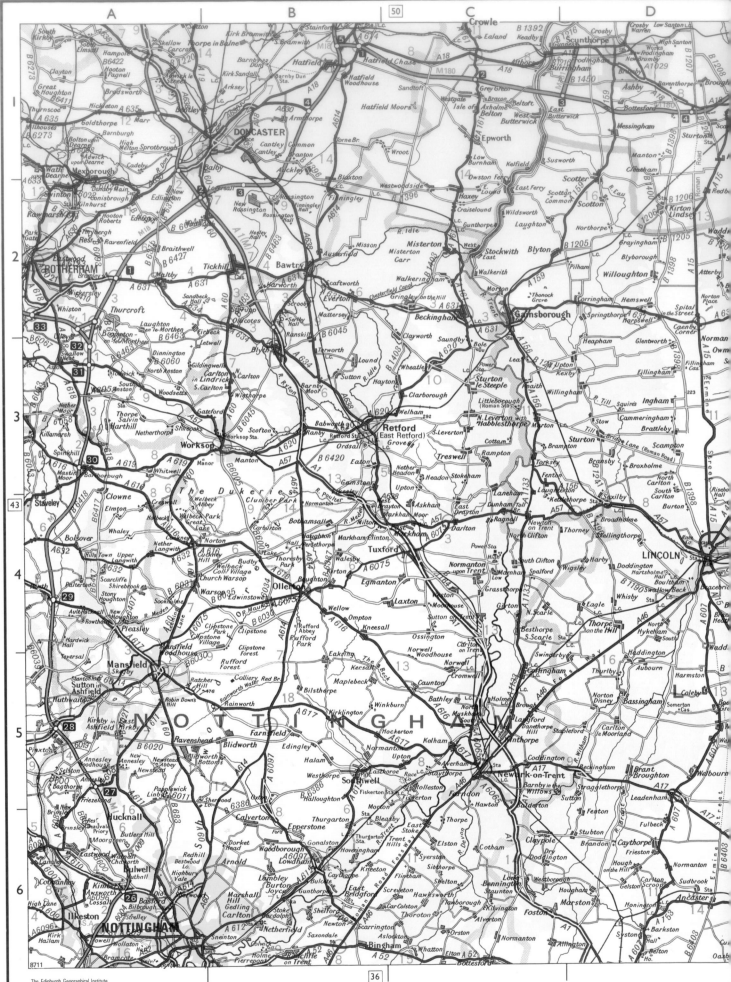

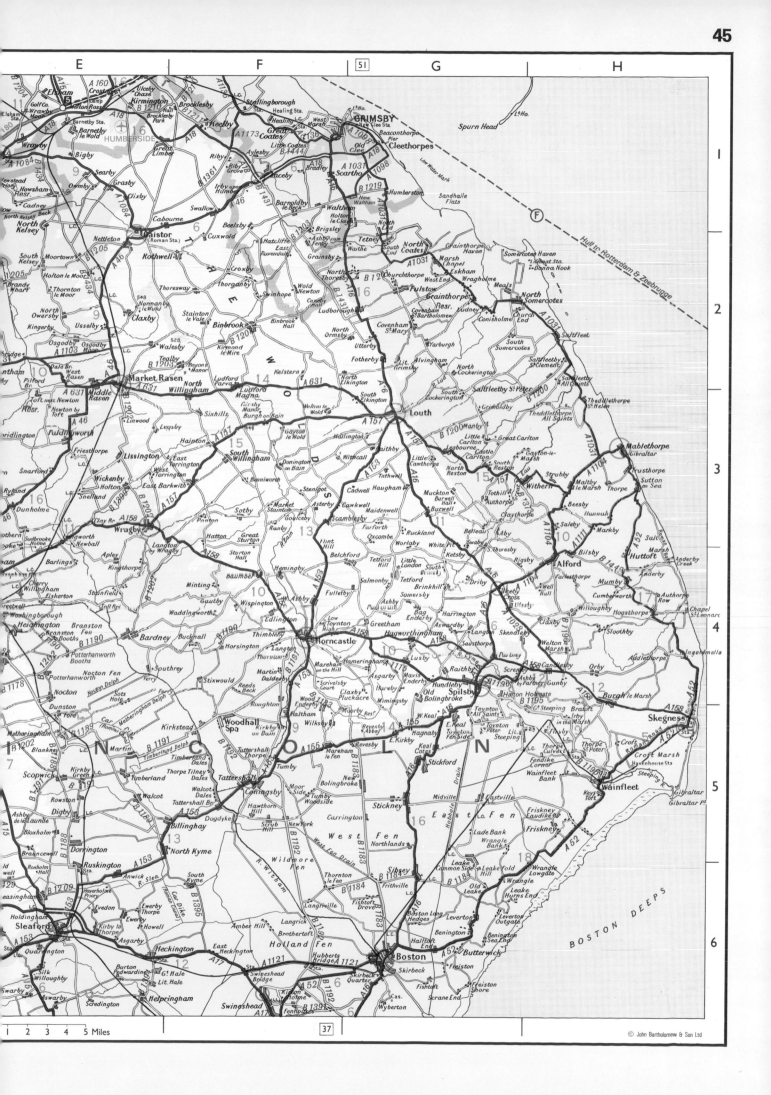

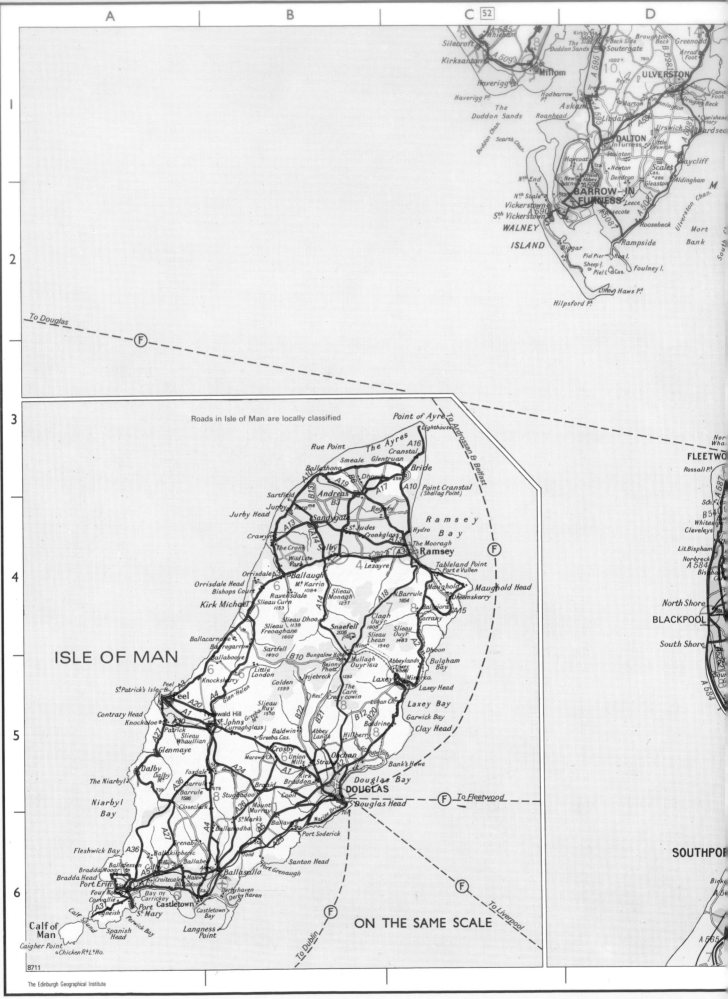

A   B   C [52]   D

Roads in Isle of Man are locally classified

ISLE OF MAN

ON THE SAME SCALE

The Edinburgh Geographical Institute

8711

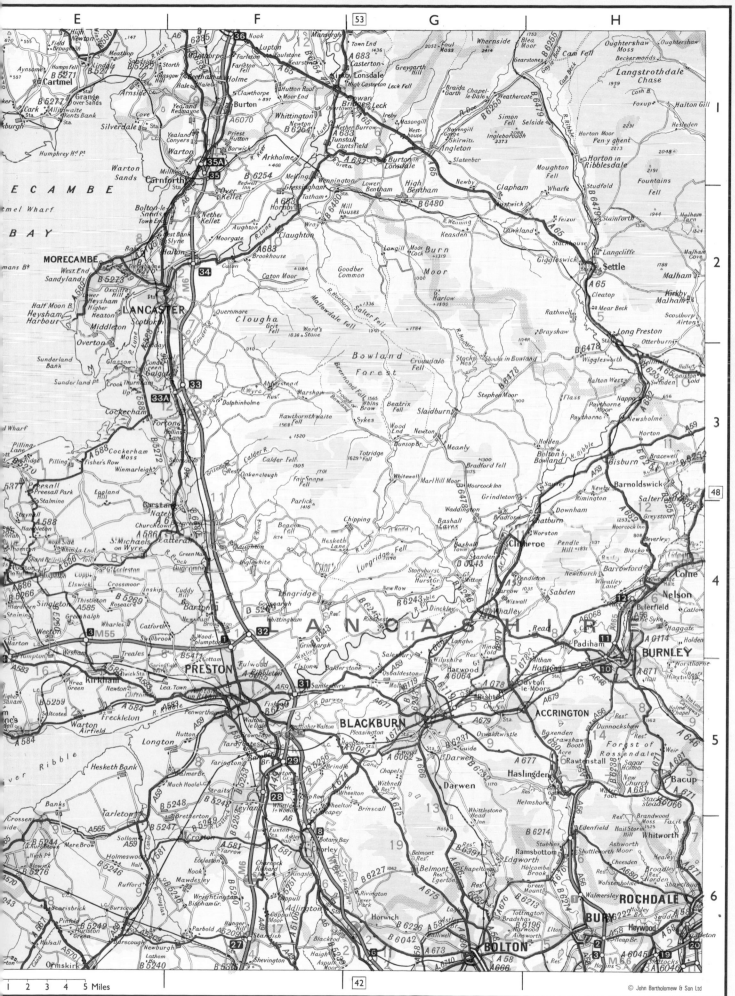

© John Bartholomew & Son Ltd

1 2 3 4 5 Miles

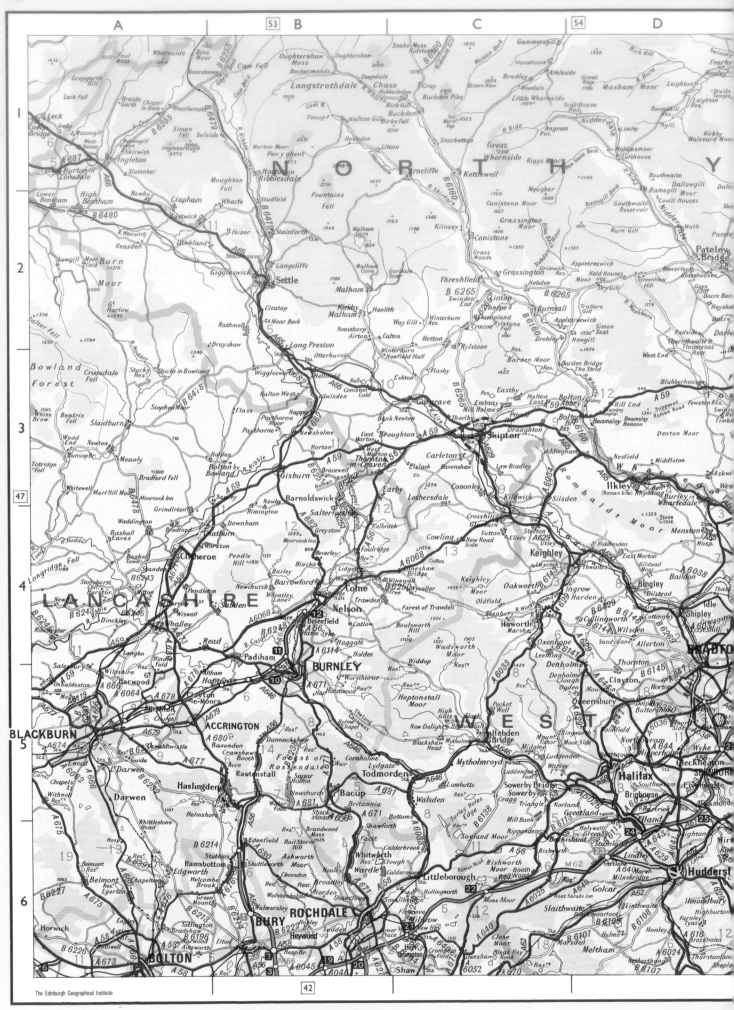

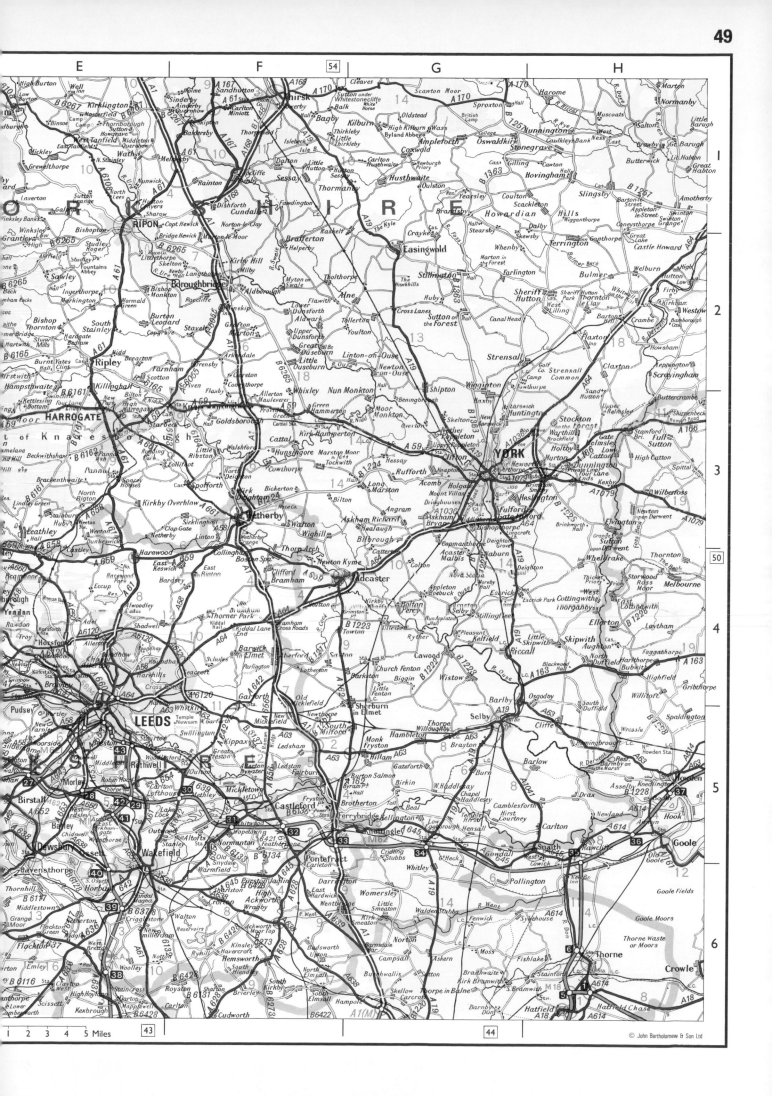

1 2 3 4 5 Miles

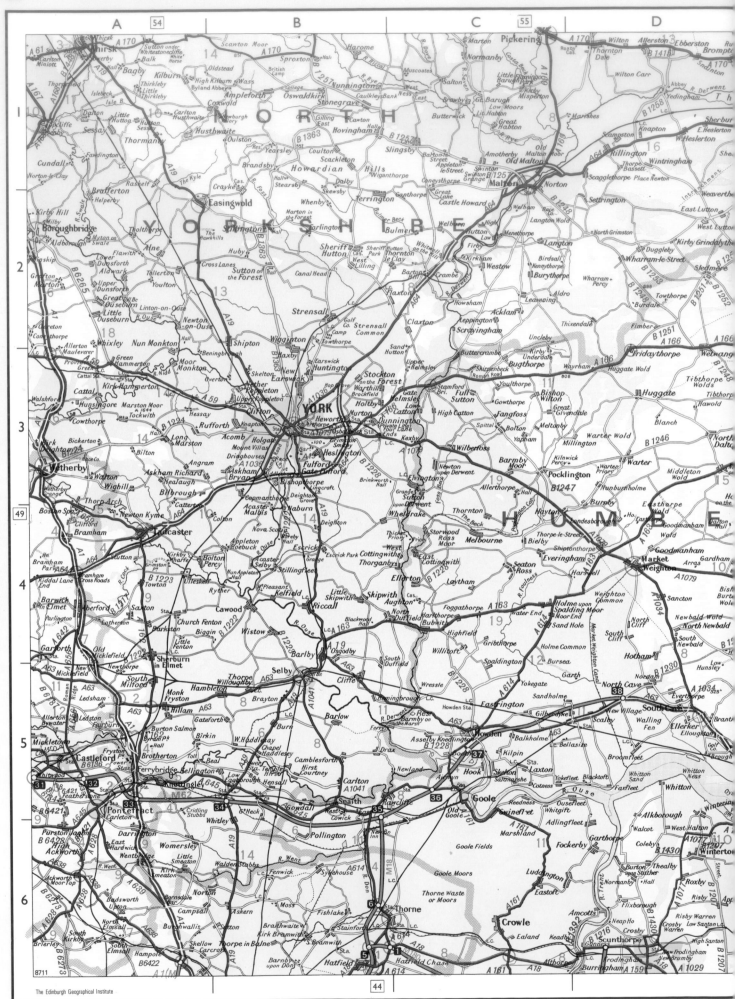

The Edinburgh Geographical Institute

1 2 3 4 5 Miles

© John Bartholomew & Son Ltd

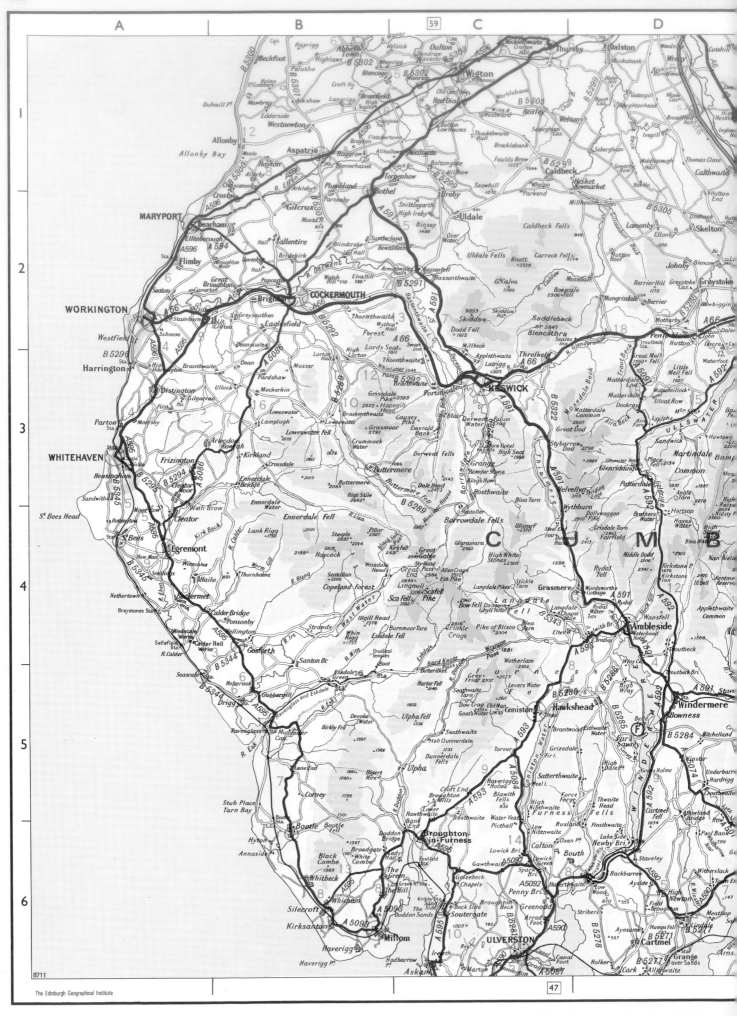

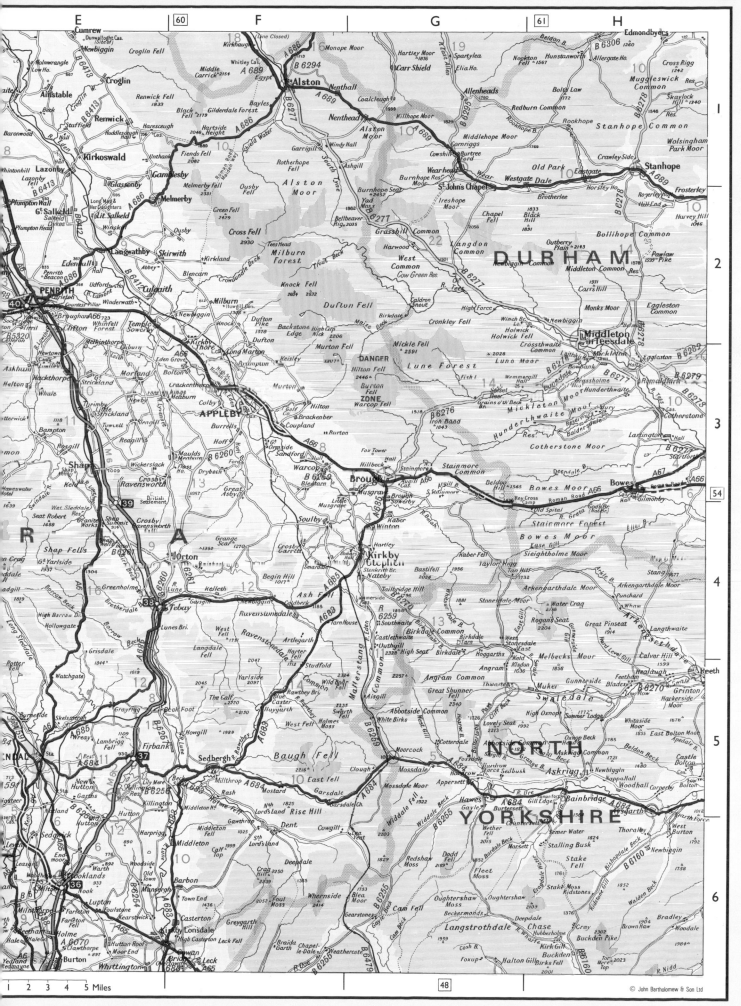

E 60 F G 61 H

Cumrew
Dunwallought Cas.
Newbiggin
Holmwrangle
Low Ho.
Ainstable
Croglin
Baronwood
Staffield
Renwick Fell
1833
Renwick
Huddlescough Hall
Hartside Height
2046
Kirkhaugh
(Line Closed)
Whitley Cas.
Egypt
A 686
B 6294
Monope Moor
Hartley Moor
1676
Carr Shield
19
Spartylea
B 6306
Beldon B.
1260
Nookton
Fell
1567
Hunstanworth
Allergate Ho.
Edmondbyers
Cross Rigg
1242
Muggleswick
Common
Skaylock
Hill
1340

I

Kirkoswald
Lazonby
Gamblesby
Glassonby
Middle Carrick
2154
A 689
Alston
Nenthall
Bayles
Nenthead
Coalcleugh
1958
Killhope Moor
Allenheads
1760
Redburn Common
Bolts Law
1772
Rookhope B.
Old Park
Crawley Side
Stanhope
Stanhope Common
Wolsingham
Park Moor
10

Plumpton Wall
Gt. Salkeld
Lit. Salkeld
Dykes
Melmerby
Skirwith
Kirkland
Gilderdale Forest
Black Fell
2119
Fiends Fell
2082
Garrigill
Windy Hall
Ashgill
Alston Moor
Rotherhope Fell
South Tyne
Burnhope Res.
Moor
Cowshill
Burtree Ford
St. John's Chapel
Wearhead
Middlehope Moor
Corriggs
Ireshope Moor
Westgate
Brotherlee
Eastgate
Horsley Hill
Rogerley Hall
Hill End
Harvey Hill
1046
Frosterley
10

2

PENRITH
Edenhall
Langwathby
Melmerby Fell
2331
Ousby
Fell
Green Fell
2479
Cross Fell
2930
Tees Head
Burnhope Seat
2452
Yad Moss
1802
Bellbeaver Rig.
2035
Grasshill Common
Harwood
West Common
Cow Green Res.
Langdon Common
Chapel Fell
2056
Black Hill
1831
Outberry Plain
2143
Newbiggin Common
Bollihope Common
Pawlaw Pike
1599
DURHAM
2

Blencarn
Crowdundle Beck
Milburn Forest
Knock Fell
2604
2632
Dufton Fell
Maize Beck
R. Tees
Caldron
Snout
High Force
Cronkley Fell
Holwick
Holwick Fell
Winch Br.
Lot
Crossthwaite Common
Newbiggin
Carrs Hill
1911
Monks Moor
Eggleston Common
2

Milburn
Howgill Ho.
612
Newbiggin
Dufton Pike
1578
Dufton
Backstone Edge
2205
High Cup Nick
2206
Murton Fell
Keisley
Mickle Fell
2591
1026
Luno Moor
Fish L.
14
Wemmergill Hall
Selset Res.
Grains o'th Beck
Middleton Moor
Hunderthwaite
Grassholme
Middleton in Teesdale
Mickleton
Eggleston
B 6282
10

3

Kirkby Thore
Long Marton
Crackenthorpe
Knock
Dufton
Hilton
Murton
DANGER
Hilton Fell
2446
Burton Fell
2349
ZONE
Warcop Fell
1578
B 6276
Iron Band
1843
2026
Hunderthwaite Moor
Romaldkirk
Cotherstone
B 6277
B 6279
B 6278
3

APPLEBY
Colby
Bongate
Hoff
Burrells
Drybeck
Coupland
Brackenber
Burton
Fox Tower
Hall
Stainmore
Common
Baldersdale
Cotherstone Moor
Deepdale B.
Startforth
B 6277
A 67
3

Temple Sowerby
Newbiggin
Kirkby Thore
Sandford
B 6260
Ormside
Warcop
B 6259
Bleatarn
Musgrave
Little Musgrave
Brough
Brough Sowerby
A66
Augill B.
A 66
Stainmore
Rey Cross Camp
Old Spital
Roman Road
Beldoo
1565
Bowes Moor
Bowes
A 66
Gilmonby
A 66
54
Hall
16

4

Soulby
Kaber
Winton
Hartley
Kirkby Stephen
Nateby
Stenkrith Br.
Kaber Fell
Begin Hill
1017
Smardale
Tailbridge Hill
1796
Bastifell
2024
Whitsun Dale B.
1956
1132
Stonesdale Moor
Arkengarthdale Moor
Punchard
Water Crag
2204
Rogans Seat
Great Pinseat
1914
Langthwaite
Calvar Hill
1599
Reeth
4

Orton
Kelleth
Newbiggin
Ash Fell
185
Ravensdale Beck
B 6259
Tarn House
Southwaite
6259
1850
Birkdale Common
Birkdale Tarn
West Stonesdale East
Hoggarths
Melbecks Moor
High Level Gill
Grinton
Hackersike Moor
4

Tebay
Gaisgill
Ravenstonedale
R. Lune
R. Eden
Castlethwaite
Uthgill
High Seat
2328
Birkdale
Angram
Kisdon
1636
Muker
Gunnerside
Swaledale
B 6270
Feetham
Blades
Healaugh
5

Greenholme
Bretherdale
Lunes Bri.
West Fell
1791
Harter Fell
1712
Studfold
2324
Mallerstang
Common
Angram Common
Great Shunner Fell
2340
Thwaite
Cliff Beck
Lovely Seat
2213
High Oxnop
Summer Lodge
Oxnop Beck
Whitaside Moor
1676
East Bolton Moor
Apedale B.
Castle Bolton
5

Langdale Fell
1844
Yarlside
2097
Wild Boar
Fell
2324
Swarth Fell
2235
2150
Holmes Moss
Aisgill
Abbotside Common
White Birks
Cotterdale
1726
Grange B.
Fossdale
Hardraw
Force Sedbush
Askrigg
Newbiggin
Nappa Hall
Woodhall
Carperby
5

The Calf
2220
Peak Foot
Grayrigg
Skelsmergh
Blue Caster
Rawthey Bri.
Howgill
West Fell
1989
Rawthey
Sedbergh
A 684
Baugh Fell
Clough
Moorcock
A 684
Mossdale
Appersett
Hawes
Gayle
Burtersett
A 684
Bainbridge
A 684
Gill Edge
Carperby
9

5

Grisdale
1818
Firbank
Middleton H.
Millthrop
Rash
East Fell
Garsdale
Garsdale Ch.
Widdale Beck
Mossdale Moor
Mossdale Fell
1922
R. Ure
Semer Water
1824
Wether Fell
2015
Stalling Busk
Thoralby
West Burton
1792
B 6160
Newbiggin
1758
6

Lily Mere
Killington
Middleton Fell
Lord's Land
Rise Hill
Dent
Cowgill
Lea Yeat
Widdale Fell
2203
Redshaw Moss
1829
Dodd Fell
2189
Bardale Beck
Marsett
Stake Fell
1761
Stake Moss
Kidstones
Bishopdale Beck
1852
6

Middleton
Harprigg
Gawthrop
Middleton Fell
1025
Sth Lord's Land
Calf Top
1999
Deepdale
Crag Hill
2250
Whernside
2414
Blea Moor
1753
Fleet Moss
Oughtershaw Moss
Oughtershaw
Deepdale Chase
1376
Bradley
1904
Brown Haw
Woodale
6

Barbon
Mansergh
Old Town
Woodside
Town End
1436
Fout Moss
2057
Gearstones
Cam Fell
Langstrothdale Chase
Hubberholme
Cray
2302
Buckden Pike
1984
R. Nidd
6

Casterton
Kirkby Lonsdale
Greygarth Hill
Braida Garth
Chapel-le-Dale
Weathercote
B 6479
B 6255
Foxup
Cosh B.
Halton Gill
1959
Birks Fell
2001
Kirk Gill
Buckden
Top Mere Top
2023
6

Leck Fell
High Casterton
Leck
A 65
Oughtershaw
Beckermonds
B 6160

1 2 3 4 5 Miles
48
© John Bartholomew & Son Ltd

NORTH

YORKSHIRE

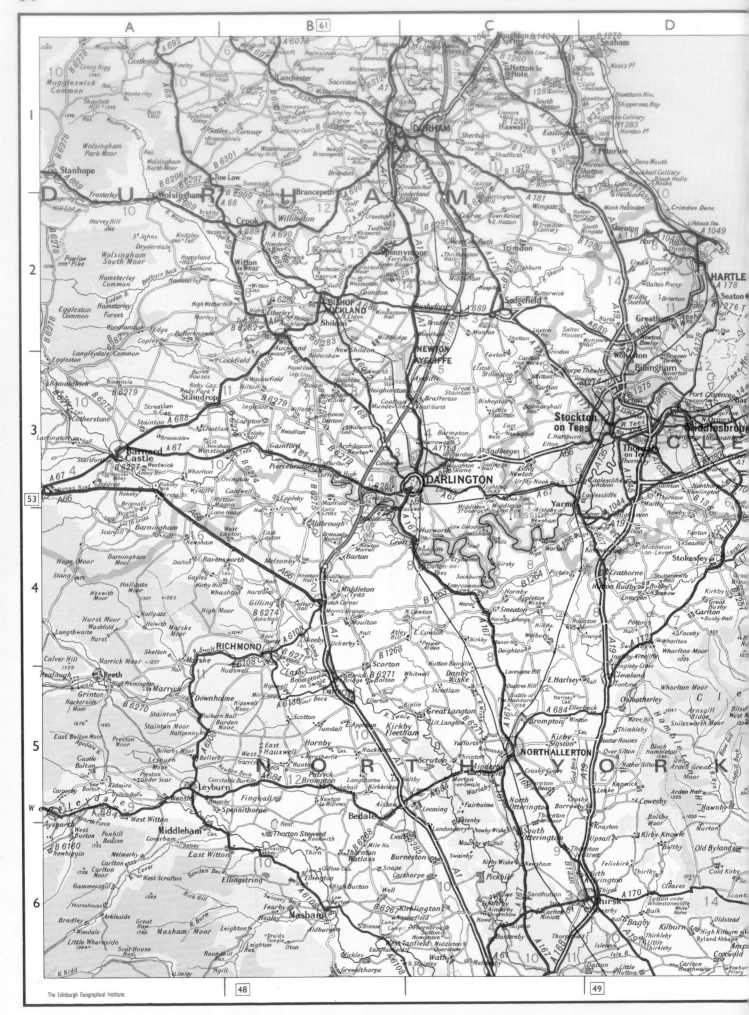

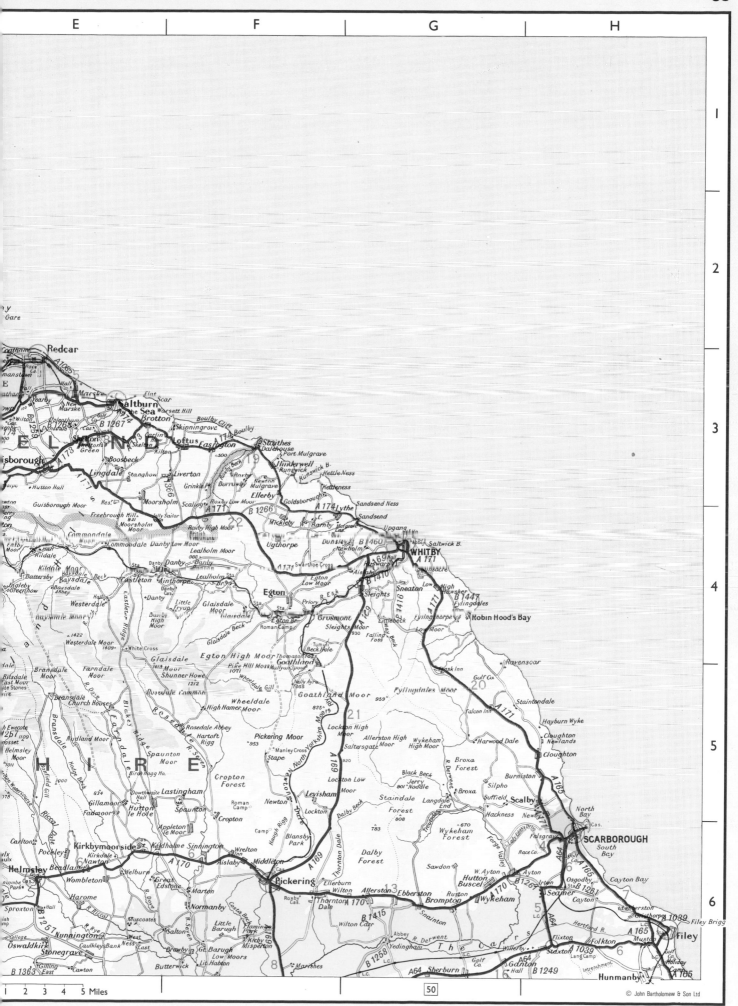

1 2 3 4 5 Miles

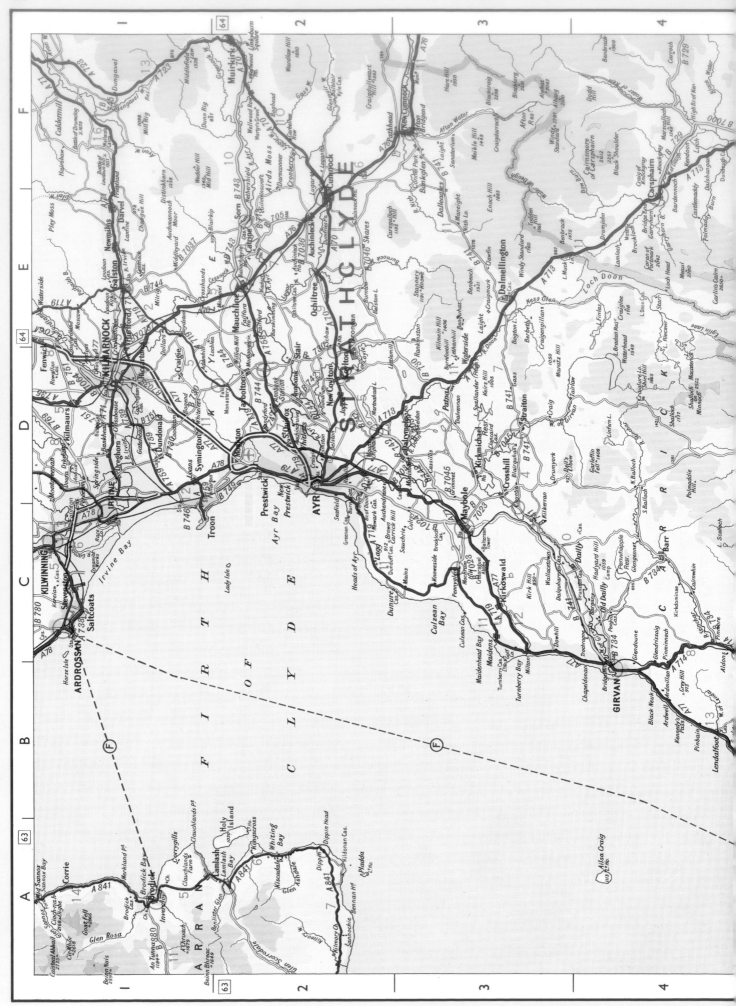

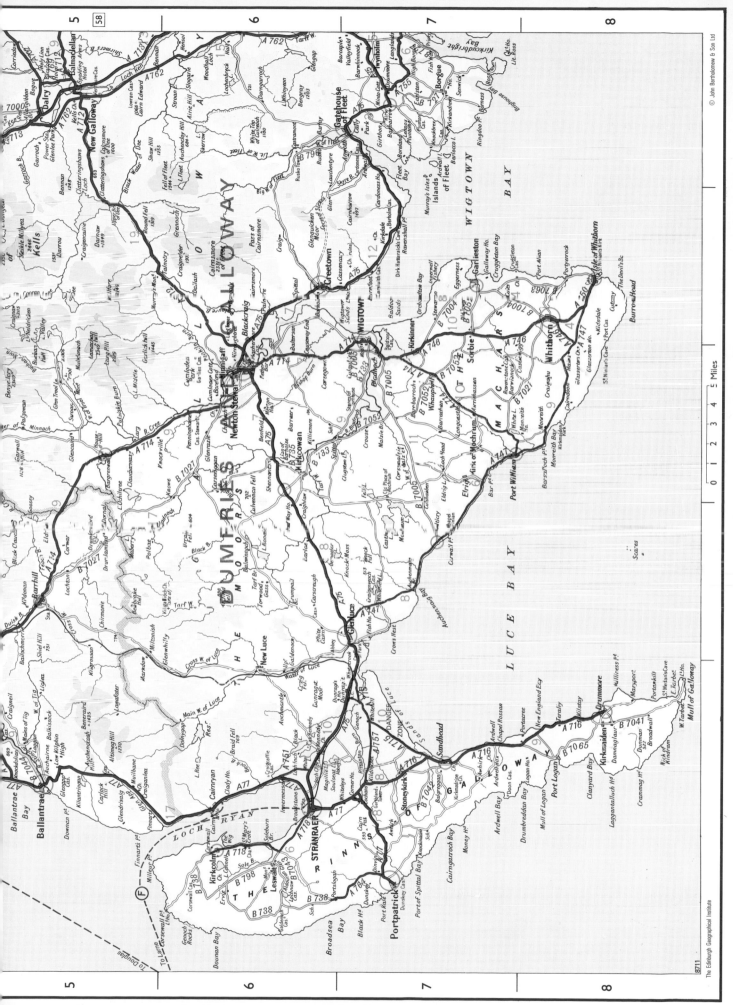

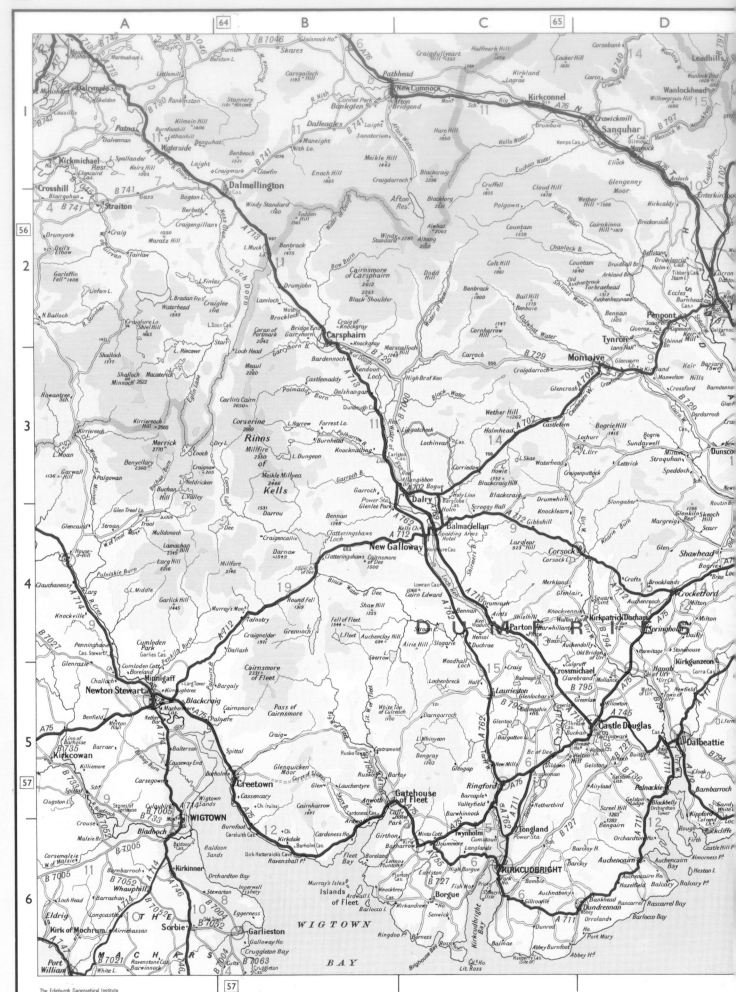

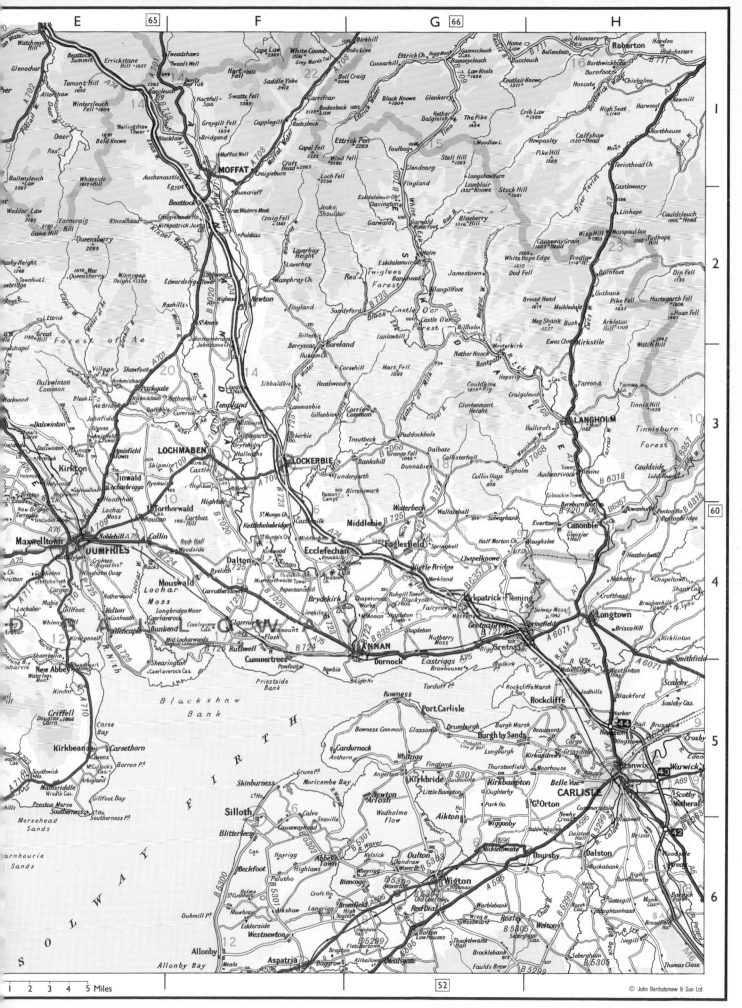

© John Bartholomew & Son Ltd

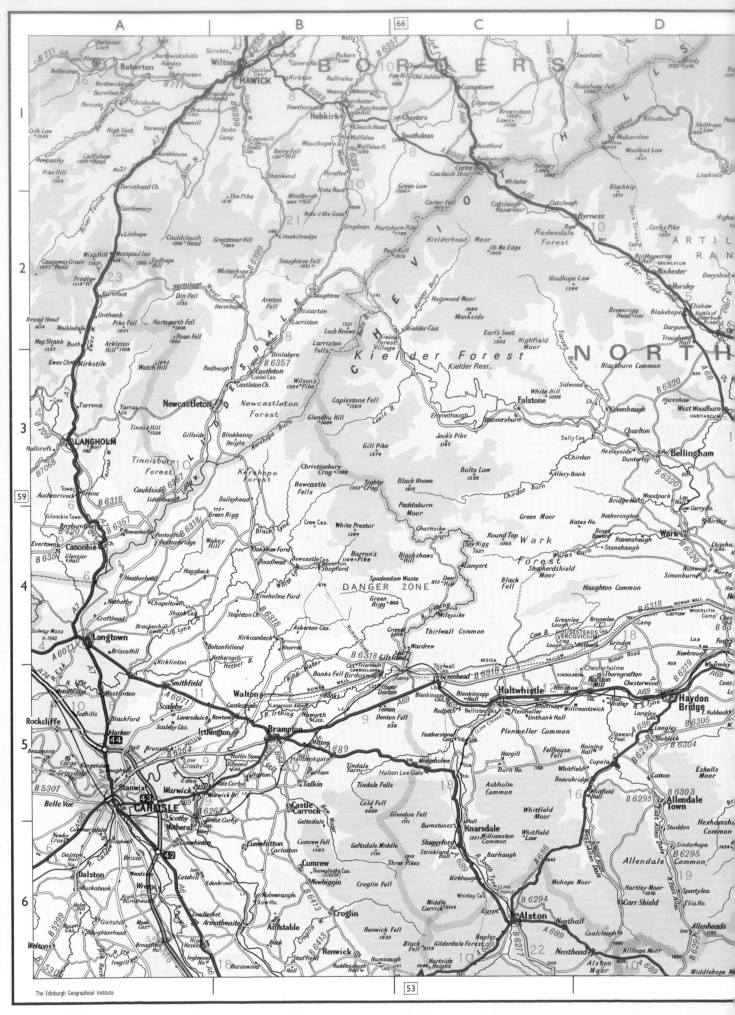

The Edinburgh Geographical Institute

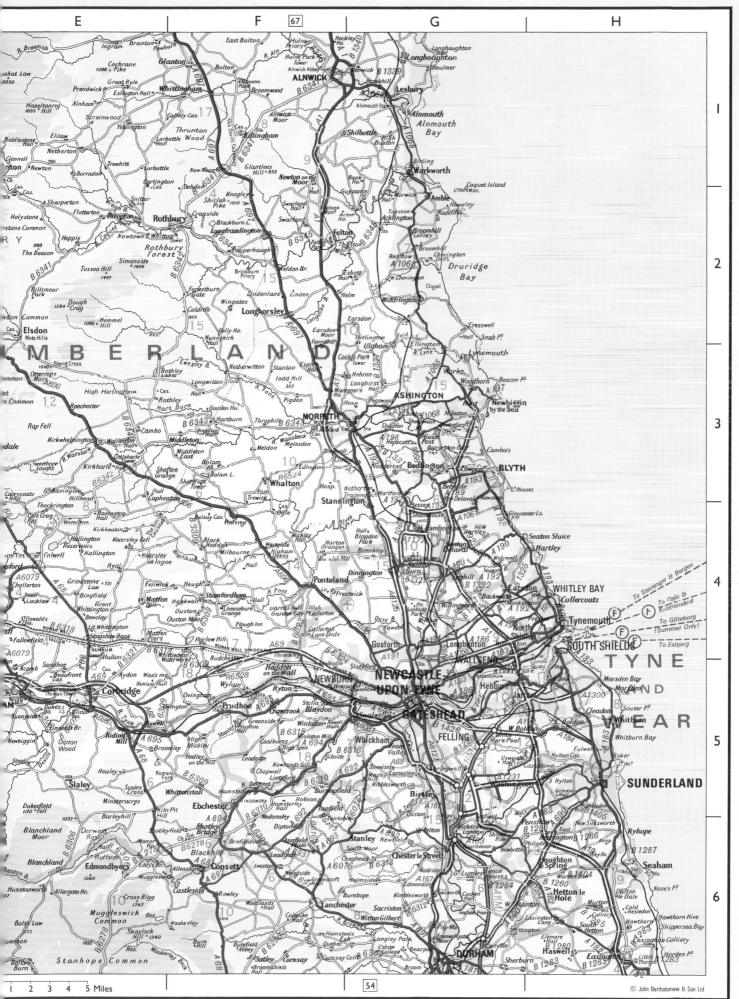

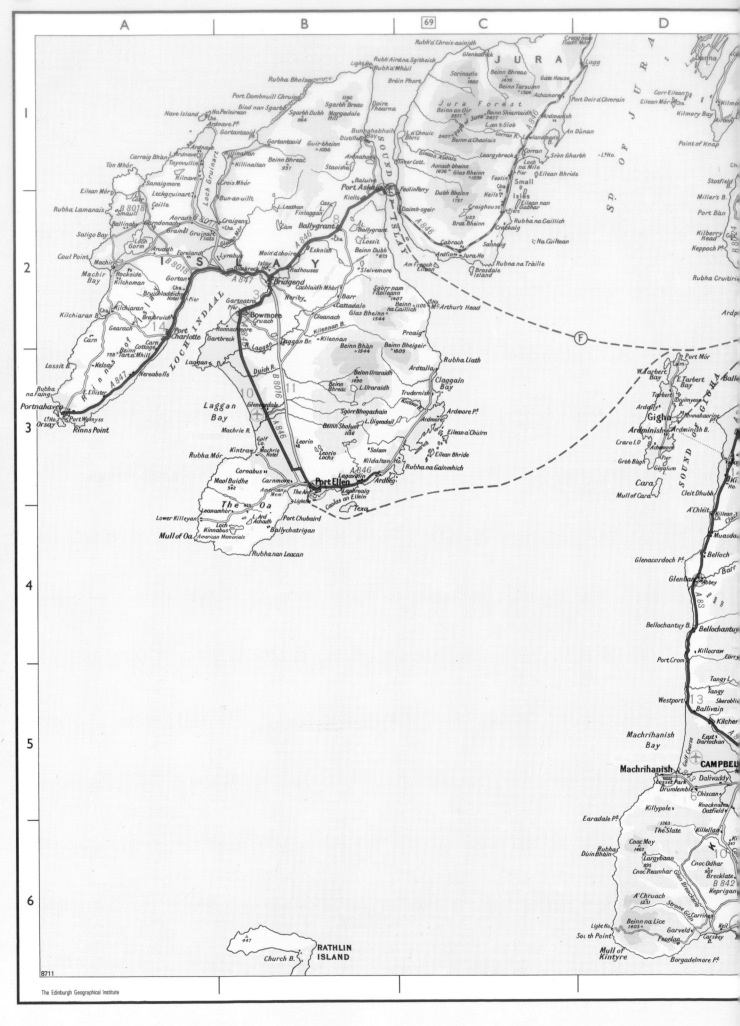

8711

The Edinburgh Geographical Institute

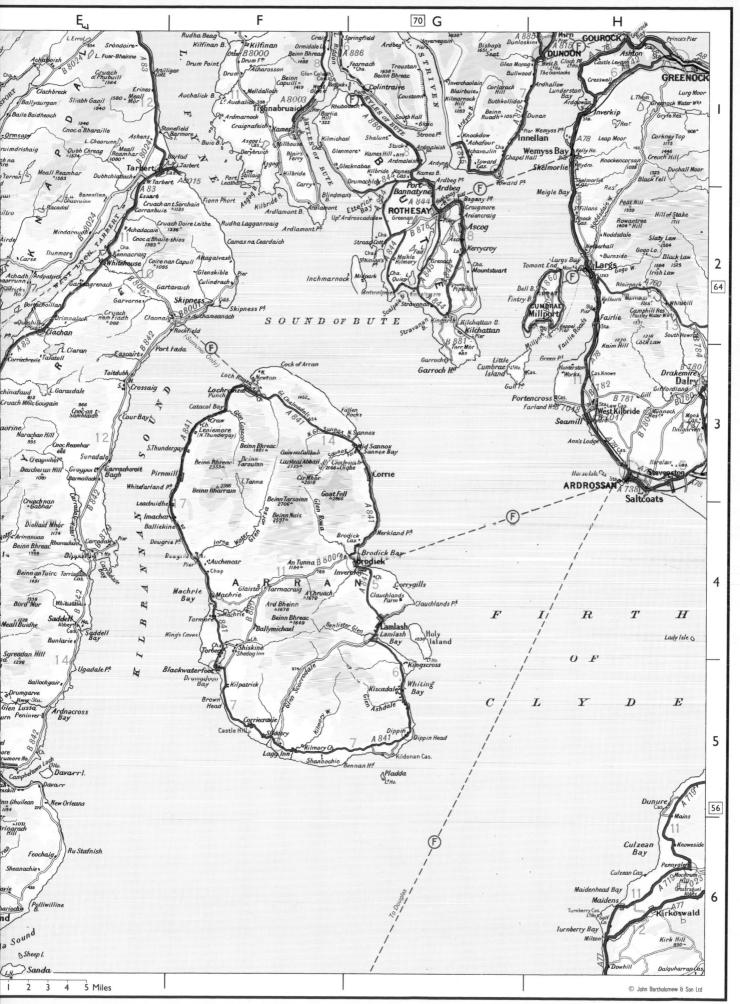

E F G H

I

2

64

3

4

56

5

6

1 2 3 4 5 Miles

© John Bartholomew & Son Ltd

64

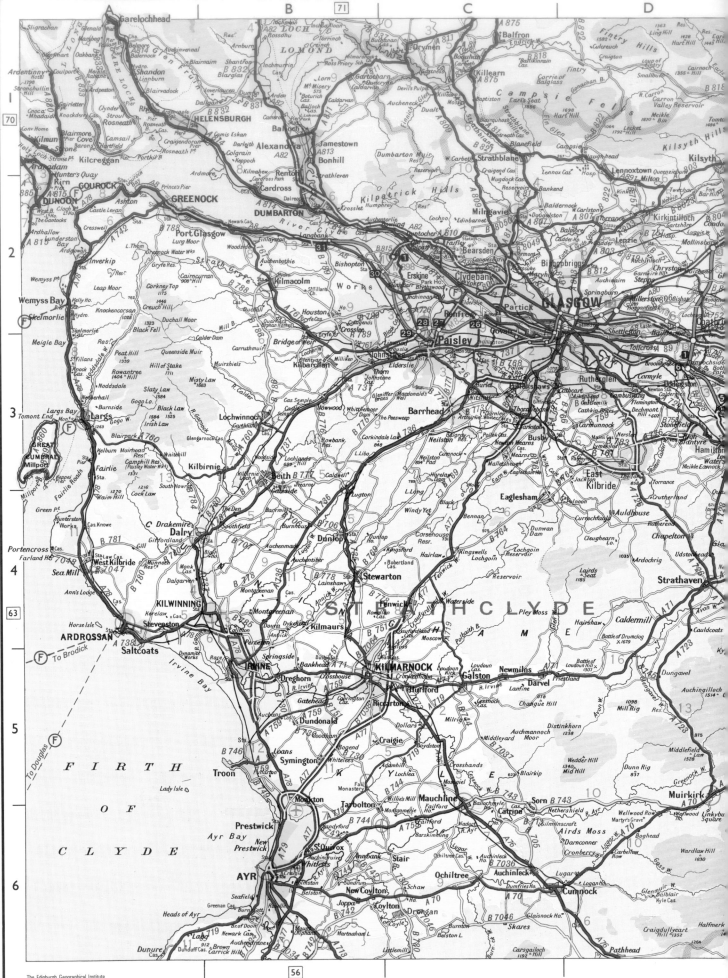

The Edinburgh Geographical Institute

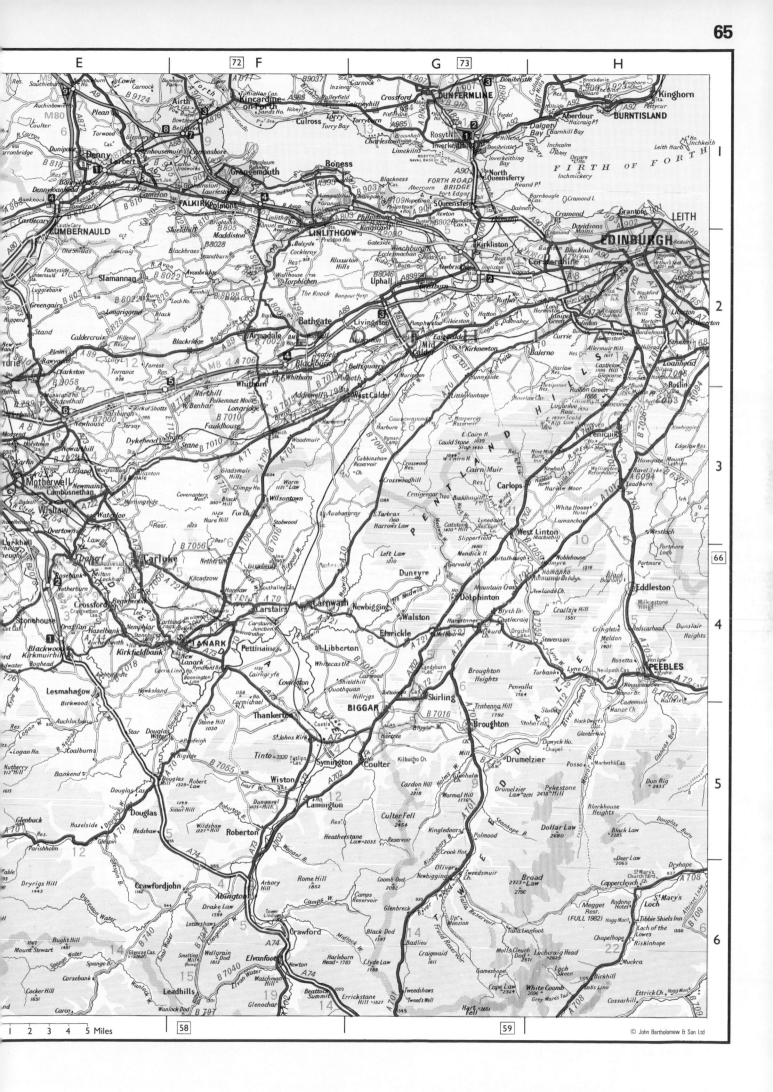

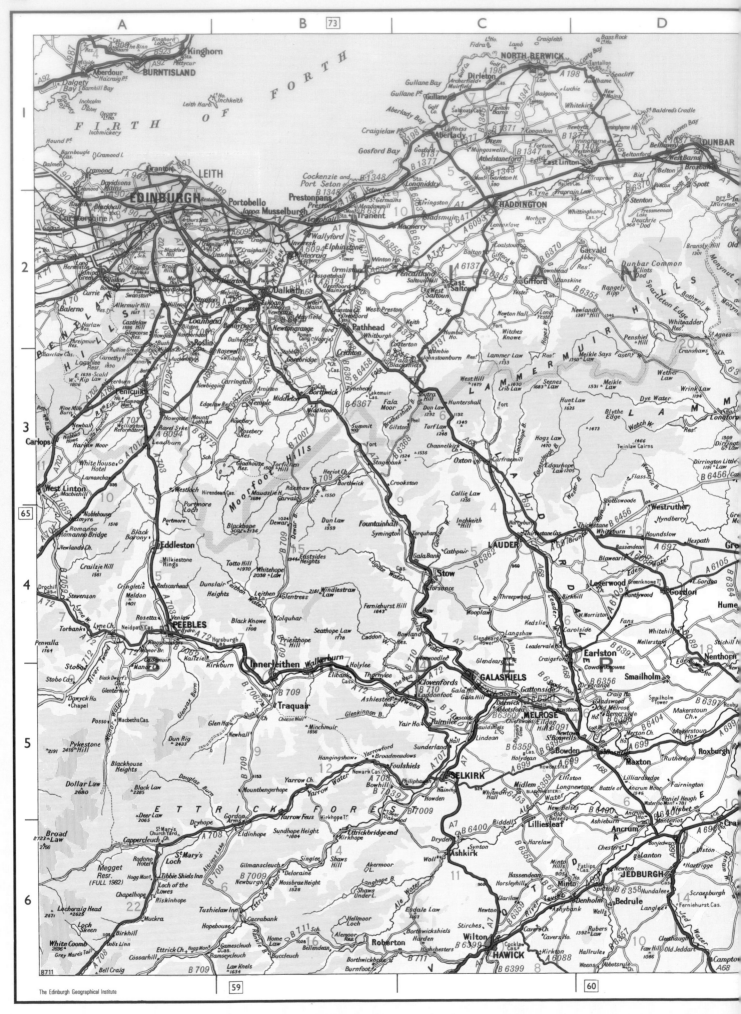

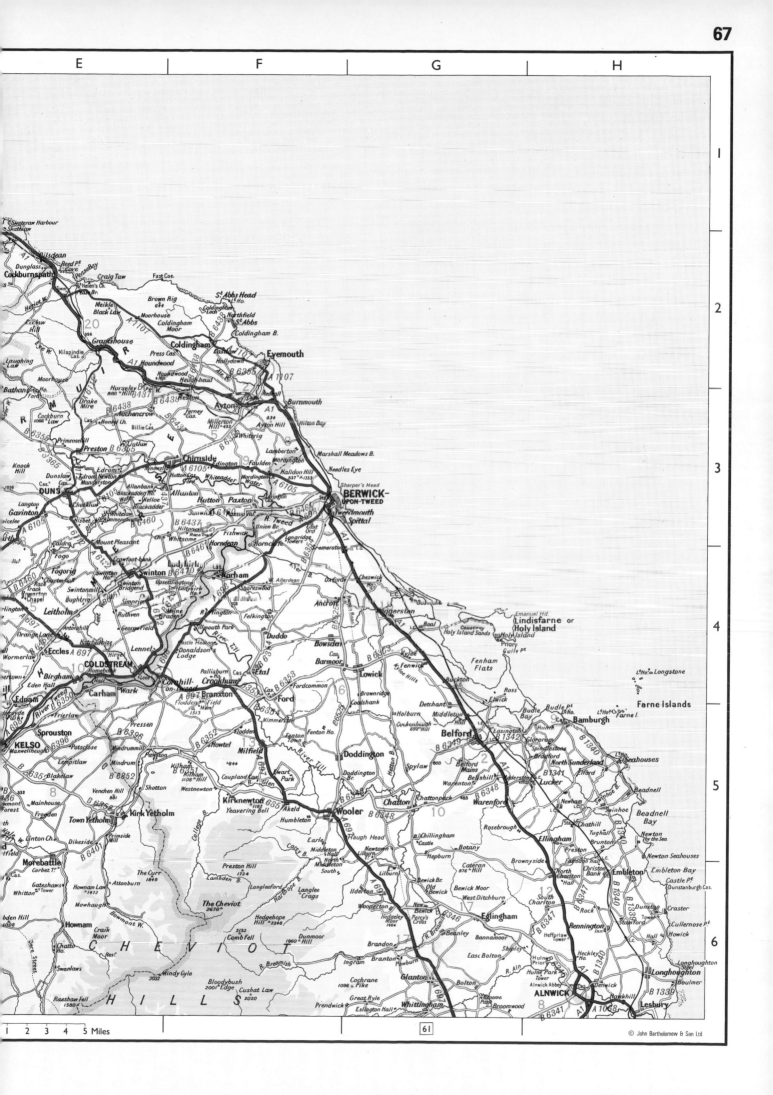

E F G H

I

2

3

4

5

6

Skateraw Harbour
Skateraw
Dunglass
Cove
Reed Pt
Cockburnspath
Penseybay
Helen's Ch.
Craig Taw
Fast Cas.
St Abbs Head
L. Ho.
Heriot W.
Meikle
Black Law
Brown Rig
634
Coldingham
Loch
Northfield
St Abbs
Coldingham B.
Moorhouse
A 1107
Grantshouse
396
Coldingham
Moor
Easton
A 1107
Eyemouth
Laughing
Law
Kilspindie
Cas.
A 1107 Houndwood
Press Cas.
Hollydown
Ale
B 6355
Burnmouth
Burnmouth
Moorhouse
Houndwood
Heughhead
Redhall
A 1107
A 1
Ayton
634
Ayton Hill
Hilton Bay
Horseley B.
B 8431
B 6438
Fernay
Cas.
Millerton
Hill 433
Whiterig
Marshall Meadows B.
Cockburn
Law 1066
Bonkyl Ch.
Billie Cas.
Lamberton
Mordington
Needles Eye
Primrosehill
Cutlaw
Whitrig
Faulden
Halidon Hill
537 1333
Sharper's Head
Preston B 6355
Chirnside
Edington
Mordington D.
Water
A 6105
BERWICK-UPON-TWEED
Spittal
Tweedmouth
Knock
Hill
Dunslaw
Edrom Newton
Manderston
Allanbank
Whiteadder
Ford
Allanton
Ord
Cas.
DUNS
Edrom
Blackadder
Wate
Hutton
Paxton
East
Ord
Union Br.
R. Tweed
Gavinton
Blackadder
Whitelaw
Nisbet
Hutton Hall
Fishwick
Longridge
Tower
Horncliffe
Mount Pleasant
Ummerchaster
Hilton
Cha
Whitsome
Horndean
Cremerston
Fogorig
Swinton
Ho.
B 6460
Lady Kirk
Norham
Shoreswood
Ancroft
Oxford
Cheswick
Cas. Ho.
B 6460
Upsettlington
Ladykirk
B 6437
Felkington
Allerdean
Boggerston
Emanuel Hd.
Lindisfarne or
Holy Island
Leitholm
Swinton
Bridgend
Simpringe
Duddo
Boal
L. Co
Holy Island Sands
Holy Island
Priory
Eccles
A 697
Antonshill
George Field
Tillmouth Park
Bowsden
Cas.
Kyloe
Fenwick
Fenham
Flats
Guile Pt
Coldstream
Donaldson's
Lodge
Duddo
Barmoor
Lowick
Kyloe
Hills
Buckton
Ross
Longstone
L. Ho.
Birgham
Homebank
Hall
Castle Heaton
Pallisburn
Cas.
Crookham
Etal
Fordcommon
Brownridge
Detchant
Elwick
Budle Pt
L. Ho.
Farne I.
Farne Islands
Carham
Wark
Cornhill-on-Tweed
A 697 Branxton
Ford
Coalshank
Holburn
Middleton
Hall
Budle
Bay
Bamburgh
River
Till
Flodden
Field 1513
Kimmerston
Fenton
Town
Fenton Ho.
Cockenheugh
692 Hill
Belford
Glororum
Sprouston
Pressen
Flodden
Howtel
Hetton B.
Spylaw
800
Belford Mains
Lasington
B 1342
Bradford
North Sunderland
KELSO
Maxwellheugh
B 6396
Mindrummill
Kilham
B 6353
Milfield
Coupland Cas.
Doddington
Doddington
Br.
Warenton
Bellshill
Adderstone
Lucker
Seahouses
Lempitlaw
Mindrum
Paxton
B 6352
Kilham 1108
Hill
Ewart
Park
River Till
Glen
Warenford
Newham
L. Co.
Swinhoe B.
Beadnell
Blakelaw
B 635
Venchen Hill
651
Shotton
Westnewton
Kirknewton
685
Akeld
Wooler
Chatton
Chattonpark
B 6348
Rosebrough
Chathill
Swinhoe
Beadnell
Bay
Mainhouse
Frogden
B 6401
Yeavering Bell
Humbleton
B 6349
Ellingham
Tughall
Kirk Yetholm
Primside Mill
Haugh Head
Earle
Chillingham
Castle
Botany
Brownyside
Preston
Brunton
Newton Seahouses
Town Yetholm
Dikeside
Middleton
Newtown
Lilburn
Hepburn
Cateran
876 Hill
North Charlton
Hall
Christon
Bank
Embleton
Embleton Bay
Morebattle
Corbet Hill
The Curr
1849
Preston Hill
1124
Middleton
South
Lilburn
Berwick Br.
Old Bewick
Bewick Moor
South
Charlton
Rock
Dunstan
Craster
Gateshaws
Tower
Attonburn
Langleeford
Lambden B.
Ilderton
West Ditchburn
B 6347
Dunstanburgh Cas.
Castle Pt
Whitton
Mowhaugh
The Cheviot
2676
Harthope B.
Langlee
Crags
Wooperton
New
Bewick
Percy's
Cross
B 6346
Eglingham
Eglingham
Rennington
Inn
Hall
Hownam
Craik
Moor
Comb Fell
1850 Hill
Dunmoor
Hill
Brandon
Hedgehope
Hill 2348
Hedgeley
Moor 1464
Beanley
Bannamoor
Heffrlaw
Tower
B 6347
Cullernose Pt
Howick
Chatto
Craig
Swanlaws
Windy Gyle
2032
Breamish
Ingram
Branton
Shipley
R. Aln
B 1340
Longhoughton
Chapel
Raeshaw Fell
1580
Bloodybush
Edge 2001
Cushat Law
2020
Cochrane
Pike 1096
Powburn
Glanton
Bolton
Broome
Hulne Park
Tower
Alnwick Abbey
Heckley
Ho.
Denwick
Boulmer
Prendwick
Great Ryle
Whittingham
Eslington Hall
Broomwood
ALNWICK
Cas.
A 1
A 1068
Lesbury
B 1339
Hawkhill

CHEVIOT HILLS

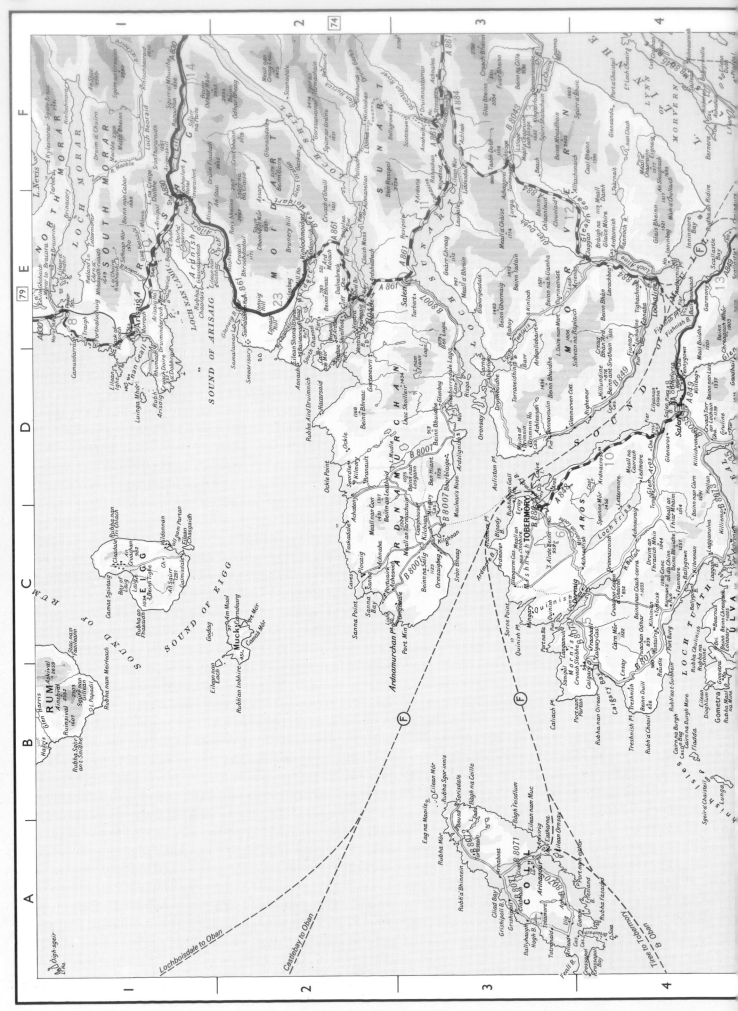

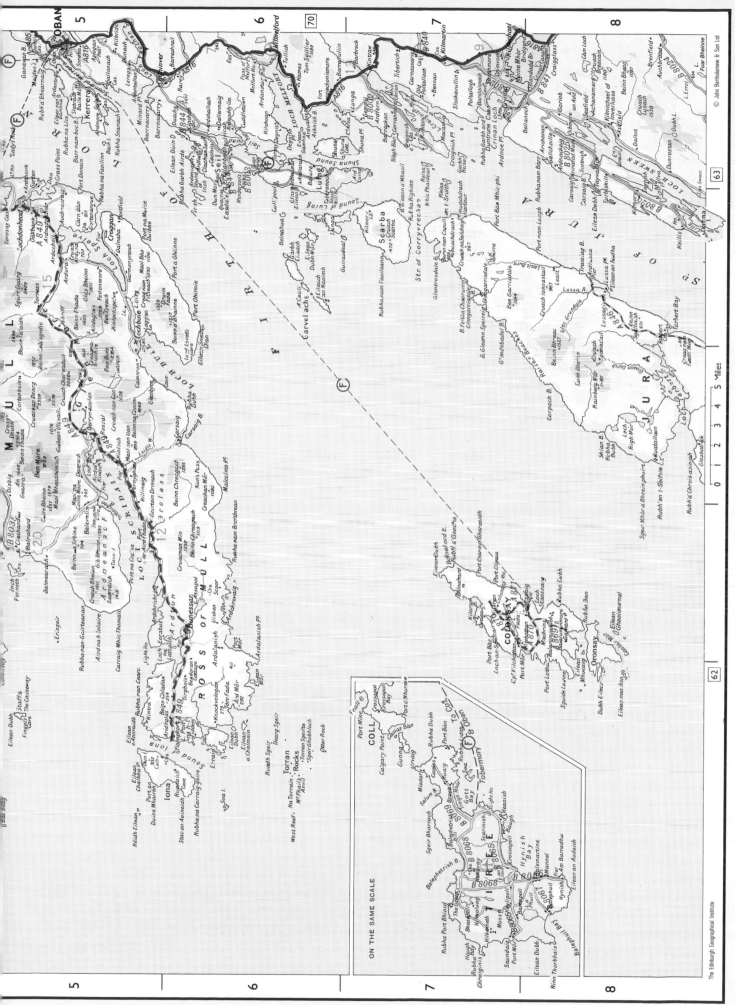

The Edinburgh Geographical Institute

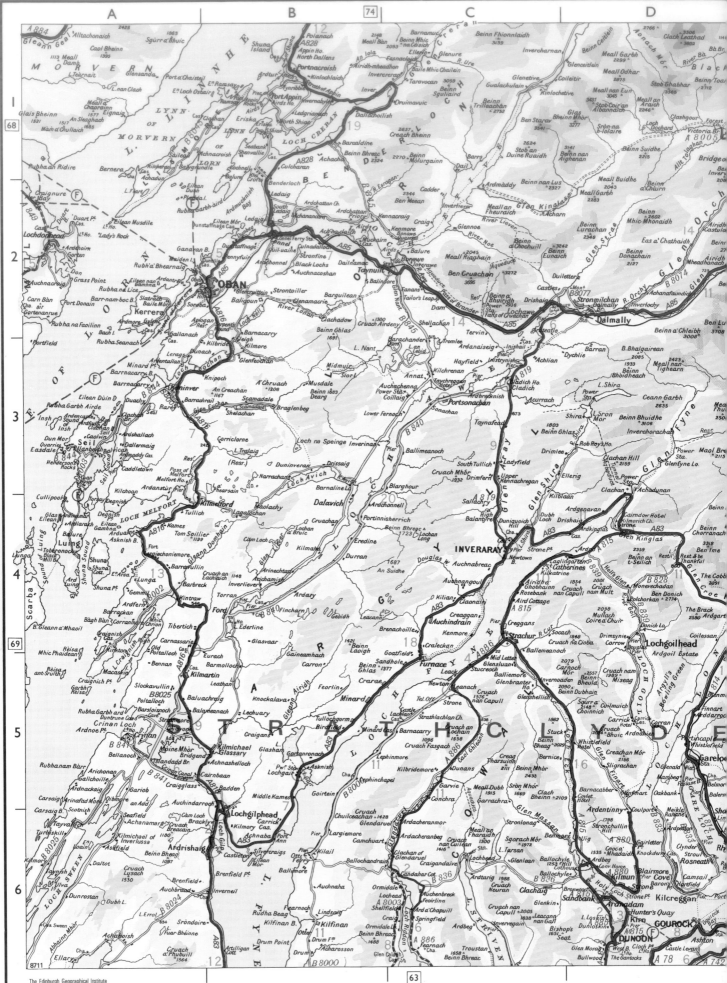

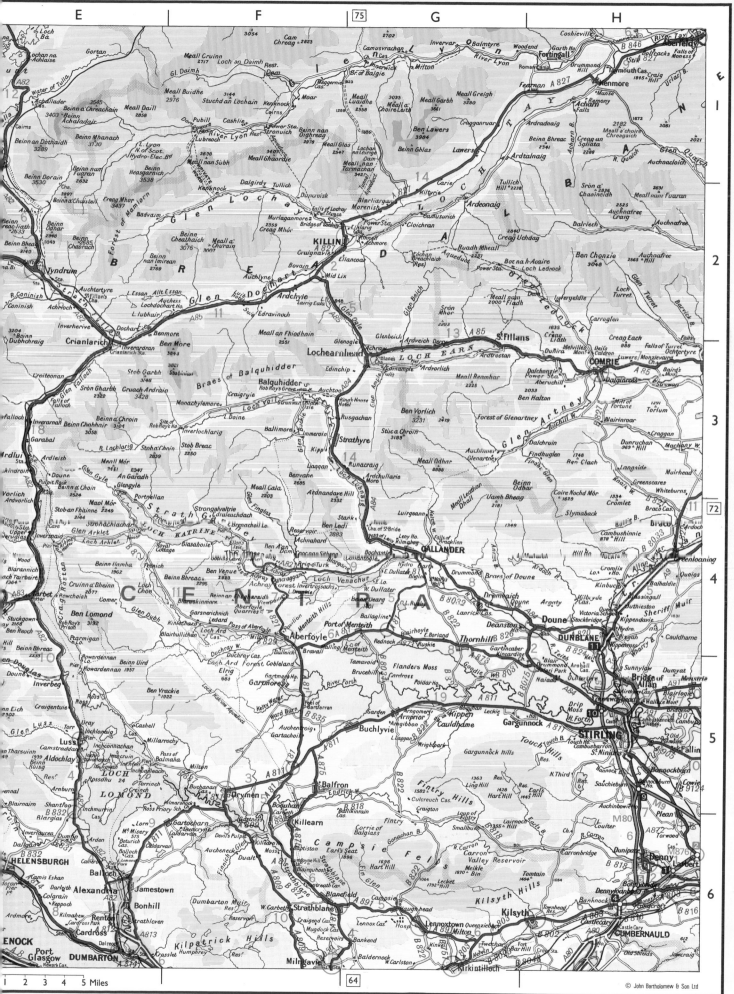

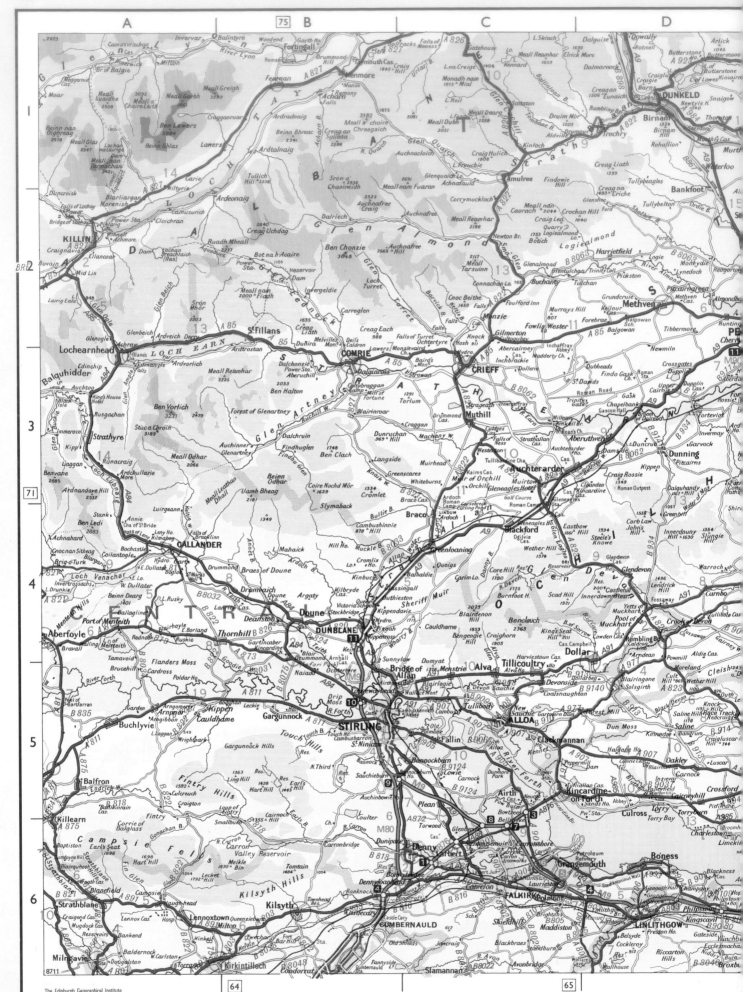

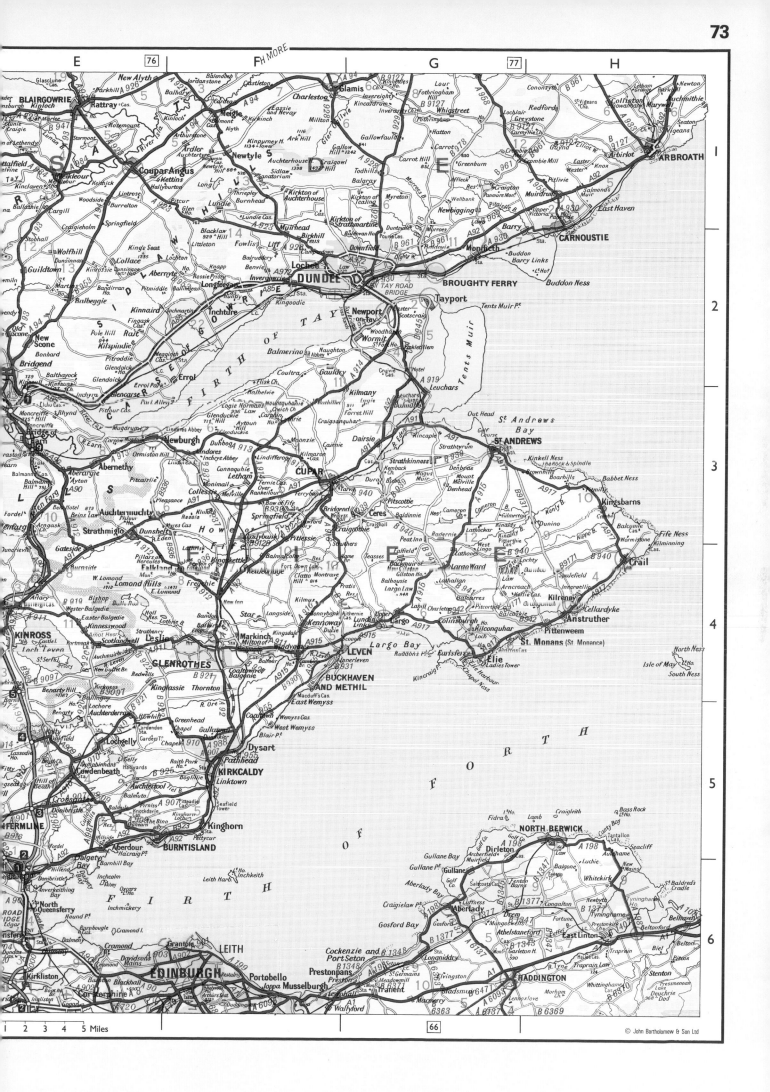

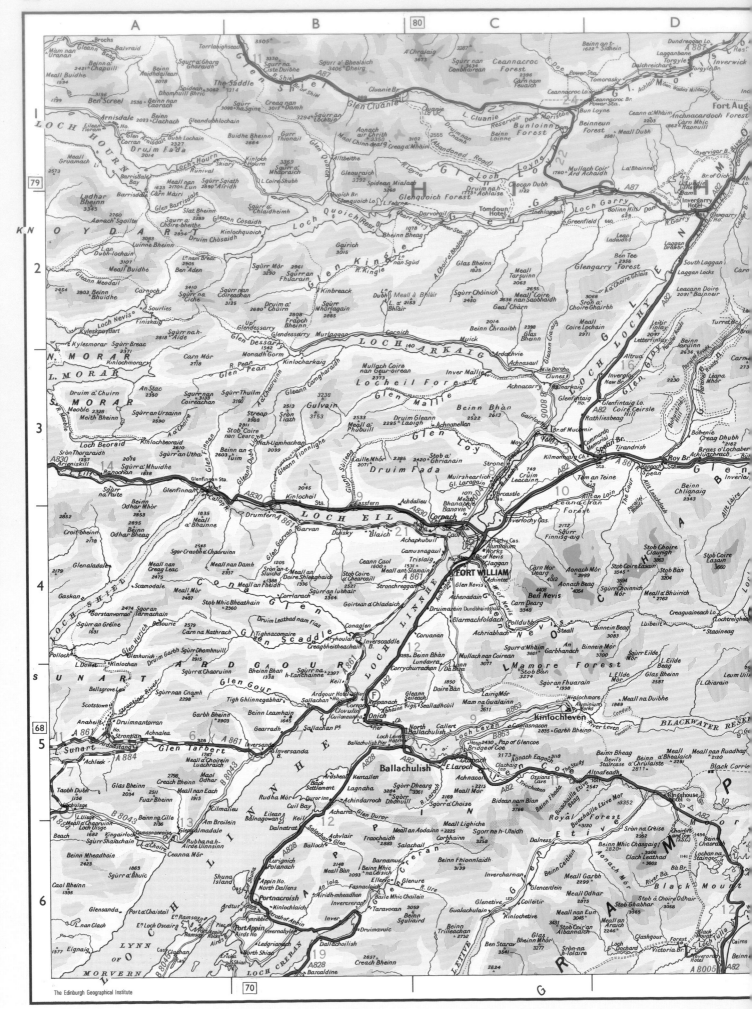

The Edinburgh Geographical Institute

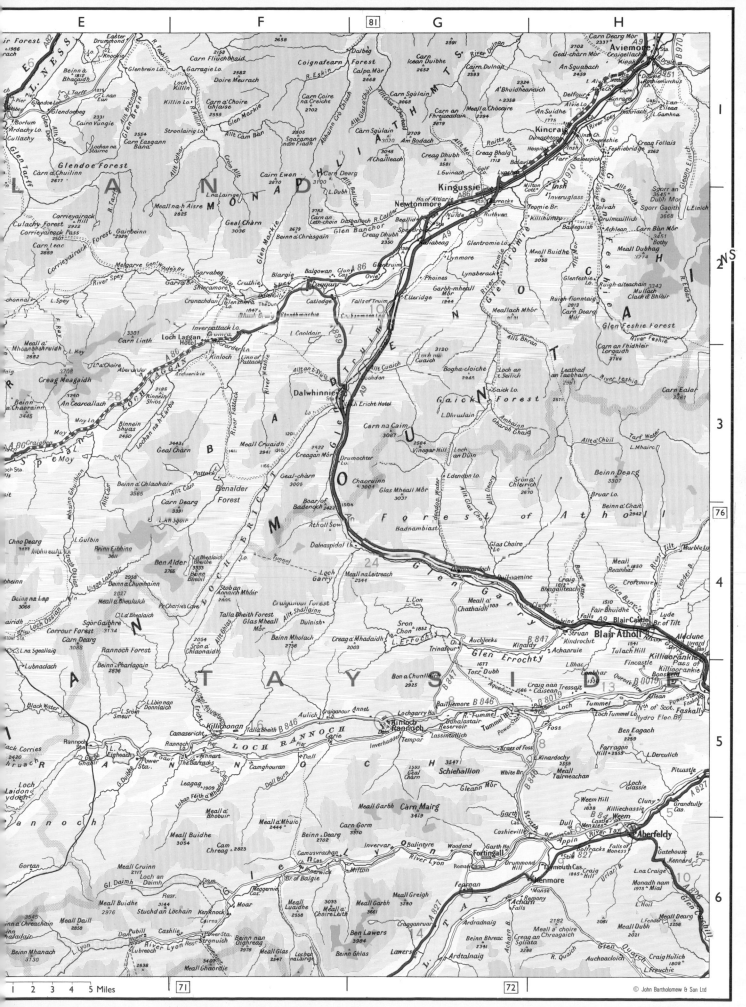

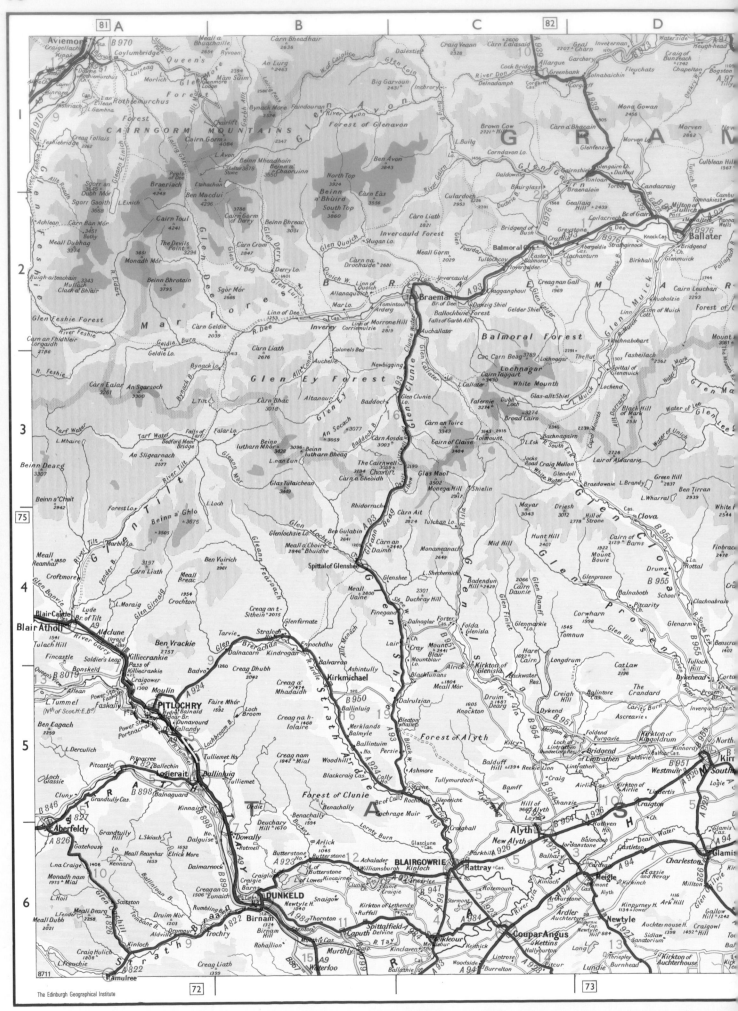

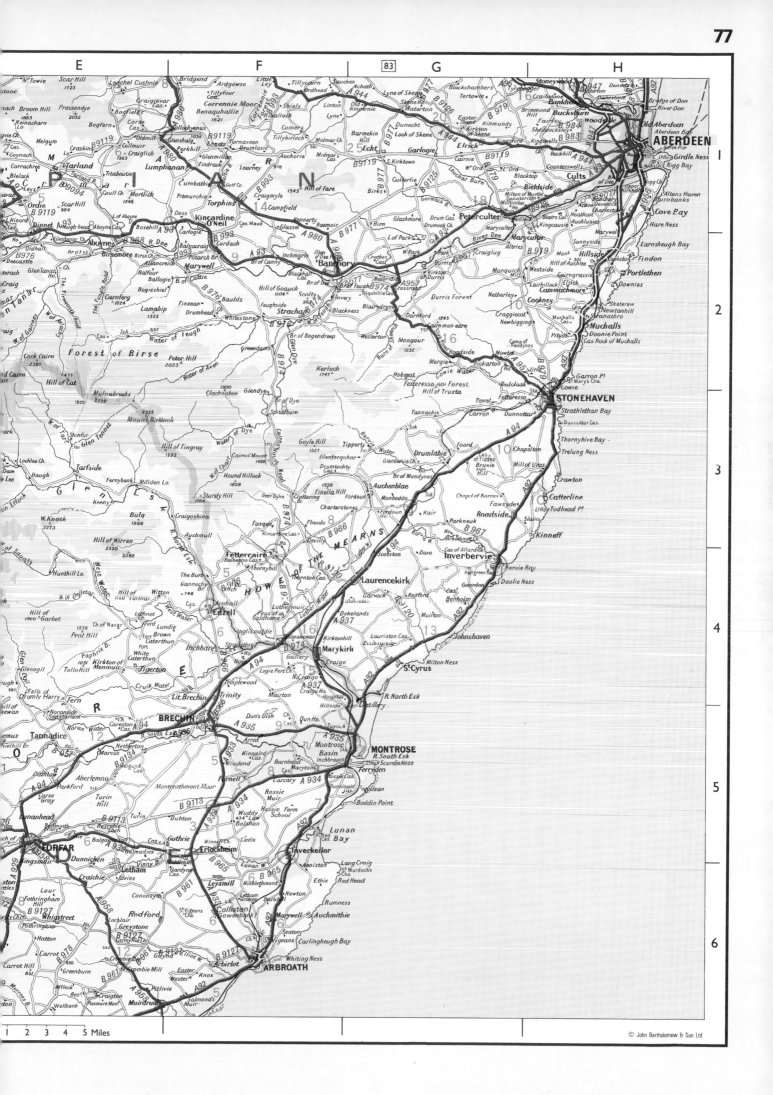

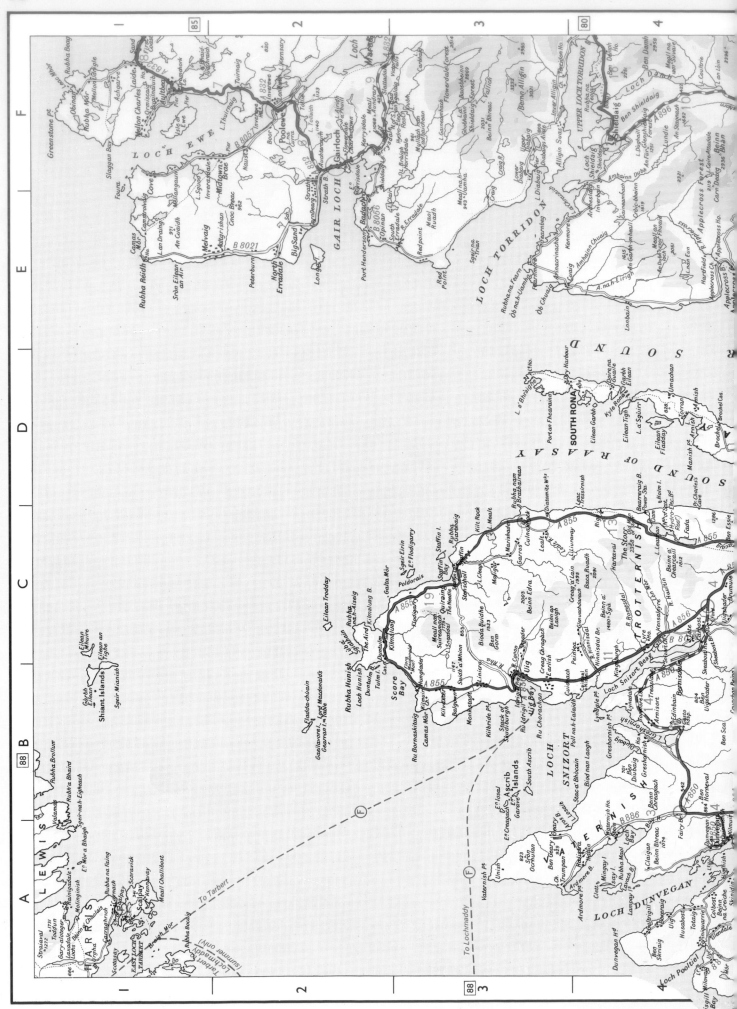

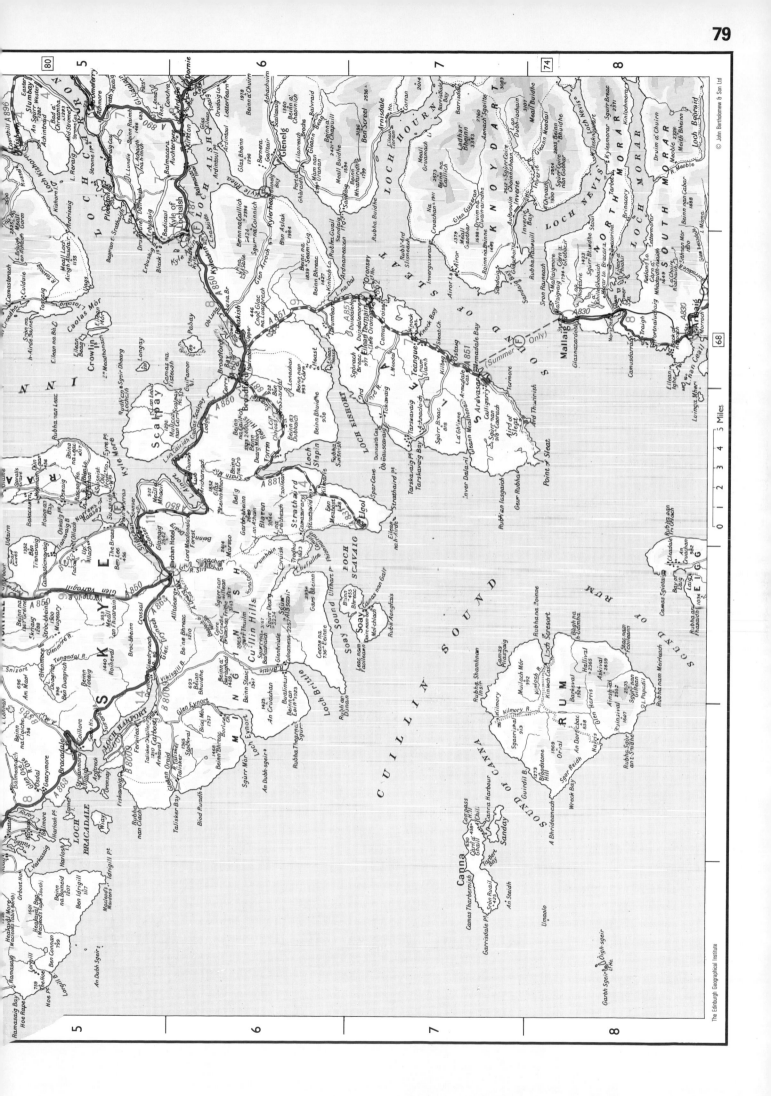

The Edinburgh Geographical Institute

0 1 2 3 4 5 Miles

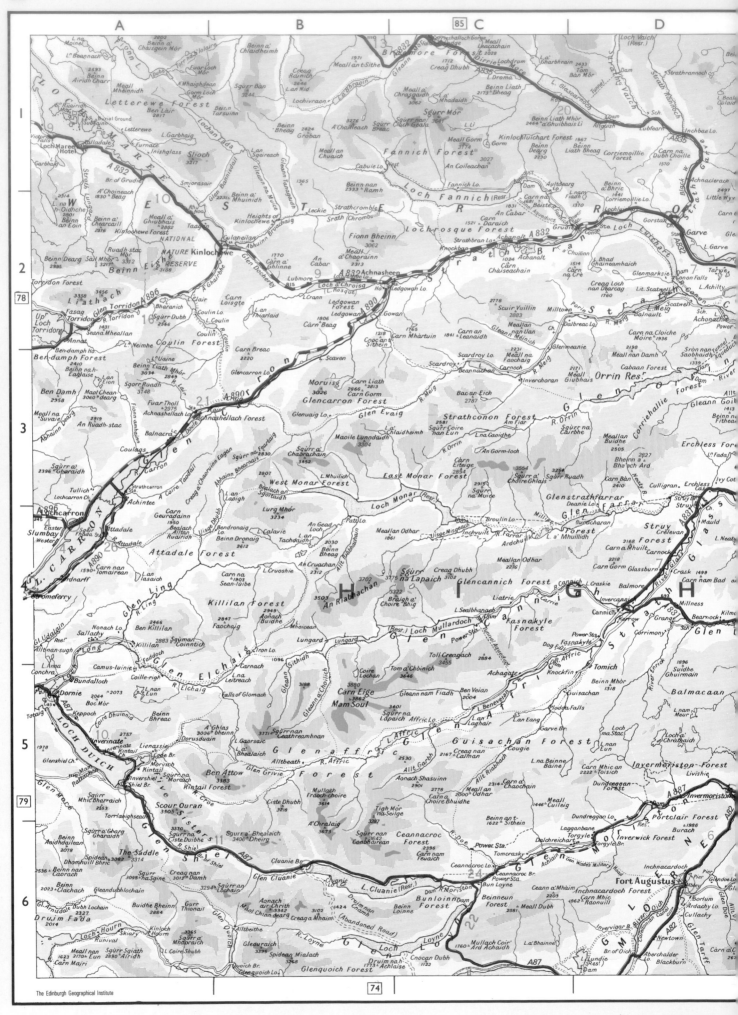

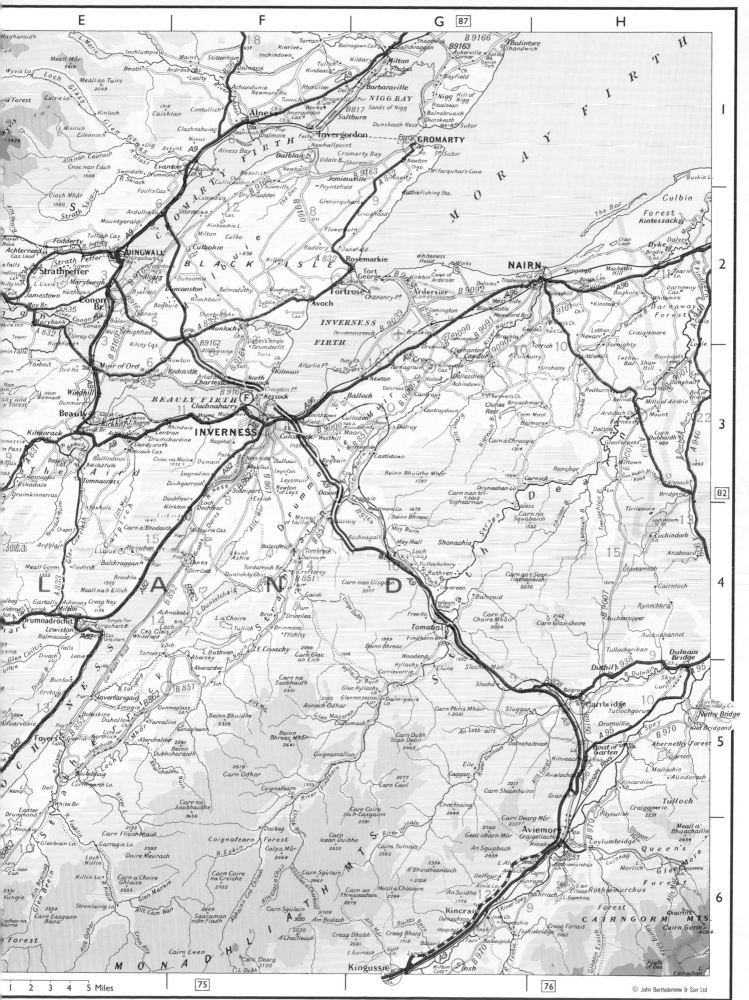

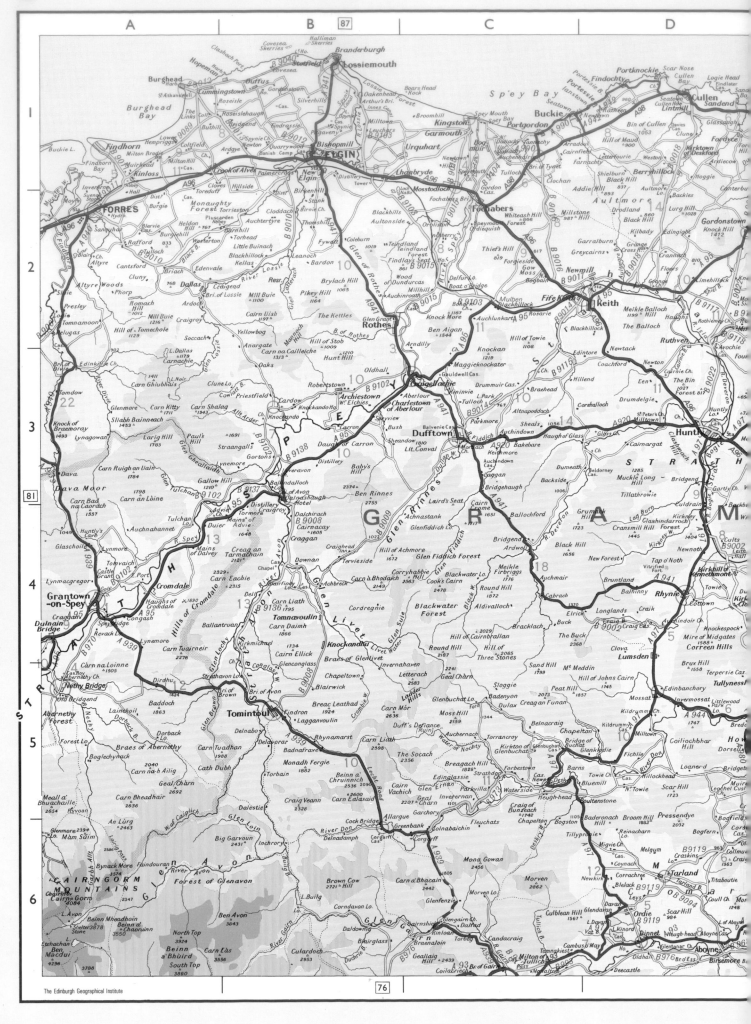

Covesea
Skerries
Halliman
Skerries
Branderburgh
B 9040
Stotfield
Lossiemouth
Hopeman
Burghead
B 9012
Duffus
Covesea
Boars Head
Rock
Sp e y Bay
Portknockie
Scar Nose
Findochty
Logie Head
Cullen Bay
Portessie
Cullen
Sandend
Cummingstown
Gordonstown
Silverhills
Oakenhead
Forest
Arthur's Bri.
Innes Ho.
Spey Mouth
Spey Bay
Buckie
Portgordon
Findlater
Findhorn
Burghead
Bay
The
Links
Roseisle
Bridgend
Spynie
R. Lossie
Milltown
Kingston
Garmouth
Boar
muir
A 990
A 98
Bin of Cullen
1053
Hill of Maud
900
Deskford
Kirktown
of Deskford
Ardiecow

FORRES
ELGIN
Bishopmill
New
Elgin
Lhanbryde
Fochabers
A 96
Keith
Huntly

Monaughty
Forest
Pluscarden
Abbey
Glen of Rothes
Speymouth
Forest
Aultmore

Dallas
Glen Grant
Rothes
Ben Aigan
1544
Fife Keith
Keith
Meikle Balloch
Ruthven

Craigellachie
Aberlour
Charlestown
of Aberlour
Dufftown
STRATH

Archiestown
Wr. Elchies

Glenlivet
Tomnavoulin

Tomintoul

CAIRNGORM
MOUNTAINS
Cairn
Gorm
4084
Forest of Glenavon

Grantown
-on-Spey
Dulnain
Bridge
Nethy
Bridge

The Edinburgh Geographical Institute

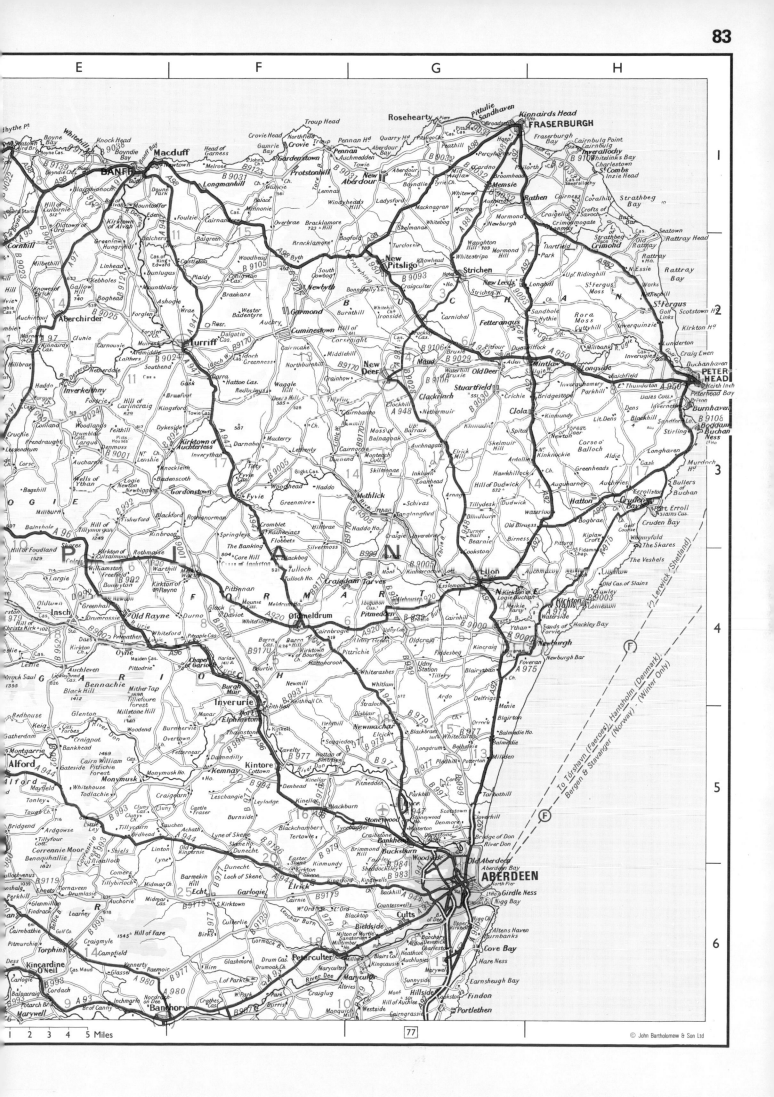

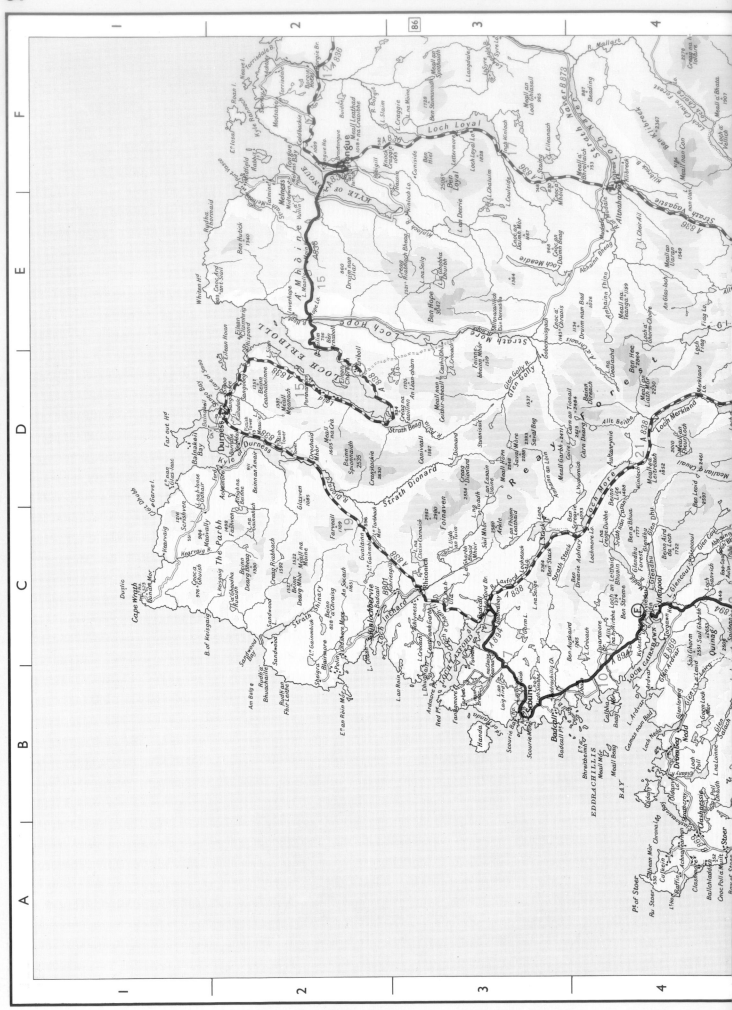

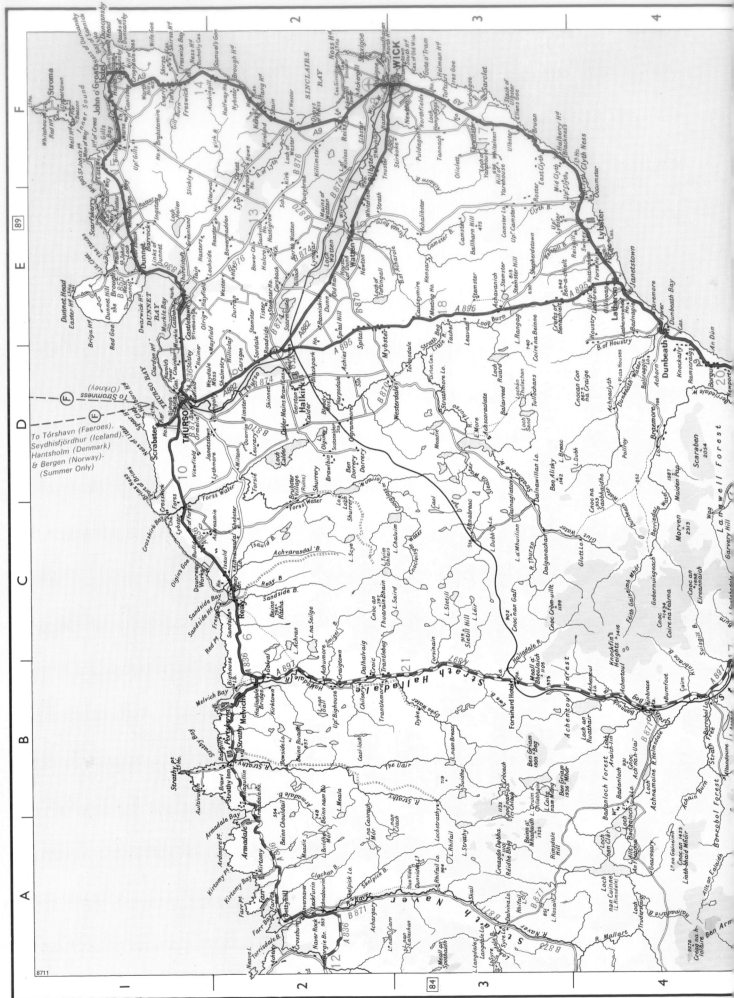

The Edinburgh Geographical Institute

5 Miles

0 1 2 3 4 5

B2

81

85

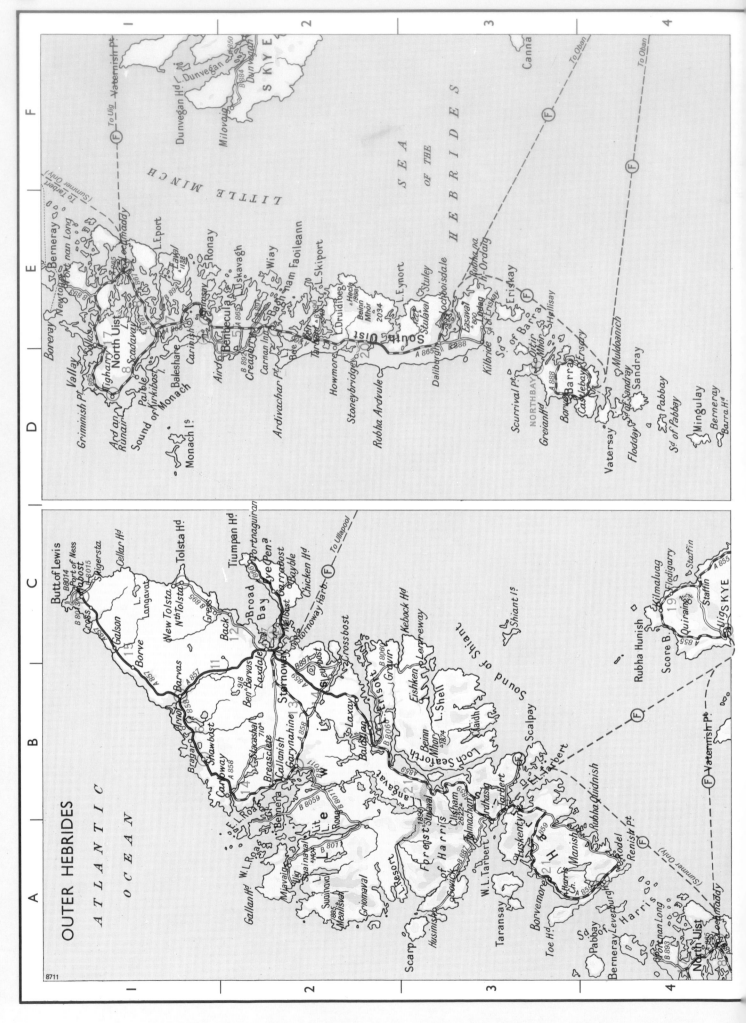

OUTER HEBRIDES

ATLANTIC

OCEAN

Butt of Lewis
B8014
Port of Ness
B8015
Skigersta
Cellar Hd.
Habost
Cross
13
Galson
Shader
Borve
L.Langavat
11
Arnol
Barvas
A857
Bragar
Shawbost
Carloway
14
Breasclete
Callanish
Garynahine
Bernera
W.L.Road
Gallan Hd.
M(a)vaig
Uig
Swainabost
Mealista
Scarp
Husinish
Griomaval
Resort
Forest of Harris
Taransay
W.L.Tarbert
Toe Hd.
Pabbay
Sd
Berneray
Leverburgh
Harris
Borvemore
Rodel
Renish Pt.
North Uist
Lochmaddy
Shiant I.s
Sound of Shiant
Scalpay
E.L.Tarbert
Tarbert
Luskentyre
Manish
Rubha Chudnish
Rubha Hunish
Score B.
Kilmaluag
19 Flodigarry
Quiraing
Staffin
A855
UIG SKYE
To Ullapool
Tolsta Hd.
New Tolsta
Nth Tolsta
Back
12
Gress
Broad Bay
Tiumpan Hd.
Portnaguiran
Eye Pen.a
Garrabost
Aignish
Chicken Hd.
Stornoway
A859
A857
Laxdale
Newmarket
Balallan
Laxay
Crossbost
Keose
Lemreway
Gravir
Keback Hd.
Eishken
L.Shell
Loch Seaforth
Beinn Mhor
Ardvourlie
Clisham
Ardhasig
Scalpay
SKYE
LITTLE MINCH

SEA

OF THE

HEBRIDES

Berneray
Newtonferry
Port nan Long
Boreray
Vallay
Griminish Pt.
Scolpay
Tigharry
North Uist
Scadavay
Ardan
Runair
Baleshare
Monach I.s
Monach Is
Sound of Monach
Lochmaddy
L.Eport
Lochmaddy
Ronay
Kallin
Grimsay
Benbecula
Creagorry
Carnan
Carnan Inn
Aird
Carinish
Wiay
Iskavagh
Baghnam Faoileann
Ardivachar Pt.
Howmore
L.Skiport
L.Druidibeg
Stoneybridge
Rubha Ardvule
South Uist
Beinn Mhor
2034
Hecla
L.Eynort
Stulaval
Staley
Dalibrughie
Kilbride
Lochboisdale
Rubha na
h Ordaig
Eriskay
Lingay
Ludaig
Lasaval
Scurrival Pt.
Greianhd
NORTHBAY
Barra
Castlebay
Eersdy
Vatersay
Flodday
Sandray
Pabbay
Sd of Pabbay
Mingulay
Berneray
Barra Hd.
SKYE
Dunvegan Hd.
L.Dunvegan
Milovaig
Dunvegan
To Uig Waternish Pt.
To Tarbert
(Summer Only)
To Oban
Canna
Muldoanich

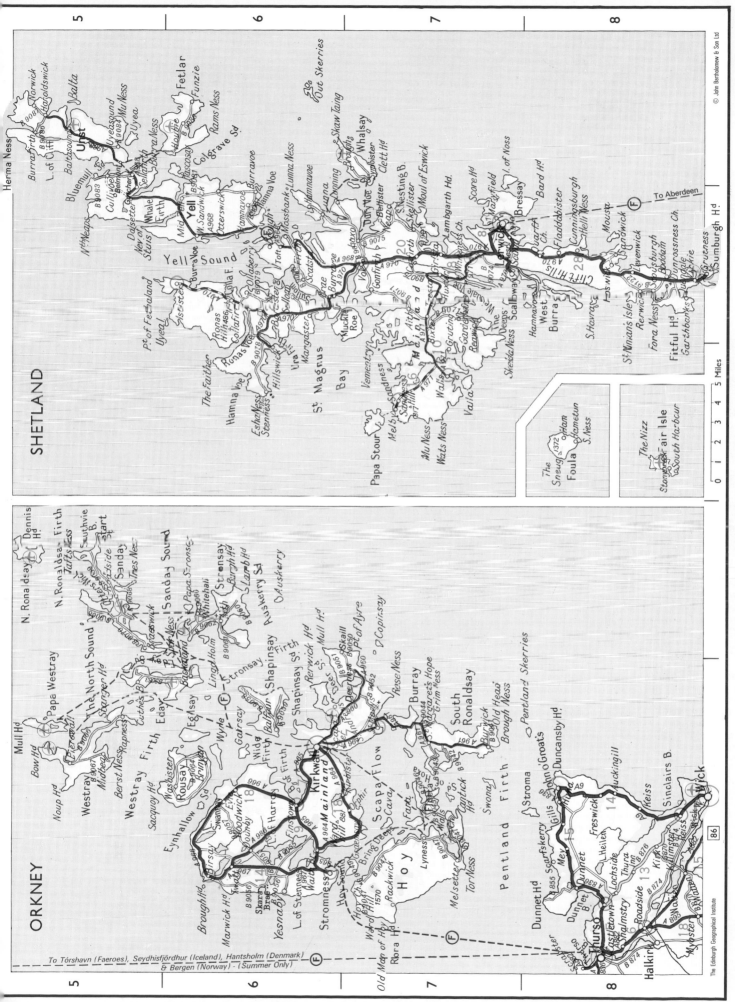

89

SHETLAND

ORKNEY

© John Bartholomew & Son Ltd

The Edinburgh Geographical Institute

To Aberdeen

To Tórshavn (Faeroes), Seydhisfjördhur (Iceland), Hantsholm (Denmark)
& Bergen (Norway) - (Summer Only)

0 1 2 3 4 5 Miles

86

Foula

Fair Isle

ROUTE PLANNING

DISTANCEFINDER DIAGRAMS

Fifteen Primary Route Centres — key points in the nation's primary route network of motorways and main roads — have been selected to represent different areas throughout Britain. They are as follows:

London
Aberdeen
Birmingham
Bristol
Cardiff
Edinburgh
Exeter
Glasgow
Inverness
Leeds
Liverpool
Manchester
Newcastle
Norwich
Southampton

For each Primary Route Centre a set of useful destinations has been selected e.g. major cities, holiday resorts, cross-channel ferry ports — and the road distances to these destinations using the nation's primary route network are indicated. The figure is shown in miles, but can be converted to kilometres by using the conversion scale at the foot of each page.

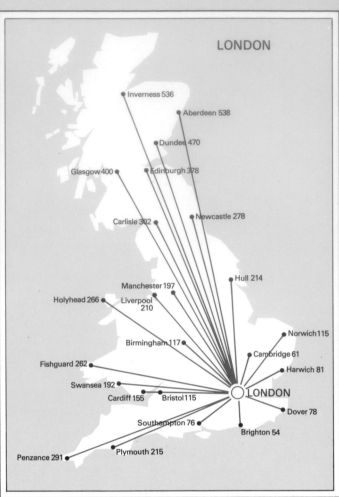

LONDON

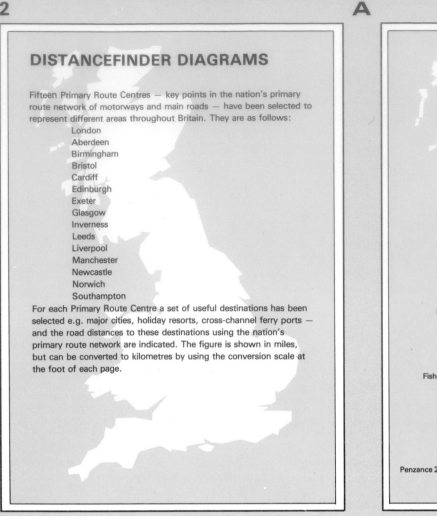

ABERDEEN

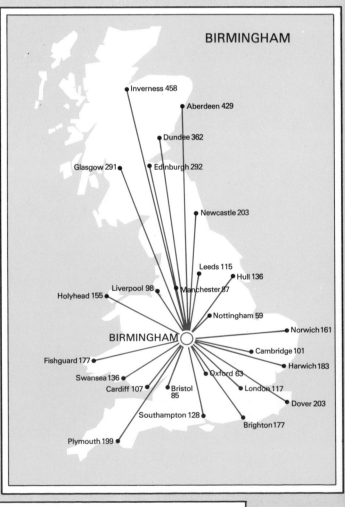

BIRMINGHAM

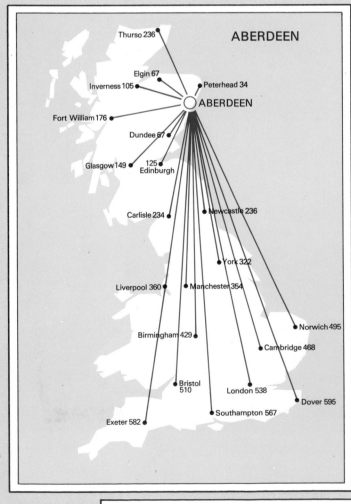

Conversion Scale

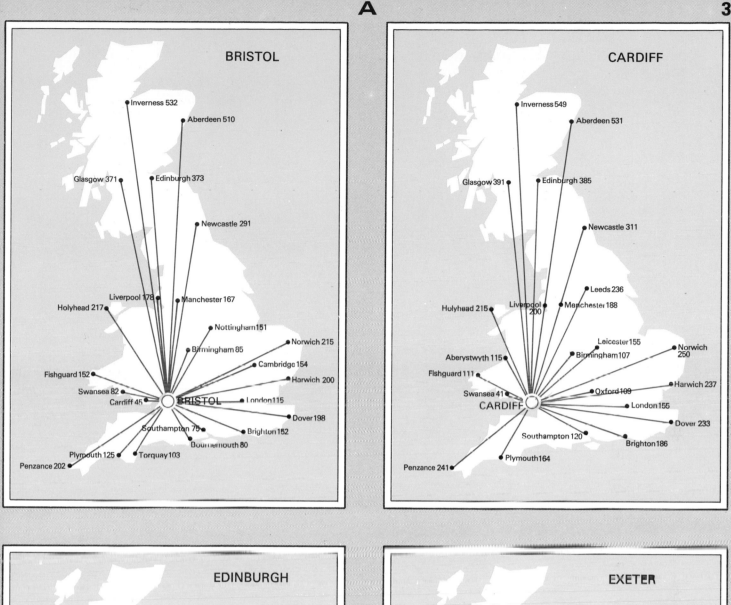

BRISTOL

- Inverness 532
- Aberdeen 510
- Glasgow 371
- Edinburgh 373
- Newcastle 291
- Liverpool 178
- Manchester 167
- Holyhead 217
- Nottingham 151
- Birmingham 85
- Norwich 215
- Cambridge 154
- Fishguard 152
- Harwich 200
- Swansea 82
- Cardiff 45
- London 115
- BRISTOL
- Dover 198
- Southampton 75
- Brighton 152
- Bournemouth 80
- Plymouth 125
- Torquay 103
- Penzance 202

CARDIFF

- Inverness 549
- Aberdeen 531
- Glasgow 391
- Edinburgh 385
- Newcastle 311
- Leeds 236
- Holyhead 215
- Liverpool 200
- Manchester 188
- Leicester 155
- Norwich 250
- Aberystwyth 115
- Birmingham 107
- Fishguard 111
- Oxford 109
- Harwich 237
- Swansea 41
- London 155
- CARDIFF
- Dover 233
- Southampton 120
- Brighton 186
- Plymouth 164
- Penzance 241

EDINBURGH

- Inverness 158
- Aberdeen 125
- Fort William 127
- Perth 44
- Dundee 56
- Glasgow 44
- EDINBURGH
- Berwick upon Tweed 57
- Stranraer 129
- Newcastle 109
- Carlisle 96
- Leeds 205
- Hull 225
- Liverpool 224
- Manchester 214
- Birmingham 292
- Norwich 370
- Swansea 425
- Oxford 357
- Cardiff 385
- Bristol 373
- London 378
- Southampton 433
- Dover 449
- Brighton 430
- Plymouth 496

EXETER

- Inverness 603
- Aberdeen 582
- Glasgow 444
- Edinburgh 446
- Newcastle 361
- Leeds 288
- Hull 297
- Liverpool 250
- Manchester 239
- Holyhead 289
- Nottingham 222
- Birmingham 158
- Northampton 183
- Norwich 293
- Cambridge 232
- Fishguard 228
- Swansea 158
- Cardiff 119
- Bristol 79
- London 170
- Dover 247
- EXETER
- Southampton 108
- Bournemouth 82
- Penzance 121
- Plymouth 45

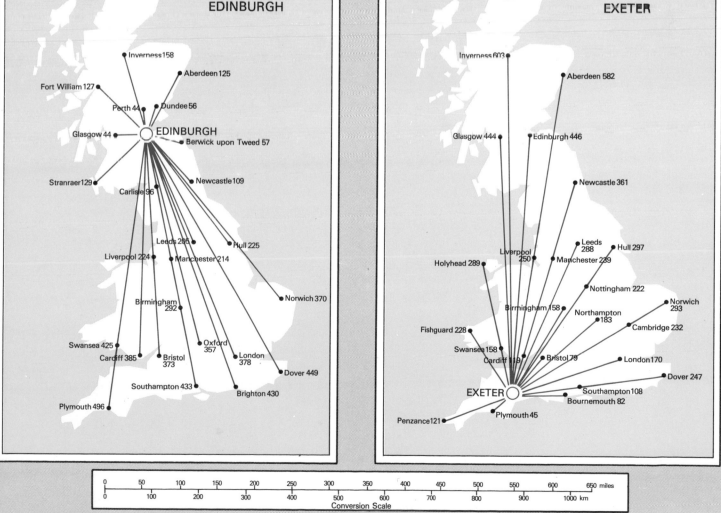

0	50	100	150	200	250	300	350	400	450	500	550	600	650 miles

0	100	200	300	400	500	600	700	800	900	1000 km

Conversion Scale

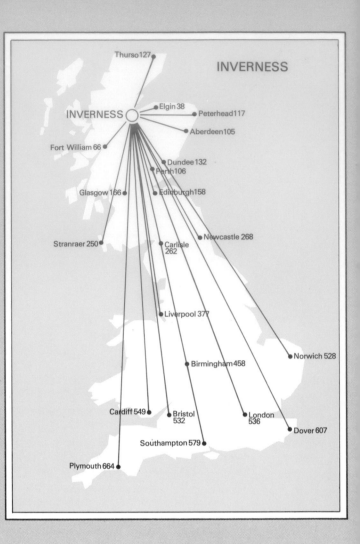

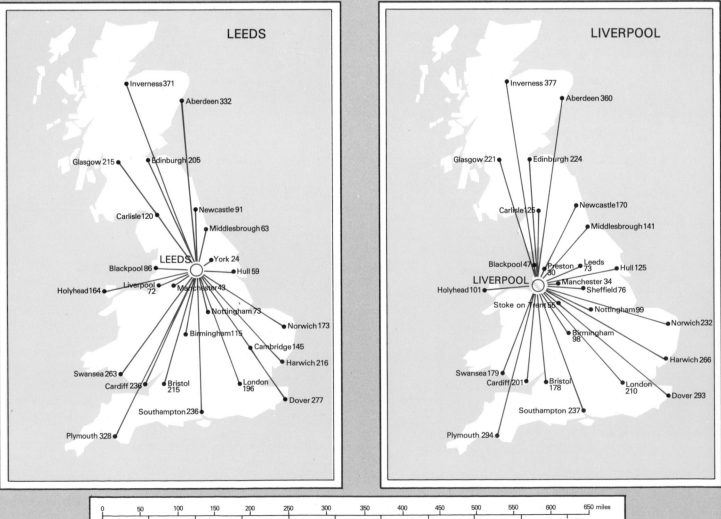

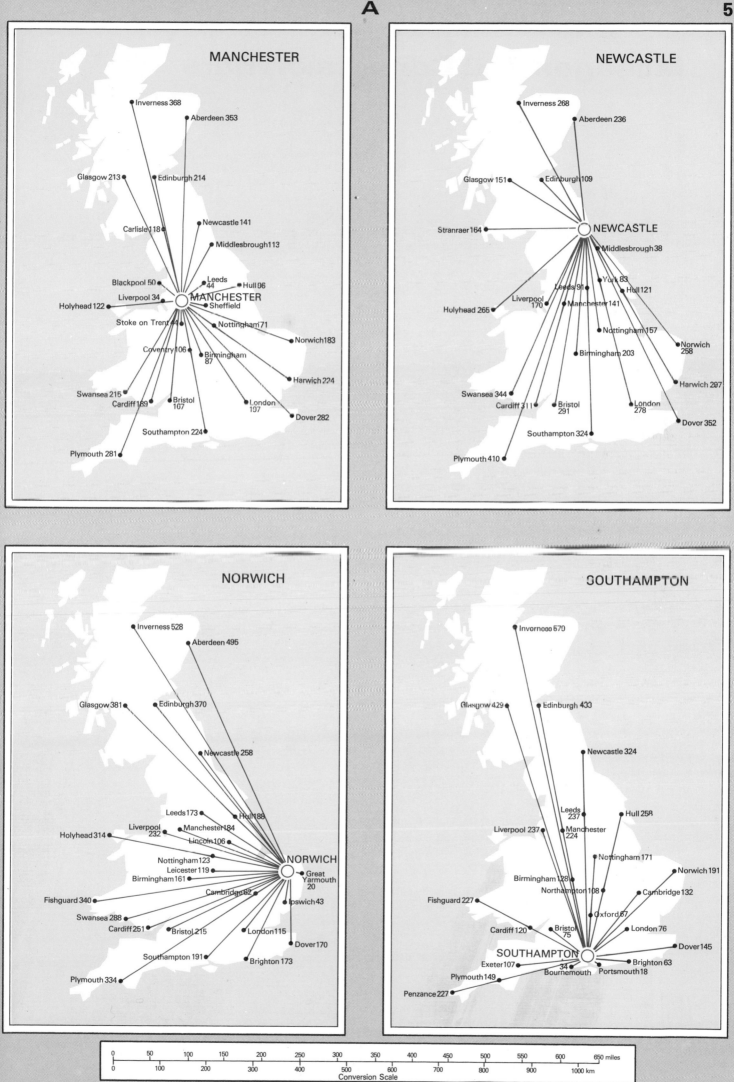

MANCHESTER

Inverness 368
Aberdeen 353
Glasgow 213
Edinburgh 214
Carlisle 118
Newcastle 141
Middlesbrough113
Blackpool 50
Leeds 44
Hull 86
Liverpool 34
MANCHESTER
Holyhead 122
Sheffield
Stoke on Trent 44
Nottingham 71
Coventry 106
Birmingham 87
Norwich 183
Swansea 215
Harwich 224
Cardiff 189
Bristol 107
London 197
Dover 282
Southampton 224
Plymouth 281

NEWCASTLE

Inverness 268
Aberdeen 236
Glasgow 151
Edinburgh 109
Stranraer 164
NEWCASTLE
Middlesbrough 38
York 83
Leeds 91
Hull 121
Liverpool 170
Manchester 141
Holyhead 265
Nottingham 157
Birmingham 203
Norwich 258
Harwich 297
Swansea 344
Cardiff 311
Bristol 291
London 278
Dover 352
Southampton 324
Plymouth 410

NORWICH

Inverness 528
Aberdeen 495
Glasgow 381
Edinburgh 370
Newcastle 258
Leeds 173
Hull 188
Liverpool 232
Manchester 184
Holyhead 314
Lincoln 106
Nottingham 123
Leicester 119
Birmingham 161
NORWICH
Great Yarmouth 20
Cambridge 82
Fishguard 340
Ipswich 43
Swansea 288
Cardiff 251
Bristol 215
London 115
Dover 170
Southampton 191
Brighton 173
Plymouth 334

SOUTHAMPTON

Inverness 570
Glasgow 429
Edinburgh 433
Newcastle 324
Hull 258
Leeds 237
Liverpool 237
Manchester 224
Nottingham 171
Norwich 191
Birmingham 128
Northampton 108
Cambridge 132
Fishguard 227
Oxford 67
Cardiff 120
Bristol 75
London 76
Dover 145
SOUTHAMPTON
Exeter 107
Brighton 63
Plymouth 149
Bournemouth 34
Portsmouth 18
Penzance 227

```
0    50   100   150   200   250   300   350   400   450   500   550   600   650 miles
0      100      200      300      400      500      600      700      800      900      1000 km
                              Conversion Scale
```

Mileages and Conversion Bars

Conversion bars:
- miles / km: 0, 10, 20, 30, 40, 50, 60, 70, 80, 90, 100
- °C −17.77 / °F 0: 0, 20, 40, 60, 80, 100, 120, 140
- kg/cm² / lbs/in² 16, 18, 20, 22, 24, 26, 28 : 1:2, 1:4, 1:6, 1:8
- gallons / litres
- litres / pints

Ireland inset (partial):
- Athlone: 141 | 81 | 134 | 114
- Belfast: 182 | 264 | 112 | 1
- Castlebar: 177 | 94 | 1
- Cork: 250 | 1
- Donegal: 1
- Dublin

	Aberdeen	Aberystwyth	Ayr	Birmingham	Bradford	Bristol	Cambridge	Cardiff	Carlisle	Coventry	Derby	Doncaster	Dover	Edinburgh	Exeter	Fishguard	Fort William	Glasgow	Gloucester	Harwich	Holyhead	Hull	Inverness	Kendal	Leeds	Leicester	Lincoln	Liverpool	Manchester	Newcastle upon Tyne	Norwich	Nottingham	Oxford	Penzance	Perth
Aberystwyth	445																																		
Ayr	175	309																																	
Birmingham	420	114	285																																
Bradford	318	167	200	108																															
Bristol	493	125	362	81	188																														
Cambridge	458	214	346	100	152	159																													
Cardiff	491	105	366	103	202	45	179																												
Carlisle	221	224	90	196	110	277	264	289																											
Coventry	417	132	299	18	114	91	81	114	209																										
Derby	384	138	266	40	74	127	96	142	176	40																									
Doncaster	344	176	229	94	34	175	116	197	142	92	54																								
Dover	576	286	455	176	260	186	115	238	372	163	196	231																							
Edinburgh	125	320	73	292	194	373	334	385	96	303	263	219	449																						
Exeter	569	201	437	157	266	76	211	121	353	167	203	251	248	450																					
Fishguard	491	56	364	170	216	154	270	112	280	185	194	233	331	376	230																				
Fort William	165	430	132	392	307	473	460	485	196	406	373	338	568	146	549	486																			
Glasgow	145	320	33	292	204	373	360	385	96	303	270	238	468	42	449	376	104																		
Gloucester	468	102	330	56	156	35	123	56	237	57	93	150	180	334	111	153	433	333																	
Harwich	505	281	413	167	220	191	67	246	336	141	163	194	125	413	248	337	532	432	178																
Holyhead	439	111	305	148	157	206	248	216	212	167	157	167	339	308	282	167	408	308	180	315															
Hull	346	223	240	123	64	203	123	224	158	111	88	42	232	216	278	280	354	254	168	185	214														
Inverness	105	486	198	458	350	539	493	549	262	459	419	351	607	158	618	542	66	166	504	545	474	374													
Kendal	253	174	135	150	65	227	215	231	45	164	131	99	324	138	302	229	242	139	195	282	170	124	294												
Leeds	327	181	206	113	9	194	145	220	119	110	70	29	260	202	270	237	315	215	159	223	164	55	360	71											
Leicester	414	153	295	39	100	120	68	142	206	24	28	74	168	283	196	209	402	302	85	135	163	87	462	160	95										
Lincoln	383	199	268	90	74	171	85	192	181	74	52	39	202	258	247	255	377	277	136	155	200	37	427	136	68	51									
Liverpool	341	104	208	93	66	161	168	169	120	107	81	86	273	216	237	160	316	216	126	235	92	130	382	72	75	100	118								
Manchester	340	141	208	80	34	161	151	172	119	94	59	51	256	215	235	197	315	215	126	239	124	95	373	72	40	92	84	35							
Newcastle upon Tyne	235	273	144	207	97	288	230	304	59	202	161	114	345	110	364	329	253	148	253	308	247	121	268	84	92	187	159	155	132						
Norwich	475	276	374	166	178	221	62	241	289	138	139	147	172	366	297	330	485	385	186	73	293	143	498	245	176	119	105	220	185	264					
Nottingham	379	164	272	50	74	145	83	153	181	48	16	43	193	262	221	220	377	277	110	150	171	90	430	135	70	25	35	98	63	157	122				
Oxford	483	154	347	64	165	74	83	108	260	50	90	145	128	357	129	205	456	356	52	126	209	158	515	210	168	73	124	157	144	260	145	98			
Penzance	660	304	545	268	374	185	330	225	451	275	311	364	353	542	111	330	650	545	217	354	393	386	703	410	375	299	350	340	342	465	390	320	250		
Perth	81	353	94	325	235	406	372	411	136	345	305	253	483	44	483	409	105	61	377	436	351	264	112	180	235	322	290	251	251	150	400	295	390	590	
	615	238	479	203	308	122	257	167	399	209	245	297	289	496	46	276	595	495	157	294	328	320	664	340	316	242	293	283	283	410	343	267	175	78	525
	560	222	425	141	242	97	124	142	337	127	167	222	130	435	118	251	533	433	108	146	286	233	592	290	244	150	201	234	221	337	186	175	77	234	468
	514	170	397	111	220	52	131	93	304	105	145	196	157	397	88	198	500	395	70	156	247	215	550	260	215	128	175	195	190	304	191	151	60	200	441
	360	159	235	76	37	167	120	179	152	78	37	18	230	235	237	215	348	248	126	187	149	65	393	100	33	62	46	72	38	125	146	37	135	346	266
	399	77	260	45	99	103	142	111	176	61	64	99	221	274	179	133	372	272	77	220	103	146	438	124	109	84	117	58	69	201	205	82	106	282	305
	547	201	412	128	227	76	131	121	324	114	154	209	143	421	105	225	520	420	93	153	273	220	579	270	232	137	188	211	208	324	193	162	65	217	454
	503	252	406	150	212	156	60	194	316	132	163	175	68	388	210	290	513	410	145	59	299	183	542	294	207	128	146	237	214	289	98	144	97	321	427
	361	110	244	42	69	124	124	137	150	57	34	65	219	244	198	164	347	243	89	190	121	107	400	105	72	55	85	50	36	162	172	49	105	306	290
	228	325	51	297	211	378	365	390	101	310	277	243	473	124	454	381	184	84	343	410	313	251	250	145	220	307	282	221	220	158	390	290	362	551	144
	226	590	315	565	472	643	606	647	371	581	541	489	715	278	718	645	183	285	611	672	586	500	132	416	469	558	528	490	489	384	634	533	627	826	237
	423	101	305	26	128	60	115	75	215	44	65	117	185	308	136	148	412	309	25	181	155	165	460	170	132	64	112	102	100	225	176	76	58	243	350
	319	205	203	130	33	211	150	244	121	126	88	34	264	194	287	261	317	217	176	228	188	37	352	85	24	108	75	99	64	84	181	77	181	391	227
	503	211	390	105	195	115	54	167	301	92	123	159	71	378	172	260	497	397	109	76	268	168	536	250	189	97	131	202	185	274	114	122	57	281	415

Distances assume the use of ferries where appropriate.

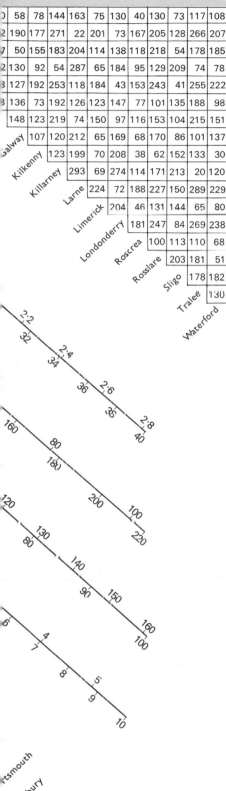

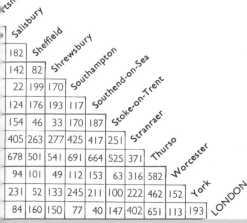

Sign Language

The array of road signs on British roads seems at first bewildering and even perhaps confusing. Some explanation can help the road user to realise that road signs are in fact carefully grouped and that the groupings in themselves can help towards a better understanding of road craft and lead to better driving.

Official road signs in Britain fall into three main categories. These are:

WARNING SIGNS such as those warning of bends or junctions, or of animals straying onto the road.

COMMAND SIGNS such as those indicating that certain types of vehicle are prohibited or that there should be no overtaking or stopping.

INFORMATION SIGNS such as those indicating a car park or a hospital or a one way street.

The three categories are readily identifiable from far off or when approached at speed, by their shape:

WARNING SIGNS are triangular, for example:-

| Wild Animals | Quayside or river bank | Uneven road | Slippery road |

COMMAND SIGNS are circular, for example:-

| No stopping (Clearway) | School crossing patrol | Maximum speed | Ahead only |

INFORMATION SIGNS are rectangular, for example:-

| Route available for pedal cyclists | One-way street | Hospital |

Hospital ahead

Within these shapes different colours are used to sub-divide the three basic classes. Triangles are all coloured red, but circles can be blue or red: blue circles give positive commands, e.g.

| Turn left ahead | Turn left |

while red rings or circles give negative instructions, e.g.

| No left turn | No U turns |

Blue rectangles denote general information, as in the case of

Parking place or lay-by

There are few exceptions to these rules and such exceptions serve to give greater emphasis to certain signs.

Directional Signs.

On all motorways, directional signs are shown as white lettering on a blue background, whereas on Primary Routes (see below) directional signs have a green background. On other routes, directional signs have a white background, the lettering being black. Local directional signs are white with a blue border and black lettering. These indicate places or public services, for example toilets or camping and caravan sites within the locality. Special signs denoting ring routes are indicated on primary and other routes - coloured approriately - by an R sign. Holiday routes, sometimes seasonal, are indicated by the letters HR in black on a yellow background.

Special signing systems are used on motorways for giving specific types of information, for example:-

| Temporary maximum speed | Change Lane |

These illuminated signs are found either beside the hard shoulder, on the central reserve or on gantries or bridges over the motorway. These signs are blank under normal conditions, but under special conditions are lit up to tell drivers what action they must take. Those signs beside the hard shoulder and on the central reserve concern all drivers. Signs over the motorway concern only those drivers in the lane below the sign.

Primary Routes form a national network of recommended through routes complementing the motorway network. Selected places along these routes are known as Primary Route Destinations. Distance and directions to such places are repeated on traffic signs on primary routes and motorways, providing an on-going guide to directions from one Primary Route Destination to the next.

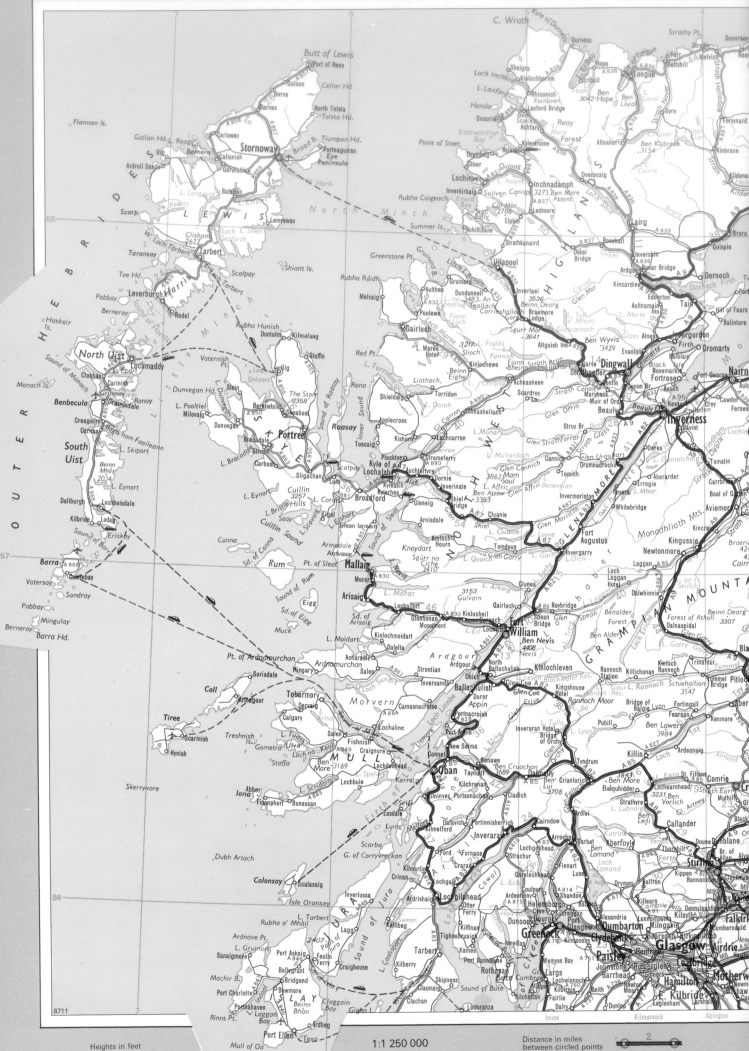

Heights in feet

1:1 250 000

Distance in miles between circled points

ORKNEY

Mull Head
North Ronaldsay
Westray
Nth. Ronaldsay Firth
Pierowall
The
North Sd.
Papness
Overbister
Sanday
Rousay
Eday
Sanday Sd.
Backaland
Brinyan
Egilsay
Brough Hd.
The Barony
Whitehall
Marwick Hd.
Dounby
Stronsay
Skara Brae
Stronsay Firth
Firth
Auskerry
Balfour
Shapinsay
Stenness
Finstown
Kirkwall
Stromness
Graemsay
Skaill
St. Mary's
Ward Hill
1570
Rora Hd.
Hoy
Scapa Flow
Burray
Coplinsay
Lyness
St. Margaret's Hope
Wateringhouse
South Ronaldsay
Pentland Firth
Burwick
Brough Ness
Dunnet Head
Stroma
John o' Groats
Scrabster

SHETLAND

Muckle Flugga
Burra Firth
Herma Ness
Norwick
Haroldswick
Unst
Baltasound
Balta
Quiivoe
Uyeasound
Dalsetter
Belmont
Gutcher Uyea
Mid Yell
Funzie
South-haa
Yell
Fetlar
The Faither
Sandwick
Otterswick Sd.
North Collafirth
Ollaberry
Burravoe
Esha Ness
Hillswick
Mossbank
Heoga Ness
Stenness
Scatsta
Out Skerries
St Magnus Bay
Brae
Lunna
Muckle Roe
Voe
Papa Stour
Laxo
Whalsay
Sandness
Aith
Mainland
Sandsting
Walls
Fresta
Vaila
Reawick
Lerwick
Foula
Ham
Scalloway
Bressay
Hamnavoe
I. of Noss
West Burra
Cunningsburgh
Bressay Sd.
Sandwick
Mousa
Soouoburgh
Fitful Head
Tolob
Sumburgh Head
Sumburgh
Stonybreck
Fair Isle

Stromness
John o' Groats
Duncansby Hd.
Mey
Castletown
Dunnet
Keiss
Sinclair's B.
Halkirk
Watten
Noss Hd.
Wick
L. More
Latheron
Lybster
Dunbeath
Berriedale

Hopeman
Lossiemouth
Findochty Portknockie
Rosehearty
Fraserburgh
Elgin
Buckie
Banff Macduff
Inverallochy
Garmouth
Gardenstown
Rattray Hd.
Fochabers
Portsoy
Strichen
Fife Keith
New Pitsligo
Keith
Aberchirder
Cuminestown Mintlaw
Peterhead
Rothes
Turriff
New Deer Maud
Longside
Boddam
Craigellachie
Rothienorman
Hatton
Dufftown
Huntly
Methlick
Cruden Bay
Ballindalloch
Fyvie
Ellon
Tomnavoulin
Rhynie
Uldmeldrum
Cabrach
Oyne
Pitmedden
Newburgh
Knockandhu
Tarves
Bridge of Alford
Inverurie
Tomintoul
Strathdon
Alford
Kintore
Balmedie
Cock Bridge
Komnay
Dunecht
Skene
Aberdeen
Macdui
Torphins
Peterculter
2862
Aboyne
Banchory
Crathie
Dallater
Muchalls
Braemar
Balmoral Castle
Strachan
Inverey
Lochnagar
Mt Keen
Stonehaven
3786
3077
Tarfside
Cairn o' Mount
1488
Clova
Inverbervie
Fordoun
Gourdon
Glen Esk
Fettercairn
Laurencekirk
Edzell
Marykirk
Dykehead
Brechin
St. Cyrus
Glenisla
Tannadice
Montrose
Kirriemuir
Br. of Cally
Friockheim
Alyth
Glamis
Inverkeilor
Blairgowrie
Forfar
Birnam
Newtyle
Arbroath
Coupar Angus
Meikleour
Carnoustie
Stanley
Monifieth
Buddon Ness
New Scone
Dundee
Bell Rock
Broughty Ferry
Perth
Tayport
Newport on Tay
Wormit
Bridge of Earn
Newburgh
Leuchars
Glencarse
St. Andrews
rarder
Abernethy
Dairsie
Glenfarg
Auchtermuchty
Cupar
Falkland
Pitscottie
Fife Ness
Milnathort
Ceres
Kinross
Strathmiglo
Largoward
Crail
Leslie
Lundin
Kennoway
Anstruther
Pittenweem
Rumblingbridge
Markinch
Links
St. Monans
Cowdenbeath
Leven
I. of May
Kirkcaldy
Buckhaven
Dunfermline
Kinghorn
North Berwick
Burntisland
Bass Rock
Inchkeith
Gullane
Inverkeithing
Dunbar
Queensferry
Prestonpans
Kirkliston
Musselburgh
Haddington
Leith
E. Linton
Cockburnspath
Edinburgh
Preston
St Abb's Hd.
Balerno
Gifford
St. Abbs
Newtongrange
Coldingham
Eyemouth
Penicuik
Ayton
Pentland Hills
Soutra Hill
Duns
Chirnside
Paxton
Berwick-upon-Tweed
Carfraemill
Tweedmouth
Carlops
Moorfoot Hills
Duns
W. Linton
Eddleston
Lauder
Westruther
Greenlaw

Abington
Galashiels
Alnwick

NORTH SEA

0   10   20   30   40   50 Miles
0 10 20 30 40 50 60 70 80 Kilometres

John Bartholomew & Son Ltd

A

Distances in miles
between circled points

1:1 250 000

Heights in feet

John Bartholomew & Son Ltd

0	10	20	30	40	50 Miles
0	10	20	30	40	50 60 70 80 Kilometres

Distances in miles
between circled points ⟨—— 2 ——⟩

1:1 250 000

Heights in feet

John Bartholomew & Son Ltd

Comparative Heights and Depths in the British Isles

Heights and depths shown in metres

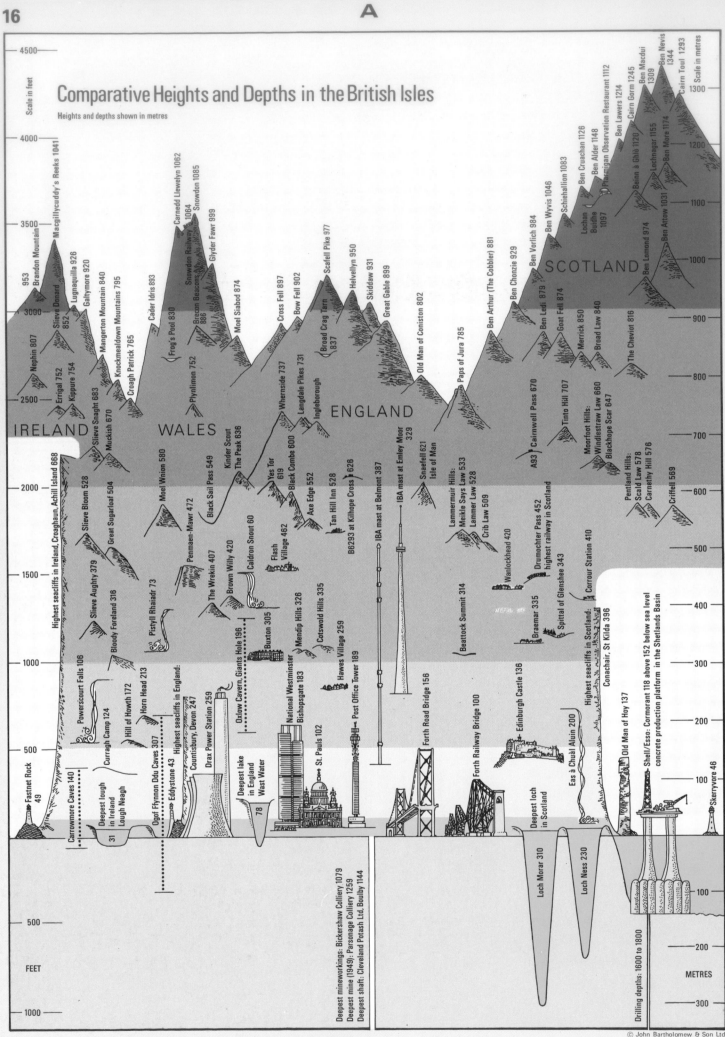

Scale in feet

4500
4000
3500
3000
2500
2000
1500
1000
500

FEET

500
1000

Scale in metres

1300
1200
1100
1000
900
800
700
600
500
400
300
200
100

100

200

METRES

300

IRELAND

Macgillycuddy's Reeks 1041
Brandon Mountain 953
Slieve Donard 852
Lugnaquilla 926
Galtymore 920
Mangerton Mountain 840
Knockmealdown Mountains 795
Nephin 807
Croagh Patrick 765
Errigal 752
Kippure 754
Slieve Snaght 683
Muckish 670
Slieve Bloom 528
Great Sugarloaf 504
Slieve Aughty 379
Bloody Foreland 316
Highest seacliffs in Ireland, Croaghaun, Achill Island 668
Powerscourt Falls 106
Hill of Howth 172
Horn Head 213
Fastnet Rock 49
Carrowmore Caves 140
Deepest lough in Ireland Lough Neagh 31

WALES

Carnedd Llewelyn 1062
Snowdon Railway 1064
Snowdon 1085
Glyder Fawr 999
Cader Idris 893
Frog's Pool 830
Brecon Beacons 886
Moel Siabod 874
Plynlimon 752
Moel Wnion 580
Penmaen-Mawr 472
Black Sail Pass 549
The Wrekin 407
Pistyll Rhaiadr 73

ENGLAND

Scafell Pike 977
Helvellyn 950
Skiddaw 931
Cross Fell 897
Bow Fell 902
Great Gable 899
Broad Crag Tarn 837
Whernside 737
Langdale Pikes 731
Ingleborough
Old Man of Coniston 802
Kinder Scout
The Peak 636
Yes Tor 619
Black Combe 600
Axe Edge 552
Tan Hill Inn 528
Brown Willy 420
B6293 at Kilhope Cross 626
IBA mast at Belmont 387
IBA mast at Emley Moor 329
Caldron Snout 60
Flash Village 462
Buxton 305
Mendip Hills 326
Cotswold Hills 335
Oxlow Cavern, Giants Hole 196
Hawes Village 259
Post Office Tower 189
National Westminster Bishopsgate 183
Drax Power Station 259
Countisbury, Devon 247
Highest seacliffs in England:
Ogof Ffynnon Ddu Caves 307
Eddystone 43
St. Pauls 102
Deepest lake in England Wast Water 78

SCOTLAND

Ben Nevis 1344
Ben Macdui 1309
Cairn Toul 1293
Cairn Gorm 1245
Ben Lawers 1214
Braeriach
Ben Macdui 1174
Lochnagar 1155
Ptarmigan Observation Restaurant 1112
Ben Cruachan 1126
Ben Alder 1148
Schiehallion 1083
Ben More 1174
Ben Attow 1031
Beinn à Ghlo 1120
Lochan Buidhe 1097
Ben Wyvis 1046
Ben Lomond 974
Ben Vorlich 984
Ben Chonzie 929
Ben Arthur (The Cobbler) 881
Ben Ledi 879
Goat Fell 874
Broad Law 840
Merrick 850
The Cheviot 816
Paps of Jura 785
Cairnwell Pass 670
Tinto Hill 707
A93
Lammermuir Hills: Meikle Says Law 533 Lammer Law 528
Crib Law 509
Wanlockhead 420
Drumochter Pass 452 highest railway in Scotland
Spittal of Glenshee 343
Corrour Station 410
Beattock Summit 314
Braemar 335
Moorfoot Hills: Windlestraw Law 660 Blackhope Scar 647
Pentland Hills: Scald Law 578 Carnethy Hill 576
Criffell 569
Snaefell 621 Isle of Man
Edinburgh Castle 136
Forth Road Bridge 156
Forth Railway Bridge 100
Eas à Chual Aluin 200
Highest seacliffs in Scotland: Conachair, St Kilda 396
Old Man of Hoy 137
Shell/Esso: Cormorant 118 above 152 below sea level concrete production platform in the Shetlands Basin
Skerryvore 46
Deepest loch in Scotland
Loch Morar 310
Loch Ness 230
Drilling depths: 1600 to 1800

Deepest mineworkings: Bickershaw Colliery 1079
Deepest mine (1949): Parsonage Colliery 1259
Deepest shaft: Cleveland Potash Ltd, Boulby 1144

© John Bartholomew & Son Ltd

TOWN & CITY PLANS

SEE WHITE PAGES AT END OF SECTION FOR DETAILED LONDON STREET PLAN

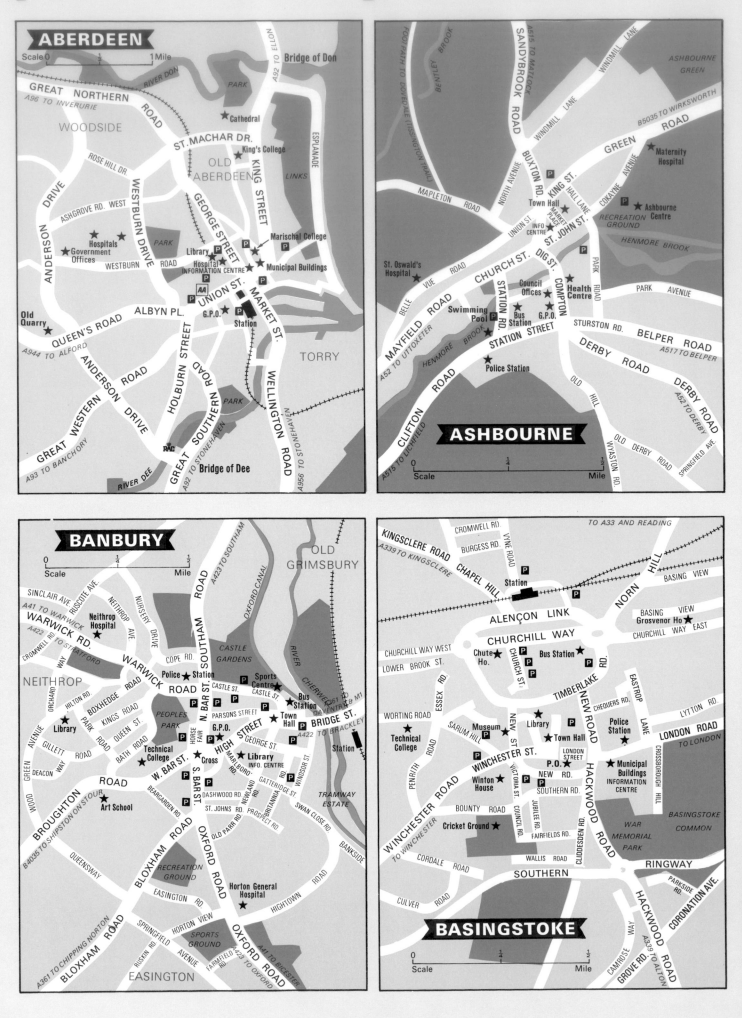

B

3

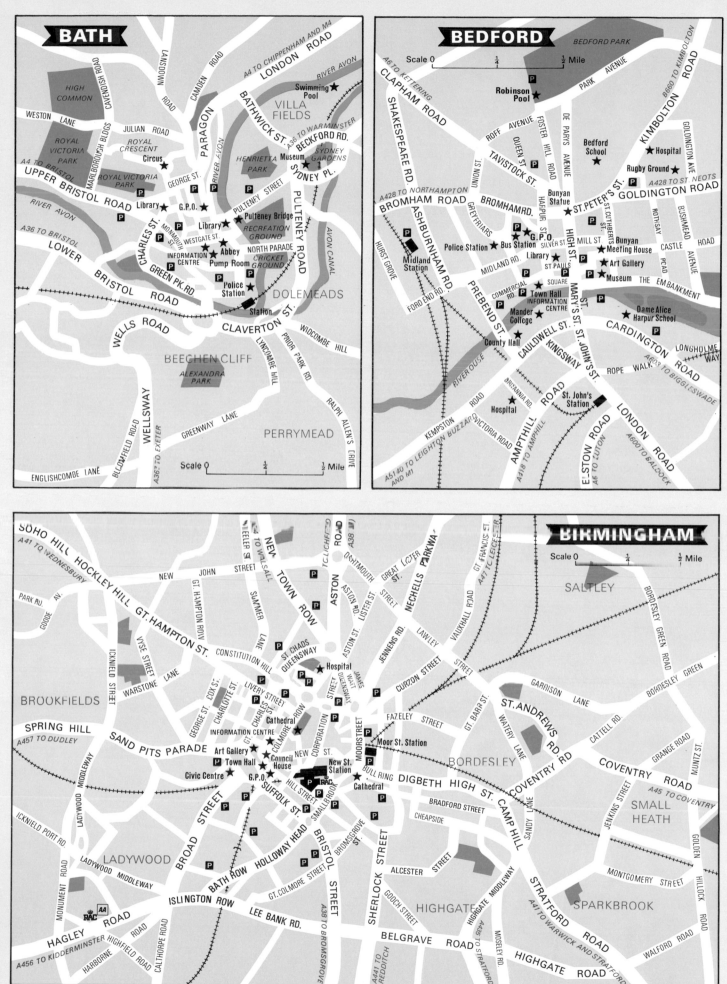

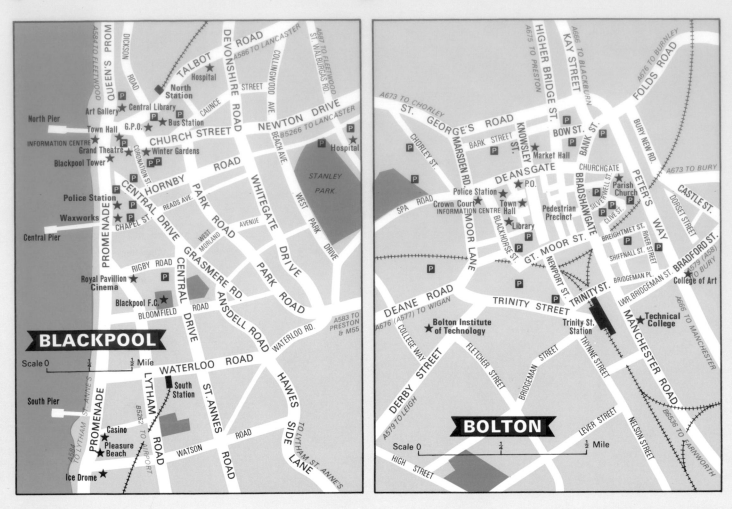

BLACKPOOL

North Pier
North Pier
Central Pier
South Pier

Queen's Prom
Dickson Road
Devonshire Road
Talbot Road
A586 to Lancaster
A587 to Fleetwood
St. Walburgas Rd.
Collingwood Ave.
Hospital
North Station
Art Gallery
Central Library
Town Hall
G.P.O.
Bus Station
Church Street
Newton Drive
A586 to Lancaster
B5266 to Lancaster
Information Centre
Grand Theatre
Winter Gardens
Blackpool Tower
Caunce Street
Whitegate Drive
West Park Drive
Stanley Park
Hospital
Police Station
Waxworks
Promenade
Central Drive
Hornby Road
Chapel St.
Coronation St.
Reads Ave.
Park Road
West Morland Avenue
Rigby Road
Royal Pavilion Cinema
Blackpool F.C.
Grasmere Rd.
Ansdell Road
Central Drive
Bloomfield Road
Waterloo Rd.
A583 to Preston & M55
Scale 0 ¼ ½ Mile
Lytham Road
St. Annes Road
Waterloo Road
Hawes Side Lane
South Station
Watson Road
To Lytham St. Annes
A584 to Lytham St. Annes
B5262 to Airport
Promenade
Casino
Pleasure Beach
Ice Drome

BOLTON

Higher Bridge St.
Kay Street
A666 to Blackburn
A675 to Preston
A676 to Burnley
Folds Road
A676 to Bury
St. George's Road
Chorley St.
Marsden Rd.
Bark Street
Knowsley St.
Bow St.
A673 to Chorley
Deansgate
Market Hall
Churchgate
Peter's Way
Castle St.
A673 to Bury
Police Station
P.O.
Parish Church
Crown Court
Town Hall
Bradshawgate
Dorset Street
Information Centre
Library
Pedestrian Precinct
Silverwell St.
Clive St.
Bradford St.
A579 (A58) to Bury
Spa Road
Blackhorse St.
Great Moor St.
Breightmet St.
Shiffnall St.
Bridgeman Pl.
College of Art
Moor Lane
Newport St.
Lwr. Bridgeman St.
River Street
Deane Road
A676 (A577) to Wigan
Trinity Street
Trinity St.
Technical College
A666 to Manchester
A579 to Leigh
Bolton Institute of Technology
College Way
Fletcher Street
Bridgeman Street
Trinity St. Station
Thynne Street
Manchester Road
B6536 to Farnworth
Derby Street
Lever Street
Nelson Street
High Street
Scale 0 ¼ ½ Mile

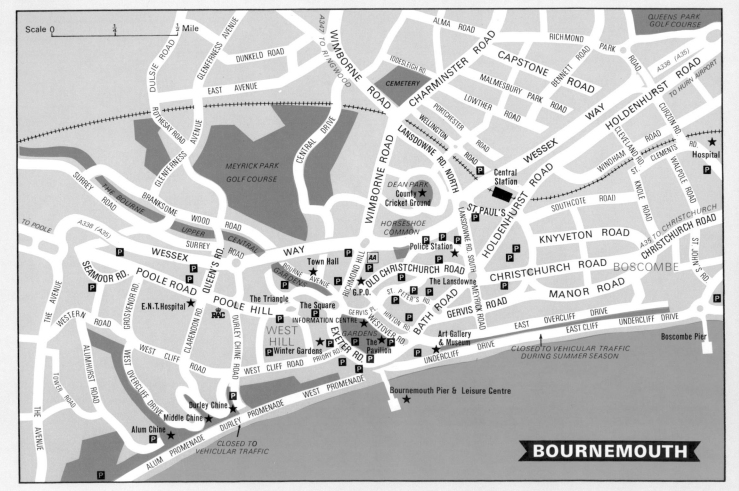

BOURNEMOUTH

Scale 0 ¼ ½ Mile
Dulsie Road
Glenferness Avenue
Dunkeld Road
Wimborne Road
A347 to Ringwood
Alma Road
Richmond Park Road
Queens Park Golf Course
A338 (A35)
East Avenue
Rothesay Road
Iddesleigh Rd.
Cemetery
Charminster Road
Capstone Road
Bennett Road
Holdenhurst Road
To Hurn Airport
Curzon Rd.
Meyrick Park Golf Course
Central Drive
Wellington Road
Malmesbury Park Road
Lowther Road
Portchester Road
Wessex Way
Cleveland Rd.
Windham Rd.
St. Clements Rd.
Hospital
Surrey Road
The Bourne
Branksome
Wood Road
Upper Central Road
Glenferness
Lansdowne Rd. North
Central Station
Holdenhurst Road
Knole Road
A35 to Christchurch
Wessex Way
Dean Park
County Cricket Ground
St. Paul's
Lansdowne Rd. South
Southcote Road
Christchurch Road
Horseshoe Common
Boscombe
To Poole
Seamoor Rd.
Poole Road
Surrey Road
Wessex Way
Queen's Rd.
Town Hall
Bourne Gardens
AA
Richmond Hill
Old Christchurch Road
Police Station
The Lansdowne
Knyveton Road
Christchurch Road
St. John's Rd.
The Avenue
Western Road
Grosvenor Rd.
Poole Hill
The Triangle
The Square
G.P.O.
St. Peter's Rd.
Bath Road
Gervis Road
Manor Road
Christchurch Road
E.N.T. Hospital
RAC
Information Centre
Gervis Place
St. Hinton Rd.
Meyrick Road
East Overcliff Drive
Undercliff Drive
Clarendon Rd.
West Hill
Westover Rd.
Art Gallery & Museum
East Cliff
Boscombe Pier
Alumhurst Road
West Cliff Road
Durley Chine Road
Priory Rd.
Exeter Rd.
Winter Gardens
The Pavilion
Gardens
Undercliff Drive
Closed to Vehicular Traffic during Summer Season
Tower Road
West Overcliff Drive
West Cliff Road
West Promenade
Bournemouth Pier & Leisure Centre
The Avenue
Durley Chine
Middle Chine
Alum Promenade
Durley Promenade
West Promenade
Alum Chine
Closed to Vehicular Traffic

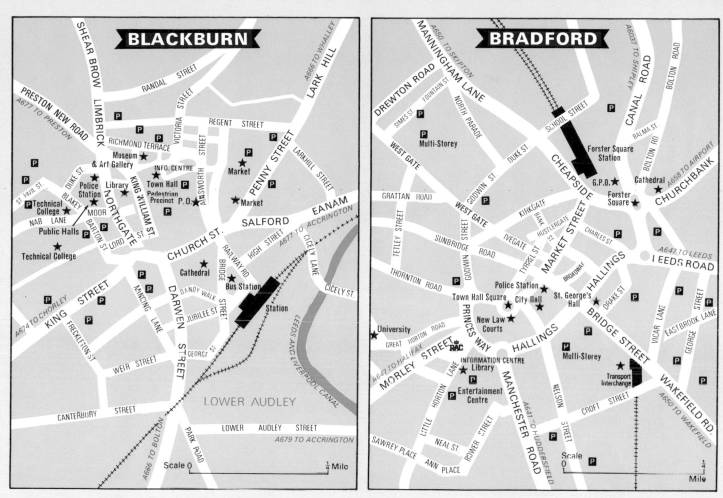

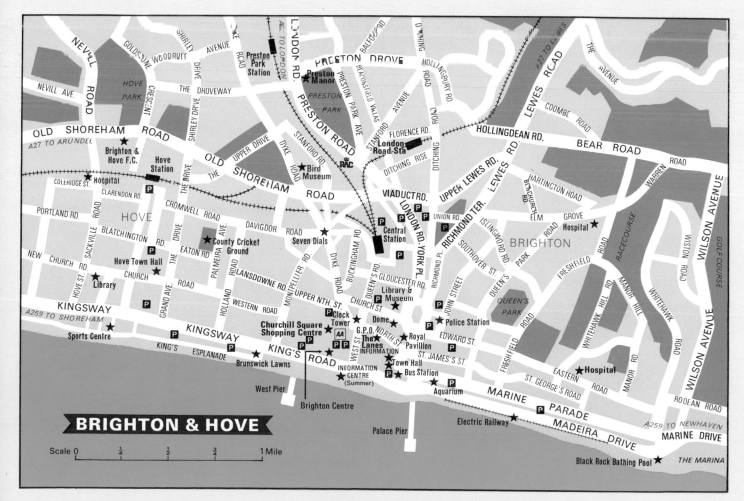

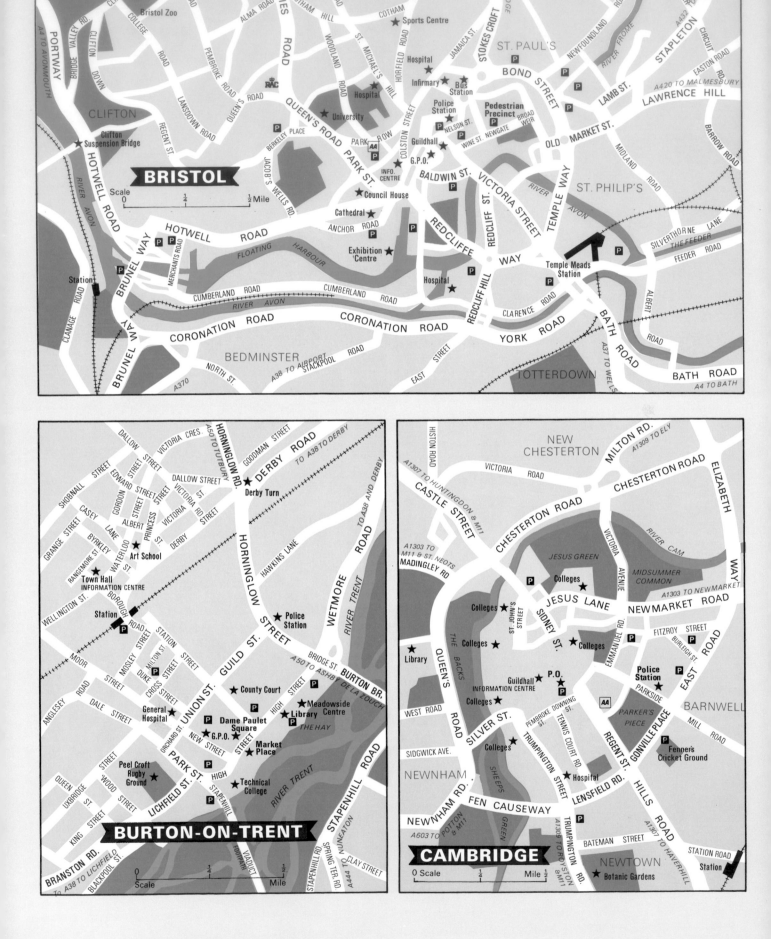

BRISTOL

CLIFTON DOWN

Station

MONTPELIER

COTHAM

CLIFTON

Bristol Zoo

★ Sports Centre

ST. PAUL'S

★ Hospital

Infirmary ★

★ Hospital

★ University

Clifton Suspension Bridge ★

Police Station ★

Pedestrian Precinct

BOND STREET

LAMB ST.

LAWRENCE HILL

Bus Station

Guildhall ★

G.P.O. ★

OLD MARKET ST.

★ Council House

BALDWIN ST.

ST. PHILIP'S

Cathedral ★

INFO. CENTRE

Exhibition Centre ★

HOTWELL ROAD

FLOATING HARBOUR

Hospital ★

Temple Meads Station

Station

CUMBERLAND ROAD

CUMBERLAND ROAD

RIVER AVON

CORONATION ROAD

CORONATION ROAD

YORK ROAD

BATH ROAD

BEDMINSTER

TOTTERDOWN

BATH ROAD

Scale 0 ¼ ½ Mile

BURTON-ON-TRENT

DERBY ROAD

Derby Turn ★

Art School ★

Town Hall ★
INFORMATION CENTRE

Station

Police Station ★

County Court ★

Meadowside Centre ★

General Hospital ★

Dame Paulet Square

Library ★

G.P.O.

THE HAY

Market Place ★

Peel Croft Rugby Ground ★

Technical College ★

LICHFIELD ST.

STAPENHILL ROAD

BRANSTON RD.

Scale 0 ¼ ½ Mile

CAMBRIDGE

NEW CHESTERTON

MILTON RD.

CHESTERTON ROAD

Jesus Green

CASTLE STREET

Colleges ★

JESUS LANE

MIDSUMMER COMMON

NEWMARKET ROAD

Colleges ★

Colleges ★

Colleges ★

Library ★

P.O. ★

Guildhall ★
INFORMATION CENTRE

Police Station ★

BARNWELL

Colleges ★

Parker's Piece

Fenner's Cricket Ground ★

SILVER ST.

Colleges ★

Hospital ★

NEWNHAM

FEN CAUSEWAY

NEWTOWN

Botanic Gardens ★

Station

0 Scale ¼ ½ Mile

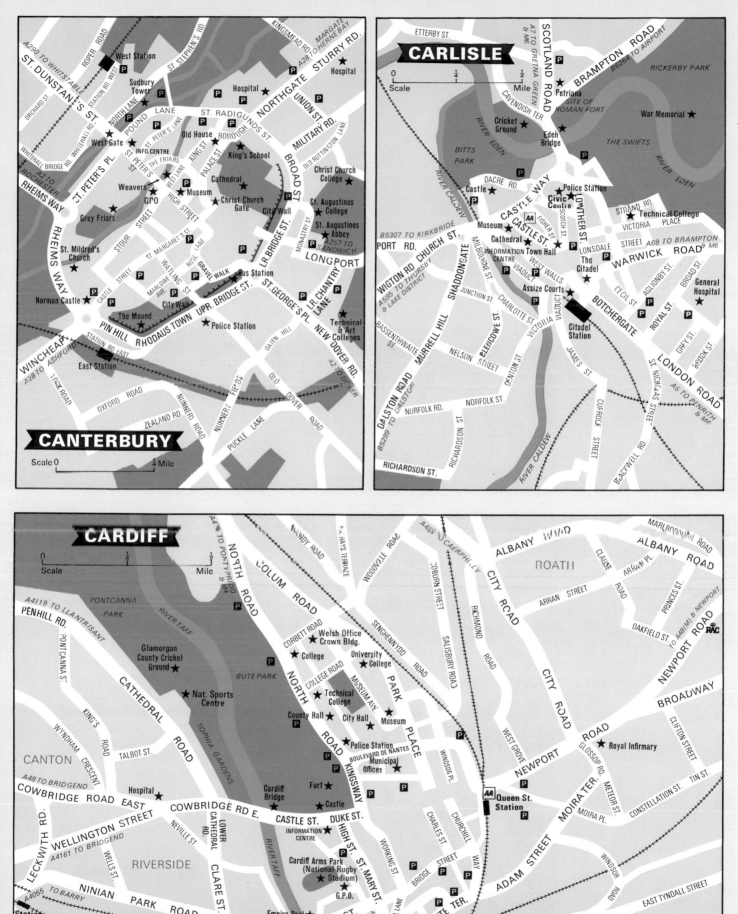

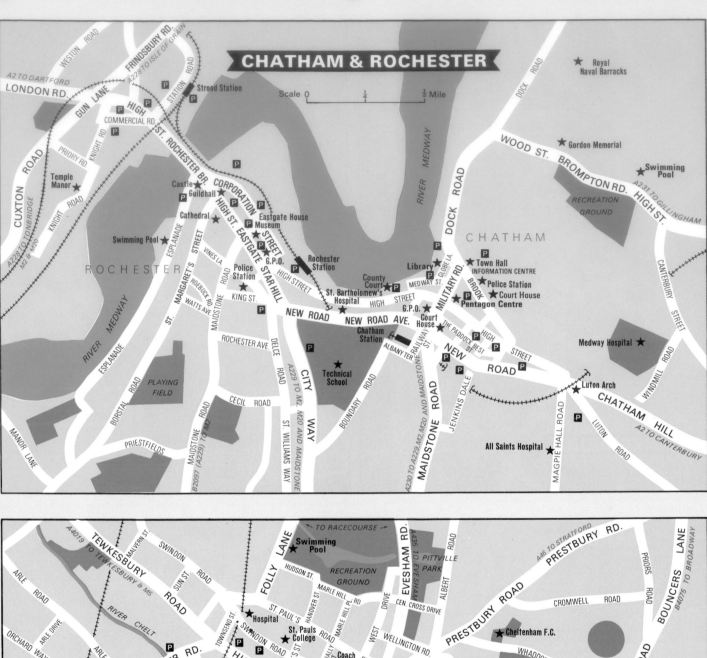

CHATHAM & ROCHESTER

Scale 0 ¼ ½ Mile

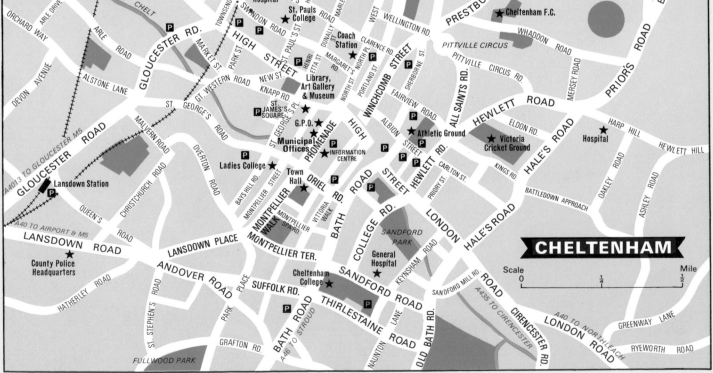

CHELTENHAM

Scale 0 ¼ ½ Mile

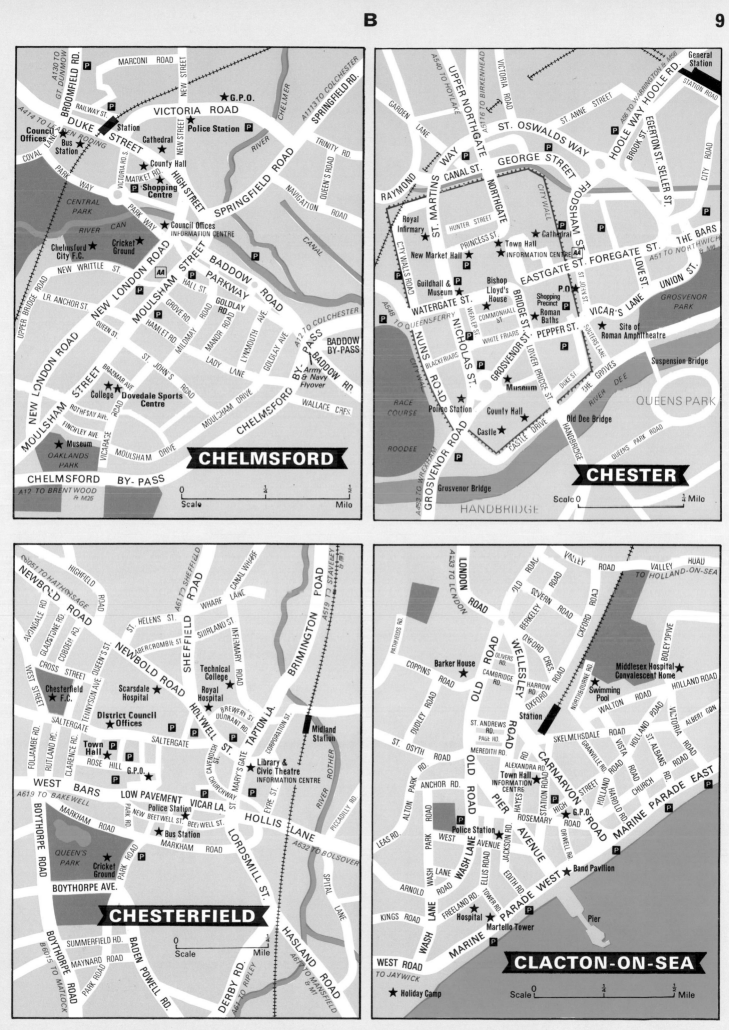

CHELMSFORD

CHESTER

CHESTERFIELD

CLACTON-ON-SEA

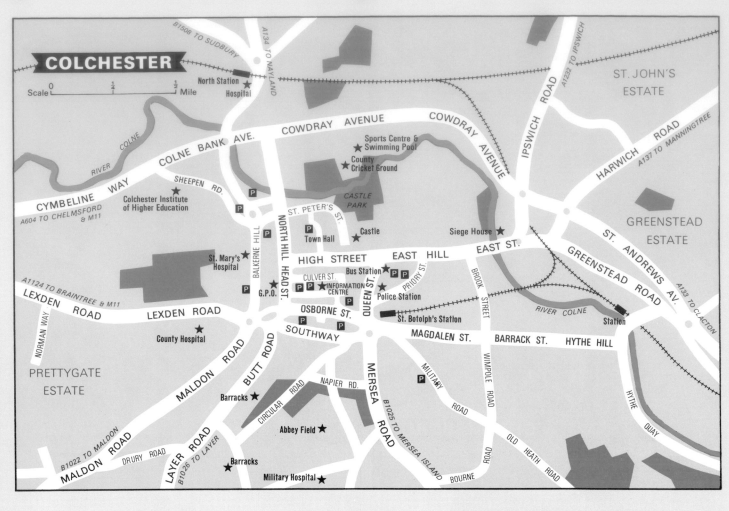

COLCHESTER

Scale 0 — ¼ — ½ Mile

B1508 TO SUDBURY
A134 TO NAYLAND
A1232 TO IPSWICH

ST. JOHN'S ESTATE

North Station
Hospital

RIVER COLNE

COWDRAY AVENUE

COWDRAY AVENUE

IPSWICH ROAD

HARWICH ROAD

A137 TO MANNINGTREE

Sports Centre & Swimming Pool ★

County ★ Cricket Ground

CYMBELINE WAY

COLNE BANK AVE.

ST. ANDREWS AV.

A133 TO CLACTON

GREENSTEAD ESTATE

A604 TO CHELMSFORD & M11

SHEEPEN RD.

Colchester Institute of Higher Education

CASTLE PARK

ST. PETER'S ST.

GREENSTEAD ROAD

St. Mary's Hospital

BALKERNE HILL

NORTH HILL HEAD ST.

P

P Town Hall

★ Castle

Siege House ★

HIGH STREET

EAST HILL

EAST ST.

A1124 TO BRAINTREE & M11

LEXDEN ROAD

LEXDEN ROAD

CULVER ST.

G.P.O. P

P

INFORMATION CENTRE

Bus Station P

QUEEN ST.

Police Station

PRIORY ST.

BROOK STREET

RIVER COLNE

Station

NORMAN WAY

OSBORNE ST.

SOUTHWAY

St. Botolph's Station

MAGDALEN ST.

BARRACK ST.

HYTHE HILL

PRETTYGATE ESTATE

County Hospital ★

MALDON ROAD

BUTT ROAD

MERSEA ROAD

MILITARY ★ ROAD

WIMPOLE ROAD

OLD HEATH ROAD

HYTHE QUAY

Barracks ★

NAPIER RD.

CIRCULAR ROAD

B1025 TO MERSEA ISLAND

B1022 TO MALDON

Abbey Field ★

DRURY ROAD

LAYER ROAD

B1026 TO LAYER

MALDON ROAD

Barracks ★

Military Hospital ★

BOURNE

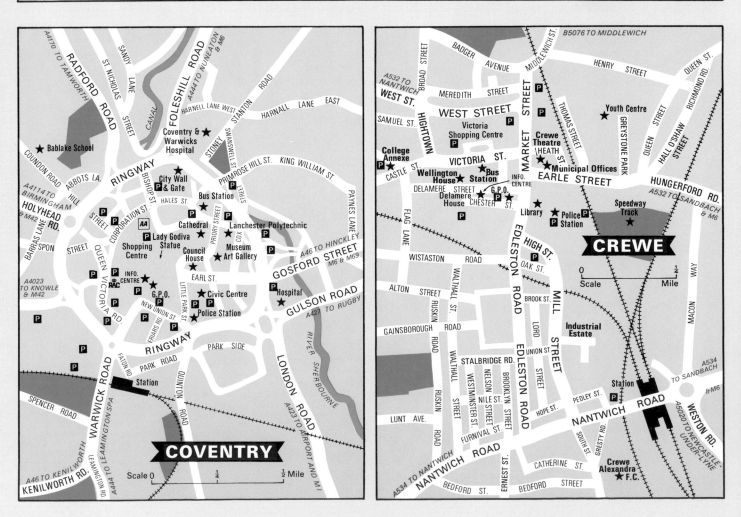

COVENTRY

Scale 0 — ¼ — ½ Mile

A4770 TO TAMWORTH

RADFORD ROAD

SANDY LANE

ST. NICHOLAS STREET

FOLESHILL ROAD

A444 TO NUNEATON & M6

B5076 TO MIDDLEWICH

BADGER AVENUE

BROAD STREET

MIDDLEWICH ST.

HENRY STREET

QUEEN ST.

Bablake School ★

CANAL

HARNELL LANE WEST

HARNALL LANE EAST

STANTON ROAD

A532 TO NANTWICH

WEST ST.

MEREDITH STREET

WEST STREET

MARKET STREET

THOMAS STREET

Youth Centre ★

RICHMOND RD.

Coventry & Warwicks Hospital ★

STONEY STANTON RD.

SWANSWELL ST.

SAMUEL ST.

HIGHTOWN

Victoria Shopping Centre

P

Crewe Theatre

HEATH ST.

GREYSTONE PARK

QUEEN STREET

HALL O'SHAW STREET

COUNDON ROAD

ABBOTS LA.

RINGWAY

HILL

BISHOP ST.

City Wall P & Gate

PRIMROSE HILL ST.

KING WILLIAM ST.

College Annexe

VICTORIA ST.

Municipal Offices

EARLE STREET

HUNGERFORD RD.

A4114 TO BIRMINGHAM

CORPORATION ST.

HALES ST.

Bus Station

PRIORY STREET

CASTLE ST.

Wellington House ★

Bus Station

INFO. CENTRE

A532 TO SANDBACH & M6

HOLYHEAD RD. & M42

BARRAS LANE

SPON STREET

QUEEN VICTORIA RD.

AA

P Lady Godiva Statue

Cathedral ★

Lanchester Polytechnic

PAYNES LANE

DELAMERE STREET

Delamere House

G.P.O. P CHESTER ST.

HIGH ST.

Library

Police P Station

Speedway Track

P

CREWE

A4023 TO KNOWLE & M42

Shopping Centre

COX ★

Museum Art Gallery ★

GOSFORD STREET

A46 TO HINCKLEY

FLAG LANE

OAK ST.

Scale 0 — ¼ — ½ Mile

INFO. CENTRE ★

G.P.O. ★

Council House ★

EARL ST.

Civic Centre ★

Hospital P

A46 TO M6 & M69

WISTASTON ROAD

ALTON STREET

WALTHALL ST.

BROOK ST.

NEW UNION ST.

LITTLE PARK ST.

Police Station ★

GULSON ROAD

A427 TO RUGBY

GAINSBOROUGH ROAD

RUSKIN ST.

LORD ST.

EDLESTON ROAD

Industrial Estate

A534 TO SANDBACH

FRIARS RD.

RINGWAY

PARK SIDE

PARK ROAD

RIVER SHERBOURNE

STALBRIDGE RD.

NELSON STREET

UNION ST.

MILL STREET

SPENCER ROAD

WARWICK ROAD

FATON RD.

QUINTON ROAD

Station

LONDON ROAD

A423 TO AIRPORT AND M1

LUNT AVE.

RUSKIN ST.

WALTHALL ST.

WESTMINSTER STREET

NILE ST.

BROOKLYN STREET

HOPE ST.

PEDLEY ST.

Station

P

NANTWICH ROAD

A534 TO NEWCASTLE UNDER LINE

KENILWORTH RD.

A46 TO KENILWORTH

A444 TO LEAMINGTON SPA

LEAMINGTON RD.

A534 TO NANTWICH

NANTWICH ROAD

FURNIVAL ST.

ERNEST ST.

CATHERINE STREET

SOUTH ST.

GRESTY RD.

Crewe Alexandra F.C. ★

A4620 TO NEWCASTLE UNDER LINE

WESTON RD.

& M6

BEDFORD ST.

BEDFORD STREET

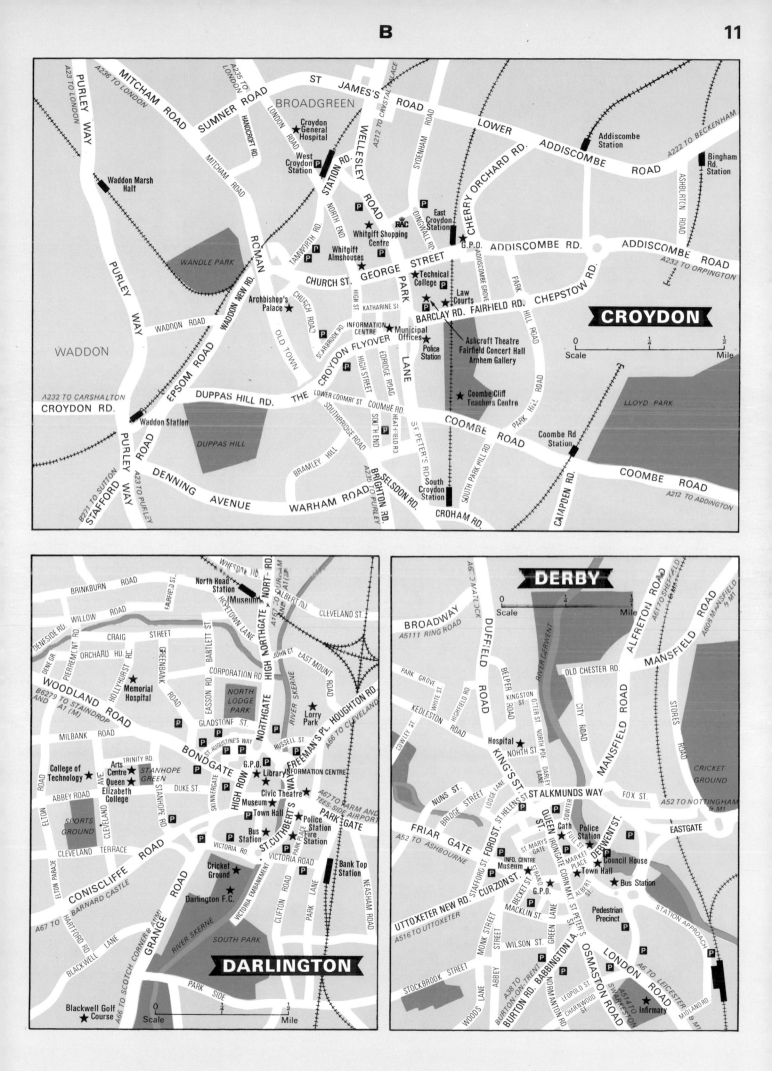

CROYDON

PURLEY WAY · A23 TO LONDON · A236 TO LONDON · MITCHAM ROAD · A235 TO LONDON · SUMNER ROAD · HANDCROFT RD. · LONDON ROAD · STATION RD. · ST JAMES'S ROAD · BROADGREEN · WELLESLEY ROAD · A212 TO CRYSTAL PALACE · SYDENHAM ROAD · LOWER · ADDISCOMBE · ROAD · A222 TO BECKENHAM

Waddon Marsh Halt · Croydon General Hospital · West Croydon Station · Addiscombe Station · Bingham Rd. Station · ASHBURTON ROAD

WANDLE PARK · ROMAN · WADDON NEW RD. · MITCHAM ROAD · NORTH END · TAMWORTH RD. · Whitgift Shopping Centre · RAC · East Croydon Station · CHERRY ORCHARD RD. · ADDISCOMBE · G.P.O. · ADDISCOMBE RD. · ADDISCOMBE ROAD · A232 TO ORPINGTON

WADDON · PURLEY WAY · WADDON ROAD · EPSOM ROAD · Archbishop's Palace · CHURCH ST. · GEORGE STREET · Whitgift Almshouses · Technical College · HIGH ST. · KATHARINE ST. · ADDISCOMBE GROVE · Law Courts · PARK · CHEPSTOW RD. · HILL ROAD · CROYDON

Information Centre · SCARBROOK RD. · CHURCH ROAD · OLD TOWN · CROYDON FLYOVER · Municipal Offices · BARCLAY RD. FAIRFIELD RD. · Police Station · Ashcroft Theatre Fairfield Concert Hall Arnhem Gallery · PARK HILL ROAD

Scale 0 ¼ ½ Mile

A232 TO CARSHALTON · CROYDON RD. · DUPPAS HILL RD. · THE · LOWER COOMBE ST. · HIGH STREET · EDRIDGE ROAD · COOMBE RD. · HEATHFIELD RD. · Coombe Cliff Teachers Centre · LLOYD PARK

DUPPAS HILL · SOUTHBRIDGE ROAD · SOUTH END · Waddon Station · PURLEY WAY · STAFFORD RD. · DENNING AVENUE · BRAMLEY HILL · WARHAM ROAD · BRIGHTON RD. · A235 TO PURLEY · ST PETER'S RD. · COOMBE ROAD · Coombe Rd Station · CAMPDEN RD. · COOMBE ROAD · A212 TO ADDINGTON

B271 TO SUTTON · A23 TO PURLEY · BRAMLEY HILL · BRIGHTON RD. · SELSDON RD. · South Croydon Station · CROHAM RD.

DARLINGTON

BRINKBURN ROAD · FAIRFIELD ST. · WHESSOE RD. · NORTH RD. · A167 TO DURHAM · ALBERT RD. · CLEVELAND ST. · North Road Station (Museum)

WILLOW ROAD · CRAIG STREET · GREENBANK ROAD · BARTLETT ST. · HIGH NORTHGATE · HOPETOWN LANE · JOHN ST. · EAST MOUNT ROAD

DENESIDE RD. · ORCHARD RD. · PIERREMONT RD. · HOLLYHURST RD. · EASSON RD. · CORPORATION RD. · NORTH LODGE PARK · RIVER SKERNE · Lorry Park

WOODLAND ROAD · B6279 TO STAINDROP AND A1 (M) · Memorial Hospital · GLADSTONE ST. · ST. AUGUSTINE'S WAY · NORTHGATE · RUSSELL ST. · FREEMAN'S PL. · HOUGHTON RD. · A66 TO CLEVELAND

MILBANK ROAD · Arts Centre · TRINITY RD. · STANHOPE GREEN · BONDGATE · G.P.O. · Library · INFORMATION CENTRE · A67 TO YARM AND TEES-SIDE AIRPORT

College of Technology · Queen Elizabeth College · ABBEY RD. · STANHOPE RD. · DUKE ST. · SKINNERGATE · HIGH ROW · Civic Theatre · Museum · Town Hall · PARKGATE

ELTON RD. · CLEVELAND AVE · SPORTS GROUND · Bus Station · ST. CUTHBERT'S WAY · PARK PLACE · Police Station Fire Station

ELTON PARADE · CLEVELAND TERRACE · VICTORIA RD. · VICTORIA ROAD · Bank Top Station

CONISCLIFFE ROAD · BARNARD CASTLE · Cricket Ground · CLIFTON ROAD · PARK LANE · NEASHAM ROAD

A67 TO HARTFORD RD. · GRANGE ROAD · Darlington F.C. · VICTORIA EMBANKMENT · A66 TO SCOTCH CORNER & A1 (M) · BLACKWELL LANE · RIVER SKERNE · SOUTH PARK · PARK SIDE

Blackwell Golf Course · Scale 0 ¼ ½ Mile

DERBY

A6 TO MATLOCK · BROADWAY · A5111 RING ROAD · DUFFIELD ROAD · RIVER DERWENT · OLD CHESTER RD. · ALFRETON ROAD · A61 TO SHEFFIELD · A6 TO MATLOCK · A608 MANSFIELD 5 MT · MANSFIELD ROAD · A610 TO SHEFFIELD

Scale 0 ¼ ½ Mile

PARK GROVE · BELPER ROAD · KINGSTON ST. · OTTER ST. · CITY ROAD · STORES ROAD · CRICKET GROUND

KEDLESTON ROAD · WHITE ST. · HIGHFIELD RD. · NORTH PDE. · DARLEY LANE · Hospital · NORTH ST. · COWLEY ST. · ST ALKMUNDS WAY · FOX ST. · A52 TO NOTTINGHAM & M1

NUNS ST. · BRIDGE STREET · LODGE LANE · ST. HELEN'S ST. · QUEEN ST. · Cath · Police Station · DERWENT ST. · EASTGATE

FRIAR GATE · A52 TO ASHBOURNE · ST MARYS GATE · IRONGATE · Market Place · Council House · Town Hall · Bus Station

FORD ST. · STAFFORD ST. · INFO. CENTRE · Museum · KING'S ST. · QUEEN ST. · CORN MKT · STRAND · ALBERT ST. · ST PETER'S ST. · G.P.O. · Pedestrian Precinct

UTTOXETER NEW RD. · A516 TO UTTOXETER · CURZON ST. · BECKET ST. · MACKLIN ST. · MONK STREET · WILSON ST. · GREEN LANE · BABBINGTON LA. · OSMASTON ROAD · LONDON ROAD · A6 TO LEICESTER · STATION APPROACH

STOCKBROOK STREET · WOOD'S LANE · ABBEY ST. · A38 TO BURTON-ON-TRENT · BURTON RD. · NORMANTON RD. · LEOPOLD ST. · CHARNWOOD ST. · A514 TO SWARKSTON · A6 TO MIDLAND & M1 · Infirmary · MIDLAND RD.

DONCASTER

Scale 0 — ½ Mile

Lorries
RIVER DON NEW CUT
GREY FRIARS ROAD
NORTH BRIDGE RD.
A638 TO WAKEFIELD
LOW FISHERGATE
HIGH FISHERGATE
CHURCH WAY
MARKET RD.
COPLEY ROAD
CHRIST ROAD
HIGHFIELD ROAD
KING'S ROAD
DON ST.
BECKETT ROAD
ST. MARY'S ROAD
QUEEN'S ROAD
BROXHOLME LANE

Northern Bus Station
Corn Exchange
Police Station
MARKET PLACE
Arndale Centre
G.P.O.
Mansion House
Station
HIGH STREET
SCOT LA.
SILVER ST.
PRINCE'S ST.
NETHER HALL ROAD
CHURCH ROAD
PARK RD.
EAST LAITHGATE
THORNE ROAD
HALL GATE
SOUTH PARADE
A638 TO BAWTRY
A18 TO SCUNTHORPE M18 & M180
TOWN FIELD

TRAFFORD WAY
A630 TO ROTHERHAM & A1(M)
CLEVELAND STREET
ST. JAMES BR.
ST. SEPULCHRE GATE
SPRING GDNS.
DUKE ST.
COLLEGE RD.
Southern Bus Station
WATERDALE
WOOD ST.
County Court
CATHERINE STREET
BENTINCK ST.
ST. JAMES STREET
CHEQUER ROAD
INFO. CENTRE
Technical College
Museum & Art Gallery
APLEY ROAD
ELMFIELD ROAD
CHEQUER ROAD
ELMFIELD PARK
CARR HOUSE ROAD
GREEN DYKE LANE
CUNNINGHAM RD.
CARR LANE
PALMER STREET

DOVER

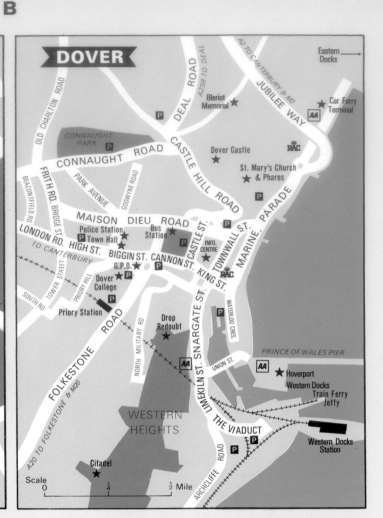

A2 TO DEAL
A2 TO CANTERBURY & M2
Eastern Docks
DEAL ROAD
OLD CHARLTON ROAD
A258 TO DEAL
JUBILEE WAY
Bleriot Memorial
AA
Car Ferry Terminal
CONNAUGHT PARK
CONNAUGHT ROAD
CASTLE HILL ROAD
Dover Castle
RAC
St. Mary's Church & Pharos
FRITH RD.
BRIDGE ST.
BEACONSFIELD RD.
PARK AVENUE
GODWYNE ROAD
MAISON DIEU ROAD
CASTLE ST.
TOWNWALL ST.
MARINE PARADE
LONDON RD.
HIGH ST.
TO CANTERBURY
Police Station
Town Hall
Bus Station
INFO. CENTRE
KING ST.
BIGGIN ST.
CANNON ST.
SNARGATE ST.
WATERLOO CRES.
G.P.O.
Dover College
TOWER STREET
PRIORY HILL
RAC
Priory Station
SOUTH RD.
FOLKESTONE ROAD
A20 TO FOLKESTONE & M20
NORTH MILITARY RD.
Drop Redoubt
LIMEKILN ST.
UNION ST.
AA
PRINCE OF WALES PIER
AA
Hoverport
Western Docks Train Ferry Jetty
WESTERN HEIGHTS
THE VIADUCT
ARCHCLIFFE ROAD
Western Docks Station
Citadel
Scale 0 — ¼ — ½ Mile

DUDLEY

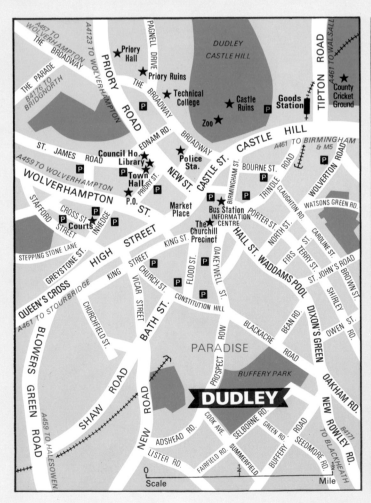

A457 TO WOLVERHAMPTON
A4123 TO WOLVERHAMPTON
PAGNELL DRIVE
TIPTON ROAD
A461 TO WALSALL
THE BROADWAY
THE PARADE
B4176 TO BRIDGNORTH
Priory Hall
Priory Ruins
PRIORY ROAD
THE BROADWAY
Technical College
DUDLEY CASTLE HILL
Castle Ruins
Zoo
Goods Station
County Cricket Ground
ST. JAMES ROAD
A459 TO WOLVERHAMPTON
Council Ho.
Library
Town Hall
EDNAM RD.
BROADWAY
NEW ST.
Police Sta.
CASTLE ST.
CASTLE HILL
A461 TO BIRMINGHAM & M5
WOLVERHAMPTON STREET
P.O.
Market Place
PRIORY ST.
BOURNE ST.
BIRMINGHAM ST.
TRINDLE ROAD
CLAUGHTON RD.
WOLVERTON ROAD
WATSONS GREEN RD.
STAFFORD STREET
CROSS ST.
Courts
INHEDGE
HIGH STREET
The Churchill Precinct
Bus Station
INFORMATION CENTRE
PORTER ST.
NORTH ST.
FIRS ST.
CAROLINE ST.
ST. JOHN'S ROAD
BROWN ST.
GREYSTONE ST.
STEPPING STONE LANE
QUEEN'S CROSS
A461 TO STOURBRIDGE
KING STREET
VICAR STREET
CHURCH ST.
FLOOD ST.
OAKEYWELL ST.
KING ST.
HALL ST.
WADDAMSPOOL
TERRY ST.
SHIRLEY ROAD
OWEN ST.
DIXON'S GREEN
OAKHAM ROAD
BLOWERS GREEN ROAD
SHAW ROAD
NEW ROAD
BATH ST.
CHURCHFIELD ST.
CONSTITUTION HILL
PROSPECT ROW
BLACKACRE ROAD
BEAN ST.
PARADISE
BUFFERY PARK
A459 TO HALESOWEN
ADSHEAD RD.
COOK AVE.
SELBORNE RD.
GREEN RD.
SEEDMORE RD.
B4171 NEW ROWLEY RD.
TO BLACKHEATH
LISTER RD.
FAIRFIELD RD.
SUMMERFIELD
BUFFERY RD.
Scale 0 — ½ Mile

DUNDEE

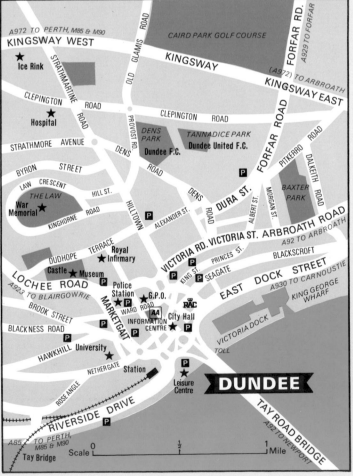

A972 TO PERTH, M85 & M90
FORFAR RD.
A929 TO FORFAR
KINGSWAY WEST
GLAMIS ROAD
CAIRD PARK GOLF COURSE
KINGSWAY
(A972) TO ARBROATH
KINGSWAY EAST
Ice Rink
STRATHMARTINE ROAD
OLD GLAMIS ROAD
CLEPINGTON ROAD
PROVOST RD.
CLEPINGTON ROAD
Hospital
DENS PARK
TANNADICE PARK
FORFAR ROAD
PITKERRO ROAD
DALKEITH ROAD
STRATHMORE AVENUE
Dundee F.C.
Dundee United F.C.
BYRON STREET
DENS ROAD
BAXTER PARK
LAW CRESCENT
THE LAW
War Memorial
KINGHORNE ROAD
HILL ST.
HILLTOWN
ALEXANDER ST.
ALBERT ST.
DURA ST.
MORGAN ST.
VICTORIA RD.
VICTORIA ST.
ARBROATH ROAD
A92 TO ARBROATH
DUDHOPE TERRACE
Royal Infirmary
Castle
Museum
Police Station
King ST.
PRINCES ST.
SEAGATE
BLACKSCROFT
EAST DOCK STREET
A930 TO CARNOUSTIE
KING GEORGE WHARF
LOCHEE ROAD
A923 TO BLAIRGOWRIE
BROOK STREET
G.P.O.
City Hall
WARD ROAD
RAC
AA
MARKETGAIT
INFORMATION CENTRE
BLACKNESS ROAD
HAWKHILL
University
NETHERGATE
Station
Leisure Centre
VICTORIA DOCK
TOLL
ROSE ANGLE
RIVERSIDE DRIVE
A85 TO PERTH, M85 & M90
Tay Bridge
TAY ROAD BRIDGE
A929 TO NEWPORT
Scale 0 — ½ — 1 Mile

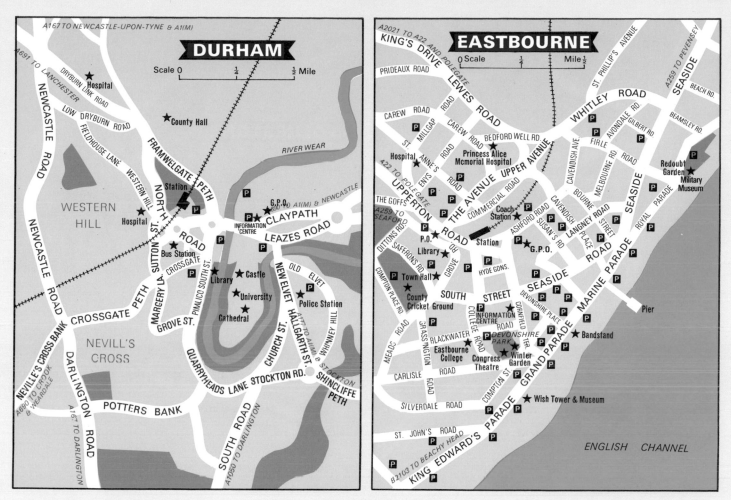

DURHAM

Scale 0   ¼   ½ Mile

A167 TO NEWCASTLE-UPON-TYNE & A1(M)

A691 TO LANCHESTER
DRYBURN LINK ROAD
★ Hospital
LOW DRYBURN ROAD
★ County Hall
FIELDHOUSE LANE
WESTERN HILL
NEWCASTLE ROAD
NORTH ROAD
FRAMWELGATE PETH
Station
★ Hospital
RIVER WEAR
G.P.O.
A690 TO A1(M) & NEWCASTLE
CLAYPATH
INFORMATION CENTRE
LEAZES ROAD
WESTERN HILL
MARGERY LA.
SUTTON ST.
Bus Station
CROSSGATE
PIMLICO SOUTH ST.
★ Library ★ Castle
NEW ELVET
OLD ELVET
GROVE ST.
★ University
★ Police Station
CHURCH ST.
HALLGARTH ST.
A177 TO A1(M) & STOCKTON
★ Cathedral
WHINNEY HILL
A1050 TO STOCKTON
SHINCLIFFE PETH
CROSSGATE PETH
NEVILLE'S CROSS BANK
A690 TO CROOK & WEARDALE
NEVILL'S CROSS
DARLINGTON ROAD
A167 TO DARLINGTON
QUARRYHEADS LANE
STOCKTON RD.
POTTERS BANK
SOUTH ROAD
A1050 TO DARLINGTON

EASTBOURNE

Scale 0   ¼   Mile ½

A2021 TO A22 AND POLEGATE
KING'S DRIVE
LEWES ROAD
PRIDEAUX ROAD
A259 TO PEVENSEY
SEASIDE
ST. PHILLIP'S AVENUE
BEACH RD.
WHITLEY ROAD
BEAMSLEY RD.
CAREW ROAD
ST. MILLGAP
CAREW ROAD
BEDFORD WELL RD.
CAVENDISH AVE.
FIRLE
AVONDALE RD.
GILBERT RD.
Princess Alice Memorial Hospital
UPPER AVENUE
THE AVENUE
MELBOURNE RD.
BOURNE ST.
A259 TO SEAFORD
A22 TO POLEGATE
★ Hospital
ST. ANNE'S ROAD
ENYS RD.
COMMERCIAL ROAD
Redoubt Garden
Military Museum
UPPERTON ROAD
THE GOFFS
Coach Station
ASHFORD ROAD
CAVENDISH RD.
SUSAN'S RD.
LANGNEY ROAD
SEASIDE
ROYAL PARADE
Station
P.O.
Library
G.P.O.
DITTONS RD.
SAFFRONS RD.
GROVE
HYDE GDNS.
SEASIDE
MARINE PARADE
★ Town Hall
COMPTON PLACE RD.
County Cricket Ground
SOUTH STREET
DEVONSHIRE PLACE
CORNFIELD ROAD
INFORMATION CENTRE
Pier
MEADS ROAD
GRASSINGTON
COLLEGE ROAD
★ BLACKWATER
DEVONSHIRE PARK
★ Bandstand
CARLISLE ROAD
Eastbourne College
Congress Theatre
★ Winter Garden
GRAND PARADE
SILVERDALE ROAD
COMPTON ST.
★ Wish Tower & Museum
ST. JOHN'S ROAD
KING EDWARD'S PARADE
B2103 TO BEACHY HEAD
ENGLISH CHANNEL

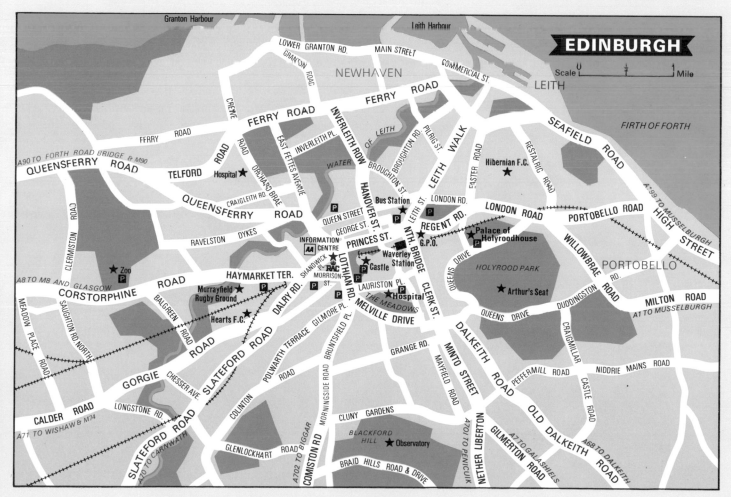

EDINBURGH

Scale 0   ½   1 Mile

Granton Harbour
Leith Harbour
LOWER GRANTON RD.
MAIN STREET
EDINBURGH
GRANTON ROAD
NEWHAVEN
COMMERCIAL ST.
LEITH
FERRY ROAD
FERRY ROAD
CREWE
FERRY ROAD
FIRTH OF FORTH
INVERLEITH ROW
FERRY ROAD
INVERLEITH PL.
SEAFIELD ROAD
EAST FETTES AVENUE
WATER OF LEITH
BROUGHTON ST.
PILRIG ST.
LEITH WALK
A90 TO FORTH ROAD BRIDGE & M90
QUEENSFERRY ROAD
TELFORD ROAD
★ Hospital
ORCHARD BRAE
RESTALRIG ROAD
A99 TO MUSSELBURGH
★ Hibernian F.C.
HIGH STREET
QUEENSFERRY ROAD
CRAIGLEITH RD.
EASTER ROAD
LONDON ROAD
PORTOBELLO ROAD
CLERMISTON ROAD
Queen Street
George St.
HANOVER ST.
Bus Station
LEITH ST.
LONDON RD.
REGENT RD.
G.P.O.
RAVELSTON DYKES
INFORMATION CENTRE
PRINCES ST.
NTH. BRIDGE
Palace of Holyroodhouse
WILLOWBRAE RD.
PORTOBELLO
★ Zoo
A8 TO M8 AND GLASGOW
Waverley Station
★ Castle
HOLYROOD PARK
CORSTORPHINE ROAD
HAYMARKET TER.
SHANDWICK PL.
RAC
LOTHIAN RD.
QUEENS DRIVE
MILTON ROAD
A1 TO MUSSELBURGH
Murrayfield Rugby Ground ★
MORRISON ST.
LAURISTON PL.
★ Hospital
★ Arthur's Seat
DALRY RD.
THE MEADOWS
CLERK ST.
QUEENS DRIVE
DUDDINGSTON
BALGREEN ROAD
MELVILLE DRIVE
CRAIGMILLAR
Hearts F.C. ★
GILMORE PL.
GRANGE RD.
DALKEITH ROAD
MEADOW PLACE
SAUGHTON RD. NORTH
POLWARTH TERRACE
BRUNTSFIELD PL.
MINTO STREET
MAYFIELD ROAD
PEFFERMILL ROAD
NIDDRIE MAINS ROAD
CALDER ROAD
GORGIE
CHESSER AVE.
SLATEFORD ROAD
COLINTON RD.
MORNINGSIDE ROAD
CASTLE ROAD
A71 TO WISHAW & M74
LONGSTONE RD.
CLUNY GARDENS
OLD DALKEITH ROAD
SLATEFORD ROAD
A70 TO CARNWATH
GLENLOCKHART ROAD
COMISTON RD.
A702 TO BIGGAR
BLACKFORD HILL
★ Observatory
NETHER LIBERTON
GILMERTON ROAD
A703 TO PENICUIK
A772 TO GALASHIELS
DALKEITH ROAD
A68 TO DALKEITH
BRAID HILLS ROAD & DRIVE

14

B

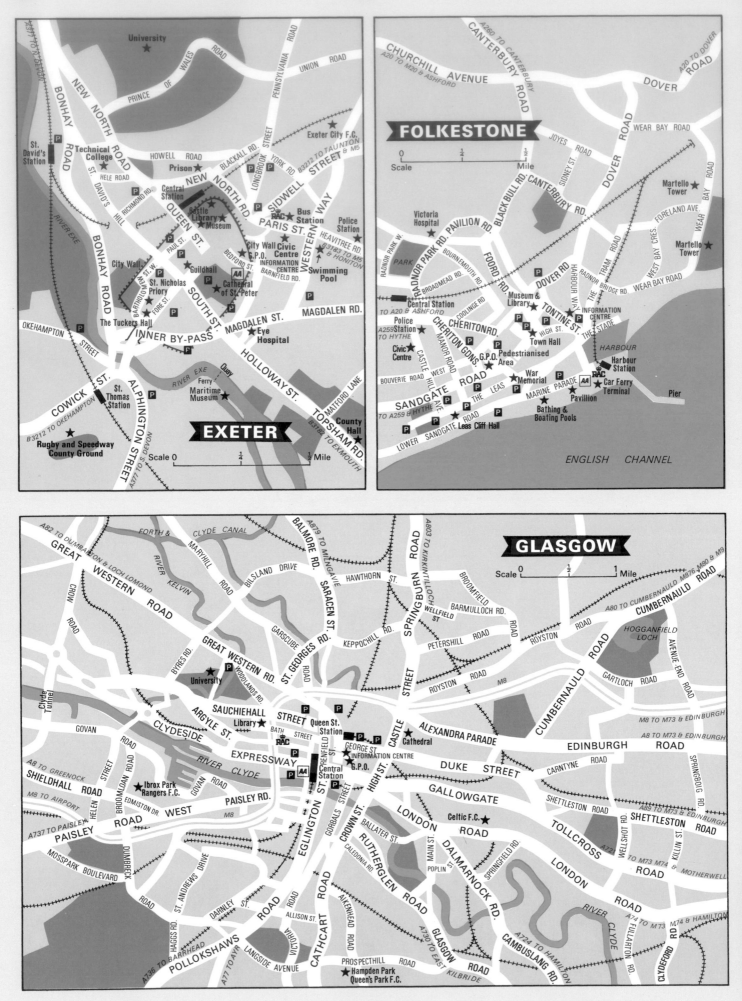

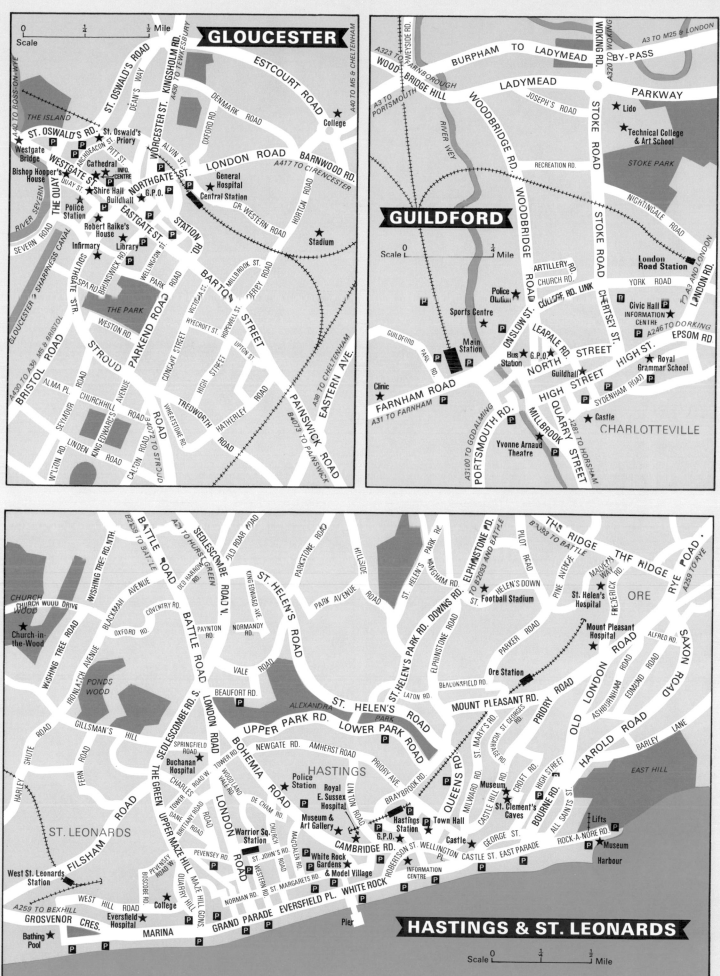

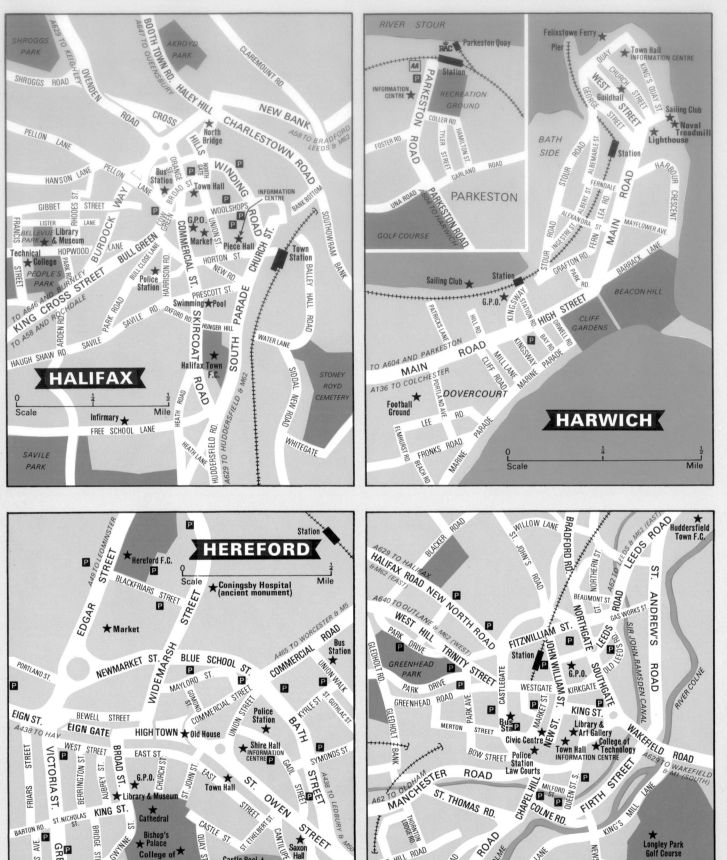
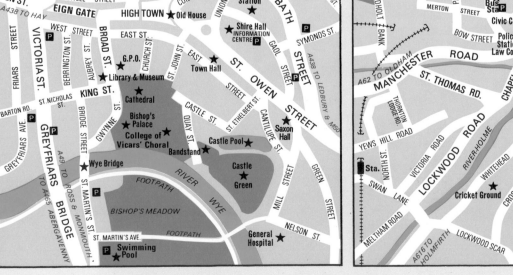

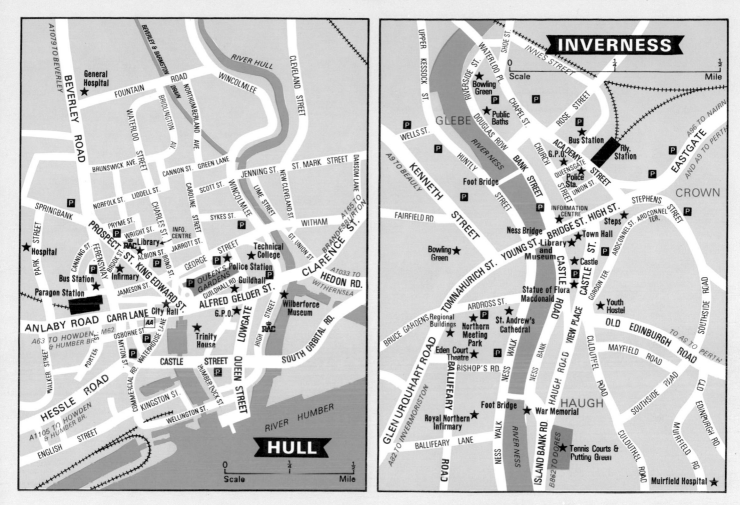

HULL

General Hospital
A1079 TO BEVERLEY
RIVER HULL
CLEVELAND STREET
FOUNTAIN ROAD
WINCOLMLEE
BEVERLEY ROAD
WATERLOO STREET
BRIDLINGTON
NORTHUMBERLAND AV.
BRUNSWICK AVE.
GREEN LANE
CANNON ST.
JENNING ST.
ST. MARK STREET
DANSOM LANE
A165 TO SUTTON
NEW CLEVELAND ST.
LIDDELL ST.
NORFOLK ST.
CAROLINE STREET
SCOTT ST.
WINCOLMLEE
LIME STREET
WITHAM
GT. UNION ST.
BRANDESBURTON ST.
CLARENCE ST.
A1033 TO HEDON RD.
WITHERNSEA
SPRINGBANK
PARK STREET
Hospital
PROSPECT ST.
PRYME ST.
WRIGHT ST.
ALBION ST.
CHARLES ST.
BOND ST.
GEORGE STREET
SYKES ST.
RAC
Library
INFO. CENTRE
Technical College
Bus Station
Infirmary
FERENSWAY
KING EDWARD ST.
Queen's Gardens
Police Station
Guildhall
JARROTT ST.
GUILDHALL RD.
ALFRED GELDER ST.
Paragon Station
CANNING ST.
JAMESON ST.
City Hall
G.P.O.
LOWGATE
HIGH STREET
Wilberforce Museum
ANLABY ROAD
CARR LANE
AA
Trinity House
RAC
A63 TO HOWDEN & HUMBER BRS.
M62
OSBORNE ST.
WATERHOUSE LANE
MYTON ST.
COMMERCIAL RD.
CASTLE STREET
QUEEN STREET
SOUTH ORBITAL RD.
HESSLE ROAD
WALKER STREET
PORTER
KINGSTON ST.
WELLINGTON ST.
A1105 TO HOWDEN & HUMBER BR.
ENGLISH STREET
RIVER HUMBER
Scale 0 ¼ ½ Mile

INVERNESS

Scale 0 ¼ ½ Mile
UPPER KESSOCK ST.
SHOE ST.
INNES STREET
WATERLOO ST.
RIVERSIDE ST.
Bowling Green
CHAPEL ST.
ROSE STREET
A96 TO NAIRN AND A9 TO PERTH
GLEBE
Public Baths
DOUGLAS ROW
WELLS ST.
A9 TO BEAULY
KENNETH STREET
HUNTLY STREET
RIVER NESS
BANK STREET
CHURCH STREET
ACADEMY ST.
G.P.O.
QUEENSGATE
UNION ST.
Bus Station
Rly. Station
EASTGATE
CROWN
FAIRFIELD RD.
Foot Bridge
INFORMATION CENTRE
STEPHENS
Bowling Green
Ness Bridge
BRIDGE ST.
YOUNG ST.
HIGH ST.
Steps
CASTLE ST.
Town Hall
Library and Museum
Castle
ARDCONNEL TER.
TOMNAHURICH ST.
Statue of Flora Macdonald
CASTLE ROAD
GORDON TER.
Youth Hostel
SOUTHSIDE ROAD
ARDROSS ST.
St. Andrew's Cathedral
VIEW PLACE
OLD EDINBURGH ROAD
TO A8 TO PERTH
GLEN URQUHART ROAD
BRUCE GARDENS
Regional Buildings
Northern Meeting Park
Eden Court Theatre
BISHOP'S RD.
BALLIFEARY
NESS WALK
NESS BANK
HAUGH RD.
CULDUTHEL ROAD
MAYFIELD ROAD
SOUTHSIDE ROAD
OLD EDINBURGH RD.
A862 TO INVERMORISTON
Royal Northern Infirmary
Foot Bridge
War Memorial
HAUGH
SOUTHSIDE ROAD
MUIRFIELD RD.
BALLIFEARY LANE
NESS WALK
RIVER NESS
ISLAND BANK RD.
CULDUTHEL ROAD
Tennis Courts & Putting Green
B862 TO DORES
Muirfield Hospital

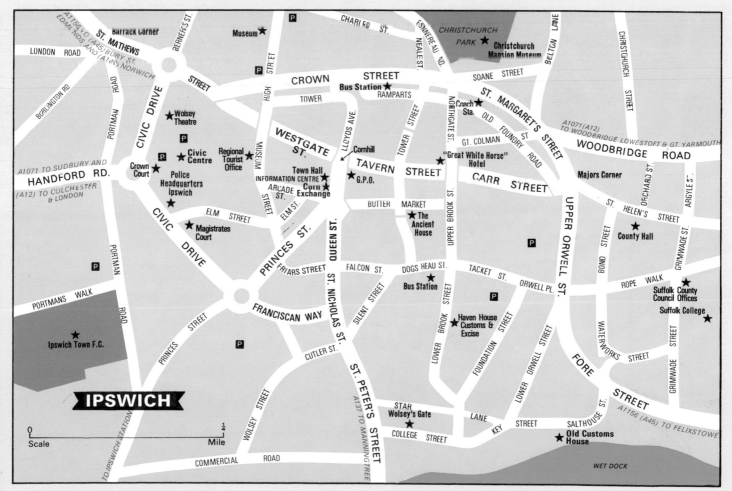

IPSWICH

A1156 TO EDMUNDS AND (A45) NORWICH
Barrack Corner
ST. MATHEWS
BERNER'S ST.
ST. MATTHEWS ST.
Museum
CHARLES ST.
NEALE ST.
CHRISTCHURCH PARK
Christchurch Mansion Museum
BELTON LANE
CHRISTCHURCH STREET
LONDON ROAD
BUCKLINGHAM RD.
PORTMAN ROAD
CIVIC DRIVE
HIGH STREET
CROWN STREET
Bus Station
RAMPARTS
SOANE STREET
ST. MARGARET'S STREET
A1071 (A12) TO WOODBRIDGE LOWESTOFT & GT. YARMOUTH
Wolsey Theatre
TOWER
WESTGATE ST.
LLOYDS AVE.
Cornhill
TOWER STREET
Coach Sta.
NORTHGATE ST.
OLD FOUNDRY RD.
GT. COLMAN ST.
WOODBRIDGE ROAD
A1071 TO SUDBURY AND HANDFORD RD.
Civic Centre
Regional Tourist Office
MUSEUM STREET
Town Hall
INFORMATION CENTRE
TAVERN STREET
"Great White Horse" Hotel
CARR STREET
Majors Corner
ORCHARD ST.
ST. HELEN'S STREET
ARGYLE ST.
(A12) TO COLCHESTER & LONDON
Crown Court
Police Headquarters Ipswich
ARCADE ST.
Corn Exchange
G.P.O.
BUTTER MARKET
UPPER BROOK ST.
UPPER ORWELL ST.
County Hall
BOND ST.
CIVIC DRIVE
ELM STREET
ELM ST.
PRINCES ST.
The Ancient House
GRIMWADE ST.
PORTMAN
FRIARS STREET
QUEEN ST.
FALCON ST.
DOGS HEAD ST.
TACKET ST.
ORWELL PL.
Rope Walk
WATERWORKS STREET
Magistrates Court
SILENT STREET
Bus Station
LOWER BROOK ST.
Suffolk County Council Offices
PORTMAN ROAD
Ipswich Town F.C.
FRANCISCAN WAY
ST. NICHOLAS ST.
Haven House Customs & Excise
FOUNDATION STREET
LOWER ORWELL STREET
FORE STREET
Suffolk College
PORTMANS WALK
PRINCES STREET
CUTLER ST.
WOLSEY STREET
ST. PETER'S STREET
A137 TO MANNINGTREE
Star Wolsey's Gate
COLLEGE STREET
KEY STREET
SALTHOUSE ST.
A1156 (A45) TO FELIXSTOWE
Old Customs House
TO IPSWICH STATION
COMMERCIAL ROAD
WET DOCK
Scale 0 ¼ Mile

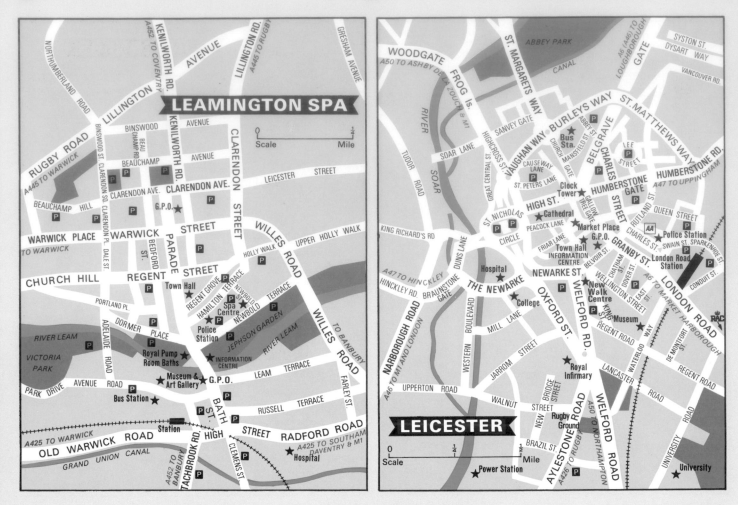

LEAMINGTON SPA

Scale 0 — ½ Mile

NORTHUMBERLAND ROAD · A452 TO COVENTRY · KENILWORTH RD. · LILLINGTON AVENUE · LILLINGTON RD. · A425 TO RUGBY · GRESHAM AVENUE

RUGBY ROAD · LILLINGTON AVENUE · KENILWORTH RD. · CLARENDON AVENUE · LEICESTER STREET · CLARENDON STREET

BINSWOOD AVENUE · BINSWOOD ST. · BEAUCHAMP · BEAU CHAMP ST. · CLARENDON SQ. · CLARENDON PL. · DALE ST. · CLARENDON AVE. · CLARENDON AVE.

G.P.O. ★

BEAUCHAMP HILL

WARWICK PLACE · WARWICK STREET · PARADE · WILLES ROAD · UPPER HOLLY WALK

TO WARWICK · BEDFORD ST. · HOLLY WALK

CHURCH HILL · REGENT STREET · Town Hall · REGENT GROVE · HAMILTON TERRACE · NEWBOLD TERRACE · NEWBOLD TERRACE

PORTLAND PL. · Spa Centre · Police Station

DORMER PLACE · Jephson Garden

RIVER LEAM · ADELAIDE ROAD · Royal Pump Room Baths ★ · Information Centre · River Leam · LEAM TERRACE

VICTORIA PARK · Museum & Art Gallery ★ · G.P.O. ★ · RUSSELL TERRACE

PARK DRIVE · AVENUE · ROAD · Bus Station ★ · BATH ST. · FARLEY ST.

OLD WARWICK ROAD · Station ★ · HIGH STREET · RADFORD ROAD

A425 TO WARWICK · GRAND UNION CANAL · TACHBROOK RD. · A452 TO BANBURY · CLEMENS ST. · Hospital ★ · A425 TO SOUTHAM DAVENTRY & M1

LEICESTER

Scale 0 — ¼ — ½ Mile

WOODGATE · A50 TO ASHBY DE LA ZOUCH & M1 · ST. MARGARETS WAY · ABBEY PARK · CANAL · SYSTON ST. · DYSART WAY

RIVER SOAR · TUDOR ROAD · SANVEY GATE · VAUGHAN WAY · BURLEYS WAY · ST. MATTHEWS WAY · VANCOUVER RD.

HIGHCROSS ST. · GREAT CENTRAL ST. · CAUSEWAY LANE · ST. PETERS LANE · Bus Sta. · BELGRAVE GATE · CHARLES STREET · LEE STREET · HUMBERSTONE RD.

KING RICHARD'S RD. · ST. NICHOLAS CIRCLE · Clock Tower ★ · HIGH ST. · HUMBERSTONE GATE · QUEEN STREET

A47 TO HINCKLEY · DUNS LANE · Cathedral ★ · PEACOCK LANE · Market Place · RUTLAND ST. · A47 TO UPPINGHAM

Hospital ★ · FRIAR LANE · Town Hall · G.P.O. ★ · GRANBY ST. · CHARLES ST. · AA · Police Station · SWAIN ST. · SPARKENHOE ST.

THE NEWARKE · BELVOIR ST. · INFORMATION CENTRE · BELGRAVE GATE · London Road Station

HINCKLEY RD. · BRAUNSTONE GATE · MILL LANE · College · NEWARKE ST. · New Walk Centre · WELLINGTON STREET · A6 TO MARKET HARBOROUGH

WESTERN BOULEVARD · OXFORD ST. · WELFORD RD. · King Museum ★ · REGENT ROAD · RAC

A47 TO M1 AND LONDON · JARROM STREET · Royal Infirmary ★ · LANCASTER ROAD · REGENT ROAD

NARBOROUGH ROAD · UPPERTON ROAD · WALNUT STREET · NEW BRIDGE STREET · Rugby Ground · BRAZIL ST. · DE MONTFORT ST. · DE MONTFORT ST.

A46 TO M1 AND LONDON · AYLESTONE ROAD · A426 TO RUGBY · WELFORD ROAD · A426 TO NORTHAMPTON · UNIVERSITY ROAD

Power Station ★ · University ★

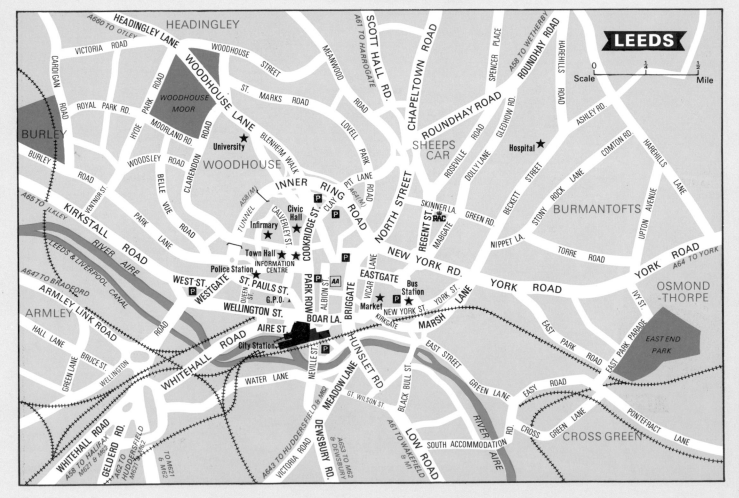

LEEDS

Scale 0 — ¼ — ½ Mile

A660 TO OTLEY · HEADINGLEY LANE · HEADINGLEY · A61 TO HARROGATE · SCOTT HALL RD. · CHAPELTOWN ROAD · SPENCER PLACE · A58 TO WETHERBY · ROUNDHAY ROAD · HAREHILLS ROAD

CARDIGAN ROAD · VICTORIA ROAD · WOODHOUSE STREET · MEANWOOD ROAD · ASHLEY RD.

ROYAL PARK RD. · PARK ROAD · WOODHOUSE MOOR · WOODHOUSE LANE · ST. MARKS ROAD · SHEEPS CAR · ROSEVILLE ROAD · GLEDHOW ROAD · COMTON RD. · HAREHILLS LANE

BURLEY · HYDE PARK ROAD · MOORLAND RD. · CLARENDON ROAD · University ★ · BLENHEIM WALK · LOVELL PARK · Hospital ★ · DOLLY LANE · ROCK STREET · STONY ROCK LANE

BURLEY ROAD · WOODSLEY ROAD · WOODHOUSE · PIT LANE · NORTH STREET · BECKETT STREET · BURMANTOFTS · UPTON AVENUE

KIRKSTALL ROAD · VENTNOR ST. · BELLE VUE ROAD · PARK LANE · INNER RING ROAD · A58(M) · A64(M) · SKINNER LA. · GREEN RD. · NIPPET LA. · TORRE ROAD · YORK ROAD

A65 TO ILKLEY · RIVER AIRE · TUNNEL · Civic Hall ★ · CLAY PIT LANE · REGENT ST. · RAC · MABGATE · YORK ROAD · A64 TO YORK

LEEDS & LIVERPOOL CANAL · Infirmary ★ · CALVERLEY ST. · COOKRIDGE ST. · NEW YORK RD. · YORK ROAD

A647 TO BRADFORD · Town Hall · INFORMATION CENTRE · Police Station · EASTGATE · Bus Station ★ · VICAR LANE · OSMOND-THORPE

ARMLEY · WEST ST. · WESTGATE · ST. PAULS ST. · G.P.O. · PARK ROW · ALBION ST. · AA · BRIGGATE · Market ★ · NEW YORK ST. · YORK ST. · MARSH LANE · IVY ST.

ARMLEY LINK ROAD · WELLINGTON ST. · QUEEN ST. · BOAR LA. · KIRKGATE · EAST PARK PARADE · EAST END PARK

HALL LANE · BRUCE ST. · WELLINGTON ROAD · AIRE ST. · City Station ★ · NEVILLE ST. · EAST STREET · EAST PARK ROAD

GREEN LANE · WHITEHALL ROAD · WATER LANE · MEADOW LANE · HUNSLET RD. · GT. WILSON ST. · BLACK BULL ST. · GREEN LANE · EASY ROAD · PONTEFRACT LANE

GELDERD RD. · A62 TO HUDDERSFIELD · A58 TO HALIFAX · A621 TO M621 & M62 · A643 TO M62 VICTORIA ROAD · DEWSBURY RD. · A643 TO M62 & DEWSBURY · LOW ROAD · A61 TO WAKEFIELD & M1 · RIVER AIRE · SOUTH ACCOMMODATION RD. · CROSS GREEN LANE · CROSS GREEN

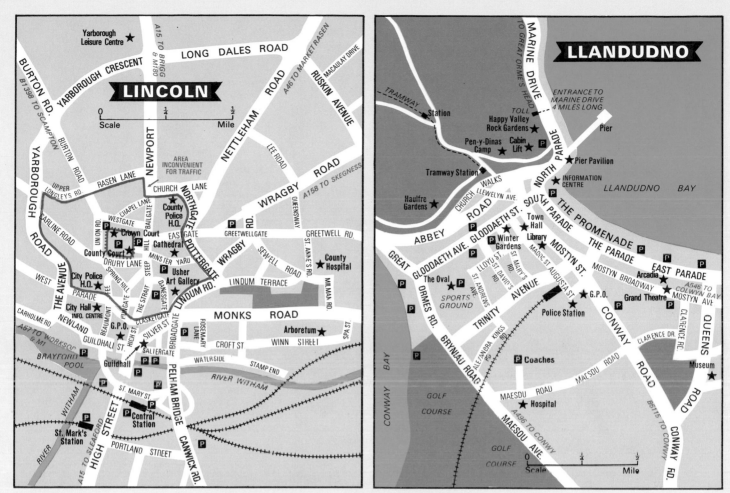

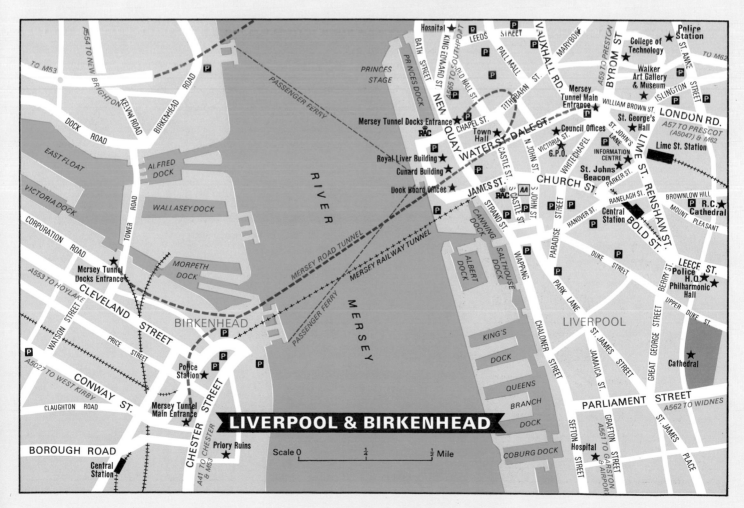

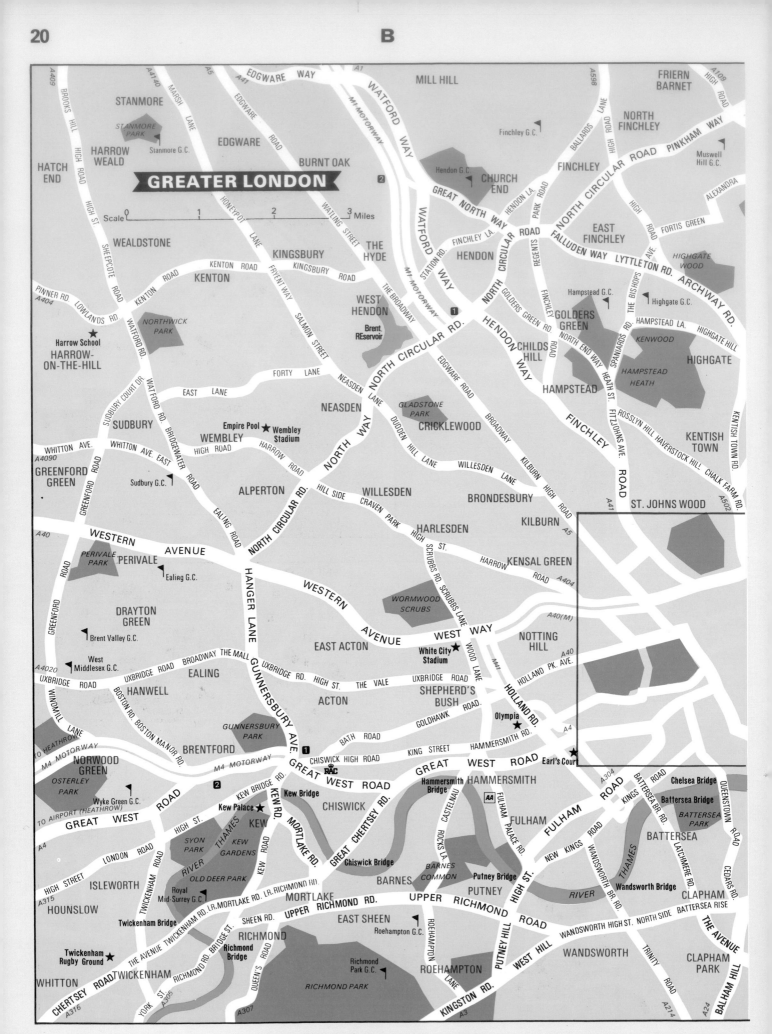

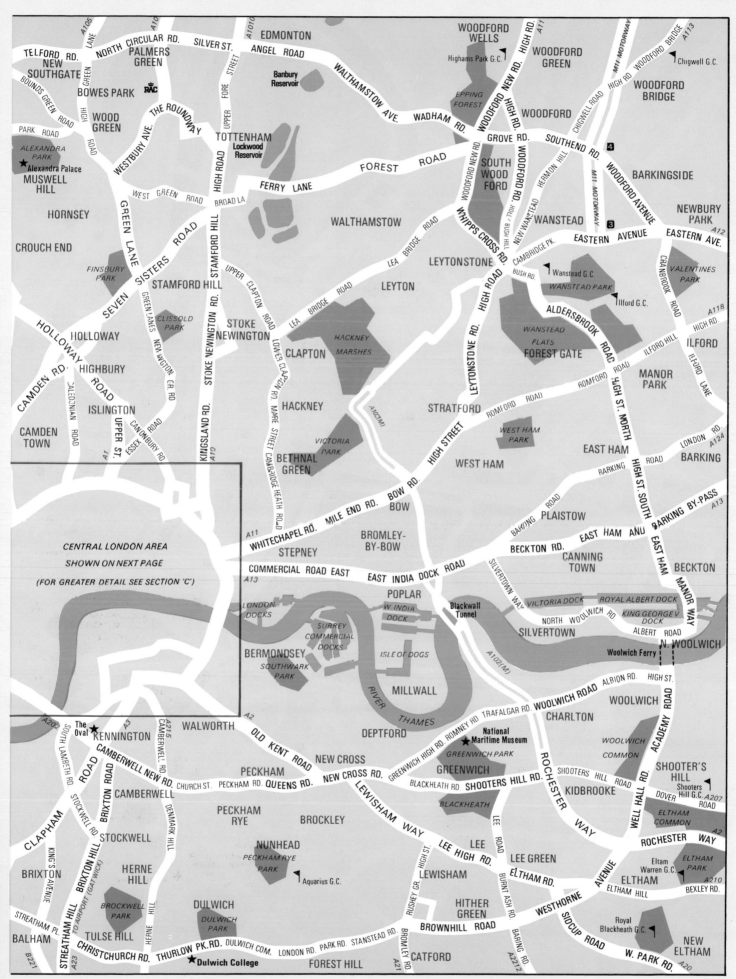

TELFORD RD. NORTH CIRCULAR RD. SILVER ST. ANGEL ROAD EDMONTON WOODFORD WELLS
NEW SOUTHGATE PALMERS GREEN WOODFORD GREEN
Highams Park G.C. Chigwell G.C.
BOWES PARK RAC Banbury Reservoir WALTHAMSTOW AVE. WADHAM RD. EPPING FOREST WOODFORD WOODFORD BRIDGE
BOUNDS GREEN ROAD WOOD GREEN THE ROUNDWAY TOTTENHAM FORE STREET UPPER FORE STREET
PARK ROAD WESTBURY AVE. Lockwood Reservoir GROVE RD. SOUTHEND RD. 4 M11 MOTORWAY WOODFORD BRIDGE
ALEXANDRA PARK Alexandra Palace HIGH ROAD FERRY LANE BROAD LA. FOREST ROAD SOUTH WOOD FORD WOODFORD RD. HERMON HILL WOODFORD AVENUE BARKINGSIDE
MUSWELL HILL WEST GREEN ROAD WALTHAMSTOW NEWBURY PARK
HORNSEY WHIPPS CROSS RD. WANSTEAD EASTERN AVENUE EASTERN AVE. A12
CROUCH END GREEN LANE SEVEN SISTERS ROAD STAMFORD HILL UPPER CLAPTON ROAD LEYTONSTONE CAMBRIDGE PK. BUSH RD. Wanstead G.C. CRANBROOK ROAD VALENTINES PARK
FINSBURY PARK LEA BRIDGE ROAD LEYTON WANSTEAD PARK Ilford G.C. A118
HOLLOWAY STAMFORD HILL CLISSOLD PARK STOKE NEWINGTON LOWER CLAPTON RD. CLAPTON HACKNEY MARSHES ALDERSBROOK HIGH RD. ILFORD
HOLLOWAY GREEN LANES NEW INGTON GR. RD. STOKE NEWINGTON RD. WANSTEAD FLATS ILFORD HILL ILFORD LANE
HIGHBURY CAMBRIDGE HEATH ROAD HACKNEY VICTORIA PARK FOREST GATE ROMFORD ROAD MANOR PARK
CAMDEN RD. CALEDONIAN ISLINGTON MARE STREET STRATFORD LEYTONSTONE RD. HIGH ROAD ROMFORD ROAD HIGH ST. NORTH EAST HAM BARKING
CAMDEN TOWN UPPER ST. ESSEX RD. CANONBURY RD. KINGSLAND RD. A10 BETHNAL GREEN HIGH STREET WEST HAM WEST HAM PARK ROAD A124
A1 A11 MILE END RD. BOW RD. BOW WEST HAM BARKING ROAD HIGH ST. SOUTH BARKING BY-PASS A13
WHITECHAPEL RD. BROMLEY-BY-BOW PLAISTOW EAST HAM AND BECKTON
A13 STEPNEY CANNING TOWN BECKTON
COMMERCIAL ROAD EAST EAST INDIA DOCK ROAD BECKTON RD. EAST HAM
CENTRAL LONDON AREA POPLAR SILVERTOWN WAY VICTORIA DOCK ROYAL ALBERT DOCK MANOR WAY
SHOWN ON NEXT PAGE LONDON DOCKS W. INDIA DOCK Blackwall Tunnel NORTH WOOLWICH RD. KING GEORGE V DOCK
(FOR GREATER DETAIL SEE SECTION 'C') SURREY COMMERCIAL DOCKS SILVERTOWN N. WOOLWICH
BERMONDSEY ISLE OF DOGS A102(M) ALBERT ROAD Woolwich Ferry
SOUTHWARK PARK RIVER THAMES MILLWALL ALBION RD. HIGH ST.
The Oval KENNINGTON WALWORTH A2 OLD KENT ROAD DEPTFORD WOOLWICH ROAD WOOLWICH
A202 A3 CAMBERWELL ROMNEY RD. Trafalgar Rd. CHARLTON ACADEMY ROAD
SOUTH LAMBETH RD. CAMBERWELL NEW RD. CHURCH ST. PECKHAM RD. QUEENS RD. NEW CROSS RD. National Maritime Museum WOOLWICH COMMON
CAMBERWELL PECKHAM GREENWICH HIGH RD. GREENWICH PARK GREENWICH SHOOTERS HILL ROAD SHOOTER'S HILL
CLAPHAM STOCKWELL RD. BRIXTON ROAD PECKHAM RYE BROCKLEY LEWISHAM WAY BLACKHEATH RD. SHOOTERS HILL RD. KIDBROOKE Shooters Hill G.C. DOVER A207
KING'S AVENUE BRIXTON HILL STOCKWELL DENMARK HILL NUNHEAD BLACKHEATH LEE HIGH RD. LEE ROAD WELL HALL RD. ROCHESTER WAY ELTHAM COMMON A2
BRIXTON HERNE HILL PECKHAM RYE PARK Aquarius G.C. LEE GREEN ELTHAM RD. Eltam Warren G.C. ELTHAM PARK ROCHESTER WAY
STREATHAM PL. BROCKWELL PARK DULWICH HITHER GREEN BURNT ASH RD. ELTHAM ELTHAM HILL A210
BALHAM B221 STREATHAM HILL A23 CHRISTCHURCH ROAD THURLOW PK. RD. TULSE HILL HERNE DULWICH PARK DULWICH COM. LONDON RD. PARK RD. STANSTEAD RD. BROWNHILL ROAD CATFORD Royal Blackheath G.C. BEXLEY RD. NEW ELTHAM
KING'S AVENUE TO AIRPORT (GATWICK) Dulwich College FOREST HILL RUSHEY GR. HIGH ST. BROMLEY RD. A21 A2212 SIDCUP ROAD W. PARK RD. A20

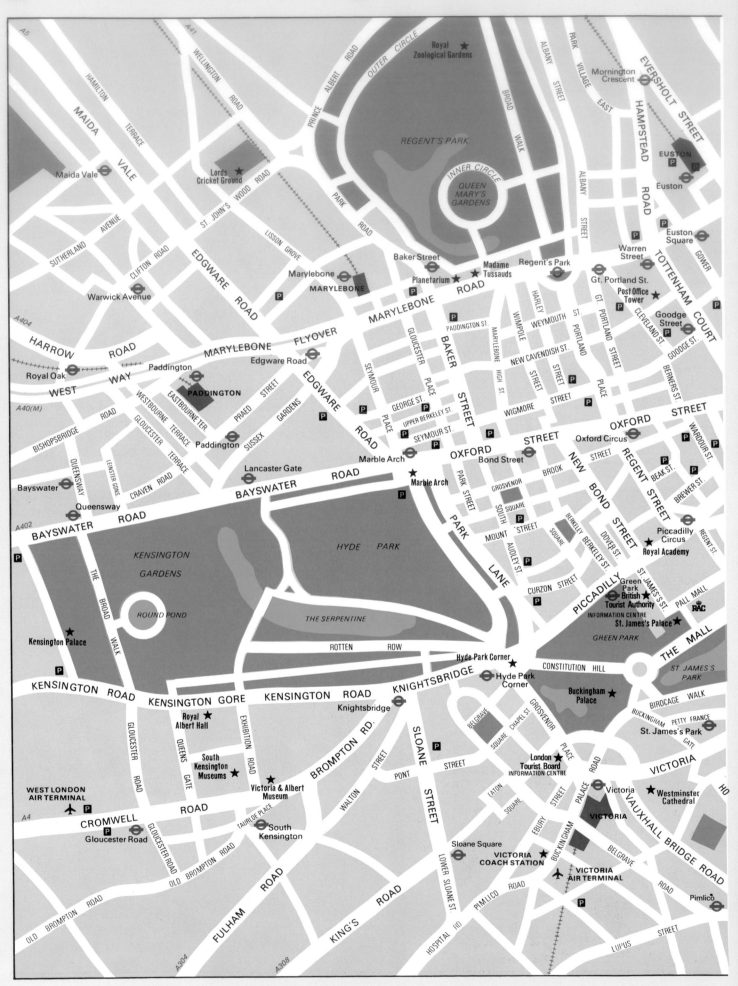

Royal Zoological Gardens

Mornington Crescent

EVERSHOLT STREET
HAMPSTEAD ROAD
ALBANY STREET
PARK VILLAGE EAST

REGENT'S PARK

EUSTON
Euston
Euston Square

MAIDA VALE
HAMILTON TERRACE
WELLINGTON ROAD
A41
A5

Maida Vale

Lords Cricket Ground

ST. JOHN'S WOOD ROAD

PARK ROAD

INNER CIRCLE
QUEEN MARY'S GARDENS

OUTER CIRCLE

BROAD WALK

Warren Street

SUTHERLAND AVENUE
CLIFTON ROAD
Warwick Avenue

LISSON GROVE

Baker Street
Regent's Park
Gt. Portland St.

ALBANY STREET

Post Office Tower
Goodge Street

GOWER STREET
CLEVELAND ST.
BERNERS ST.
TOTTENHAM COURT ROAD

EDGWARE ROAD

Marylebone
MARYLEBONE

Marylebone Planetarium
Madame Tussauds

HARROW ROAD
WEST WAY
A40(M)

Royal Oak
Paddington
Edgware Road
MARYLEBONE FLYOVER

MARYLEBONE ROAD

PADDINGTON ST.
WEYMOUTH ST.
GLOUCESTER PLACE
BAKER STREET
WIMPOLE STREET
HARLEY STREET
MARYLEBONE HIGH ST.
PORTLAND PLACE
NEW CAVENDISH ST.
GT. PORTLAND STREET

Goodge Street

BISHOPSBRIDGE ROAD
WESTBOURNE TERRACE
EASTBOURNE TER.
PADDINGTON
GLOUCESTER TERRACE
PRAED STREET
Paddington
SUSSEX GARDENS

SEYMOUR STREET
GEORGE ST.
UPPER BERKELEY ST.
SEYMOUR ST.

WIGMORE STREET

Oxford Circus
WARDOUR ST.

A404

LEINSTER GDNS.
CRAVEN ROAD
Lancaster Gate

Marble Arch

OXFORD STREET
Bond Street

REGENT STREET
NEW BOND STREET
BEAK ST.
BREWER ST.

Bayswater
QUEENSWAY
Queensway

EDGWARE ROAD
BAYSWATER ROAD

Marble Arch

PARK STREET
GROSVENOR
BROOK STREET
SOUTH AUDLEY ST.
MOUNT STREET
BERKELEY SQUARE
DOVER ST.
Piccadilly Circus
Royal Academy
REGENT ST.

A402
BAYSWATER ROAD

KENSINGTON GARDENS

HYDE PARK

PARK LANE
MOUNT STREET
CURZON STREET

PICCADILLY
Green Park
British Tourist Authority
St. James's Palace
PALL MALL
RAC

ROUND POND

THE SERPENTINE

INFORMATION CENTRE
ST. JAMES'S ST.
GREEN PARK

Kensington Palace

THE BROAD WALK

ROTTEN ROW

Hyde Park Corner

CONSTITUTION HILL

THE MALL
ST JAMES'S PARK

KENSINGTON ROAD

KENSINGTON GORE
KENSINGTON ROAD
KNIGHTSBRIDGE

Hyde Park Corner

Buckingham Palace

BIRDCAGE WALK
BUCKINGHAM GATE
PETTY FRANCE
St. James's Park

Knightsbridge

Royal Albert Hall
EXHIBITION ROAD
BROMPTON RD.
SLOANE STREET
BELGRAVE SQUARE
CHAPEL ST.
GROSVENOR PLACE

VICTORIA

GLOUCESTER ROAD
QUEENS GATE
South Kensington Museums
Victoria & Albert Museum

WALTON STREET
PONT STREET

EATON SQUARE

London Tourist Board INFORMATION CENTRE

Victoria
Westminster Cathedral
VICTORIA

WEST LONDON AIR TERMINAL
A4

CROMWELL ROAD
Gloucester Road
TAURLOE PLACE
South Kensington

PALACE STREET

BUCKINGHAM PALACE ROAD

VAUXHALL BRIDGE ROAD
HO

OLD BROMPTON ROAD
OLD BROMPTON ROAD

FULHAM ROAD
KING'S ROAD

Sloane Square

SLOANE STREET
LOWER SLOANE ST.
EBURY STREET

VICTORIA COACH STATION

BELGRAVE ROAD

VICTORIA AIR TERMINAL

Pimlico

A304
A308

HOSPITAL RD
PIMLICO ROAD

LUPUS STREET

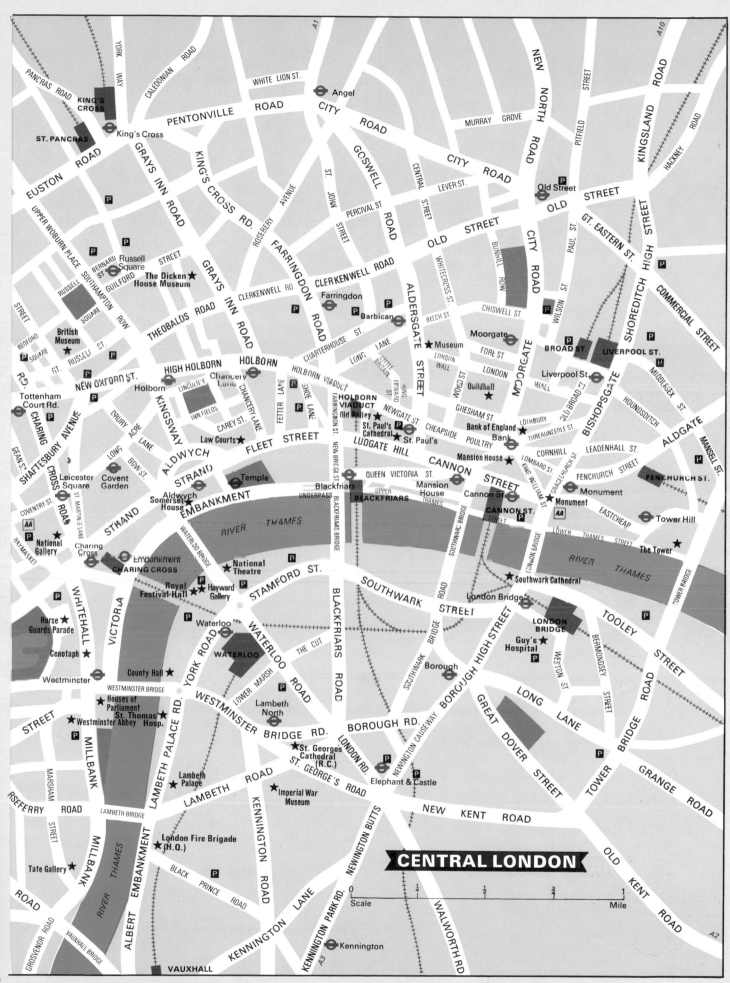

CENTRAL LONDON

Scale 0 ¼ ½ ¾ 1 Mile

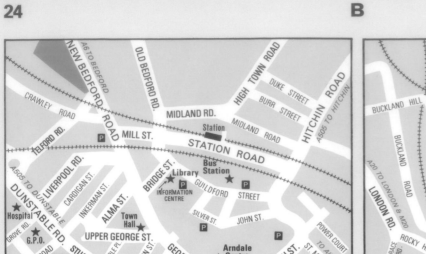

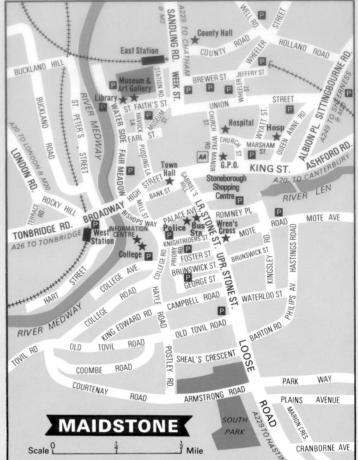

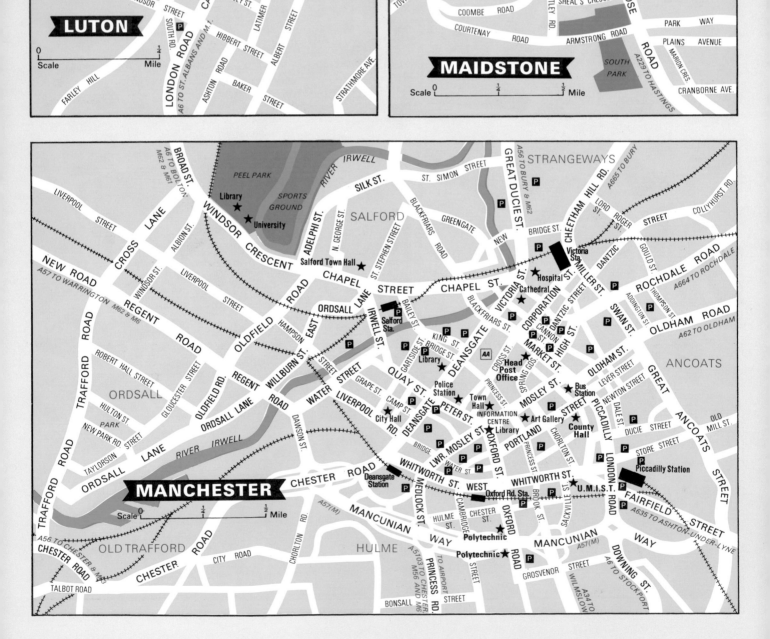

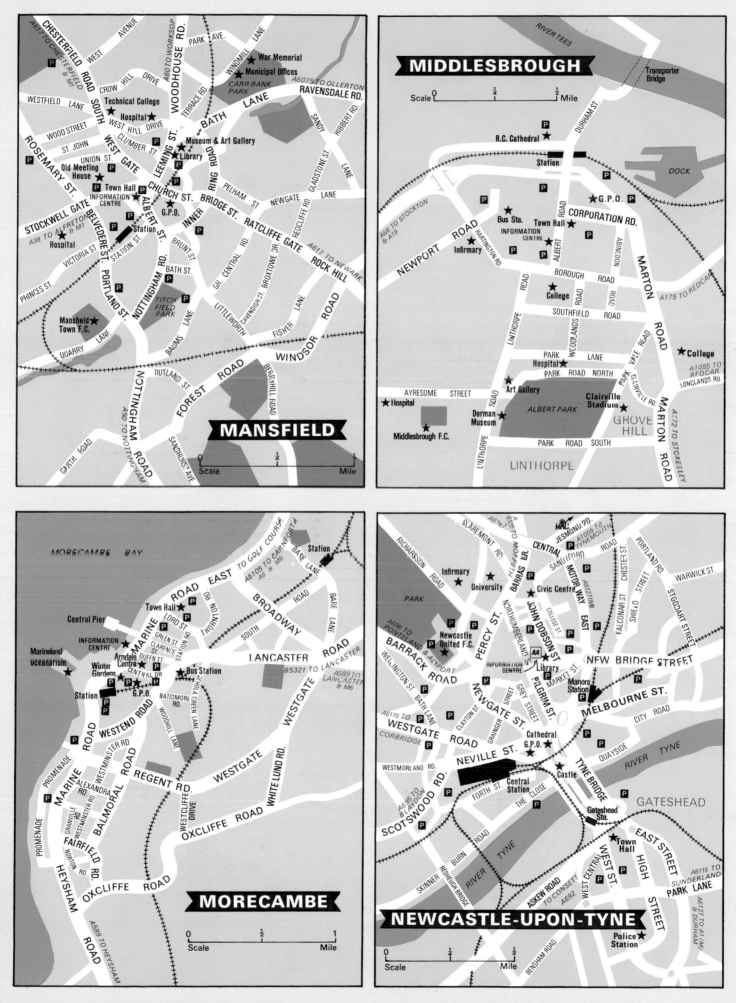

MANSFIELD

A6177 TO CHESTERFIELD & M1
CHESTERFIELD ROAD SOUTH
WEST AVENUE
WOODHOUSE RD.
PARK AVE.
WINDMILL LANE
War Memorial
Municipal Offices
A6075 TO OLLERTON
RAVENSDALE RD.
CROW HILL DRIVE
WESTFIELD LANE
Technical College
CARR BANK PARK
WOOD STREET
Hospital
WEST HILL DRIVE
TERRACE RD.
BATH LANE
SANDY LANE
HIBBERT RD.
ST. JOHN
CLUMBER ST.
Museum & Art Gallery
LEEMING ST.
WEST GATE
ROSEMARY ST.
UNION ST.
Old Meeting House
Library
RING ROAD
PELHAM ST.
NEWGATE LANE
GLADSTONE RD.
REDCLIFFE RD.
Town Hall
CHURCH ST.
ALBERT ST.
BRIDGE ST.
RATCLIFFE GATE
INFORMATION CENTRE
G.P.O.
INNER
A38 TO ALFRETON & M1
STOCKWELL GATE
BELVEDERE ST.
BRUNT ST.
ROCK HILL
A617 TO NEWARK
Station
STATION ST.
Hospital
VICTORIA ST.
PORTLAND ST.
NOTTINGHAM RD.
BATH ST.
GR. CENTRAL RD.
CAVENDISH ST.
BROXTOWE DR.
TITCH FIELD PARK
PRINCES ST.
Mansfield Town F.C.
QUARRY LANE
RUTLAND ST.
BAUMS LANE
LITTLEWORTH LANE
FISHER LANE
WINDSOR ROAD
GARTH ROAD
NOTTINGHAM ROAD
A50 TO NOTTINGHAM
FOREST ROAD
BERRYHILL ROAD
SANDHURST AVE.
Scale 0 ¼ ½ Mile

MIDDLESBROUGH

Scale 0 ¼ ½ Mile
RIVER TEES
Transporter Bridge
DURHAM ST.
R.C. Cathedral
Station
DOCK
G.P.O.
CORPORATION RD.
A66 TO STOCKTON & A19
NEWPORT ROAD
Bus Sta.
Town Hall
INFORMATION CENTRE
MARTON ROAD
Infirmary
HARTINGTON RD.
Albert
ABINGDON ROAD
BOROUGH ROAD
A175 TO REDCAR
College
LINTHORPE ROAD
WOODLANDS ROAD
SOUTHFIELD ROAD
PARK VALE ROAD
A1085 TO REDCAR LONGLANDS RD.
College
PARK LANE
Hospital
Park ROAD NORTH
CLAIRVILLE RD.
A172 TO STOKESLEY
AYRESOME STREET
Hospital
Art Gallery
ALBERT PARK
Clairville Stadium
MARTON ROAD
GROVE HILL
Dorman Museum
Middlesbrough F.C.
LINTHORPE
PARK ROAD SOUTH

MORECAMBE

MORECAMBE BAY
TO GOLF COURSE
A5105 TO CARNFORTH A6 & M6
Station
ROAD EAST
BARE LANE
BROADWAY
Town Hall
MARINE RD.
THORNTON RD.
LORD ST.
GREEN ST.
Central Pier
BARE LANE
INFORMATION CENTRE
CLARENCE ST.
QUEEN ST.
SOUTH ROAD
LANCASTER ROAD
Marineland Oceanarium
Arndale Centre
CENTRAL DR.
B5321 TO LANCASTER
Winter Gardens
A589 TO LANCASTER & M6
Bus Station
Station
G.P.O.
BATISMORE RD.
LULLA GREEN LANE
WESTGATE ROAD
WESTEND ROAD
WOODHILL LANE
MARINE ROAD
WESTMINSTER RD.
BALMORAL ROAD
REGENT RD.
WESTGATE
WHITE LUND RD.
PROMENADE
ALEXANDRA RD.
WESTMINSTER ST.
WESTCLIFFE DRIVE
OXCLIFFE ROAD
GRANVILLE RD.
FAIRFIELD RD.
NORTON RD.
HEYSHAM
OXCLIFFE ROAD
A589 TO HEYSHAM
Scale 0 ½ 1 Mile

NEWCASTLE-UPON-TYNE

A6125 TO MORPETH
JESMOND RD.
A1058 TO TYNEMOUTH
CLAREMONT RD.
CENTRAL
RICHARDSON ROAD
SANDYFORD ROAD
PORTLAND RD.
CHESTER ST.
Infirmary
University
BARRAS LR.
MOTOR WAY
A6127(M)
WARWICK ST.
PARK
Civic Centre
PERCY ST.
JOHN DOBSON ST.
COLLEGE ST.
FALCONAR ST.
SHIELD STREET
STODDART STREET
A696 TO PONTELAND & AIRPORT
Newcastle United F.C.
NORTHUMBERLAND ST.
AA
NEW BRIDGE STREET
BARRACK ROAD
INFORMATION CENTRE
Library
MARKET ST.
Manors Station
MELBOURNE ST.
WELLINGTON ST.
BATH LANE
PILGRIM ST.
GREY ST.
CITY ROAD
A6115 TO
NEWGATE ST.
CLAYTON ST.
GRAINGER ST.
Cathedral
G.P.O.
QUAYSIDE
RIVER TYNE
WESTGATE ROAD
CORBRIDGE
NEVILLE ST.
WESTMORLAND RD.
A695 TO BLAYDON
Central Station
Castle
TYNE BRIDGE
GATESHEAD
FORTH ST.
THE CLOSE
SCOTSWOOD RD.
Gateshead Sta.
SKINNER BURN ROAD
REDHEUGH BRIDGE
RIVER TYNE
Town Hall
EAST STREET
WEST ST.
HIGH ST.
ASKEW ROAD
TO CONSETT A692
WEST CENTRAL
PARK LANE
A6115 TO SUNDERLAND
BENSHAM ROAD
A6127 TO A1(M) & DURHAM
Police Station
Scale 0 ¼ ½ Mile

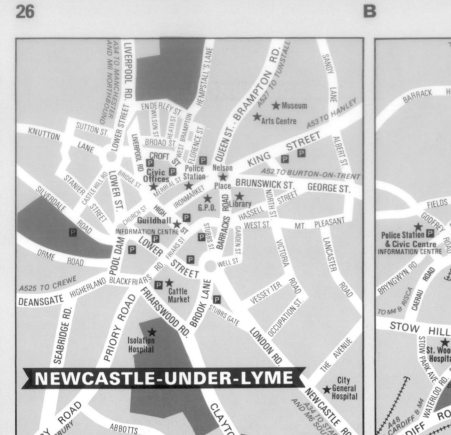

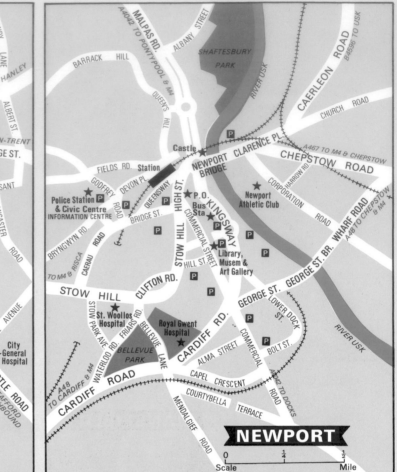

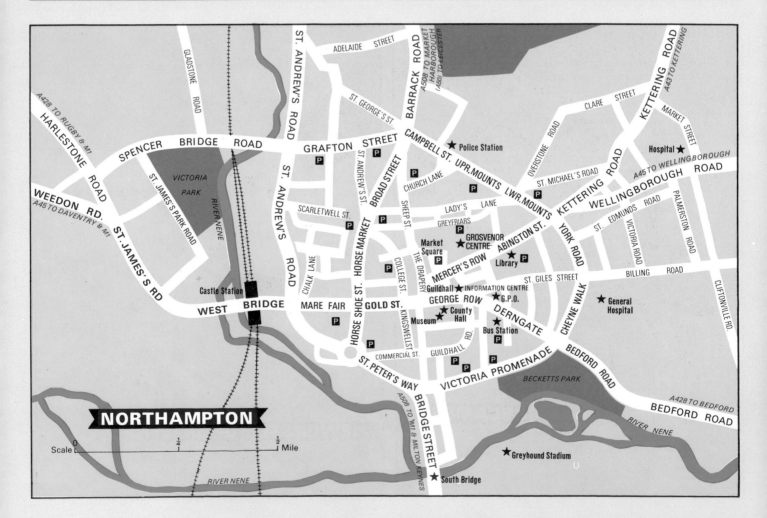

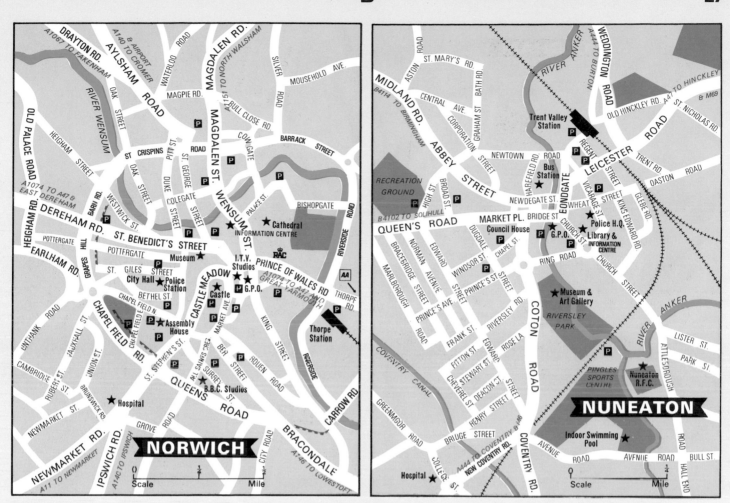

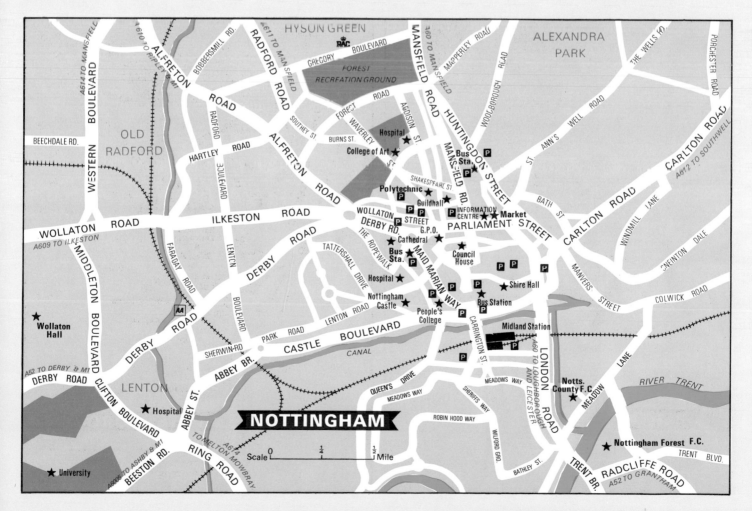

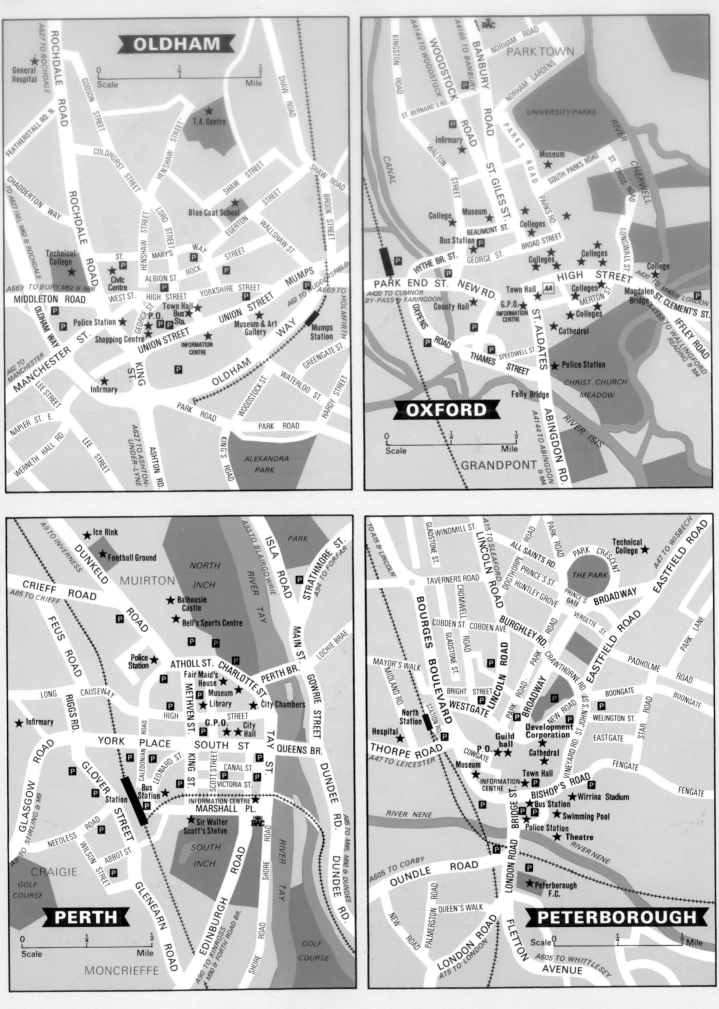

OLDHAM

General Hospital
ROCHDALE ROAD
A627 TO ROCHDALE N.
GODSON STREET
COLDHURST STREET
T. A. Centre
FEATHERSTALL RD. N.
CHADDERTON WAY
TO A627 (M), M62 & ROCHDALE
ROCHDALE ROAD
HENSHAW STREET
LORD STREET
Blue Coat School
SHAW STREET
EGERTON STREET
SHAW STREET
SHAW ROAD
BROOK STREET
Technical College
A669 TO BURY, M62 & M6
MIDDLETON ROAD
ST. MARY'S
HENSHAW STREET
WAY
ROCK STREET
ALBION ST.
Civic Centre
WEST ST.
HIGH STREET
YORKSHIRE STREET
UNION STREET
MUMPS
A62
A669 TO HUDDERSFIELD
HOLMFIRTH
OLDHAM WAY
Police Station
P.O.
GEORGE STREET
Town Hall
Bus Sta.
Museum & Art Gallery
Mumps Station
MANCHESTER ST.
A62 TO MANCHESTER
Shopping Centre
UNION STREET
KING ST.
INFORMATION CENTRE
OLDHAM WAY
GREENGATE ST.
Infirmary
LEE STREET
WATERLOO ST.
WOODSTOCK ST.
NAPIER ST. E.
WERNETH HALL RD.
LEE STREET
A627 TO ASHTON-UNDER-LYNE
KING'S ROAD
PARK ROAD
PARK ROAD
HARDY STREET
ALEXANDRA PARK

OXFORD

A4144 TO WOODSTOCK
KINGSTON ROAD
WOODSTOCK ROAD
A4165 TO BANBURY
BANBURY ROAD
NORHAM ROAD
PARK TOWN
NORHAM GARDENS
RAC
ST. BERNARD'S RD.
Infirmary
WALTON STREET
ST. GILES ST.
PARKS ROAD
UNIVERSITY PARKS
RIVER CHERWELL
ST. CROSS ROAD
CANAL
College
Museum
Museum
BEAUMONT ST.
Colleges
PARKS RD.
SOUTH PARKS ROAD
LONGWALL STREET
HYTHE BR. ST.
Bus Station
BROAD STREET
Colleges
Colleges
College
A40 TO LONDON
PARK END ST.
NEW RD.
GEORGE ST.
HIGH STREET
A420 TO CUMNOR BY-PASS & FARINGDON
Town Hall
AA
Colleges
IFFLEY ROAD
DPENS ROAD
County Hall
G.P.O. INFORMATION CENTRE
ST. ALDATES
MERTON ST.
Colleges
Magdalen Bridge
ST. CLEMENT'S ST.
A4158 TO WALLINGFORD, READING & M4
Cathedral
THAMES STREET
Speedwell St.
Police Station
CHRIST CHURCH MEADOW
Folly Bridge
ABINGDON ROAD
RIVER ISIS
A4144 TO ABINGDON & M4
GRANDPONT

PERTH

Ice Rink
A9 TO INVERNESS
DUNKELD
Football Ground
A93 TO BLAIRGOWRIE
ISLA ROAD
Park
A94 TO FORFAR
STRATHMORE ST.
CRIEFF ROAD
A85 TO CRIEFF
MUIRTON
NORTH INCH
RIVER TAY
FEUS ROAD
DUNKELD ROAD
Balhousie Castle
Bell's Sports Centre
MAIN ST.
LOCHIE BRAE
LONG CAUSEWAY
RIGGS RD.
Police Station
ATHOLL ST.
CHARLOTTE ST.
PERTH BR.
GOWRIE STREET
Fair Maid's House
Museum
Library
City Chambers
Infirmary
METHVEN ST.
HIGH STREET
G.P.O.
City Hall
GLASGOW ROAD
A9 TO STIRLING & M9
YORK PLACE
SOUTH ST.
TAY STREET
QUEENS BR.
GLOVER STREET
CALEDONIAN ROAD
LEONARD ST.
KING ST.
SCOTT STREET
CANAL ST.
VICTORIA ST.
DUNDEE RD.
A85 TO M85, M90 & DUNDEE
Bus Station
INFORMATION CENTRE
MARSHALL PL.
Sir Walter Scott's Statue
RAC
NEEDLESS ROAD
WILSON STREET
ABBOT ST.
SOUTH INCH
EDINBURGH ROAD
SHORE ROAD
RIVER TAY
DUNDEE RD.
CRAIGIE
GOLF COURSE
GLENEARN ROAD
A90 TO KINROSS, M90 & FORTH ROAD BR.
GOLF COURSE
MONCRIEFFE

PETERBOROUGH

TO A15 & LINCOLN
GLADSTONE ST.
WINDMILL ST.
A15 TO SLEAFORD & LINCOLN
LINCOLN ROAD
PARK ROAD
PARK CRESCENT
Technical College
A47 TO WISBECH
EASTFIELD ROAD
ALL SAINTS RD.
DOGTHORPE
PRINCE'S ST.
THE PARK
PRINCE'S GATE
BROADWAY
TAVERNERS ROAD
CROMWELL ROAD
HUNTLEY GROVE
VERGETTE ST.
BOURGES BOULEVARD
COBDEN ST.
COBDEN AVE.
BURGHLEY RD.
CRAWTHORNE RD.
EASTFIELD ROAD
PARK LANE
MAYOR'S WALK
GLADSTONE STREET
BRIGHT STREET
LINCOLN ROAD
PARK ROAD
BROADWAY
PADHOLME ROAD
North Station
MIDLAND RD.
WESTGATE
NEW ROAD
ST. JOHN'S ST.
BOONGATE
BOONGATE
Hospital
STATION RD.
Development Corporation
Guildhall
WELINGTON ST.
STAR ROAD
THORPE ROAD
A47 TO LEICESTER
COWGATE
P.O.
Cathedral
EASTGATE
FENGATE
Museum
INFORMATION CENTRE
Town Hall
VINEYARD RD.
FENGATE
BISHOP'S ROAD
Wirrina Stadium
BRIDGE ST.
Bus Station
Swimming Pool
RIVER NENE
Police Station
Theatre
A605 TO CORBY
OUNDLE ROAD
LONDON ROAD
RIVER NENE
Peterborough F.C.
NEW ROAD
PALMERSTON ROAD
QUEEN'S WALK
FLETTON AVENUE
LONDON ROAD
A15 TO LONDON
A605 TO WHITTLESEY

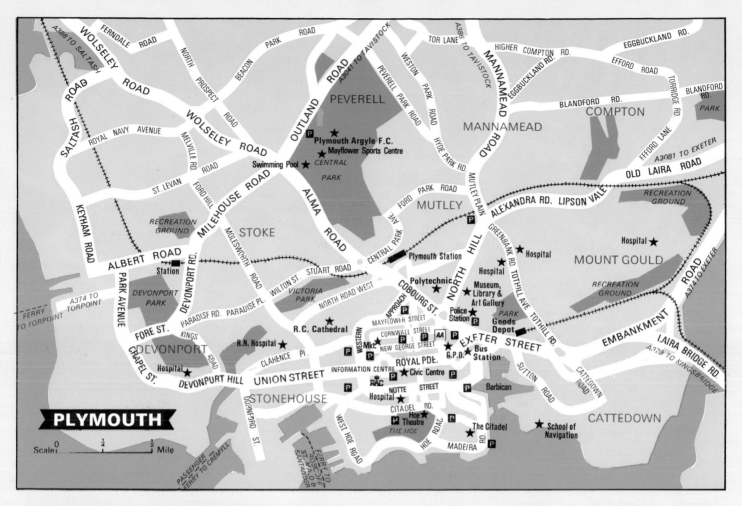

PLYMOUTH

FERNDALE ROAD
WOLSELEY ROAD
A388 TO SALTASH
NORTH PROSPECT ROAD
BEACON PARK ROAD
PARK ROAD
OUTLAND ROAD
A3041 TO TAVISTOCK
TOR LANE
HIGHER COMPTON RD.
EGGBUCKLAND RD.
EGGBUCKLAND RD.
PEVERELL PARK ROAD
WESTON PARK ROAD
A386 TO TAVISTOCK
MANNAMEAD ROAD
EFFORD ROAD
TORRIDGE RD.
BLANDFORD RD.
PEVERELL
COMPTON
SALTASH ROAD
WOLSELEY ROAD
ROYAL NAVY AVENUE
MELVILLE RD.
FORD HILL
MILEHOUSE ROAD
HYDE PARK RD.
MUTLEY PLAIN
MANNAMEAD
BLANDFORD ROAD
EFFORD LANE
A3081 TO EXETER
OLD LAIRA ROAD
ST. LEVAN
KEYHAM ROAD
ALMA ROAD
FORD PARK ROAD
MUTLEY
ALEXANDRA RD. LIPSON VALE
RECREATION GROUND
RECREATION GROUND
STOKE
MOLESWORTH ROAD
CENTRAL PARK
★ Plymouth Argyle F.C.
★ Mayflower Sports Centre
Swimming Pool ★
★ CENTRAL PARK
NORTH HILL
GREENBANK RD.
TOTHILL AVE. TOTHILL
★ Hospital
MOUNT GOULD
Hospital ★
A374 TO TORPOINT
ALBERT ROAD
Station
DEVONPORT RD.
WILTON ST.
STUART ROAD
CENTRAL PARK
Plymouth Station ★
RECREATION GROUND
A374 TO EXETER
EMBANKMENT
FERRY TO TORPOINT
PARK AVENUE
DEVONPORT PARK
PARADISE RD. PARADISE PL.
VICTORIA PARK
NORTH ROAD WEST
Polytechnic ★
Hospital ★
Museum, Library & Art Gallery ★
Police Station ★
PARK Goods Depot ★
EXETER STREET
LAIRA BRIDGE RD.
A379 TO KINGSBRIDGE
FORE ST.
KINGS ROAD
CLARENCE PL.
R.C. Cathedral ★
MAYFLOWER STREET
COBOURG ST.
APPROACH
CORNWALL STREET
AA
DEVONPORT
CHAPEL ST.
R.N. Hospital ★
WESTERN
Mkt.
NEW GEORGE STREET
G.P.O.
Bus Station
CATTEDOWN ROAD
Hospital ★
DEVONPURT HILL
UNION STREET
INFORMATION CENTRE
ROYAL PDE.
Civic Centre ★
SUTTON ROAD
STONEHOUSE
BOURNFORD ST.
RAC
NOTTE STREET
Hospital ★
Barbican ★
CATTEDOWN
CITADEL RD.
Hoe Theatre ★
CITADEL RD.
HOE ROAD
The Citadel ★
★ School of Navigation
WEST HOE ROAD
THE HOE
MADEIRA RD.

Scale: 0 — ¼ — ½ Mile

PASSENGER FERRY TO CREMYLL
FERRY TO ROSCOFF, ST. MALO & SANTANDER

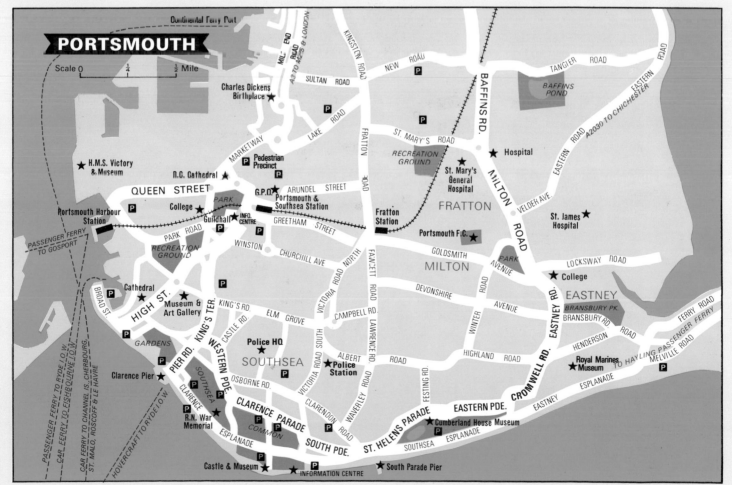

PORTSMOUTH

Scale 0 — ¼ — ½ Mile

Continental Ferry Port
MILE END
NEW ROAD
A3 TO M275 & LONDON
KINGSTON ROAD
TANGIER ROAD
ROAD
EASTERN ROAD
SULTAN ROAD
NEW ROAD
P
BAFFINS POND
Charles Dickens Birthplace ★
LAKE ROAD
FRATTON ROAD
ST. MARY'S ROAD
BAFFINS RD.
A2030 TO CHICHESTER
EASTERN ROAD
H.M.S. Victory & Museum ★
MARKETWAY
Pedestrian Precinct ★
P
RECREATION GROUND
Hospital ★
MILTON ROAD
VELDER AVE.
R.C. Cathedral ★
G.P.O. ★
ARUNDEL STREET
St. Mary's General Hospital ★
FRATTON
QUEEN STREET
PARK
College ★
P
Portsmouth & Southsea Station
Fratton Station
St. James Hospital ★
Portsmouth Harbour Station
Guildhall ★
INFO. CENTRE ★
GREETHAM STREET
Portsmouth F.C. ★
GOLDSMITH AVENUE
LOCKSWAY ROAD
PASSENGER FERRY TO GOSPORT
PARK ROAD
RECREATION GROUND
WINSTON
CHURCHILL AVE.
FAWCETT ROAD
MILTON
PARK AVENUE
★ College
BROAD ST.
Cathedral ★
HIGH ST.
Museum & Art Gallery ★
VICTORIA ROAD NORTH
DEVONSHIRE AVENUE
WINTER ROAD
EASTNEY RD.
EASTNEY
BRANSBURY PK.
BRANSBURY ROAD
FERRY ROAD
GARDENS
KING'S RD.
ELM GROVE
CAMPBELL RD.
LAWRENCE RD.
HIGHLAND ROAD
CROMWELL RD.
PASSENGER FERRY TO HAYLING
MELVILLE ROAD
PIER RD.
WESTERN PDE.
Police HQ ★
KING'S TER.
Castle RD.
VICTORIA ROAD SOUTH
ALBERT ROAD
★ Royal Marines Museum
PASSENGER FERRY TO RYDE I.O.W.
CAR FERRY TO FISHBOURNE I.O.W.
CAR FERRY TO CHANNEL IS., CHERBOURG, ST. MALO, ROSCOFF & LE HAVRE
HOVERCRAFT TO RYDE I.O.W.
SOUTHSEA
★ Police Station
OSBORNE RD.
CLARENDON ROAD
WAVERLEY ROAD
FESTING RD.
ESPLANADE
CLARENCE PARADE
CLARENCE
SOUTHSEA
Clarence Pier ★
R.N. War Memorial ★
COMMON
SOUTH PDE.
ST. HELENS PARADE
EASTERN PDE.
EASTNEY ESPLANADE
★ Cumberland House Museum
Castle & Museum ★
INFORMATION CENTRE ★
★ South Parade Pier
SOUTHSEA ESPLANADE

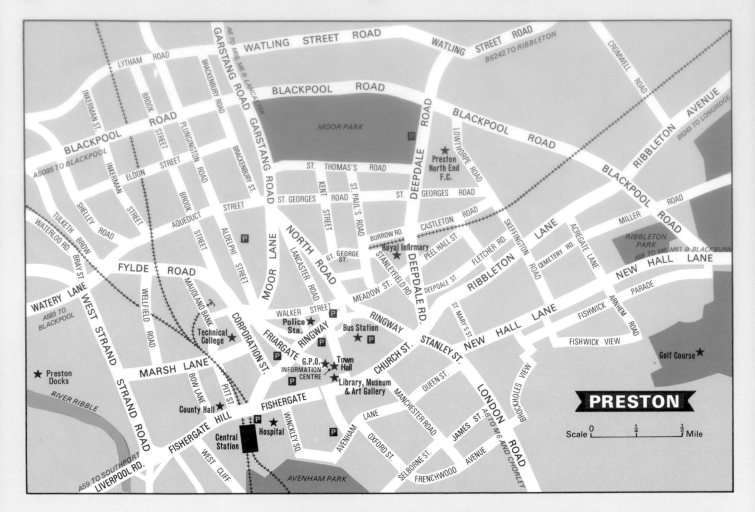

PRESTON

Scale 0 ¼ ½ Mile

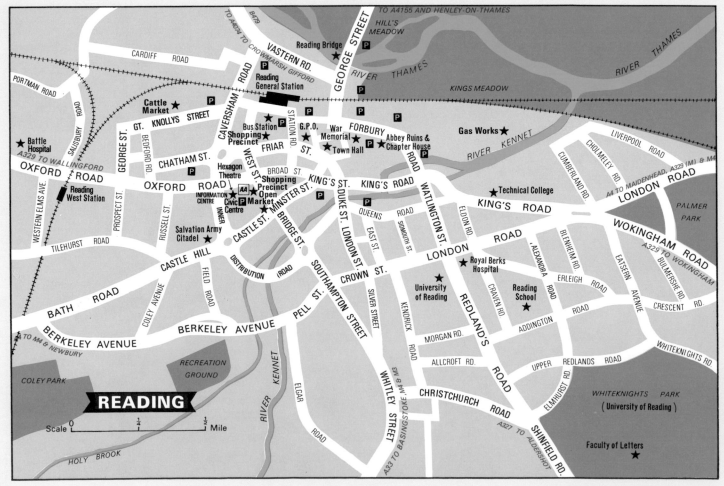

READING

Scale 0 ¼ ½ Mile

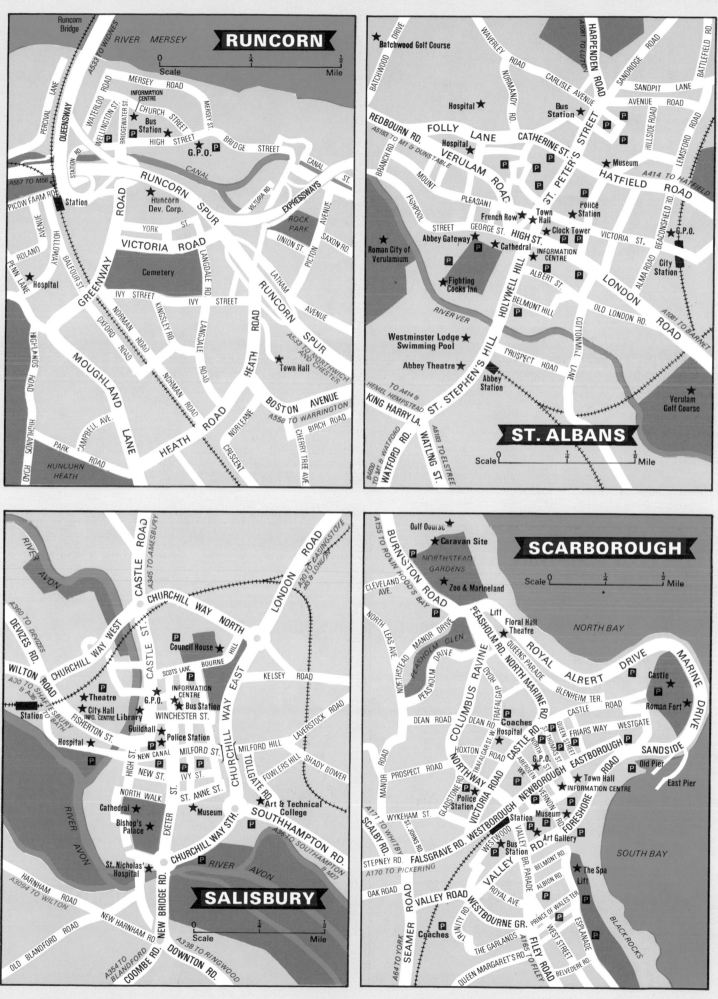

RUNCORN

Scale
0   ¼   ½
Mile

Runcorn Bridge
RIVER MERSEY
MERSEY ROAD
RIVER MERSEY
PERCIVAL LANE
QUEENSWAY
WATERLOO ROAD
WELLINGTON ST.
BRIDGEWATER ST.
CHURCH STREET
INFORMATION CENTRE
Bus Station
MERSEY ST.
HIGH STREET
G.P.O.
MERSEY ROAD
BRIDGE STREET
STATION RD.
A557 TO M56
PICOW FARM RD.
Station
RUNCORN SPUR
CANAL
CANAL
ST.
ROAD
Runcorn Dev. Corp.
VICTORIA ROAD
YORK ST.
VICTORIA RD.
UNION ST.
SAXON RD.
PICTON AVENUE
ROCK PARK
EXPRESSWAYS
ROLAND AVENUE
PENN LANE
Hospital
HOLLOWAY
BALFOUR ST.
GREENWAY
IVY STREET
OXFORD ROAD
NORMAN ROAD
KINGSLEY RD.
IVY STREET
LANGDALE RD.
Cemetery
LATHAM AVENUE
RUNCORN SPUR
A533 TO NORTHWICH AND CHESTER
HIGHLANDS ROAD
MOUGHLAND LANE
NORMAN ROAD
LANGDALE ROAD
HEATH ROAD
NORLEANE
Town Hall
HIGHLANDS ROAD
CAMPBELL AVE.
PARK ROAD
HEATH ROAD
CRESCENT
BOSTON AVENUE
A558 TO WARRINGTON
BIRCH ROAD
CHERRY TREE AVE.
RUNCORN HEATH

ST. ALBANS

Batchwood Golf Course
BATCHWOOD DRIVE
WAVERLEY ROAD
NORMANDY RD.
CARLISLE AVENUE
HARPENDEN ROAD
A1081 TO LUTON
SANDRIDGE ROAD
SANDPIT LANE
BATTLEFIELD RD.
REDBOURN RD.
A5183 TO M1 & DUNSTABLE
FOLLY LANE
Hospital
CATHERINE ST.
ST. PETER'S STREET
AVENUE ROAD
HILLSIDE ROAD
LEMSFORD ROAD
Bus Station
Hospital
VERULAM ROAD
HATFIELD
A414 TO HATFIELD
Museum
BRANCH RD.
MOUNT PLEASANT
FISHPOOL STREET
French Row
Town Hall
George St.
HIGH St.
Police Station
VICTORIA ST.
BEACONSFIELD RD.
G.P.O.
Roman City of Verulamium
Abbey Gateway
Clock Tower
Cathedral
INFORMATION CENTRE
ALBERT ST.
ALMA ROAD
City Station
Fighting Cocks Inn
HOLYWELL HILL
BELMONT HILL
OLD LONDON RD.
LONDON ROAD
A1081 TO BARNET
RIVER VER
COTTONMILL LANE
PROSPECT ROAD
Westminster Lodge Swimming Pool
ST. STEPHEN'S HILL
Abbey Theatre
Abbey Station
KING HARRY LA.
TO A414 & HEMEL HEMPSTEAD
B650 TO M1 & WATFORD
WATFORD RD.
WATLING ST.
A5183 TO ELSTREE
Verulam Golf Course

Scale
0   ¼   ½
Mile

SALISBURY

RIVER AVON
CASTLE ROAD
A360 TO DEVIZES
A345 TO AMESBURY
A30 TO BASINGSTOKE M3 & LONDON
CHURCHILL WAY NORTH
LONDON ROAD
DEVIZES RD.
CASTLE ST.
Council House
HILL
WILTON ROAD
CHURCHILL WAY WEST
A30 TO SHAFTESBURY & A36
SCOTS LANE
BOURNE
KELSEY ROAD
Theatre
Station
TO BATH
INFO. CENTRE
City Hall
G.P.O.
INFORMATION CENTRE
Bus Station
FISHERTON ST.
Library
WINCHESTER ST.
LAVERSTOCK ROAD
Hospital
Guildhall
Police Station
HIGH ST.
NEW CANAL
MILFORD ST.
MILFORD HILL
FOWLERS HILL
SHADY BOWER
CHURCHILL WAY EAST
TOLLGATE RD.
NEW ST.
IVY ST.
NORTH WALK
ST. ANNE ST.
EXETER ST.
CHURCHILL WAY STH.
Cathedral
Museum
Art & Technical College
Bishop's Palace
SOUTHAMPTON RD.
A36 TO SOUTHAMPTON & M27
RIVER AVON
St. Nicholas' Hospital
CHURCHILL WAY STH.
NEW BRIDGE RD.
RIVER AVON
HARNHAM ROAD
A3094 TO WILTON
NEW HARNHAM RD.
OLD BLANDFORD ROAD
A354 TO BLANDFORD
COOMBE RD.
DOWNTON RD.
A338 TO RINGWOOD

Scale
0   ¼
Mile

SCARBOROUGH

Golf Course
Caravan Site
A165 TO ROBIN HOOD'S BAY
BURNISTON ROAD
NORTHSTEAD GARDENS
Zoo & Marineland
CLEVELAND AVE.
Lift
Floral Hall Theatre
NORTH BAY
NORTH LEAS AVE.
MANOR DRIVE
PEASHOLM GLEN
PEASHOLM RD.
QUEENS PARADE
ROYAL ALBERT DRIVE
MARINE DRIVE
NORTHSTEAD
PEASHOLM DRIVE
NORTH MARINE RD.
BLENHEIM TER.
Castle
Roman Fort
COLUMBUS RAVINE
TRAFALGAR ROAD
CASTLE ROAD
DEAN ROAD
DEAN RD.
Coaches
FRIARS WAY
WESTGATE
SANDSIDE
MANOR ROAD
HOXTON ROAD
TRAFALGAR SW.
ABERDEEN
Hospital
CASTLE RD.
QUEEN STREET
ST. THOMAS ST.
Old Pier
PROSPECT ROAD
NORTHWAY
VICTORIA ROAD
G.P.O.
NEWBOROUGH
EASTBOROUGH
VERNON RD.
East Pier
A171 TO WHITBY
GLADSTONE RD.
Town Hall
INFORMATION CENTRE
FORESHORE ROAD
SCALBY RD.
WYKEHAM ST.
ST. JOHNS RD.
Police Station
Station
Museum
Art Gallery
SOUTH BAY
WESTBOROUGH
FALSGRAVE RD.
Bus Station
WESTWOOD
VALLEY RD.
VALLEY BR.
BELMONT RD.
STEPNEY RD.
A170 TO PICKERING
Valley
PARADE
The Spa
Lift
OAK ROAD
VALLEY ROAD
ROYAL AVE.
ALBION RD.
WESTBOURNE GR.
PRINCE OF WALES TER.
BLACK ROCKS
HARNHAM ROAD
Coaches
THE GARLANDS
TRINITY RD.
QUEEN MARGARET'S RD.
A64 TO YORK
SEAMER ROAD
WEST STREET
FILEY ROAD
A165 TO FILEY
ESPLANADE
BELVEDERE RD.

Scale
0   ¼   ½
Mile

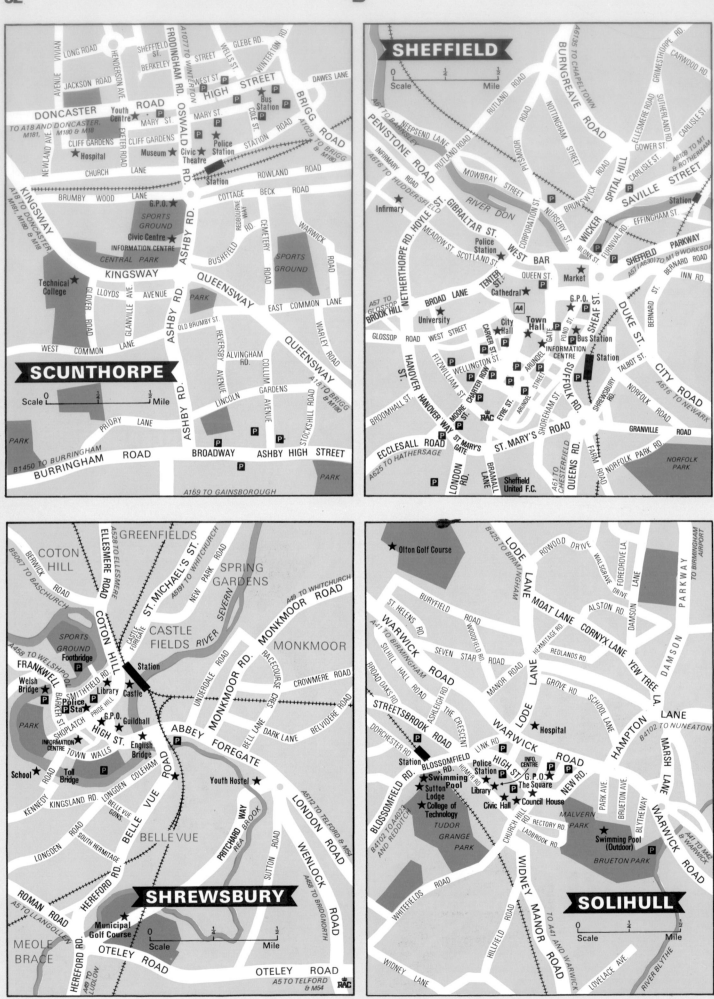

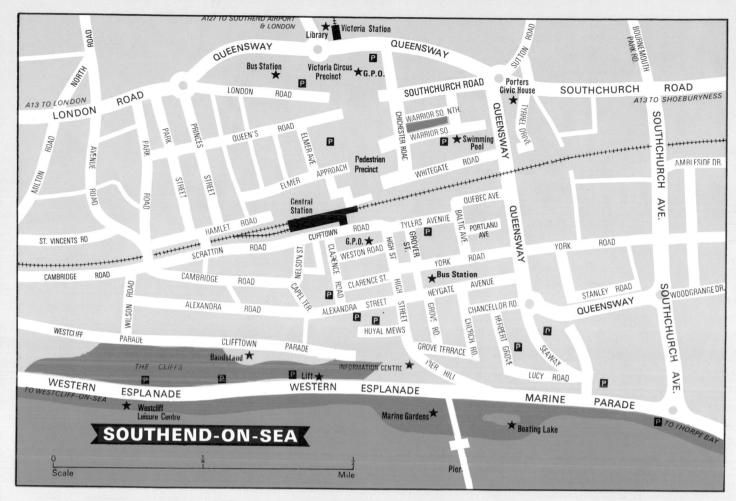

SOUTHEND-ON-SEA

A127 TO SOUTHEND AIRPORT & LONDON
Library ★ Victoria Station ★
QUEENSWAY
QUEENSWAY
A13 TO LONDON
Bus Station ★
Victoria Circus Precinct
G.P.O. ★
Porters Civic House ★
SOUTHCHURCH ROAD
SOUTHCHURCH ROAD
A13 TO SHOEBURYNESS
LONDON ROAD
LONDON ROAD
NORTH ROAD
MILTON ROAD
AVENUE ROAD
PARK STREET
PRINCES STREET
QUEEN'S ROAD
ELMER AVE.
WARRIOR SQ. NTH.
WARRIOR SQ.
Swimming Pool ★
CHICHESTER ROAD
WHITEGATE ROAD
SUTTON ROAD
QUEENSWAY
TYRREL DRIVE
BOURNEMOUTH PARK RD.
AMBLESIDE DR.
SOUTHCHURCH AVE.
ST. VINCENTS RD
ELMER APPROACH
Pedestrian Precinct
Central Station
HAMLET ROAD
CLIFFTOWN ROAD
SCRATTON ROAD
G.P.O. ★
WESTON ROAD
CLIFFTOWN ROAD
NELSON ST.
CLARENCE ROAD
CAPEL TER.
HIGH STREET
GROVER ST.
TYLERS AVENUE
BALTIC AVE.
PORTLAND AVE.
QUEBEC AVE.
YORK ROAD
QUEENSWAY
YORK ROAD
WOODGRANGE DR.
CAMBRIDGE ROAD
CAMBRIDGE ROAD
ALEXANDRA ROAD
WILSON ROAD
CLARENCE ST.
ALEXANDRA STREET
Bus Station ★
HEYGATE AVENUE
GROVE RD.
YORK ROAD
CHANCELLOR RD.
HERBERT GROVE
CHURCH ROAD
STANLEY ROAD
QUEENSWAY
SOUTHCHURCH AVE.
HUYAL MEWS
GROVE TERRACE
WESTCLIFF PARADE
CLIFFTOWN PARADE
THE CLIFFS
Bandstand ★
INFORMATION CENTRE ★
PIER HILL
SEAWAY
LUCY ROAD
WESTERN ESPLANADE
Lift ★
WESTERN ESPLANADE
MARINE PARADE
TO WESTCLIFF-ON-SEA
Westcliff Leisure Centre ★
Marine Gardens ★
Boating Lake ★
P TO THORPE BAY
Pier
Scale 0 ¼ ½ Mile

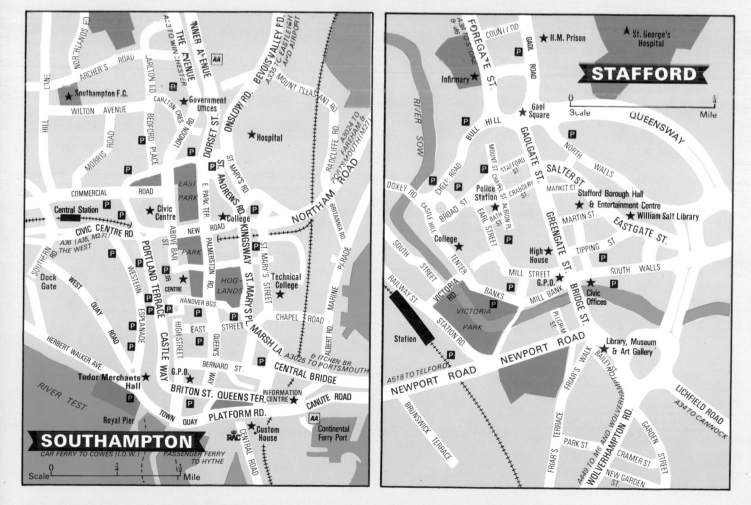

SOUTHAMPTON

INNER AVENUE
THE AVENUE
A33 TO WINCHESTER
ARCHER'S ROAD
NORTHLANDS
HILL LANE
AA
Southampton F.C. ★
Government Offices ★
WILTON AVENUE
CARLTON RD.
CARLTON CRES.
LONDON RD.
DORSET ST.
ONSLOW RD.
BEVOIS VALLEY RD.
A335 TO EASTLEIGH AND AIRPORT
MOUNT PLEASANT RD.
MORRIS ROAD
BEDFORD PLACE
Hospital ★
ST. MARY'S RD.
RADCLIFFE RD.
A3024 TO PORTSMOUTH (M27)
A3024 TO FAREHAM & PORTSMOUTH (M27)
ROAD
NORTHAM ROAD
COMMERCIAL ROAD
EAST PARK
Civic Centre ★
E. PARK TER.
ST. ANDREWS RD.
College ★
KINGSWAY
ST. MARY'S RD.
BRITANNIA RD.
Central Station
CIVIC CENTRE RD.
A36 (A35, M271) THE WEST
ABOVE BAR ST.
NEW PARK
PALMERSTON RD.
ST. MARY'S STREET
Technical College ★
MARINE PARADE
DOCK Gate
WEST QUAY ROAD
SOUTHERN ROAD
PORTLAND TERRACE
WESTERN ESPLANADE
Centre ★
HANOVER BGS.
HOG-LANDS
CHAPEL ROAD
ALBERT RD.
A3025 TO PORTSMOUTH & ITCHEN BR.
HERBERT WALKER AVE.
CASTLE WAY
HIGH STREET
EAST STREET
QUEEN'S WAY
BERNARD ST.
MARSH LA.
A3025 TO PORTSMOUTH
CENTRAL BRIDGE
RIVER TEST
Tudor Merchants Hall ★
G.P.O. ★
BRITON ST.
QUEENS TER.
INFORMATION CENTRE ★
CANUTE ROAD
Royal Pier
TOWN QUAY
PLATFORM RD.
RAC
Custom House
AA
Continental Ferry Port
CENTRAL ROAD
Scale 0 ¼ ½ Mile
CAR FERRY TO COWES (I.O.W.)
PASSENGER FERRY TO HYTHE

STAFFORD

FOREGATE ST.
COUNTY RD.
A34 TO STONE & M6
GAOL ROAD
H.M. Prison ★
St. George's Hospital ★
Infirmary ★
RIVER SOW
Gaol Square ★
BULL HILL
Scale 0 ¼ Mile
QUEENSWAY
GAOLGATE ST.
NORTH WALLS
SALTER ST.
MOUNT ST.
STAFFORD ST.
CHAPEL ST.
CRABBERY ST.
MARKET ST.
Stafford Borough Hall & Entertainment Centre ★
William Salt Library ★
DOXEY RD.
CHELL RD.
BROAD ST.
Police Station ★
ALBION PL.
BATH ST.
EARL STREET
MARTIN ST.
EASTGATE ST.
CASTLE HILL
College ★
GREENGATE ST.
High House ★
TENTER
MILL STREET
TIPPING ST.
SOUTH WALLS
RAILWAY ST.
VICTORIA RD.
SOUTH STREET
Banks ★
G.P.O. ★
MILL BANK
Civic Offices ★
Station
VICTORIA PARK
STATION RD.
BRIDGE ST.
PILGRIM ST.
A518 TO TELFORD
NEWPORT ROAD
NEWPORT ROAD
Library, Museum & Art Gallery ★
FRIAR'S WALK
LICHFIELD ROAD
A3470 CANNOCK
BRUNSWICK TERRACE
FRIAR'S TERRACE
PARK ST.
A449 TO M6 AND WOLVERHAMPTON
WOLVERHAMPTON RD.
CRAMER ST.
GARDEN STREET
NEW GARDEN ST.
BAILEY'S

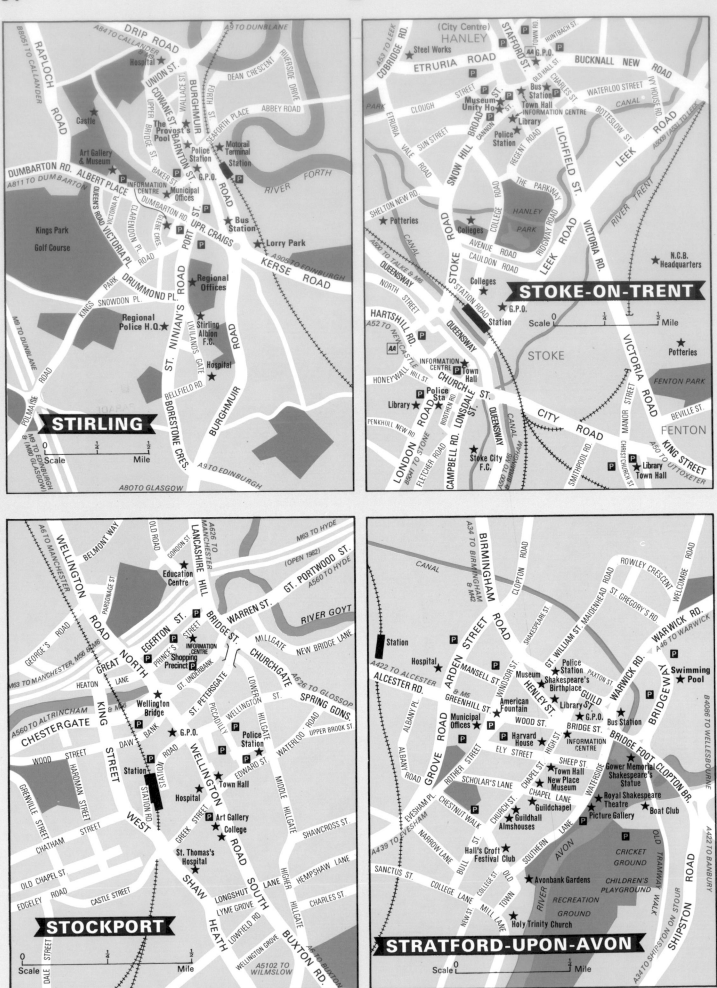

STIRLING

DRIP ROAD
A84 TO CALLANDER
A9 TO DUNBLANE
RAPLOCH ROAD
BB051 TO CALLANDER
UNION ST.
Hospital
DEAN CRESCENT
RIVERSIDE DRIVE
WALLACE ST.
COWANE ST.
BURGHMUIR
FORTH ST.
SEAFORTH PLACE
ABBEY ROAD
Castle
The Provost's Pool
UPPER BRIDGE ST.
ST. BARNTON ST.
BAKER ST.
Police Station
Motorail Terminal Station
RIVER FORTH
Art Gallery & Museum
DUMBARTON RD.
A811 TO DUMBARTON
ALBERT PLACE
INFORMATION CENTRE
QUEEN'S ROAD
VICTORIA PL.
CLARENDON PL.
GLEBE CRES.
DUMBARTON RD.
Municipal Offices
G.P.O.
PORT ST.
UPR. CRAIGS
Bus Station
Kings Park Golf Course
KINGS PARK ROAD
SNOWDON PL.
DRUMMOND PL.
ST. NINIAN'S ROAD
LINLANDS GATE
Regional Offices
Lorry Park
A905 TO EDINBURGH
KERSE ROAD
M9 TO DUNBLANE
Regional Police H.Q.
Stirling Albion F.C.
ROAD
Hospital
M9 TO EDINBURGH & M80 GLASGOW
POLMAISE
BELLFIELD RD.
BURGHMUIR ROAD
BORESTONE CRES.
A9 TO EDINBURGH
A80 TO GLASGOW
0 ¼ ½
Scale   Mile

STOKE-ON-TRENT

(City Centre)
HANLEY
A53 TO LEEK
COBRIDGE RD.
Steel Works
STAFFORD ST.
TOWN RD.
HUNTBACH ST.
AA
G.P.O.
ETRURIA ROAD
OLD HALL ST.
BUCKNALL NEW ROAD
PARK
STAFFORD ST.
CHARLES ST.
WATERLOO STREET
IVY HOUSE RD.
A5009 (A53) TO LEEK
ETRURIA VALE
BROAD ST.
Bus Station
Museum
Unity Ho.
Town Hall
INFORMATION CENTRE
CANAL
BOTTESLOW ST.
CLOUGH
SUN STREET
CANNON ST.
Library
Police Station
REGENT ROAD
LICHFIELD ST.
LEEK ROAD
SHELTON NEW RD.
COLLEGE ROAD
THE PARKWAY
RIDGWAY ROAD
HANLEY PARK
VICTORIA RD.
RIVER TRENT
Potteries
Colleges
AVENUE ROAD
CAULDON ROAD
LEEK ROAD
N.C.B. Headquarters
QUEENSWAY
NORTH STREET
STOKE ROAD
STATION ROAD
Colleges
HARTSHILL RD.
A52 TO NEWCASTLE
G.P.O.
Station
Scale 0 ¼ ½ Mile
AA
A50 TO TALKE & M6
STOKE
HONEYWALL HILL ST.
INFORMATION CENTRE
Town Hall
CHURCH ST.
Police Sta
Library
LONSDALE ST.
BOOTHEN RD.
QUEENSWAY
VICTORIA ROAD
MANOR STREET
FENTON PARK
Potteries
BEVILLE ST.
FENTON
PENKHULL NEW RD.
LONDON ROAD
B5041 TO STONE
CAMPBELL RD.
FLETCHER ROAD
CITY ROAD
SMITHPOOL RD.
CHRISTCHURCH ST.
KING STREET
A50 TO UTTOXETER
Stoke City F.C.
A500 TO M6 & BIRMINGHAM
Library Town Hall

STOCKPORT

A6 TO MANCHESTER
BELMONT WAY
OLD ROAD
LANCASHIRE HILL
GORDON ST.
A626 TO MANCHESTER
M63 TO HYDE
(OPEN 1982)
GT. PORTWOOD ST.
A560 TO HYDE
WELLINGTON ROAD
PARSONAGE ST.
Education Centre
EGERTON ST.
BRIDGE ST.
WARREN ST.
MILLGATE
NEW BRIDGE LANE
RIVER GOYT
GEORGE'S ROAD
PRINCE'S STREET
INFORMATION CENTRE
Shopping Precinct
CHURCHGATE
A626 TO GLOSSOP
M63 TO MANCHESTER
GREAT NORTH
GT. UNDERBANK
LOWER
ST. PETERSGATE
SPRING GDNS.
M56 & M6 TO ALTRINCHAM
A560 TO ALTRINCHAM
HEATON LANE
Wellington Bridge
PICCADILLY
WELLINGTON ST.
WATERLOO ST.
UPPER BROOK ST.
KING STREET
Bank
G.P.O.
Police Station
WOOD STREET
DAW
STATION ROAD
Edward St.
MIDDLE HILLGATE
HARDMAN STREET
Station
Town Hall
Hospital
WELLINGTON ROAD
GREEK STREET
Art Gallery
College
SHAWCROSS ST.
GRENVILLE STREET
St. Thomas's Hospital
CHATHAM STREET
OLD CHAPEL ST.
EDGELEY ROAD
CASTLE STREET
WEST
SHAW HEATH
LONGSHUT LANE
LYME GROVE
SOUTH
HIGHER HILLGATE
HEMPSHAW LANE
CHARLES ST.
LOWFIELD RD.
WELLINGTON GROVE
BUXTON RD.
A5102 TO WILMSLOW
A6 TO BUXTON
0 ¼ ½
Scale   Mile
DALE STREET

STRATFORD-UPON-AVON

A34 TO BIRMINGHAM & M42
CANAL
BIRMINGHAM ROAD
CLOPTON ROAD
ROWLEY CRESCENT
ST. GREGORY'S RD.
WELCOMBE ROAD
SHAKESPEARE ST.
WINDSOR ST.
ST. WILLIAM ST.
MAIDENHEAD ROAD
WARWICK RD.
A46 TO WARWICK
Station
A422 TO ALCESTER
Hospital
ARDEN STREET ROAD
MANSELL ST.
& M5
Museum
PAXTON RD.
Police Station
GUILD ST.
WARWICK RD.
BRIDGEWAY
B4086 TO WELLESBOURNE
Swimming Pool
ALCESTER RD.
GREENHILL ST.
Shakespeare's Birthplace
HENLEY ST.
American Fountain
Library
G.P.O.
Bus Station
BRIDGE FOOT
CLOPTON BR.
ALBANY PL.
GROVE ROAD
Municipal Offices
WOOD ST.
HIGH ST.
BRIDGE ST.
INFORMATION CENTRE
A422 TO BANBURY
ALBANY ROAD
Harvard House
ELY STREET
ROTHER STREET
SHEEP ST.
CHAPEL ST.
Town Hall
New Place Museum
Gower Memorial Shakespeare's Statue
WATERSIDE
SCHOLAR'S LANE
CHAPEL LANE
Royal Shakespeare Theatre
Boat Club
A439 TO EVESHAM
EVESHAM PL.
CHESTNUT WALK
CHURCH ST.
Guildchapel
Guildhall Almshouses
Picture Gallery
CLOPTON BR.
OLD TRAMWAY WALK
A422 TO BANBURY
NARROW LANE
Hall's Croft Festival Club
SOUTHERN LANE
RIVER AVON
CRICKET GROUND
SANCTUS ST.
COLLEGE LANE
BULL
TOWN
MILL LANE
Avonbank Gardens
CHILDREN'S PLAYGROUND
RECREATION GROUND
SHIPSTON ROAD
A34 TO SHIPSTON ON STOUR
NEW ST.
Holy Trinity Church
Scale 0 ¼ ½ Mile

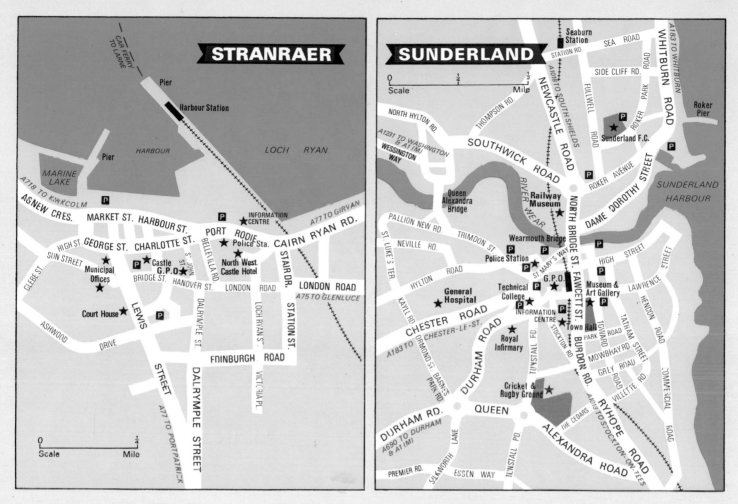

STRANRAER

CAR FERRY TO LARNE

Pier

Harbour Station

LOCH RYAN

HARBOUR

Pier

MARINE LAKE

A718 TO KIRKCOLM

ASNEW CRES.

MARKET ST. HARBOUR ST.

PORT RODIE

INFORMATION CENTRE

A77 TO GIRVAN

HIGH ST. GEORGE ST. CHARLOTTE ST.

Police Sta.

CAIRN RYAN RD.

SUN STREET

Municipal Offices

Castle G.P.O.

North West Castle Hotel

STAIR DR.

STATION ST.

GLEBE ST.

BRIDGE ST. HANOVER ST.

LONDON ROAD

LONDON ROAD

A75 TO GLENLUCE

BELLEVILLA RD.

S. JOHN

ASHWOOD

Court House

LEWIS STREET

DALRYMPLE ST.

EDINBURGH ROAD

LOCH RYAN ST.

VICTORIA PL.

DRIVE

DALRYMPLE STREET

A77 TO PORTPATRICK

0 Scale ¼ Mile

SUNDERLAND

0 Scale ¼ ½ Mile

Seaburn Station

SEA ROAD

STATION RD.

A183 TO WHITBURN

WHITBURN ROAD

NORTH HYLTON RD.

THOMPSON RD.

A1018 TO SOUTH SHIELDS

SIDE CLIFF RD.

FULWELL

ROKER PARK ROAD

Roker Pier

A1231 TO WASHINGTON & A1 (M)

SOUTHWICK ROAD

NEWCASTLE ROAD

ROKER AVENUE

Sunderland F.C.

WESSINGTON WAY

Queen Alexandra Bridge

RIVER WEAR

Railway Museum

NORTH BRIDGE ST.

DAME DOROTHY STREET

SUNDERLAND HARBOUR

PALLION NEW RD.

TRIMDON ST.

Wearmouth Bridge

FAWCETT ST.

HIGH STREET

ST. LUKE'S TER.

NEVILLE RD.

Police Station

ST. MARY'S WAY

G.P.O.

Museum & Art Gallery

LAWRENCE STREET

HYLTON ROAD

KAYLL RD.

General Hospital

Technical College

INFORMATION CENTRE

Town Hall

PARK ROAD

HENDON ROAD

TATHAM STREET

A183 TO ORMONDE ST.

CHESTER ROAD

CHESTER-LE-ST.

STOCKTON RD.

TUNSTALL RD.

BURDON RD.

MOWBRAY RD.

GRAY ROAD

COMMERCIAL ROAD

BARNES PARK RD.

DURHAM ROAD

Royal Infirmary

THE CEDARS

VILLETTE RD.

Cricket & Rugby Ground

A1018 TO STOCKTON-ON-TEES

DURHAM RD.

QUEEN

RYHOPE ROAD

A183 TO CHESTER-LE-ST.

DURHAM RD.

A690 TO DURHAM & A1 (M)

SILKSWORTH LANE

ALEXANDRA ROAD

PREMIER RD.

ESSEN WAY

TUNSTALL RD.

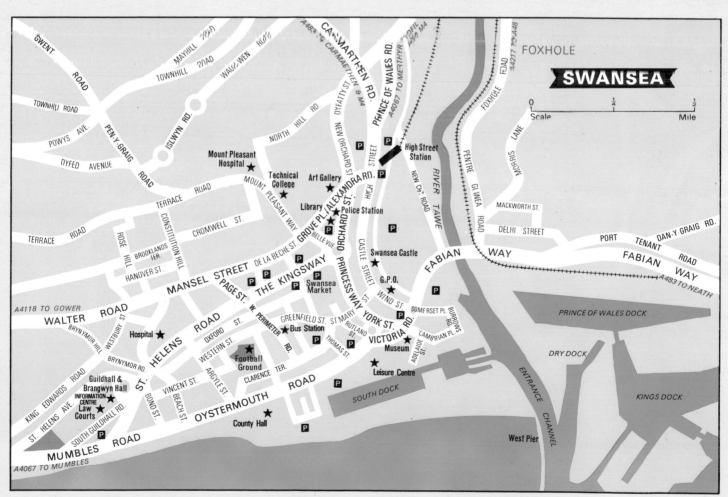

SWANSEA

FOXHOLE

0 Scale ¼ ½ Mile

GWENT ROAD

MAYHILL ROAD

WAUN WEN ROAD

CARMARTHEN RD.

A483 TO CARMARTHEN & M4

PRINCE OF WALES RD.

A4067 TO MERTHYR TYDFIL & M4

A4217/A48

FOXHOLE ROAD

TOWNHILL ROAD

ISLWYN RD.

NORTH RD.

NORTH HILL RD.

DYFATTY ST.

NEW ORCHARD ST.

High Street Station

PENTRE GUINEA ROAD

MORRIS LANE

TOWNHILL ROAD

POWYS AVE.

PEN-Y-GRAIG ROAD

Mount Pleasant Hospital

Technical College

Art Gallery

ALEXANDRA RD.

HIGH STREET

RIVER TAWE

MACKWORTH ST.

DYFED AVENUE

Library

GROVE PL.

Police Station

NEW CUT ROAD

DELHI STREET

TERRACE ROAD

MOUNT PLEASANT WAY

ORCHARD ST.

BELLE VUE

PORT TENANT ROAD

DAN-Y-GRAIG RD.

ROSE HILL

BROOKLANDS TER.

CONSTITUTION HILL

CROMWELL ST.

Swansea Castle

FABIAN WAY

FABIAN WAY

TERRACE ROAD

HANOVER ST.

DE LA BECHE ST.

CASTLE STREET

A483 TO NEATH

MANSEL STREET

PAGE ST.

THE KINGSWAY

G.P.O.

PRINCE OF WALES DOCK

A4118 TO GOWER

Swansea Market

PRINCESS WAY

WIND ST.

WALTER ROAD

BRYNMOR HILL

WESTBURY ST.

Hospital

ST. HELENS ROAD

OXFORD ST.

W. PERIMETER RD.

GREENFIELD ST.

ST. MARY ST.

YORK ST.

SOMERSET PL.

BURROWS RD.

DRY DOCK

BRYNMOR RD.

Bus Station

WESTERN ST.

RUTLAND ST.

VICTORIA

Museum

CAMBRIAN PL.

ADELAIDE ST.

Football Ground

THOMAS ST.

Guildhall & Brangwyn Hall

INFORMATION CENTRE

Law Courts

KING EDWARDS ROAD

ST. HELENS AVE.

ARGYLE ST.

VINCENT ST.

CLARENCE TER.

Leisure Centre

KINGS DOCK

BOND ST.

BEACH ST.

OYSTERMOUTH ROAD

County Hall

SOUTH DOCK

ENTRANCE CHANNEL

MUMBLES ROAD

SOUTH GUILDHALL RD.

West Pier

A4067 TO MUMBLES

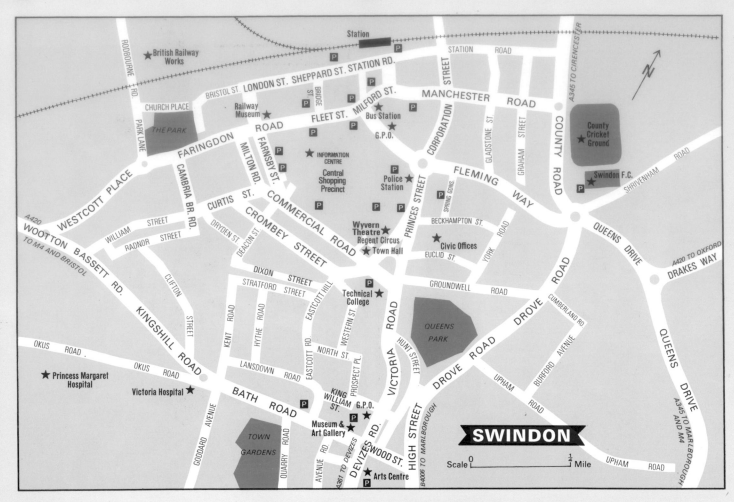

SWINDON

British Railway Works

Station

STATION ROAD

A345 TO CIRENCESTER

RODBOURNE RD.

BRISTOL ST. LONDON ST. SHEPPARD ST. STATION RD.

CHURCH PLACE

Railway Museum

FLEET ST. MILFORD ST.

Bus Station

G.P.O.

MANCHESTER ROAD

STREET

STATION

COUNTY ROAD

County Cricket Ground

Swindon F.C.

SHRIVENHAM ROAD

THE PARK

FARINGDON ROAD

FARNSBY ST.

MILTON RD.

BRIDGE ST.

Information Centre

Central Shopping Precinct

Police Station

PRINCES STREET

FLEMING WAY

GLADSTONE ST.

GRAHAM STREET

PARK LANE

WESTCOTT PLACE

CAMBRIA BR. RD.

CURTIS ST.

COMMERCIAL ROAD

DRYDEN ST.

DEACON ST.

Wyvern Theatre

Regent Circus

Town Hall

Civic Offices

SPRING GDNS.

BECKHAMPTON ST.

EUCLID ST.

YORK ROAD

QUEENS DRIVE

A420 TO OXFORD

A420

WOOTTON BASSETT RD.
TO M4 AND BRISTOL

WILLIAM STREET

RADNOR STREET

CLIFTON STREET

KINGSHILL ROAD

CROMBEY STREET

DIXON STREET

STRATFORD STREET

EASTCOTT HILL

Technical College

GROUNDWELL ROAD

DROVE ROAD

CUMBERLAND RD.

DRAKES WAY

KENT ROAD

HYTHE ROAD

EASTCOTT RD.

NORTH ST.

WESTERN ST.

PROSPECT PL.

Queens Park

BURFORD AVENUE

QUEENS DRIVE
A345 TO MARLBOROUGH AND M4

Princess Margaret Hospital

OKUS ROAD

OKUS ROAD

BATH ROAD

LANSDOWN ROAD

VICTORIA ROAD

HUNT STREET

UPHAM ROAD

Victoria Hospital

GODDARD AVENUE

QUARRY ROAD

AVENUE RD.

KING WILLIAM ST.

G.P.O.

HIGH STREET

DROVE ROAD

B4006 TO MARLBOROUGH

TOWN GARDENS

Museum & Art Gallery

DEVIZES RD.

A361 TO DEVIZES

WOOD ST.

Arts Centre

UPHAM ROAD

Scale 0 — ¼ Mile

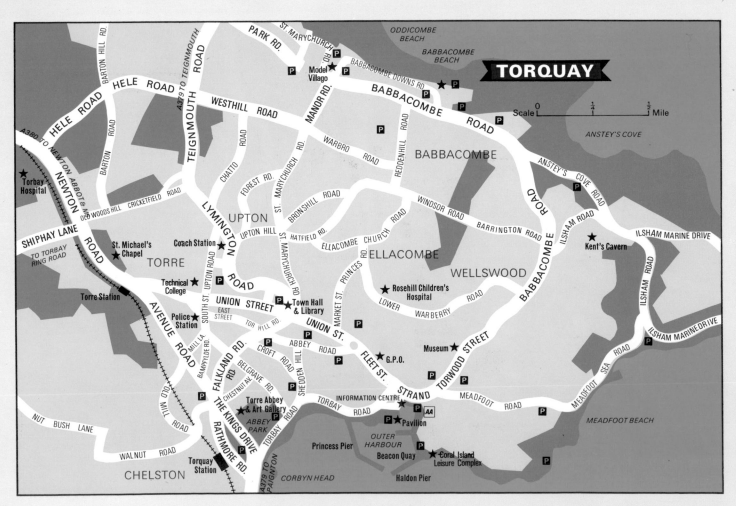

TORQUAY

ST. MARYCHURCH RD.

PARK RD.

ODDICOMBE BEACH

BABBACOMBE BEACH

BARTON HILL RD.

TEIGNMOUTH ROAD

A379 TO TEIGNMOUTH

HELE ROAD

HELE ROAD

WESTHILL ROAD

MANOR RD.

Model Village

BABBACOMBE DOWNS RD.

BABBACOMBE ROAD

Scale 0 — ¼ — ½ Mile

ANSTEY'S COVE

A380 TO NEWTON ABBOT & M5

NEWTON ROAD

BARTON ROAD

CHATTO ROAD

CRICKETFIELD ROAD

OLD WOODS HILL

FOREST RD.

WARBRO ROAD

REDDENHILL ROAD

BABBACOMBE

ANSTEY'S COVE ROAD

SHIPHAY LANE
TO TORBAY RING ROAD

Torbay Hospital

St. Michael's Chapel

TORRE

Coach Station

LYMINGTON ROAD

UPTON HILL

UPTON

ST. MARYCHURCH RD.

BRONSHILL ROAD

HATFIELD RD.

ELLACOMBE CHURCH ROAD

ELLACOMBE

WINDSOR ROAD

BARRINGTON ROAD

BABBACOMBE ROAD

ILSHAM ROAD

Kent's Cavern

ILSHAM MARINE DRIVE

Technical College

Torre Station

SOUTH ST. UPTON ROAD

UNION STREET

EAST STREET

Town Hall & Library

ST. MARYCHURCH RD.

PRINCES ROAD

WELLSWOOD

Rosehill Children's Hospital

LOWER WARBERRY ROAD

ILSHAM ROAD

AVENUE ROAD

Police Station

MILL LA.

BAMPFYLDE RD.

UNION ST.

TOR HILL RD.

MARKET ST.

FLEET ST.

G.P.O.

Museum

TORWOOD STREET

SEA ROAD

MEADFOOT SEA ROAD

ILSHAM MARINE DRIVE

NUT BUSH LANE

FALKLAND RD.

OLD MILL ROAD

CHESTNUT AV.

BELGRAVE RD.

CROFT ROAD

SHEDDEN HILL

ABBEY ROAD

Torre Abbey & Art Gallery

Information Centre

STRAND

MEADFOOT ROAD

MEADFOOT BEACH

WALNUT ROAD

THE KINGS DRIVE

RATHMORE RD.

Torquay Station

Abbey Park

TORBAY ROAD

Pavilion

AA

Princess Pier

OUTER HARBOUR

Beacon Quay

Coral Island Leisure Complex

CHELSTON

A379 TO PAIGNTON

CORBYN HEAD

Haldon Pier

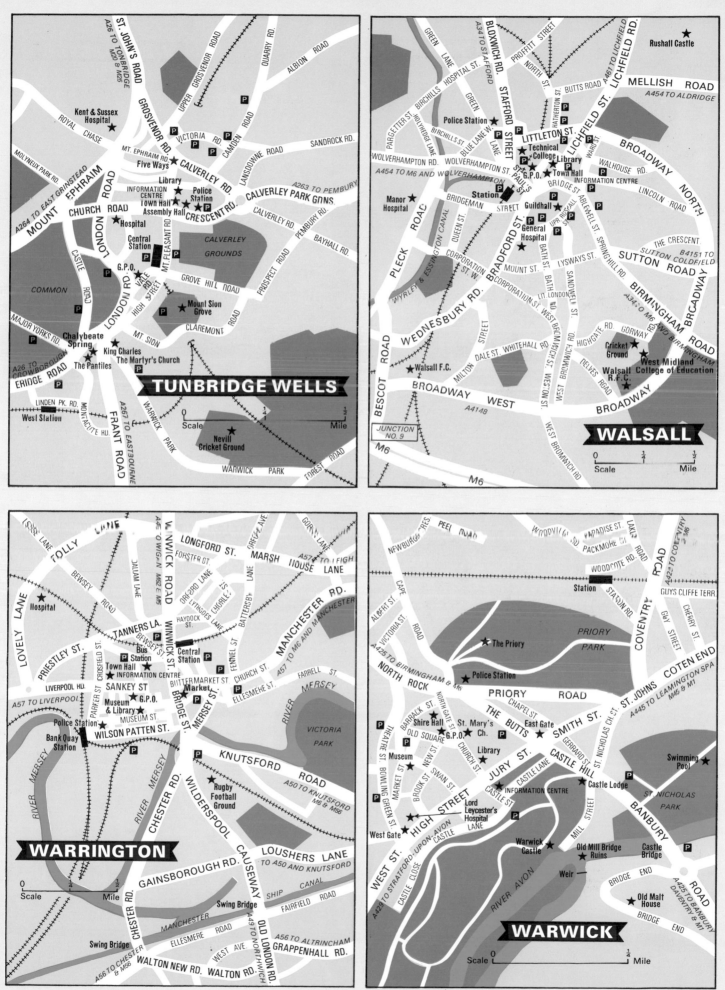

TUNBRIDGE WELLS

ST. JOHN'S ROAD
A26 TO TONBRIDGE M20 & M25
UPPER GROSVENOR ROAD
QUARRY RD.
GROSVENOR RD.
ALBION ROAD
Kent & Sussex Hospital
ROYAL CHASE
MT. EPHRAIM RD.
Five Ways
CALVERLEY RD.
VICTORIA RD.
CAMDEN ROAD
LANSDOWNE ROAD
SANDROCK RD.
MOUNT EPHRAIM
LONDON ROAD
CHURCH ROAD
Library
INFORMATION CENTRE
Town Hall
Assembly Hall
Police Station
CRESCENT RD.
CALVERLEY PARK GDNS.
A263 TO PEMBURY
Hospital
CALVERLEY RD.
PEMBURY RD.
A264 TO EAST GRINSTEAD
MOLYNEUX PARK RD.
CASTLE ROAD
Central Station
G.P.O.
VALE RD.
STREET
HIGH STREET
MT. PLEASANT RD.
CALVERLEY GROUNDS
GROVE HILL ROAD
CLAREMONT ROAD
PROSPECT ROAD
BAYHALL RD.
COMMON
Chalybeate Spring
MAJOR YORKS RD.
Mount Sion Grove
MT. SION
A26 TO CROWBOROUGH
King Charles The Martyr's Church
The Pantiles
ERIDGE ROAD
LINDEN PK. RD.
West Station
MONTACUTE HU.
FRANT ROAD
A267 TO EASTBOURNE
WARWICK PARK
Scale
0 ¼ ½ Mile
Nevill Cricket Ground
WARWICK PARK
FOREST ROAD

WALSALL

GREEN LANE
BLOXWICH RD.
A34 TO STAFFORD
PROFFITT STREET
LICHFIELD RD.
Rushall Castle
NORTH ST.
STAFFORD STREET
BUTTS ROAD
A461 TO LICHFIELD
MELLISH ROAD
A454 TO ALDRIDGE
PARGETTER ST.
BIRCHILLS ST.
HOSPITAL ST.
GREEN LANE
Police Station
HATHERTON ST.
LICHFIELD ST.
WARD ST.
BROADWAY NORTH
BIRCHILLS ST.
BLUE LANE W.
Technical College
Library
WALHOUSE RD.
WOLVERHAMPTON RD.
HOLYEDGE LANE
WOLVERHAMPTON ST.
ST. PAUL'S
G.P.O.
Town Hall
INFORMATION CENTRE
A454 TO M6 AND WOLVERHAMPTON
Manor Hospital
BRIDGEMAN ST.
Station
BRIDGE ST.
ABLEWELL ST.
LINCOLN ROAD
THE CRESCENT
PLECK ROAD
BRIDGEMAN STREET
Guildhall
UPR. RUSHALL ST.
B4151 TO SUTTON COLDFIELD
WYRLEY & ESSINGTON CANAL
QUEEN ST.
BRADFORD ST.
General Hospital
BATH ST.
SPRINGHILL RD.
SUTTON ROAD
CORPORATION ST. W.
MOUNT ST.
BATH
LYSWAYS ST.
BIRMINGHAM ROAD
WEDNESBURY RD.
CORPORATION ST.
WEST BROMWICH ST.
SANDWELL ST.
A34 TO M6 AND BIRMINGHAM
STREET
LIT. LONDON
MILTON STREET
LIT. LONDON ST.
BROADWAY
HIGHGATE RD.
GORWAY
Walsall F.C.
DALE ST.
WHITEHALL RD.
WEST BROMWICH RD.
NELVES ROAD
Cricket Ground
West Midland College of Education
BESCOT ROAD
BROADWAY WEST
A4148
WEST BROMWICH ROAD
Walsall R.F.C.
JUNCTION NO. 9
M6
M6
Scale
0 ¼ ½ Mile

WARRINGTON

FOLLY LANE
WARWICK ROAD
A49 TO WIGAN & M6
LONGFORD ST.
GREEN AVE.
MARSH HOUSE LANE
A57 TO LEIGH
GORSE LANE
FORSTER ST.
Hospital
BEWSEY ROAD
LOVELY LANE
ORFORD LANE
JALLAM LANE
M62 & M6
LYTHGOES LANE
BATTERSBY LANE
MANCHESTER RD.
A57 TO M6 AND MANCHESTER
PRIESTLEY ST.
TANNERS LA.
BEWSEY ST.
HAYDOCK ST.
WINWICK ST.
FENNEL ST.
CHURCH ST.
FARRELL ST.
Bus Station
Town Hall
INFORMATION CENTRE
Central Station
BUTTERMARKET ST.
ELLESMERE ST.
RIVER MERSEY
LIVERPOOL RD.
SANKEY ST.
CROSFIELD ST.
Market
MERSEY ST.
A57 TO LIVERPOOL
Museum & Library
G.P.O.
BRIDGE ST.
VICTORIA PARK
PARKER ST.
MUSEUM ST.
Police Station
WILSON PATTEN ST.
Bank Quay Station
CHESTER RD.
KNUTSFORD ROAD
A50 TO KNUTSFORD M6 & M56
RIVER MERSEY
WILDERSPOOL CAUSEWAY
Rugby Football Ground
RIVER MERSEY
GAINSBOROUGH RD.
LOUSHERS LANE
TO A50 AND KNUTSFORD
Scale
0 ¼ ½ Mile
Swing Bridge
SHIP CANAL
FAIRFIELD ROAD
MANCHESTER ROAD
A49 TO NORTHWICH
Swing Bridge
WEST AVE.
WALTON NEW RD. WALTON RD.
A56 TO CHESTER M56
A56 TO ALTRINCHAM
GRAPPENHALL RD.
OLD LONDON RD.

WARWICK

PEEL ROAD
NEWBURGH CRES.
WOODVILLE RD.
PARADISE ST.
PACKMORE ST.
LAKIN ROAD
A429 TO COVENTRY & M6
WOODCOTE RD.
CAPE ROAD
COVENTRY ROAD
Station
STATION RD.
GUYS CLIFFE TERR.
GUY STREET
CHERRY ST.
ALBERT ST.
VICTORIA STREET
A425 TO BIRMINGHAM & M6
PRIORY PARK
The Priory
Police Station
PRIORY ROAD
COTEN END
NORTH ROCK
CHAPEL ST.
ST. JOHNS
A445 TO LEAMINGTON SPA M6 & M1
THE BUTTS
East Gate
SMITH ST.
Shire Hall
BARRACK ST.
NORTHGATE ST.
St. Mary's Ch.
G.P.O.
GERRARD ST.
CASTLE HILL
ST. NICHOLAS CH. ST.
THEATRE ST.
OLD SQUARE
Library
JURY ST.
CASTLE LANE
Castle Lodge
Swimming Pool
BOWLING GREEN ST.
Museum
BROOK ST.
NEW ST.
CHURCH ST.
INFORMATION CENTRE
MILL STREET
ST. NICHOLAS PARK
MARKET ST.
SWAN ST.
HIGH STREET
Lord Leycester's Hospital
CASTLE LANE
BANBURY ROAD
West Gate
WEST ST.
A429 TO STRATFORD-UPON-AVON
CASTLE CLOSE
Warwick Castle
Old Mill Bridge Ruins
Weir
Castle Bridge
BRIDGE END
RIVER AVON
A425 TO BANBURY DAVENTRY & M1
Old Malt House
BRIDGE END
Scale
0 ¼ ½ Mile

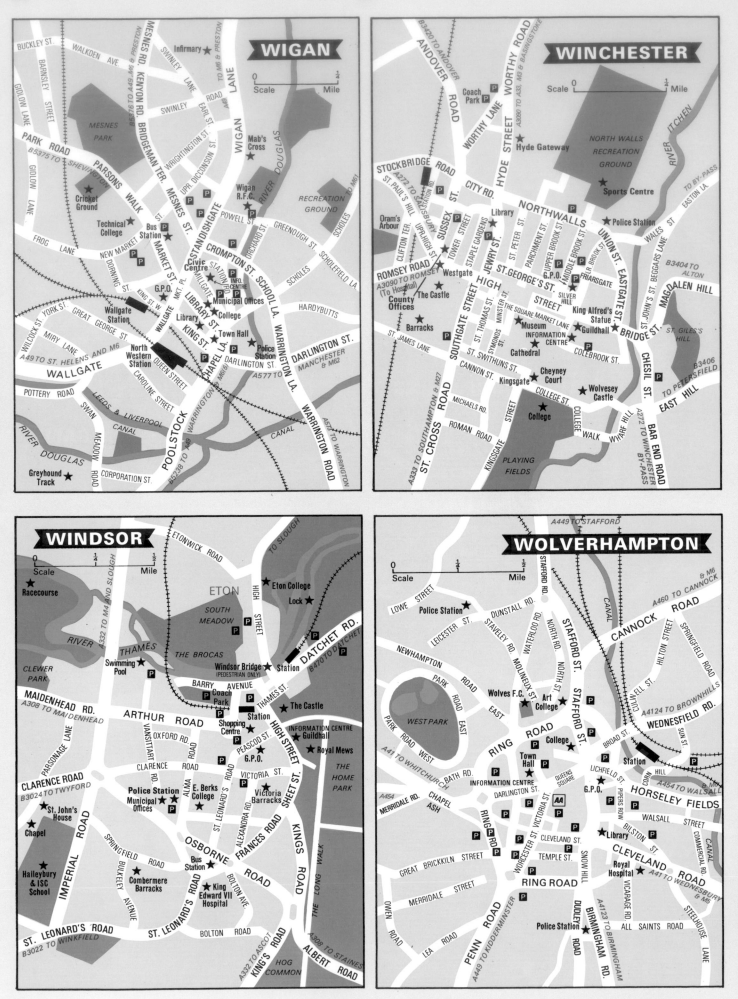

WIGAN

Scale 0 ¼ Mile

BUCKLEY ST.
BARNSLEY STREET
GIDLOW LANE
WALKDEN AVE.
MESNES RD.
KENYON RD.
B5376 TO M6 & PRESTON
BRIDGEMAN TER.
SWINLEY LANE
WIGAN LANE
EARL ST.
A49 TO M6 & PRESTON
Infirmary ★
MESNES RD.
SWINLEY
STANDISHGATE
WRIGHTINGTON ST.
UPR. DICCONSON ST.
Mab's Cross ★
Wigan R.F.C. ★
POWELL ST.
ORCHARD ST.
GREENOUGH ST.
SCHOLEFIELD LA.
RECREATION GROUND
RIVER DOUGLAS
SCHOLES
PARK ROAD
B5375 TO SHEVINGTON
PARSONS WALK
MESNES PARK
MESNES ST.
Technical College ★
Cricket Ground ★
Bus Station
NEW MARKET ST.
MARKET ST.
DORNING ST.
CROMPTON ST.
SCHOOL LA.
HARDYBUTTS
FROG LANE
Civic Centre
STATION RD.
INFO. CENTRE
Municipal Offices
G.P.O.
KING ST. W.
KING ST.
College
WALLGATE
Library ★
Town Hall ★
CHAPEL LA.
Police Station ★
DARLINGTON ST.
DARLINGTON STREET
MANCHESTER & M62
A577 TO MANCHESTER
WILCOCK ST.
YORK ST.
GREAT GEORGE ST.
MIRY LANE
Wallgate Station
North Western Station
QUEEN STREET
A49 TO ST. HELENS AND M6
WALLGATE
CAROLINE STREET
SWAN MEADOW ROAD
LEEDS & LIVERPOOL CANAL
POOLSTOCK
WARRINGTON LA.
WARRINGTON ROAD
A577 TO WARRINGTON
B5238 TO A49
CANAL
POTTERY ROAD
RIVER DOUGLAS
CORPORATION ST.
Greyhound Track ★

WINCHESTER

Scale 0 ¼ Mile

B3420 TO ANDOVER
ANDOVER ROAD
WORTHY LANE
WORTHY ROAD
HYDE STREET
Coach Park
A3090 TO A33, M3 & BASINGSTOKE
Hyde Gateway ★
NORTH WALLS RECREATION GROUND
RIVER ITCHEN
STOCKBRIDGE ROAD
A272 TO SALISBURY
ST. PAUL'S HILL
CITY RD.
NORTHWALLS
Sports Centre ★
TO BY-PASS
EASTON LA.
Oram's Arbour
CLIFTON TER.
UPR. HIGH ST.
SUSSEX ST.
TOWER STREET
Library ★
STAPLE GARDENS
ST. PETER ST.
PARCHMENT ST.
UPPER BROOK ST.
MIDDLE BROOK ST.
FR BROOK ST
UNION ST.
EASTGATE ST.
Police Station ★
WALES ST.
B3404 TO ALTON
MAGDALEN HILL
ROMSEY ROAD
A3090 TO ROMSEY (To Hospital)
JEWRY ST.
ST. GEORGE'S ST.
G.P.O.
Friarsgate ★
ST. JOHN'S ST.
BEGGARS LANE
Westgate ★
The Castle ★
County Offices
HIGH STREET
SILVER HILL
King Alfred's Statue ★
BRIDGE ST.
ST. GILES'S HILL
Barracks ★
ST. THOMAS ST.
THE SQUARE
MARKET LANE
Museum ★
INFORMATION CENTRE
Guildhall ★
COLEBROOK ST.
CHESIL ST.
SOUTHGATE STREET
ST. JAMES LANE
ST. SWITHUNS ST.
ST. SYMONDS ST.
Cathedral ★
EAST HILL
B3406 TO PETERSFIELD
CANNON ST.
Cheyney Court ★
Kingsgate ★
Wolvesey Castle ★
ST. CROSS ROAD
A333 TO SOUTHAMPTON & M27
MICHAELS RD.
ROMAN ROAD
COLLEGE ST.
COLLEGE WALK
College ★
WHARF HILL
A272 TO WINCHESTER BY-PASS
BAR END ROAD
KINGSGATE
PLAYING FIELDS

WINDSOR

Scale 0 ¼ ½ Mile

ETONWICK ROAD
TO SLOUGH
Racecourse ★
A332 TO M4 AND SLOUGH
RIVER
ETON
HIGH STREET
Eton College ★
Lock ★
SOUTH MEADOW
THE BROCAS
CLEWER PARK
THAMES
Swimming Pool ★
Windsor Bridge (PEDESTRIAN ONLY)
Station
DATCHET RD.
B470 TO DATCHET
MAIDENHEAD RD.
A308 TO MAIDENHEAD
ARTHUR ROAD
BARRY AVENUE
Coach Park
THAMES ST.
Station
The Castle ★
VANSITTART ROAD
OXFORD RD.
Shopping Centre
PEASCOD ST.
HIGH STREET
Guildhall ★
INFORMATION CENTRE
CLARENCE ROAD
G.P.O.
Royal Mews ★
CLARENCE ROAD
B3024 TO TWYFORD
IMPERIAL ROAD
VICTORIA ST.
SHEET ST.
THE HOME PARK
Police Station ★
Municipal Offices
ALMA RD.
E. Berks College ★
Victoria Barracks ★
KINGS ROAD
St. John's House ★
ST. LEONARD'S ROAD
ALEXANDRA RD.
FRANCES ROAD
Chapel ★
SPRINGFIELD ROAD
OSBORNE ROAD
BOLTON AVE.
THE LONG WALK
Haileybury & ISC School ★
BULKELEY AVENUE
Combermere Barracks ★
Bus Station ★
King Edward VII Hospital ★
ST. LEONARD'S ROAD
B3022 TO WINKFIELD
BOLTON ROAD
KING'S ROAD
A332 TO ASCOT
HOG COMMON
HOG ROAD
ALBERT ROAD
A308 TO STAINES

WOLVERHAMPTON

Scale 0 ¼ ½ Mile

A449 TO STAFFORD
LOWE STREET
Police Station ★
LEICESTER ST.
DUNSTALL RD.
STAFFORD RD.
WATERLOO RD.
NORTH RD.
STAFFORD ST.
CANAL
A460 TO CANNOCK & M6
CANNOCK ROAD
HILTON STREET
SPRINGFIELD ROAD
NEWHAMPTON ROAD
STAVELEY RD.
MOLINEUX ST.
NORTH ST.
Wolves F.C. ★
Art College ★
RING ROAD
CLEVELL ST.
A4124 TO BROWNHILLS
WEDNESFIELD RD.
SUN ST.
PARK ROAD EAST
WEST PARK
PARK ROAD WEST
College ★
BROAD ST.
A41 TO WHITCHURCH
BATH RD.
Town Hall ★
INFORMATION CENTRE
QUEENS SQUARE
Station
A4 TO WALSALL & M6
HORSELEY FIELDS
LICHFIELD ST.
CORN HILL
A454 TO WALSALL
MERRIDALE RD.
CHAPEL ASH
DARLINGTON ST.
AA
PIPERS ROW
G.P.O.
WALSALL STREET
Library ★
BILSTON ST.
A454
WORCESTER ST.
VICTORIA ST.
Cleveland ST.
CLEVELAND ROAD
COMMERCIAL RD.
CANAL
GREAT BRICKKILN STREET
TEMPLE ST.
SNOW HILL
Royal Hospital ★
A41 TO WEDNESBURY & M6
RING ROAD
MERRIDALE STREET
PENN ROAD
VICARAGE RD.
A4123 TO DUDLEY
OWEN ROAD
LEA ROAD
Police Station ★
BIRMINGHAM RD.
DUDLEY ROAD
ALL SAINTS ROAD
STEELHOUSE LANE
A4123 TO BIRMINGHAM
A449 TO KIDDERMINSTER

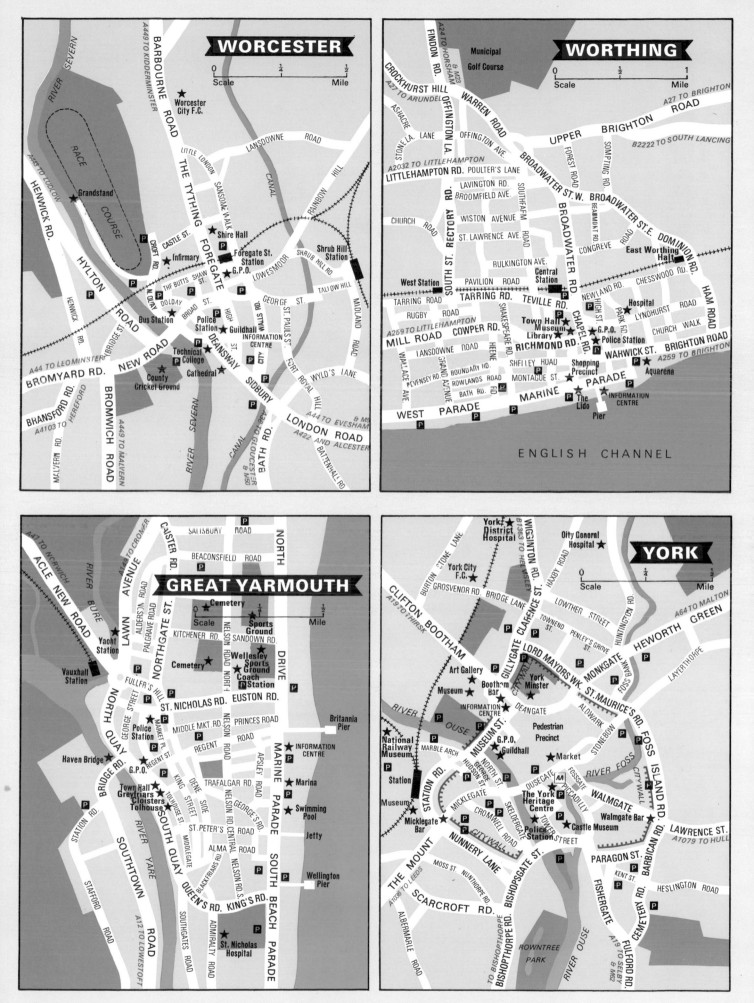

WORCESTER

Scale 0 ¼ ½ Mile

RIVER SEVERN
A449 TO KIDDERMINSTER
BARBOURNE ROAD
★ Worcester City F.C.
LANSDOWNE ROAD
LITTLE LONDON
THE TYTHING
SANSOME WALK
CANAL
RAINBOW HILL
RACE COURSE
A456 TO LUDLOW
HENWICK RD.
★ Grandstand
CROFT RD.
CASTLE ST.
★ Shire Hall
FOREGATE
P Foregate St. Station
G.P.O.
LOWESMOOR
SHRUB HILL RD.
Shrub Hill Station ■
★ Infirmary
HYLTON ROAD
HENWICK RD.
P
THE BUTTS SHAW ST.
N. QUAY
DOLDAY
Broad St.
P
George St.
St. PAULS ST.
FORT ROYAL HILL
TALLOW HILL
MIDLAND ROAD
Bus Station
Police Station ■
★ Guildhall
INFORMATION CENTRE
ST. PAULS ST.
ST. MARTINS
P
A44 TO LEOMINSTER
(BRIDGE ST.)
NEW ROAD
DEANSWAY
★ Technical College
CITY
WYLD'S LANE
BROMYARD RD.
County Cricket Ground ★
Cathedral ★
SIDBURY
P
LONDON ROAD
A44 TO EVESHAM & M5
BRANSFORD RD.
BROMWICH ROAD
A4103 TO HEREFORD
A449 TO MALVERN
McLVERN RD.
RIVER SEVERN
CANAL
BATH RD.
A38 TO GLOUCESTER & M50
A422 AND ALCESTER
A449 TO GLOUCESTER
BATTENHALL RD.

WORTHING

Scale 0 ½ 1 Mile

Municipal Golf Course
FINDON RD.
A24 TO HORSHAM
B23 TO
CROCKHURST HILL
A27 TO ARUNDEL
WARREN ROAD
OFFINGTON LA.
UPPER BRIGHTON ROAD
A27 TO BRIGHTON
ASHACRE LANE
STONE LA. LANE
OFFINGTON AVE.
BROADWATER ST. W.
FOREST ROAD
SOMPTING RD.
B2222 TO SOUTH LANCING
A2032 TO LITTLEHAMPTON
LITTLEHAMPTON RD. POULTER'S LANE
LAVINGTON RD.
SOUTHFARM
BROADWATER ST. E.
BEAUMONT RD.
DOMINION RD.
BROOMFIELD AVE.
CHURCH ROAD
RECTORY RD.
WISTON AVENUE
ST. LAWRENCE AVE.
ROAD
CONGREVE
East Worthing Halt ■
RULKINGTON AVE.
BROADWATER RD.
NEWLAND RD.
CHESSWOOD RD.
West Station ■
PAVILION ROAD
Central Station ■
P
HIGH ST.
Hospital ★
HAM ROAD
TARRING ROAD
TARRING RD.
TEVILLE RD.
NEWLAND RD.
LYNDHURST ROAD
PARK RD.
CHURCH WALK
RUGBY ROAD
CHAPEL RD.
G.P.O.
MILL ROAD
COWPER RD.
Town Hall ★ Museum
Library ★
RICHMOND RD.
Police Station ■
BRIGHTON ROAD
LANSDOWNE ROAD
HEENE
SHAKESPEARE RD.
WARWICK ST. ★ ■ A259 TO BRIGHTON
WALLACE AVE.
GRAND AVENUE
PEVENSEY RD.
BOUNDARY RD.
SHELLEY ROAD
A259 TO LITTLEHAMPTON
ROWLANDS ROAD
MONTAGUE ST.
Shopping Precinct
PARADE
Aquarena ■
BATH RD.
WEST PARADE
MARINE
P
★ The Lido
INFORMATION CENTRE
Pier ★

ENGLISH CHANNEL

GREAT YARMOUTH

SALISBURY ROAD
P
A47 TO NORWICH
A149 TO CROMER
BEACONSFIELD ROAD
NORTH
RIVER BURE
ACLE NEW ROAD
LAWN AVENUE
CAISTER RD.
NORTHGATE ST.
Cemetery ★
Scale 0 ¼ ½ Mile
Sports Ground
SANDOWN RD.
Yacht Station ★
ALDERSON RD.
PALGRAVE ROAD
KITCHENER RD.
NELSON ROAD NORTH
Cemetery ★
Wellesley Sports Ground
P Coach Station
DRIVE
Vauxhall Station ■
FULLER'S HILL
ST. NICHOLAS RD. EUSTON RD.
NORTH QUAY
GEORGE STREET
MIDDLE MKT. RD.
PRINCES ROAD
Britannia Pier
Police Station ■
Market Pl.
NELSON ROAD CENTRAL
MARINE PARADE
★ INFORMATION CENTRE
REGENT
Haven Bridge ★
BRIDGE RD.
G.P.O. ■
REGENT ST.
TRAFALGAR RD.
APSLEY ROAD
★ Marina
STATION RD.
Town Hall ★
Greyfriars ★
Cloisters
Tolhouse ★
KING STREET
DENE SIDE
GEORGE'S RD.
★ Swimming Pool
RIVER YARE
SOUTH QUAY
TOLHOUSE ST.
ST. PETER'S ROAD
NELSON RD. CENTRAL
Jetty
SOUTHTOWN
MIDDLEGATE
ALMA ROAD
BLACKFRIARS RD.
NELSON RD. S.
P
Wellington Pier ■
P
SOUTHGATES ROAD
QUEEN'S RD. KING'S RD.
SOUTH BEACH PARADE
STAFFORD ROAD
A12 TO LOWESTOFT
ADMIRALTY ROAD
St. Nicholas Hospital ★
P

YORK

York District Hospital ★
B1363 TO HELMSLEY
WIGGINTON RD.
City General Hospital ★
Scale 0 ¼ ½ Mile
BURTON STONE LANE
York City F.C. ★
GROSVENOR RD.
BRIDGE LANE
HANBY ROAD
HUNTINGTON RD.
A19 TO THIRSK
CLIFTON BOOTHAM
LOWTHER STREET
A64 TO MALTON
GILLYGATE
CLARENCE ST.
TOWNEND ST.
PENLEY'S GROVE ST.
HEWORTH GREEN
LORD MAYORS WK.
MONKGATE
LAYERTHORPE
Art Gallery ★
ST. MAURICE'S RD.
CITYWALL
Museum ★ ■
Boothom ★ Bar
York Minster ★
FOSS ISLAND RD.
RIVER OUSE
INFORMATION CENTRE
DEANGATE
ALDWARK
CITYWALL
National Railway Museum ★
MUSEUM ST.
STONEBOW
Pedestrian Precinct
Marble Arch
G.P.O. ■
Guildhall ★
★ Market
MARBLE ARCH
MUSEUM STREET
NORTH ST.
HUDSON ST.
The York Heritage Centre ★
PICCADILLY
WALMGATE
RIVER FOSS
Station ■
STATION RD.
OUSEGATE
FOSSGATE
CITYWALL
Museum ★
MICKLEGATE
George St.
SKELDERGATE
Police Station ■
Tower ★
Castle Museum ★
Walmgate Bar ■
Micklegate Bar ★
CROMWELL ROAD
Street
BARBICAN RD.
LAWRENCE ST.
THE MOUNT
NUNNERY LANE
CITYWALL
BISHOPGATE ST.
PARAGON ST.
A1079 TO HULL
A1036 TO LEEDS
MOSS ST.
NUNTHORPE RD.
KENT ST.
FISHERGATE
SCARCROFT RD.
TO BISHOPTHORPE
BISHOPTHORPE RD.
ALBEMARLE ROAD
ROWNTREE PARK
RIVER OUSE
CEMETERY RD.
FULFORD RD.
HESLINGTON ROAD
A19 TO SELBY & M62

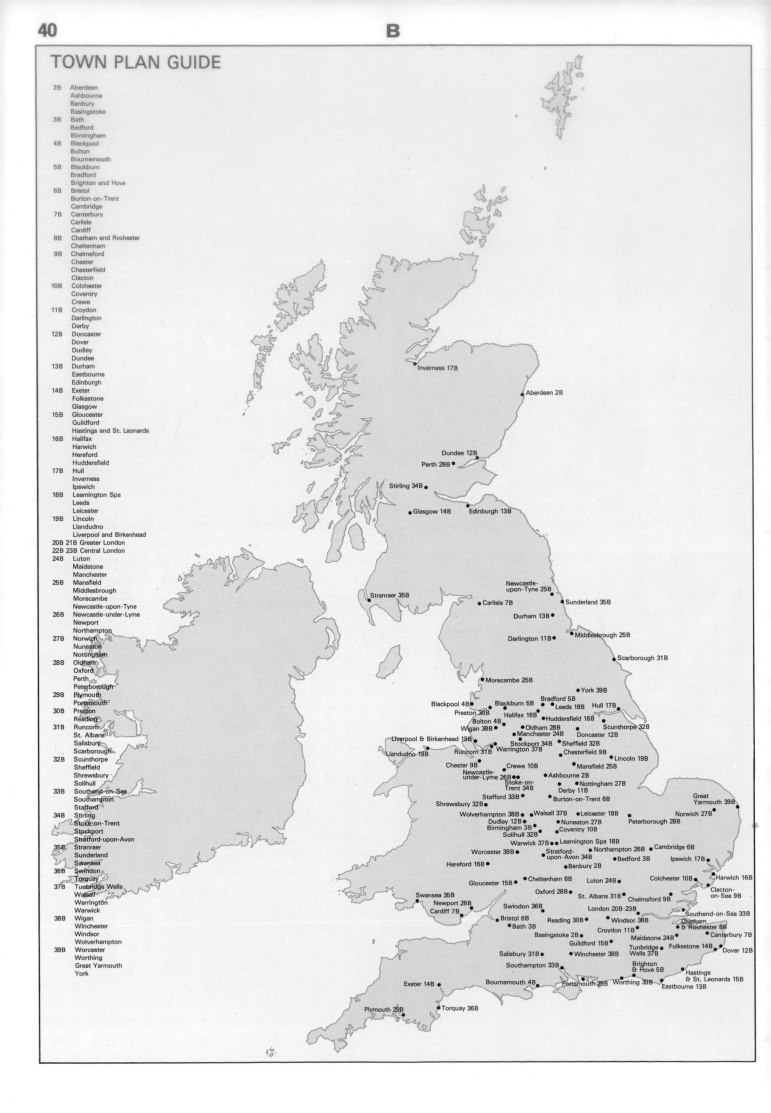

TOWN PLAN GUIDE

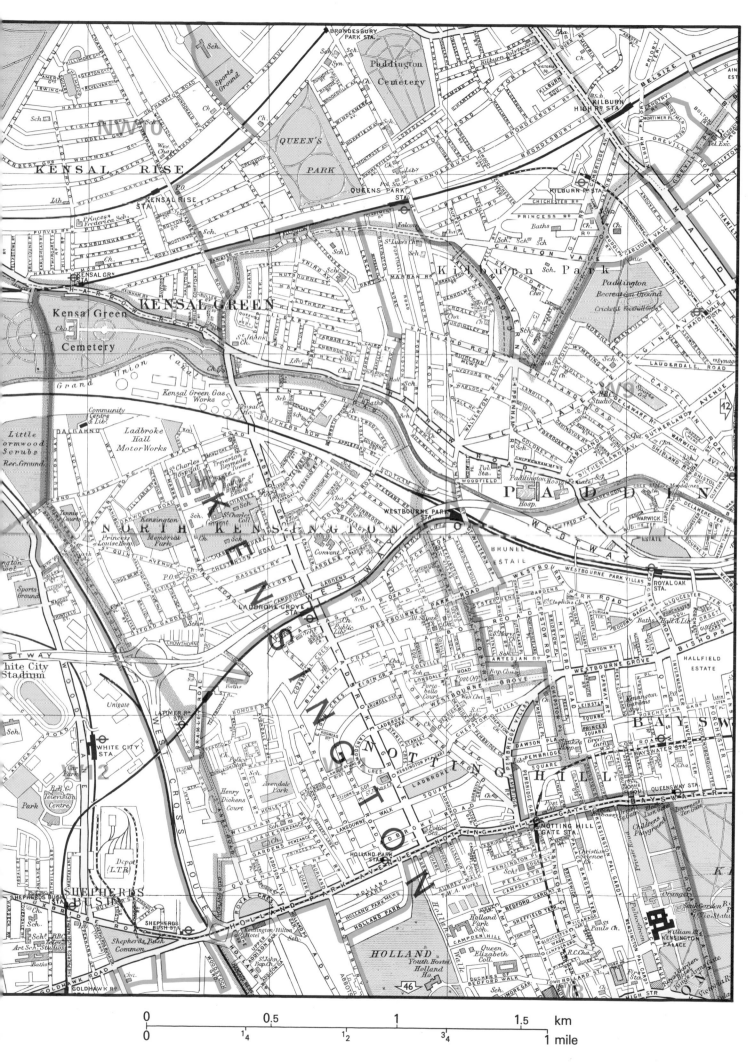

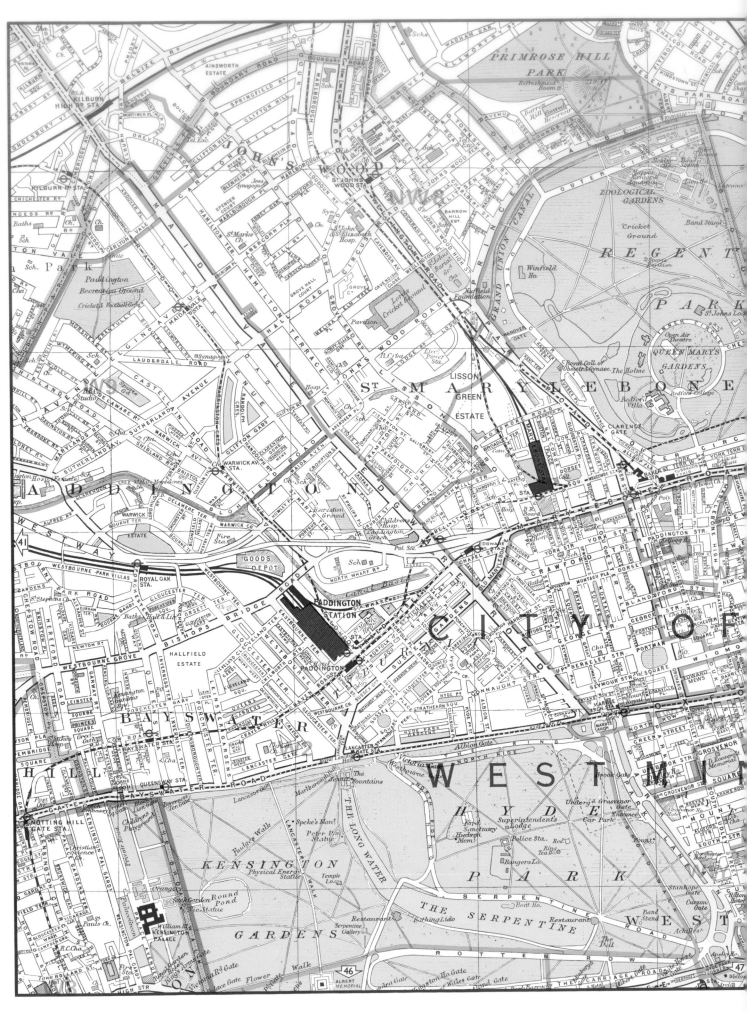

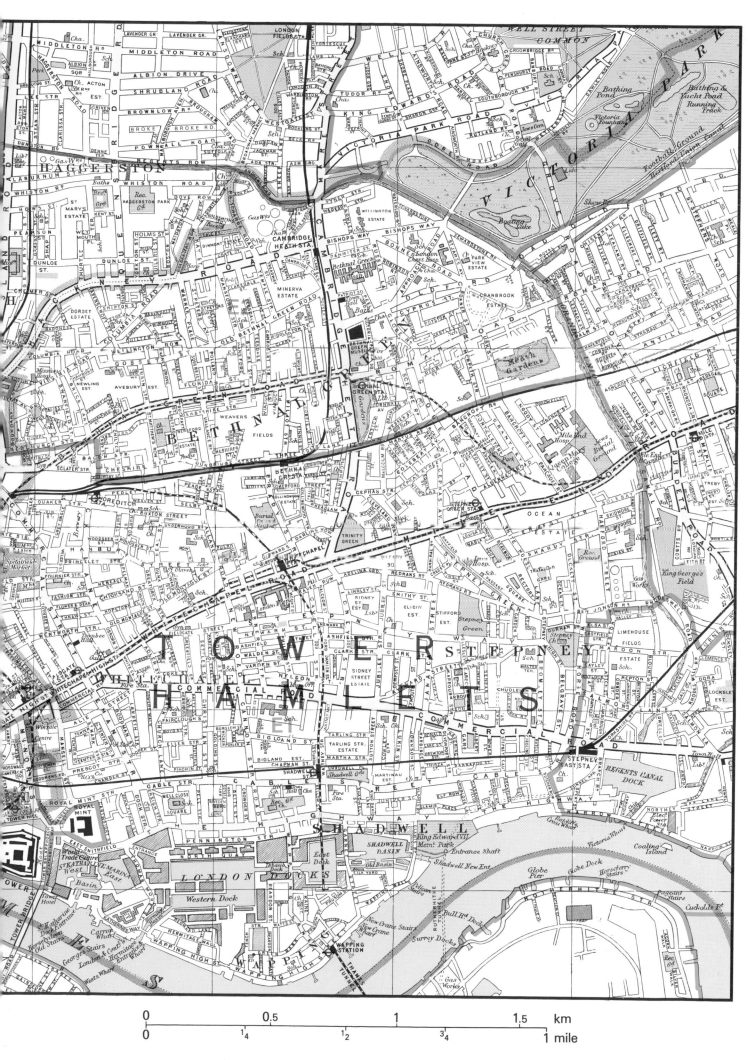

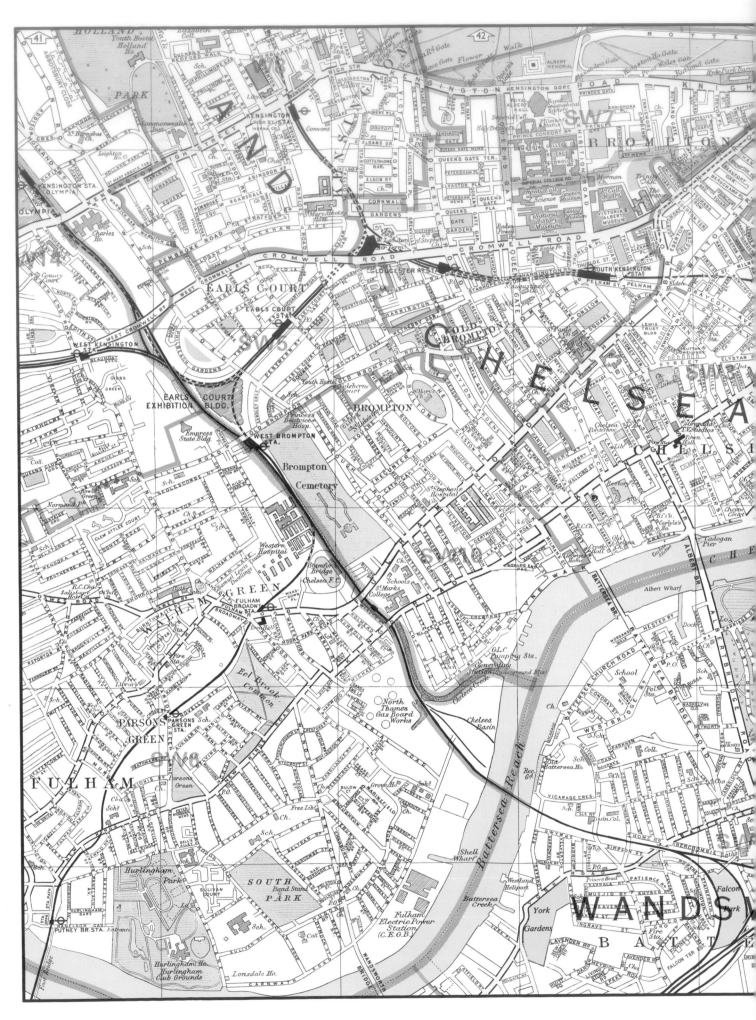

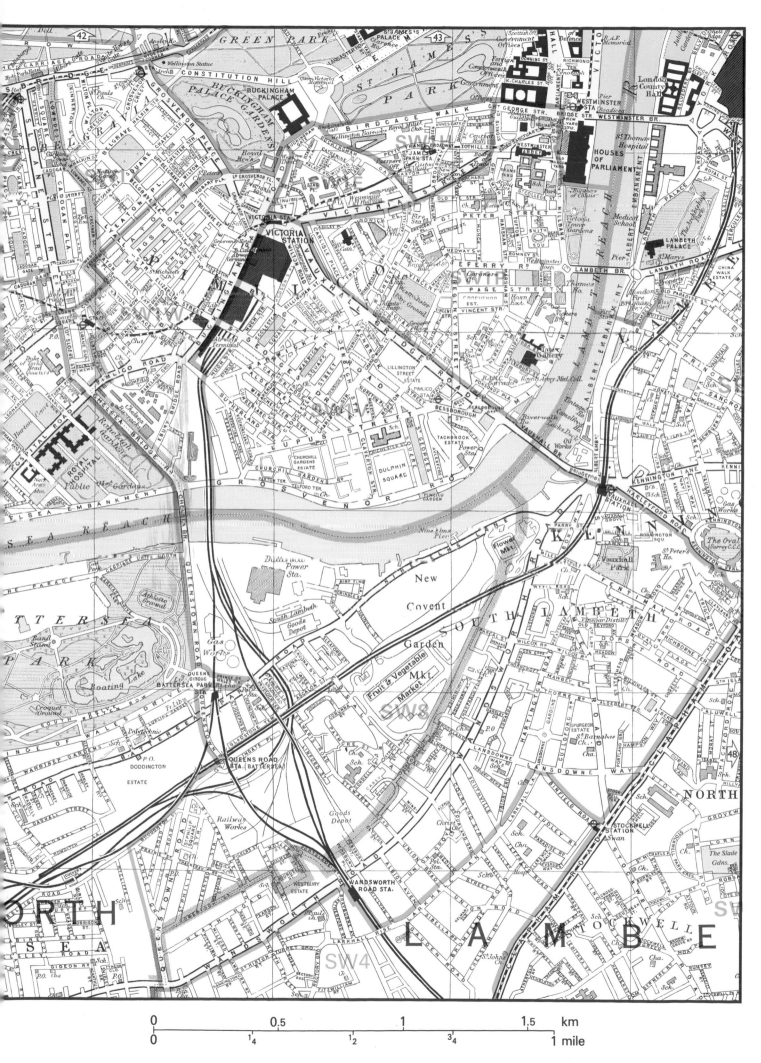

SPECIAL TOPIC MAPS

NORTHERN IRELAND
4. BALLYMONEY
5. MOYLE
6. LARNE
12. ANTRIM
13. NEWTOWNABBEY
14. CARRICKFERGUS
15. NORTH DOWN
16. ARDS
17. CASTLEREAGH
18. BELFAST
19. LISBURN
20. CRAIGAVON
24. NEWRY & MOURNE
25. BANBRIDGE
26. DOWN

CLWYD (See p. 6C)
1. COLWYN
2. RHUDDLAN
3. DELYN
4. ALYN & DEESIDE
5. WREXHAM-MAELOR
6. GLYNDWR
GWYNEDD (See p. 6C)
1. YNYS MON - ISLE OF ANGLESEY
2. ARFON
3. DWYFOR
4. ABERCONWY
5. MEIRIONNYDD

BORDERS (See p. 4C)
1. TWEEDDALE
2. ETTRICK & LAUDERDALE
3. BERWICKSHIRE
4. ROXBURGH
DUMFRIES & GALLOWAY
1. WIGTOWN
2. STEWARTRY
3. NITHSDALE
4. ANNANDALE & ESKDALE
LOTHIAN (See p. 3C)
STRATHCLYDE (See p. 2C, 4C)

CHESHIRE
1. WARRINGTON
2. HALTON
3. ELLESMERE PORT & NESTON
4. VALE ROYAL
5. MACCLESFIELD
6. CHESTER
7. CREWE & NANTWICH
8. CONGLETON
CLEVELAND
1. HARTLEPOOL
2. STOCKTON-ON-TEES
3. MIDDLESBROUGH
4. LANGBAURGH
CUMBRIA
1. CARLISLE
2. ALLERDALE
3. EDEN
4. COPELAND
5. SOUTH LAKELAND
6. BARROW-IN-FURNESS
DERBYSHIRE (See p. 7C)
1. HIGH PEAK
2. WEST DERBYSHIRE
3. NORTH EAST DERBYSHIRE
4. CHESTERFIELD
5. BOLSOVER
6. AMBER VALLEY
7. EREWASH
8. DERBY
9. SOUTH DERBYSHIRE
DURHAM
1. CHESTER-LE-STREET
2. DERWENTSIDE
3. DURHAM
4. EASINGTON
5. SEDGEFIELD
6. WEAR VALLEY
7. TEESDALE
8. DARLINGTON
HUMBERSIDE
1. NORTH WOLDS
2. HOLDERNESS
3. KINGSTON UPON HULL
4. BEVERLEY
5. BOOTHFERRY
6. SCUNTHORPE
7. GLANFORD
8. GREAT GRIMSBY
9. CLEETHORPES

LANCASHIRE
1. LANCASTER
2. WYRE
3. BLACKPOOL
4. FYLDE
5. PRESTON
6. RIBBLE VALLEY
7. PENDLE
8. BURNLEY
9. ROSSENDALE
10. HYNDBURN
11. BLACKBURN
12. CHORLEY
13. SOUTH RIBBLE
14. WEST LANCASHIRE
LINCOLNSHIRE (See p. 7C)
1. WEST LINDSEY
2. LINCOLN
3. EAST LINDSEY
4. NORTH KESTEVEN
5. BOSTON
6. SOUTH KESTEVEN
7. SOUTH HOLLAND
MANCHESTER, GREATER
1. WIGAN
2. BOLTON
3. BURY
4. ROCHDALE
5. OLDHAM
6. TAMESIDE
7. STOCKPORT
8. MANCHESTER
9. SALFORD
10. TRAFFORD
MERSEYSIDE
1. WIRRAL
2. SEFTON
3. LIVERPOOL
4. KNOWSLEY
5. ST HELENS
NORTHUMBERLAND
1. BERWICK-UPON-TWEED
2. ALNWICK
3. CASTLE MORPETH
4. WANSBECK
5. BLYTH VALLEY
6. TYNEDALE
NOTTINGHAMSHIRE (See p 7C)
1. BASSETLAW
2. MANSFIELD
3. NEWARK
4. ASHFIELD
5. GEDLING
6. BROXTOWE
7. NOTTINGHAM
8. RUSHCLIFFE
SHROPSHIRE (See p. 7C)
STAFFORDSHIRE (See p. 6C)
1. NEWCASTLE-UNDER-LYME
2. STOKE ON TRENT
3. STAFFORDSHIRE MOORLANDS
4. STAFFORD
5. EAST STAFFORDSHIRE
6. SOUTH STAFFORDSHIRE
7. CANNOCK CHASE
8. LICHFIELD
9. TAMWORTH
TYNE & WEAR
1. NEWCASTLE UPON TYNE
2. NORTH TYNESIDE
3. SOUTH TYNESIDE
4. GATESHEAD
5. SUNDERLAND
YORKSHIRE, NORTH
1. SCARBOROUGH
2. RYEDALE
3. HAMBLETON
4. RICHMONDSHIRE
5. CRAVEN
6. HARROGATE
7. SELBY
8. YORK
YORKSHIRE, SOUTH
1. BARNSLEY
2. DONCASTER
3. ROTHERHAM
4. SHEFFIELD
YORKSHIRE, WEST
1. CALDERDALE
2. BRADFORD
3. LEEDS
4. WAKEFIELD
5. KIRKLEES

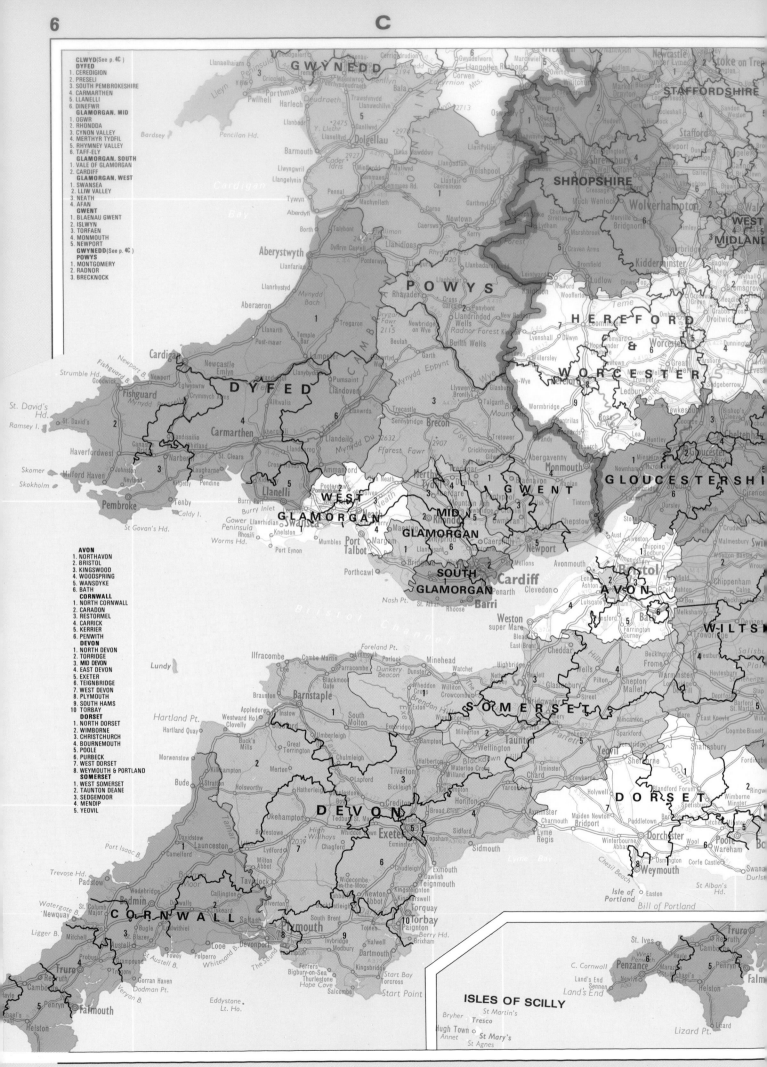

0   10   20   30   40   50 Miles
0 10 20 30 40 50 60 70 80 Kilometres

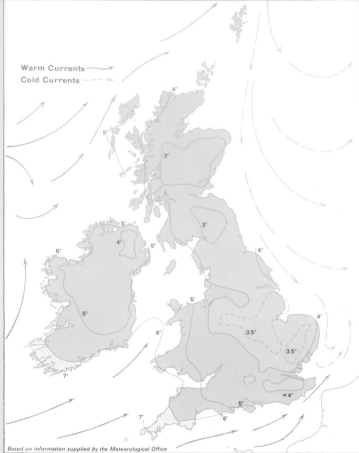

Warm Currents ⟶
Cold Currents ⟶

Based on information supplied by the Meteorological Office

TEMPERATURE (Reduced to Sea Level)
JANUARY *The Figures indicate the Temperature in °C*

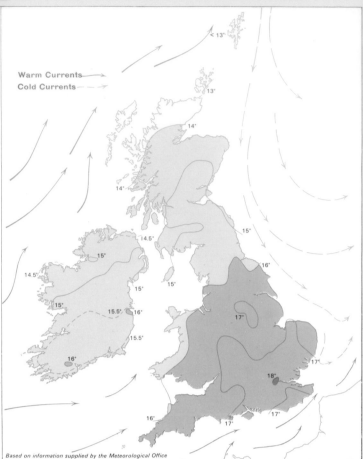

Warm Currents ⟶
Cold Currents ⟶

Based on information supplied by the Meteorological Office

TEMPERATURE (Reduced to Sea Level)
JULY *The Figures indicate the Temperature in °C*

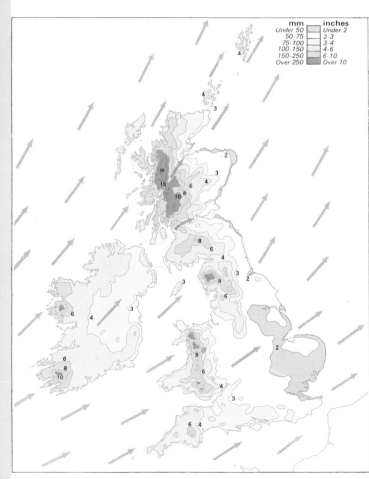

mm	inches
Under 50	Under 2
50-75	2-3
75-100	3-4
100-150	4-6
150-250	6-10
Over 250	Over 10

PRECIPITATION *The Figures indicate the Precipitation in Inches.*
JANUARY *The Prevailing Winds are shown by arrows*

mm	inches
Under 50	Under 2
50-75	2-3
75-100	3-4
100-150	4-6
Over 150	Over 6

PRECIPITATION *The Figures indicate the Precipitation in Inches.*
JULY *The Prevailing Winds are shown by arrows*

1:10 800 000

© John Bartholomew & Son Ltd

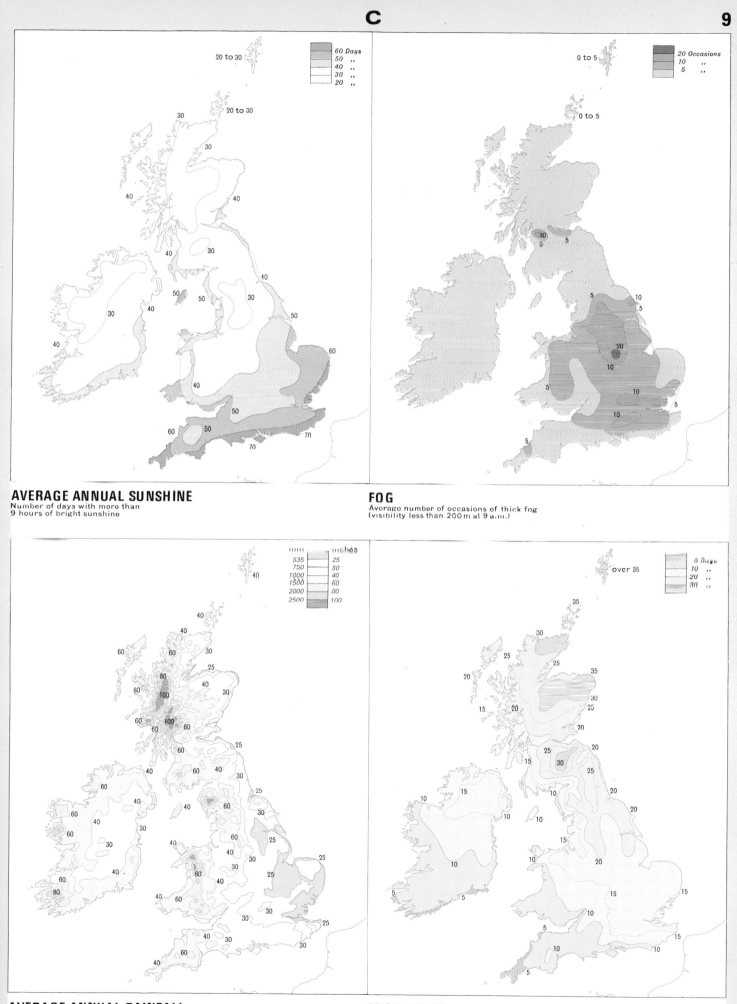

AVERAGE ANNUAL SUNSHINE
Number of days with more than
9 hours of bright sunshine

FOG
Average number of occasions of thick fog
(visibility less than 200 m at 9 a.m.)

AVERAGE ANNUAL RAINFALL *The Figures indicate the Precipitation in Inches.*

SNOW COVER
Average number of days with snow
falling on low ground.(0-60 m.)

1:10 800 000

© John Bartholomew & Son Ltd

LAND USE

Forest and Woodland
Heath, Moor and Rough Pasture
Meadow and Grassland
Mixed Wood and Grassland
Mixed Arable and Grassland
Predominantly Arable Land
Nursery Gardens and Orchards
Built-up Areas

1:6 800 000

PRINCIPAL CROPS

Wheat, Barley and Oats
Barley and Oats
Oats
Cattle Pastures
Sheep Grazing

1:6 800 000

© John Bartholomew & Son Ltd

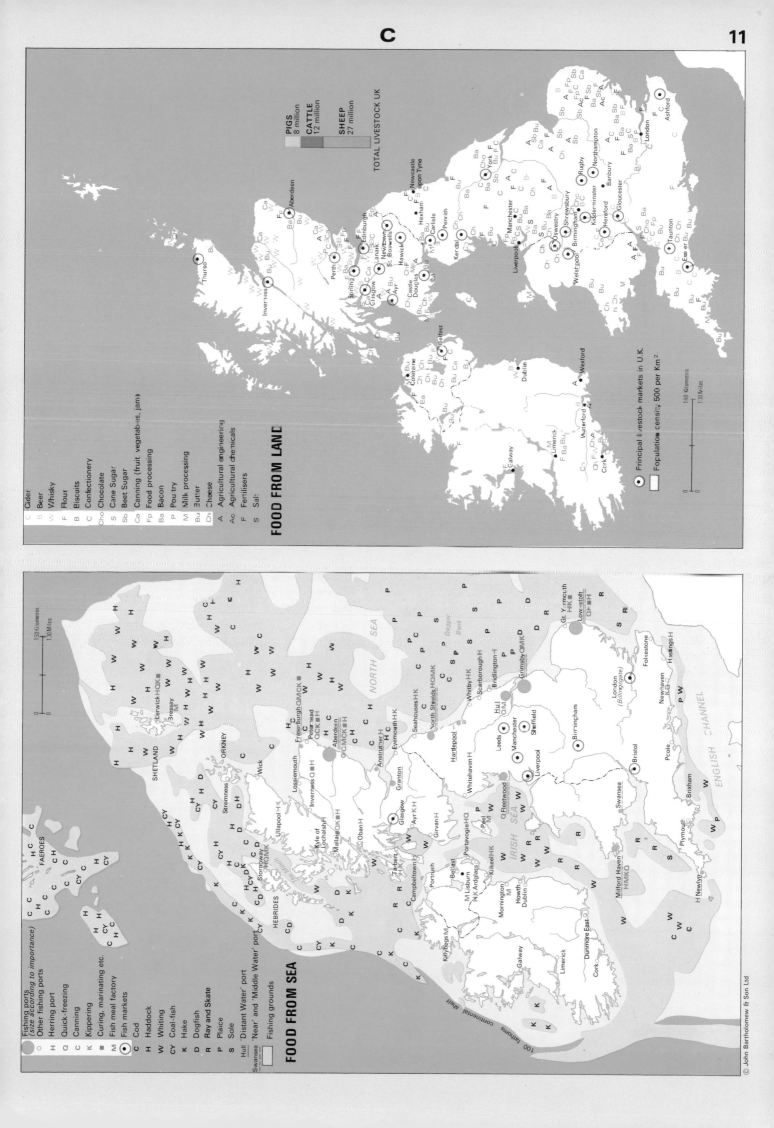

FOOD FROM SEA

FOOD FROM LAND

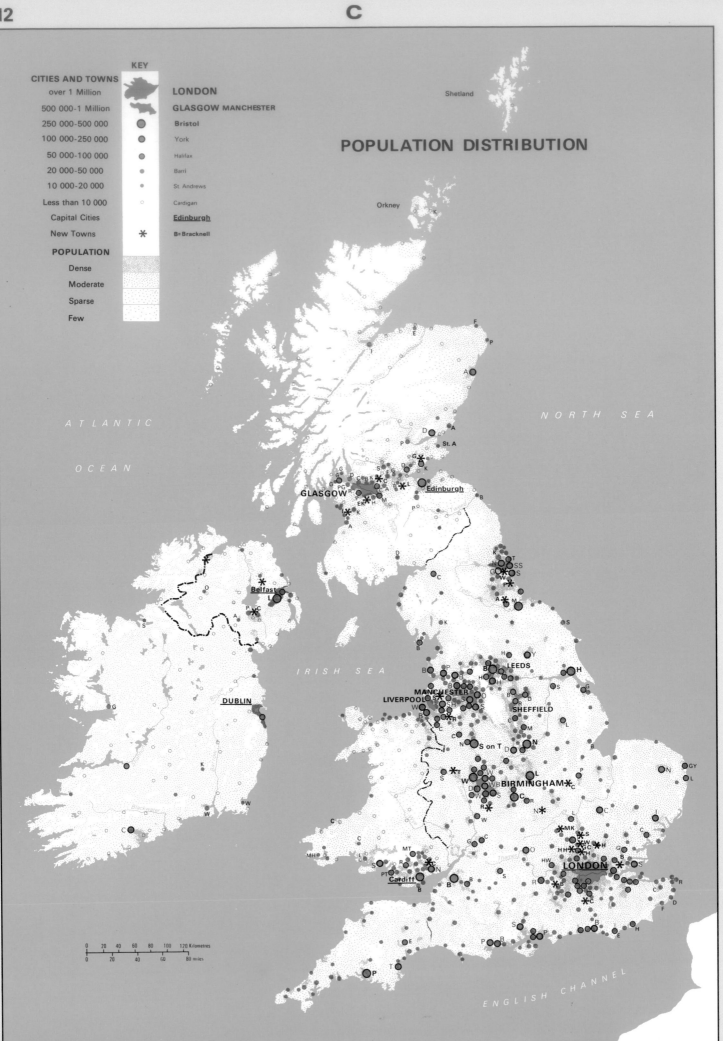

POPULATION DISTRIBUTION

KEY

CITIES AND TOWNS

over 1 Million	**LONDON**
500 000-1 Million	**GLASGOW MANCHESTER**
250 000-500 000	**Bristol**
100 000-250 000	York
50 000-100 000	Halifax
20 000-50 000	Barri
10 000-20 000	St. Andrews
Less than 10 000	Cardigan
Capital Cities	**Edinburgh**
New Towns ✳	B= Bracknell

POPULATION

Dense

Moderate

Sparse

Few

Shetland

Orkney

ATLANTIC

OCEAN

NORTH SEA

St. A

GLASGOW   **Edinburgh**

Belfast

DUBLIN

IRISH SEA

LEEDS

MANCHESTER
LIVERPOOL   **SHEFFIELD**

S on T

BIRMINGHAM

Cardiff

LONDON

ENGLISH CHANNEL

| 0 | 20 | 40 | 60 | 80 | 100 | 120 Kilometres |
| 0 | 20 | 40 | 60 | | 80 miles |

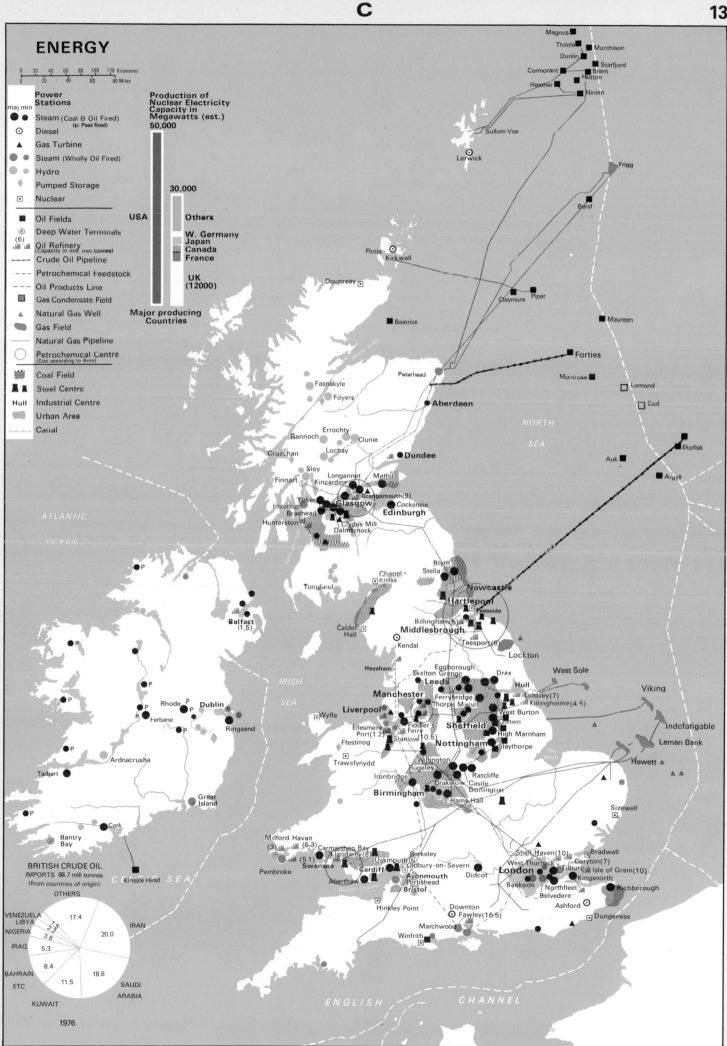

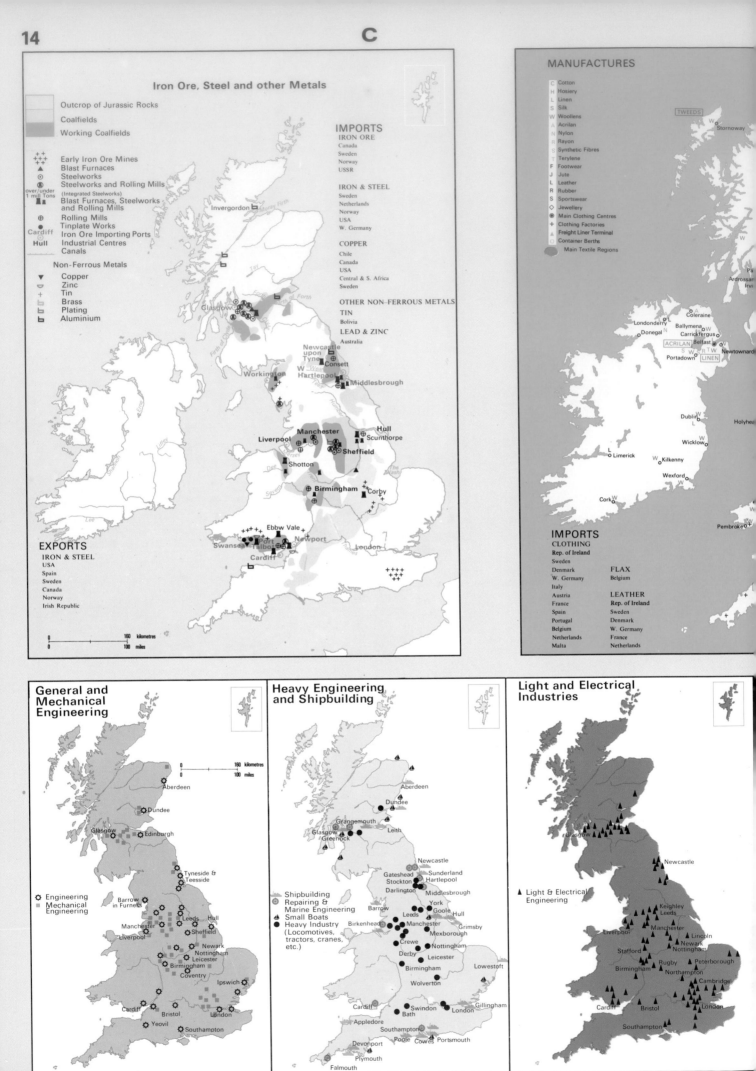

14 C

Iron Ore, Steel and other Metals

- Outcrop of Jurassic Rocks
- Coalfields
- Working Coalfields
- Early Iron Ore Mines
- Blast Furnaces
- Steelworks
- Steelworks and Rolling Mills (Integrated Steelworks)
- over/under 1 mill Tons
- Blast Furnaces, Steelworks, Steelworks and Rolling Mills
- Rolling Mills
- Tinplate Works
- Cardiff Iron Ore Importing Ports
- Hull Industrial Centres
- Canals

Non-Ferrous Metals
- Copper
- Zinc
- Tin
- Brass
- Plating
- Aluminium

IMPORTS
IRON ORE
Canada
Sweden
Norway
USSR

IRON & STEEL
Sweden
Netherlands
Norway
USA
W. Germany

COPPER
Chile
Canada
USA
Central & S. Africa
Sweden

OTHER NON-FERROUS METALS
TIN
Bolivia
LEAD & ZINC
Australia

EXPORTS
IRON & STEEL
USA
Spain
Sweden
Canada
Norway
Irish Republic

Labels: Invergordon, Glasgow, Workington, Newcastle upon Tyne, Consett, W. Hartlepool, Middlesbrough, Manchester, Liverpool, Hull, Scunthorpe, Sheffield, Shotton, Birmingham, Corby, Ebbw Vale, Newport, Swansea, Port Talbot, Cardiff, London

Scale: 0 160 kilometres / 0 100 miles

MANUFACTURES
- C Cotton
- H Hosiery
- L Linen
- S Silk
- W Woollens
- A Acrilan
- N Nylon
- R Rayon
- S Synthetic Fibres
- T Terylene
- F Footwear
- J Jute
- L Leather
- R Rubber
- S Sportswear
- Jewellery
- Main Clothing Centres
- Clothing Factories
- Freight Liner Terminal
- Container Berths
- Main Textile Regions

Labels: Stornoway, Londonderry, Coleraine, Ballymena, Donegal, Carrickfergus, Belfast, Newtownards, Portadown, ACRILAN, LINEN, TWEEDS, Dublin, Holyhead, Wicklow, Limerick, Kilkenny, Wexford, Cork, Pembroke, Ardrossan, Irvi...

IMPORTS
CLOTHING
Rep. of Ireland
Sweden
Denmark
W. Germany
Italy
Austria
France
Spain
Portugal
Belgium
Netherlands
Malta

FLAX
Belgium

LEATHER
Rep. of Ireland
Sweden
Denmark
W. Germany
France
Netherlands

General and Mechanical Engineering
- Engineering
- Mechanical Engineering

Labels: Aberdeen, Dundee, Glasgow, Edinburgh, Tyneside & Teesside, Barrow in Furness, Leeds, Hull, Manchester, Sheffield, Liverpool, Newark, Nottingham, Leicester, Birmingham, Coventry, Ipswich, Cardiff, Bristol, London, Yeovil, Southampton

Scale: 0 160 kilometres / 0 100 miles

Heavy Engineering and Shipbuilding
- Shipbuilding Repairing & Marine Engineering
- Small Boats
- Heavy Industry (Locomotives, tractors, cranes, etc.)

Labels: Aberdeen, Dundee, Grangemouth, Leith, Glasgow, Greenock, Newcastle, Gateshead, Sunderland, Stockton, Hartlepool, Darlington, Middlesbrough, York, Goole, Hull, Barrow, Birkenhead, Leeds, Manchester, Mexborough, Grimsby, Crewe, Nottingham, Derby, Leicester, Lowestoft, Birmingham, Wolverton, Gillingham, Cardiff, Swindon, London, Bath, Appledore, Southampton, Poole, Cowes, Portsmouth, Devonport, Plymouth, Falmouth

Light and Electrical Industries
- Light & Electrical Engineering

Labels: Glasgow, Newcastle, Keighley, Leeds, Liverpool, Manchester, Lincoln, Newark, Nottingham, Stafford, Rugby, Peterborough, Birmingham, Northampton, Cambridge, Cardiff, Bristol, London, Southampton

© John Bartholomew & Son Ltd

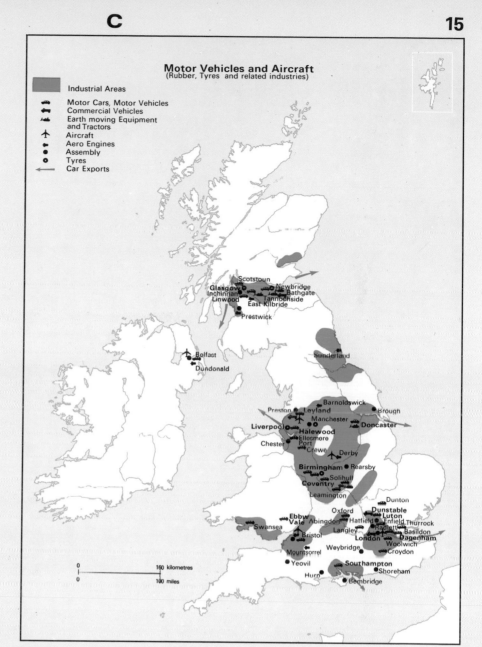

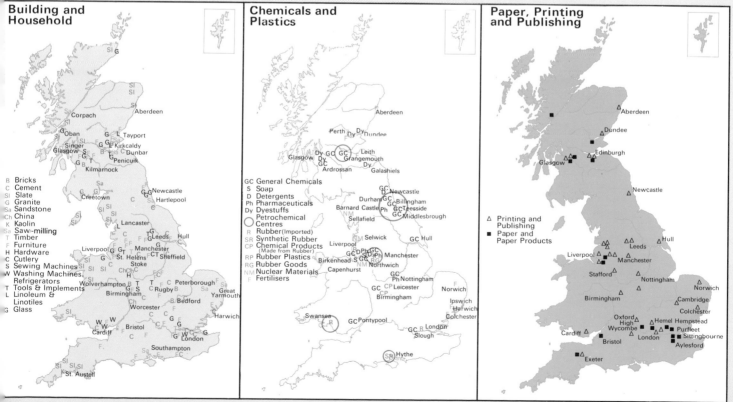

IMPORTS

FOOTWEAR
Rep. of Ireland
W. Germany
Poland
Czechoslovakia
France
Italy
Austria
Spain
Switzerland

TEXTILES
Rep. of Ireland
W. Germany
Italy
Austria
Switzerland
France
Spain
Belgium
Netherlands

HIDES, FUR & SKIN
Rep. of Ireland
Norway
Finland
W. Germany
Poland
France

WOOD
Finland
Sweden
Norway

TWEEDS
WOOLLENS
CARPETS
KNITWEAR
LACE
WORSTEDS
CARPETS
WOOLLENS
HOSIERY
LACE
NYLON
FOOTWEAR
CARPETS

Inverness
Aberdeen
Dundee
Leven
Kirkcaldy
Dunfermline
Glasgow
Edinburgh
Lanark
Kilmarnock
Darvel
Galashiels
Hawick
Dumfries
Carlisle
Newcastle upon Tyne
Kendal
Stockton
Middlesbrough
Lancaster
Heysham
Keighley
York
Preston
Bradford
Burnley
Leeds
Bolton
Halifax
Wigan
Manchester
Dewsbury
Huddersfield
Liverpool
Oldham
Grimsby
Birkenhead
Warrington
Sheffield
Macclesfield
Nottingham
Derby
Spondon
Loughborough
Kings Lynn
Wolverhampton
Hinckley
Leicester
Norwich
Kidderminster
Birmingham
Coventry
Northampton
Ipswich
Felixstowe
Harwich
Braintree
Carmarthen
Pontypool
Stroud
London
Newport
Cardiff
Bristol
Bradford-on-Avon
Camberley
Croydon
Yeovil
Wilton
Southampton
Portsmouth
Axminster
Newton Abbot

160 Kilometres
100 Miles

Motor Vehicles and Aircraft
(Rubber, Tyres and related industries)

Industrial Areas
Motor Cars, Motor Vehicles
Commercial Vehicles
Earth moving Equipment and Tractors
Aircraft
Aero Engines
Assembly
Tyres
Car Exports

Scotstoun
Glasgow
Newbridge
Inchinnan
Bathgate
Linwood
Tannochside
East Kilbride
Prestwick
Belfast
Dundonald
Sunderland
Barnoldswick
Preston
Leyland
Brough
Manchester
Liverpool
Doncaster
Halewood
Chester
Ellesmore Port
Crewe
Derby
Birmingham
Rearsby
Solihull
Coventry
Leamington
Dunton
Oxford
Dunstable
Luton
Ebbw Vale
Abingdon
Hatfield
Enfield
Thurrock
Swansea
Langley
Hadley
Basildon
Bristol
London
Dagenham
Mountsorrel
Weybridge
Woolwich
Croydon
Yeovil
Southampton
Shoreham
Hurn
Bembridge

160 kilometres
100 miles

Building and Household

B Bricks
C Cement
Sl Slate
G Granite
Sa Sandstone
Ch China
K Kaolin
Sa Saw-milling
T Timber
F Furniture
H Hardware
C Cutlery
S Sewing Machines
Refrigerators
W Washing Machines
T Tools & Implements
L Linoleum & Linotiles
G Glass

Aberdeen
Corpach
Oban
Tayport
Singer
Kirkcaldy
Glasgow
Dunbar
Penicuik
Kilmarnock
Newcastle
Creetown
Hartlepool
Lancaster
Leeds
Hull
Liverpool
Manchester
St. Helens
Sheffield
Stoke
Peterborough
Wolverhampton
Rugby
Great Yarmouth
Birmingham
Bedford
Worcester
Harwich
Bristol
London
Cardiff
Southampton
St. Austell

Chemicals and Plastics

GC General Chemicals
S Soap
D Detergents
Ph Pharmaceuticals
Dy Dyestuffs
◯ Petrochemical Centres
R Rubber (Imported)
SR Synthetic Rubber
CP Chemical Products (Made from Rubber)
RP Rubber Plastics
RG Rubber Goods
NM Nuclear Materials
F Fertilisers

Aberdeen
Perth
Dundee
Glasgow
Leith
Grangemouth
Ardrossan
Galashiels
Newcastle
Durham
Billingham
Barnard Castle
Teesside
Sellafield
Middlesbrough
Selwick
Hull
Liverpool
Manchester
Birkenhead
Northwich
Capenhurst
Nottingham
Leicester
Birmingham
Norwich
Ipswich
Colchester
Swansea
Pontypool
London
Slough
Hythe

Paper, Printing and Publishing

△ Printing and Publishing
■ Paper and Paper Products

Aberdeen
Dundee
Edinburgh
Glasgow
Newcastle
Leeds
Hull
Liverpool
Manchester
Stafford
Nottingham
Norwich
Birmingham
Cambridge
Colchester
Oxford
High Wycombe
Hemel Hempstead
Purfleet
Cardiff
London
Sittingbourne
Bristol
Aylesford
Exeter

Pentland Firth 89 A7
Pentland Hills 65 G3
Pentraeth *Gwyn* 40 C4
Pentrefoelas *Gwyn* 41 E6
Penzance *Corn* 2 A5
Perranporth *Corn* 2 C3
Pershore *Heref/Worcs* 26 D3
Perth *Tay* 72 D2
Peterborough *Cambs* 37 G4
Peterculter *Gramp* 77 G1
Peterhead *Gramp* 83 H2
Peterlee *Durham* 54 D1
Petersfield *Hants* 10 D3
Petworth *W Sussex* 11 F3
Pewsey *Wilts* 17 F5
Philleigh *Corn* 2 D4
Pickering *N Yorks* 55 F6
Pickering, Vale of *N Yorks* 50 C2
Piercebridge *Durham* 54 B3
Pill *Som* 16 A4
Pinner *London* 19 E3
Pinwherry *S'clyde* 56 C4
Pistyll Rhaiadr, waterfall *Powys* 33 G2
Pitchcombe *Glos* 16 D1
Pitlochry *Tay* 76 A5
Pittenweem *Fife* 73 H4
Plockton *H'land* 79 F5
Pluckley *Kent* 13 E3
Plumpton *E Sussex* 12 A5
Plymouth *Devon* 4 B5
Plympton *Devon* 4 C5
Plynlimon Fawr, mts *Dyfed* 33 E5
Pocklington *Humber* 50 C3
Pologate *E Sussex* 12 C6
Polesden Lacey *Surrey* 19 E6
Pollokshaws *S'clyde* 64 C3
Polmont *Cent* 65 F1
Polperro *Corn* 3 G3
Polruan *Corn* 3 F3
Ponders End *London* 19 G2
Pont-erwyd *Dyfed* 33 E6
Pont-y-Berem *Dyfed* 23 F4
Pontardawe *W Glam* 23 H5
Pontarddulais *W Glam* 23 G5
Pontefract *W Yorks* 49 F5
Ponteland *N'land* 61 F4
Pontrhydfendigaid *Dyfed* 24 C2
Pontrilas *Heref/Worcs* 25 H5
Pontypool *Gwent* 15 G2
Pontypridd *Mid Glam* 15 F3
Poole *Dorset* 9 G5
Poolewe *H'lands* 78 F2
Porlock *Som* 7 F1
Port Appin *S'clyde* 74 B6
Port Askaig *Islay* 62 B1
Port Carlisle *Cumb* 59 G5
Port Charlotte *Islay* 62 A2
Port Ellen *Islay* 62 B3
Port Erin *I of Man* 46 A6
Port Erroll *Gramp* 83 H3
Port Eynon *W Glam* 14 B3
Port Glasgow *S'clyde* 64 B2
Port of Menteith *Cent* 72 A4
Port of Ness *Lewis* 88 C1
Port St Mary *I of Man* 46 A6
Port Seton *Loth* 66 B1
Port Talbot *W Glam* 14 D3
Port William *Dumf/Gal* 57 D7
Portencross *S'clyde* 64 A4
Portessie *Gramp* 82 D1
Portgordon *Gramp* 82 C1
Porthcawl *Mid Glam* 14 D4
Porthleven *Corn* 2 C5
Porthmadog *Gwyn* 32 D1
Portinscale *Cumb* 52 C3
Portishead *Avon* 16 A4
Portknockie *Gramp* 82 D1
Portland *Dorset* 9 E6
Portlethen *Gramp* 77 H2
Portmahomack *H'land* 87 C7
Portnacroish *S'clyde* 74 B6
Portnahaven *Islay* 62 A3
Portpatrick *Dumf/Gal* 57 A7
Portreath *Corn* 2 C4
Portree *Skye* 79 C5
Portsea *Hants* 10 D4
Portskewett *Gwent* 16 A3
Portslade-by-sea *E Sussex* 11 H4
Portsmouth *Hants* 10 D4
Portsonachan *S'clyde* 70 C3
Portsoy *Gramp* 83 E1
Postbridge *Devon* 4 C3
Potters Bar *Herts* 19 F2
Potton *Beds* 29 F3
Poulton-le-Fylde *Lancs* 47 E4
Powys, co 25 E3
Praze-an-Beeble *Corn* 2 C5
Preesall *Lancs* 47 E3
Prendergast *Dyfed* 22 C4
Prescott *Mersey* 42 A2
Prestatyn *Clwyd* 41 G3
Presteigne *Powys* 25 G2
Preston *Lancs* 47 F5
Preston Candover *Hants* 10 C1
Prestonpans *Loth* 66 B2
Prestwich *Lancs* 42 D1
Prestwick *S'clyde* 64 B6
Princes Risborough *Bucks* 18 C2
Princetown *Devon* 4 C3
Probus *Corn* 2 D3
Prudhoe *N'land* 61 F5
Puckeridge *Herts* 29 G5
Puddletown *Dorset* 9 E5
Pudsey *W Yorks* 49 E5
Pulborough *E Sussex* 11 F3
Pumpsaint *Dyfed* 24 C4
Purbeck, I of *Dorset* 9 F6
Purfleet *Essex* 20 B4
Purley *London* 19 G5
Purston Jaglin *W Yorks* 49 F6
Putford E & W *Devon* 6 C4
Putsham *Som* 16 F6
Pwllheli *Gwyn* 32 B2
Quantock Hills *Som* 8 A1
Queensborough *Kent* 21 E4
Queensbury *W Yorks* 48 D5
Queensferry, N *Fife* 73 E6
Queensferry, S *Loth* 73 E6
Quiraing, mt *Skye* 78 C3
Quoich, Loch *H'land* 74 B2
Quoich Bridge *H'land* 74 B2
Raasay, I *H'land* 79 D5
Radcliffe *Gtr Man* 42 D1
Radcliffe-on-Trent *Notts* 36 C1
Radlett *Herts* 19 F2
Radnor Forest *Powys* 25 F2
Radstock *Avon* 16 C5
Raglan *Gwent* 15 H1
Rainford *Lancs* 42 B2
Rainham *London* 20 B3
Ram *Dyfed* 24 B3
Ramasaig *Skye* 79 A5
Rampside *Lancs* 46 D2
Ramsbottom *Gtr Man* 47 H6
Ramsey *Cambs* 37 G5
Ramsey *I of Man* 46 C4
Ramsey I *Dyfed* 22 A3
Ramsgate *Kent* 13 H1
Rannoch, Loch *Tay* 75 F5
Rannoch, Moor of *S'clyde/Tay* 75 E6
Ratho *Loth* 65 G2
Ratinghope *Salop* 34 B4
Rattlesden *Suff* 30 D2
Rattray *Tay* 73 E1
Raunds *Northants* 29 E1
Ravenglass *Cumb* 52 B5
Ravenscar *N Yorks* 55 G4
Ravensthorpe *W Yorks* 49 E6
Rawdon *W Yorks* 49 E4
Rawmarsh *S Yorks* 43 H2
Rawtenstall *Lancs* 47 H5
Rayleigh *Essex* 20 D3
Raynham *Norf* 38 D2
Reading *Berks* 18 C4
Reay *H'land* 86 C2
Redbourn *Herts* 19 E1
Redbridge *London* 19 G3
Redcar *Clev* 55 E3
Redditch *Heref/Worcs* 27 E1
Redhill *Surrey* 19 G6
Redruth *Corn* 2 C4
Redwick *Glos* 16 B3
Reedham *Norf* 39 H4
Reekie Linn, waterfall *Tay* 76 C5
Reepham *Norf* 39 E3
Reeth *N Yorks* 54 A5
Regent's Park *London* 19 F3
Reigate *Surrey* 19 F6
Reighton *N Yorks* 51 F1
Rempstone *Notts* 36 B2
Renfrew *S'clyde* 64 C2
Renton *S'clyde* 64 B1
Rest and be Thankful *S'clyde* 70 D4
Reston *Borders* 67 F3
Retford (East Retford) *Notts* 44 B3
Rhayader *Powys* 25 E2
Rhayadr Mawr = Aber Falls
Rhayadr-y-Wennol = Swallow Falls
Rhiconich *H'land* 84 C3
Rhondda *Mid Glam* 15 E2
Rhoose *S Glam* 15 F4
Rhos *Dyfed* 23 E2
Rhosili *W Glam* 14 A3
Rhosllanerchrugog *Clwyd* 41 H6
Rhosneigr *Gwyn* 40 A4
Rhu *S'clyde* 64 A1
Rhuddlan *Clwyd* 41 F4
Rhyd Owen *Dyfed* 24 A4
Rhydtalog *Clwyd* 41 H5
Rhyl *Clwyd* 41 F3
Rhymney *Mid Glam* 15 F1
Riccall *N Yorks* 50 B4
Riccarton *S'clyde* 64 B5
Richards Castle *Salop* 26 A1
Richmond *N Yorks* 54 B4
Richmond *London* 19 F4
Rickinghall *Suff* 31 E1
Rickmansworth *Herts* 19 E2
Riding Mill *N'land* 61 E5
Ridsdale *N'land* 61 E3
Rievaulx *N Yorks* 55 E6
Ringford *Dumf/Gal* 58 C5
Ringway *Gtr Man* 42 D3
Ringwood *Hants* 9 H4
Rinns of Galloway 57 A6
Rinns of Islay 62 A3
Rinns of Kells *Dumf/Gal* 58 B3
Ripley *Derby* 43 H5
Ripley *N Yorks* 49 E2
Ripley *Surrey* 19 E5
Ripon *N Yorks* 49 E1
Ripponden *W Yorks* 48 C6
Risca *Gwent* 15 G3
Rishton *Lancs* 47 G5
Rivington *Lancs* 47 G6
Robertsbridge *E Sussex* 12 D4
Robin Hood's Bay *N Yorks* 55 G4
Roborough *Devon* 4 B4
Rochdale *Gtr Man* 42 D1
Roche *Corn* 3 E2
Rochester *Kent* 20 D5
Rochford *Essex* 20 E3
Rockcliffe *Cumb* 59 H5
Rode *Som* 16 C5
Rodel *Harris* 88 A4
Romford *London* 19 H3
Romiley *Ches* 42 E2
Romney Marsh *Kent* 13 F4
Romsey *Hants* 10 A3
Rosehearty *Gramp* 83 G1
Rosemarkie *H'land* 81 G2
Roslin *Loth* 66 A2
Ross-on-Wye *Heref/Worcs* 26 B5
Rosyth *Fife* 73 E6
Rothbury *N'land* 61 F2
Rotherfield *E Sussex* 12 B4
Rotherham *S Yorks* 43 H2
Rothes *Gramp* 82 B2
Rothesay *S'clyde* 63 G2
Rothwell *Northants* 36 D6
Rothwell *W Yorks* 49 E5
Rouken Glen *S'clyde* 64 C3
Rousay, I *Orkney* 89 B6
Rowardennan *Cent* 71 E5
Rowley Regis *W Mid* 35 F5
Roxburgh *Borders* 66 D5
Roy Bridge *H'land* 74 D3
Royal Leamington Spa = Leamington Spa, Royal
Royal Tunbridge Wells = Tunbridge Wells, Royal
Roydon *Essex* 20 B1
Royston *Herts* 29 G4
Royston *S Yorks* 43 H1
Royton *Gtr Man* 42 D1
Ruabon *Clwyd* 34 A1
Ruddington *Notts* 36 B2
Rufforth *N Yorks* 50 A3
Rufus's Stone *Hants* 10 A3
Rugby *Warks* 27 H1
Rugeley *Staffs* 35 F3
Ruislip *London* 19 E3
Rum, I *H'land* 68 B1
Rumbling Bridge *Tay* 72 D4
Runcorn *Ches* 42 B3
Rushden *Northants* 28 D1
Rushyford *Durham* 54 C2
Rutherglen *S'clyde* 64 D3
Ruthin *Clwyd* 41 G5
Ryde *I of Wight* 10 C5
Rye *E Sussex* 13 E5
Ryhope *Tyne/Wear* 61 H6
Ryton *Tyne/Wear* 61 F5
Saddleback (Blencathra), mt *Cumb* 52 C2
Saddleworth *Gtr Man* 43 E1
Saffron Walden *Essex* 30 A4
St Abb's Hd *Borders* 67 F2
St Agnes *Corn* 2 C3
St Albans *Herts* 19 F1
St Andrews *Fife* 73 G3
St Arvans *Gwent* 16 A2
St Asaph *Clwyd* 41 F4
St Austell *Corn* 3 E3
St Bees *Cumb* 52 A4
St Blazey *Corn* 3 F3
St Boswells *Borders* 66 D5
St Briavels *Glos* 16 B1
St Bride's B *Dyfed* 22 A4
St Buryan *Corn* 2 A5
St Catherines Pt *I of Wight* 10 B6
St Clears *Dyfed* 23 E4
St Columb Major *Corn* 3 E2
St Cyrus *Gramp* 77 G4
St David's *Dyfed* 22 A3
St Day *Corn* 2 C4
St Dennis *Corn* 3 E3
St Dogmaels *Dyfed* 22 D2
St Eval *Corn* 2 D2
St Fillans *Tay* 72 B2
St Helens *I of Wight* 10 C5
St Helens *Mersey* 42 B2
St Ives *Corn* 2 B4
St Ives *Cambs* 29 G1
St Johns *I of Man* 46 B5
St John's Chapel *Durham* 53 G1
St Just *Corn* 2 A5
St Keverne *Corn* 2 D6
St Leonard's *E Sussex* 12 D5
St Margaret's-at-Cliffe *Kent* 13 H3
St Mary's *Isles of Scilly* 2 A1
St Mary's Loch *Borders* 66 A6
St Mawes *Corn* 2 D5
St Mawgan *Corn* 2 D2
St Merryn *Corn* 2 D1
St Michaels-on-Wye *Lancs* 47 E4
St Monans (St Monance) *Fife* 73 H4
St Neots *Cambs* 29 F2
St Osyth *Essex* 31 E6
St Peter Port *Channel Is* 3 G5
St Peter's *Kent* 13 H1
Salcombe *Devon* 4 D6
Sale *Gtr Man* 42 D2
Salen *H'land* 68 E3
Salen *Mull* 68 D4
Salford *Gtr Man* 42 D2
Salisbury *Wilts* 9 H2
Salisbury Plain *Wilts* 17 E6
Salop, co 34 B4
Saltaire *W Yorks* 48 D4
Saltash *Corn* 3 H2
Saltburn-by-the-Sea *Clev* 55 E3
Saltcoats *S'clyde* 64 A5
Saltoun, E & W *Loth* 66 C2
Sampford Peverell *Devon* 7 G4
Sandal Magna *W Yorks* 49 E6
Sanday, I *Orkney* 89 C5
Sandbach *Ches* 42 D5
Sandbank *S'clyde* 70 D6
Sandbanks *Dorset* 9 G5
Sandford on Thames *Oxon* 18 A2
Sandgate *Kent* 13 G3
Sandhaven *Gramp* 83 G1
Sandhurst *Berks* 18 C5
Sandown *I of Wight* 10 C6
Sandown *Surrey* 19 E5
Sandringham *Norf* 38 B2
Sandwich *Kent* 13 H2
Sandy *Beds* 29 F3
Sanquhar *Dumf/Gal* 58 D1
Sarn Meylteyrn *Gwyn* 32 A2
Satterthwaite *Cumb* 52 C5
Saundersfoot *Dyfed* 22 D5
Sawbridgeworth *Herts* 30 A6
Sawtry *Cambs* 37 F6
Saxilby *Lincs* 44 D4
Saxmundham *Suff* 31 G2
Saxthorpe *Norf* 39 E2
Scafell Pike, mt *Cumb* 52 C4
Scalby *N Yorks* 55 H5
Scale Force, waterfall *Cumb* 52 B3
Scaleber Force, waterfall *N Yorks* 47 H2
Scalloway *Shet* 89 E7
Scalpay, I *Skye* 79 D5
Scampton *Lincs* 44 D3
Scapa Flow *Orkney* 89 B7
Scarba, I *S'clyde* 69 E7
Scarborough *N Yorks* 55 H6
Scarinish *S'clyde* 69 A7
Schiehallion, mt *Tay* 75 G5
Scilly, Isles of 2 A1
Scole *Norf* 39 F6
Scotch Corner *N Yorks* 54 B4
Scotforth *Lancs* 47 F2
Scourie *H'land* 84 B3
Scrabster *H'land* 86 D1
Sculthorpe *Norf* 38 D2
Scunthorpe *Humber* 44 D1
Scwd Henrhyd *Powys* 14 D1
Sea Houses *N'land* 67 H5
Seaford *E Sussex* 12 B6
Seaforth, Loch *Lewis* 88 B3
Seaham *Durham* 61 H6
Seamer *N Yorks* 55 H6
Seascale *Cumb* 52 A5
Seaton *Devon* 5 G2
Seaton Delaval *N'land* 61 G4
Seaton Sluice *N'land* 61 H4
Seaton Valley *N'land* 61 G4
Sedbergh *Cumb* 53 F5
Sedgfield *Durham* 54 C2
Sedgley *Staffs* 35 E5
Seil, I *S'clyde* 70 A3
Selbourne *Hants* 10 D2
Selby *N Yorks* 49 G5
Selkirk *Borders* 66 C5
Selsey *E Sussex* 11 E5
Sennybridge *Powys* 25 E5
Settle *N Yorks* 47 H2
Sevenoaks *Kent* 12 B2
Severn, R 16 A3
Severn Beach *Avon* 16 A3
Shaftesbury *Dorset* 9 F2
Shalford *Surrey* 19 E6
Shanklin *I of Wight* 10 C6
Shap *Cumb* 53 E3
Shapinsay, I *Orkney* 89 B6
Sharnbrook *Beds* 29 E2
Sharpness *Glos* 16 B2
Shaw *Gtr Man* 43 E1
Shawbury *Salop* 34 C2
Sheerness *Kent* 21 E4
Sheffield *S Yorks* 43 H3
Shefford *Beds* 29 F4
Shell Bay *Dorset* 9 G5
Shelve *Salop* 34 A4
Shenfield *Essex* 20 C2
Shenley *Herts* 19 F2
Shepperton *Surrey* 19 F5
Sheppey, I *Kent* 21 E4
Shepshed *Leics* 36 B3
Shepton Mallet *Som* 16 B6
Sherborne *Dorset* 8 D3
Sherburn-in-Elmet *N Yorks* 49 G5
Shere *Surrey* 19 E6
Sheriff Hutton *N Yorks* 49 H2
Sheriff Muir *Cent* 72 C4
Sheringham *Norf* 39 F1
Sherston *Wilts* 16 D3
Sherwood Forest 44 B5
Shetland Is, and reg 89
Shiel, Loch *H'land* 68 F2
Shiel Bridge *H'land* 68 E2
Shiel Bridge *H'land* 80 A5
Shieldaig *H'land* 78 F4
Shifnal *Salop* 34 D3
Shilbottle *N'land* 61 G1
Shildon *Durham* 54 B2
Shillinglee Park *W Sussex* 11 F2
Shin, Loch *H'land* 85 E5
Shipley *W Yorks* 48 D4
Shipston-on-Stour *Warks* 27 G3
Shipton-under-Wychwood *Oxon* 27 G5
Shirehampton *Avon* 16 A4
Shirenewton *Gwent* 16 A2
Shirrell Heath *Hants* 10 C3
Shoeburyness *Essex* 21 E3
Shoreham-by-Sea *W Sussex* 11 H4
Shorwell *I of Wight* 10 B6
Shotley Bridge *Durham* 61 F6
Shottermill *Surrey* 11 E2
Shotts *S'clyde* 65 F3
Shrewsbury *Salop* 34 C3
Sidlaw Hills *Tay* 73 E2
Sidmouth *Devon* 5 G2
Siggleshorne *Humber* 51 F4
Silchester *Hants* 18 B5
Silloth *Cumb* 59 F6
Silsden *W Yorks* 48 C4
Silsoe *Beds* 29 E4
Silverstone *Northants* 28 B3
Singleton *W Sussex* 11 E4
Sissinghurst *Kent* 12 D3
Sittingbourne *Kent* 13 E1
Sizewell *Suff* 31 H2
Skateraw *Gramp* 77 H2
Skegness *Lincs* 45 H5
Skelmanthorpe *W Yorks* 43 G1
Skelmersdale *Lancs* 42 A1
Skelton *Cumb* 52 D2
Skelton *Clev* 55 E3
Skelwith Force, waterfall *Lancs* 52 D4
Skewen *W Glam* 14 C2
Skiddaw, mt *Cumb* 52 C2
Skipton *N Yorks* 48 C3
Skipwith *N Yorks* 49 H4
Skirling *Borders* 65 G4
Skye, I *H'land* 79 C5
Slaidburn *Lancs* 47 G3
Slaithwaite *W Yorks* 48 D6
Slaley *N'land* 61 E5
Slamannan *Cent* 65 E2
Sleaford *Lincs* 37 F1
Sleat, Sound of *H'land* 79 E7
Sligachan Hotel *Skye* 79 C6
Slimbridge *Glos* 26 C6
Slingsby *N Yorks* 50 C1
Slioch, mt *H'land* 80 A1
Slough *Berks* 18 D3
Sma' Glen *Tay* 72 C2
Smailholm *Borders* 66 D5
Smethwick *W Mid* 35 F5
Smoo Cave *H'land* 84 D2
Snaefell, mt *I of Man* 46 B4
Snaith *Humber* 49 H5
Snape *Suff* 31 G2
Snetterton *Norf* 38 D5
Snitterfield *Warks* 27 F2
Snizort, Loch *Skye* 78 B3
Snowdon *Gwyn* 40 C6
Soay, I *Skye* 79 C7
Soham *Cambs* 30 B1
Solent, The 10 C5
Solihull *W Mid* 35 G6
Solva *Dyfed* 22 A3
Somercoates *Derby* 43 H5
Somerset, co 8 A1
Somersham *Cambs* 29 B1
Somerton *Som* 8 C2
Sonning *Berks* 18 C4
Soutergate *Lancs* 46 D1
South Bank *Clev* 54 D3
South Brent *Devon* 4 D4
South Cave *Humber* 50 D5
South Cerney *Glos* 17 E2
South Downs *E & W Sussex* 11 E3
South Foreland *Kent* 13 H3
South Glamorgan, co 15 F4
South Kirkby *W Yorks* 49 F6
South Molton *Devon* 7 E3
South Ockendon *Essex* 20 C3
South Petherton *Som* 8 C3
South Rona *H'land* 78 D3
South Ronaldsay, I *Orkney* 89 B7
South Shields *Tyne/Wear* 61 H4
South Uist, I *W Isles* 88 E3
South Willingham *Lincs* 45 F3
South Yorkshire, co 44
Southam *Warks* 27 H2
Southampton *Hants* 10 B3
Southampton Water *Hants* 10 B4
Southborough *Kent* 12 C3
Southend *S'clyde* 62 D6
Southend-on-Sea *Essex* 21 E3
Southery *Norf* 38 B5
Southminster *Essex* 21 E2
Southport *Mersey* 46 D6
Southrop *Glos* 27 G6
Southsea *Hants* 10 D6
Southwark *London* 19 G4
Southwell *Notts* 44 B5
Southwick *W Sussex* 11 H4
Southwold *Suff* 31 H1
Soutra Hill *Loth* 66 C3
Sowerby Bridge *W Yorks* 48 C5
Spalding *Lincs* 37 G2
Sparkford *Som* 8 D2
Spean Bridge *H'land* 74 D3
Speeton *N Yorks* 51 F1
Speke *Lancs* 42 A3
Spenborough *W Yorks* 48 D5
Spencers Wood *Berks* 18 C5
Spennymoor *Durham* 54 B2
Spey, R 81 H5
Spey Bay *Gramp* 82 C1
Spilsby *Lincs* 45 G4
Spithead 10 C5
Spittal of Glenshee *Tay* 76 B4
Spofforth *N Yorks* 49 F3
Springfield *Fife* 73 F3
Sproatley *Humber* 51 F5
Sprouston *Borders* 67 E5
Squires Gate *Lancs* 46 D5
Stadhampton *Oxon* 18 B2
Staffa, I *S'clyde* 69 B5
Staffin *Skye* 78 C3
Stafford *Staffs* 35 F2
Staffordshire, co 35 E2
Stagshaw Bank *N'land* 61 E4
Staindrop *Durham* 54 A3
Staines *Surrey* 19 E4
Stainforth *S Yorks* 49 H6
Staithes *N Yorks* 55 F3
Stalbridge *Dorset* 9 E3
Stalham *Norf* 39 G2
Stalybridge *Gtr Man* 43 E2
Stamford *Lincs* 37 E4
Stamfordham *N'land* 61 F4
Standish *Lancs* 42 B1
Standlake *Oxon* 17 G2
Stanford-in-the-Vale *Oxon* 17 G2
Stanford-le-Hope *Essex* 20 C3
Stanhope *Durham* 53 H1
Stanley *Durham* 61 G6
Stanley *Tay* 73 E2
Stanley *W Yorks* 49 E5
Stanley Force, waterfall *Cumb* 52 B5
Stannington *N'land* 61 G4
Stansted *Essex* 29 H5
Stanton *Suff* 30 D1
Stanton Harcourt *Oxon* 17 H1
Stanwix *Cumb* 60 A5
Stapleford *Cambs* 29 H3
Stapleford *Notts* 36 B1
Stapleford *Wilts* 9 G1
Stapleford Abbotts *Essex* 20 B2
Starbeck *N Yorks* 49 E3
Start Pt *Devon* 5 E6
Staunton *Glos* 26 C4
Staunton *Glos* 26 B6
Staunton-on-Wye *Heref/Worcs* 25 H3
Staveley *Cumb* 52 D6
Staveley *Derby* 43 H4
Staverton *Glos* 26 D5
Steall Fall *H'land* 74 C4
Steeple Aston *Oxon* 27 H5
Stevenage *Herts* 29 F5
Stevenston *S'clyde* 64 A4
Stewarton *S'clyde* 64 B4
Steyning *W Sussex* 11 G4
Stibb Cross *Devon* 6 C4
Stickford *Lincs* 45 G5

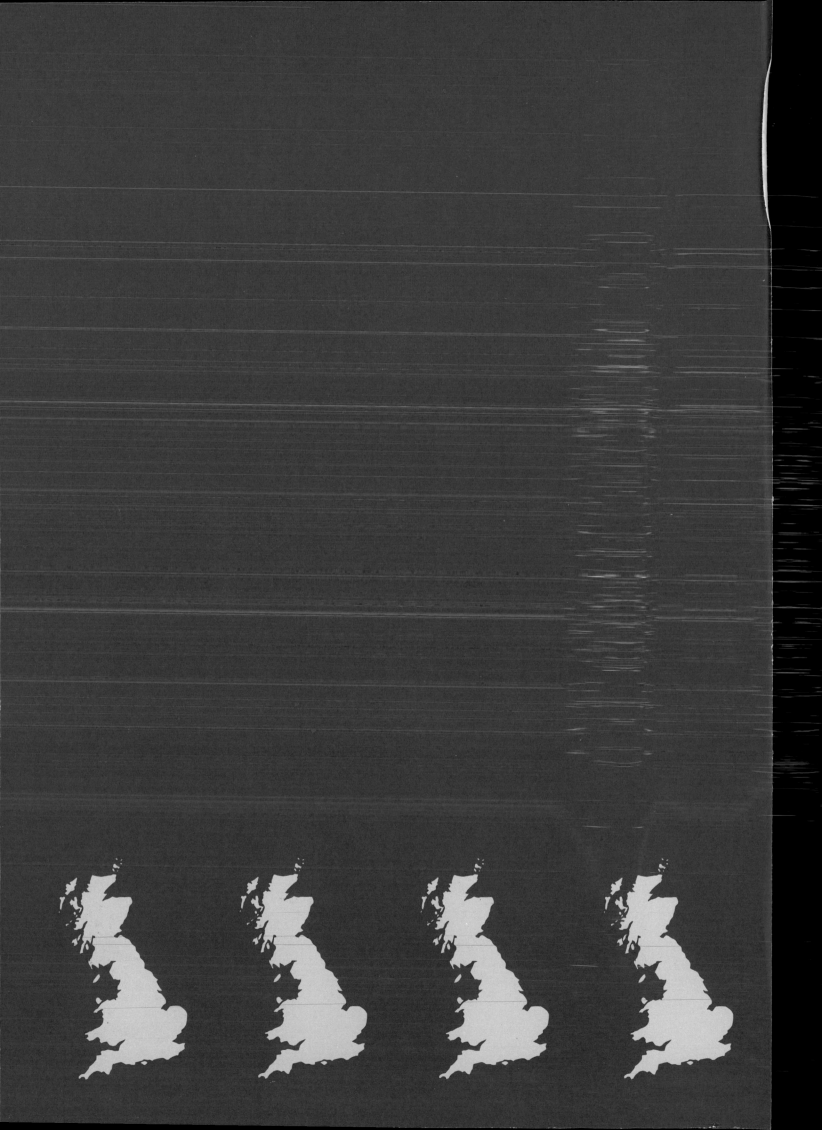

Index Abbreviations

Abbreviation	Name
—	Avon
Beds	Bedfordshire
Berks	Berkshire
—	Borders
Bucks	Buckinghamshire
Cambs	Cambridgeshire
Cent	Central
Ches	Cheshire
Clev	Cleveland
—	Clwyd
Corn	Cornwall
Cumb	Cumbria
Derby	Derbyshire
Devon	Devonshire
—	Dorset
Dumf/Gal	Dumfries and Galloway
—	Durham
—	Dyfed
E Sussex	East Sussex
—	Essex
—	Fife
Glos	Glostershire
Gramp	Grampian
Gtr Man	Greater Manchester
—	Gwent
Gwyn	Gwynedd
Hants	Hampshire
Heref/Worcs	Hereford and Worcester
Herts	Hetfordshire
H'land	Highland
Humber	Humberside
I of Man	Isle of Man
I of Wight	Isle of Wight
—	Kent
Lancs	Lancashire
Leics	Leicestershire
Lincs	Lincolnshire
—	London
Loth	Lothian
Mersey	Merseyside
Mid Glam	Mid Glamorgan
Norf	Norfolk
N Yorks	North Yorkshire
Northants	Northamptonshire
N'land	Northumberland
Notts	Nottinghamshire
—	Orkney
Oxon	Oxfordshire
—	Powys
Salop	Shropshire
Shet	Shetland
Som	Somerset
S Glam	South Glamorgan
S Yorks	South Yorkshire
Staffs	Staffordshire
S'clyde	Strathclyde
Suff	Suffolk
—	Surrey
Tay	Tayside
Tyne/Wear	Tyne and Wear
Warks	Warwickshire
W Glam	West Glamorgan
W Mid	West Midland
W Sussex	West Sussex
W Yorks	W Yorkshire
W isles	Western Isles
Wilts	Wiltshire

Abbreviation	Meaning
B	Bay
Br	Bridge
C	Cape
co	county
div	division
E	East
Hd	Head
I	Island
L	Lake, Loch, Lough
mt	Mountain
N	North
pen	Peninsula
Pt	Point
R	River
reg	Region
Res	Reservoir
S	South
St	Saint
W	West
=	cross reference

Index refers to Touring Map section, pages 2-89

Abbey St Bathans *Borders* **67 E 3**
Abbey Town *Cumb* **59 F 6**
Abbeystead *Lancs* **47 F 3**
Abbots Bromley *Staffs* **35 G2**
Abbotsbury *Dorset* **8 D5**
Abbotsford *Borders* **66 C5**
Abbotsinch *S'clyde* **64 C2**
Aber Falls *Gwyn* **40 D4**
Aber Glaslyn, Pass of *Gwyn* **40 C6**
Aberaeron *Dyfed* **24 A2**
Aberavon *W Glam* **14 D3**
Aberbeeg *Gwent* **15 G2**
Abercarn *Gwent* **15 G2**
Aberchirder *Gramp* **83 E 2**
Aberdare *Mid Glam* **15 E 2**
Aberdaron *Gwyn* **32 A2**
Aberdeen *Gramp* **83 G6**
Aberdour *Fife* **73 E 5**
Aberdyfi *Gwyn* **32 D5**
Aberfeldy *Tay* **76 A6**
Aberffraw *Gwyn* **40 A4**
Aberford *W Yorks* **49 F 4**
Aberfoyle *Cent* **71 F 4**
Abergavenny *Gwent* **15 G1**
Abergele *Clwyd* **41 F 4**
Abergiar *Dyfed* **24 B4**
Abergwili *Dyfed* **24 A5**
Aberlady *Loth* **66 C1**
Aberlour *Gramp* **82 B3**
Abernethy *Tay* **73 E 3**
Aberporth *Dyfed* **23 E 1**
Abersoch *Gwyn* **32 B2**
Abersychan *Gwent* **15 G1**
Aberthaw *S Glam* **15 F 4**
Abertillery *Gwent* **15 G1**
Aberystwyth *Dyfed* **32 D6**
Abingdon *Oxon* **17 H2**
Abinger Common *Surrey* **11 G1**
Abington *S'clyde* **65 F 6**
Aboyne *Gramp* **77 E 2**
Abram *Lancs* **42 B2**
Accrington *Lancs* **47 H5**
Acharacle *H'land* **68 E 2**
Achiltibuie *H'land* **85 A6**
Achnasheen *H'land* **80 C2**
Achray, Loch *Cent* **71 F 4**
Achterneed *H'land* **81 E 2**
Acle *Norf* **39 G4**
Acocks Green *W Mid* **35 G5**
Acton *London* **19 F 3**
Acton Turville *Glos* **16 C3**
Adderbury *Oxon* **27 H4**
Addlestone *Surrey* **19 E 5**
Adlington *Lancs* **42 B1**
Adwick-le-Street *S Yorks* **44 A1**
Ailort, Loch *H'land* **68 E 2**
Ailsa Craig, I *S'clyde* **56 A4**
Aintree *Lancs* **42 A2**
Aira Force, waterfall *Cumb* **52 D3**
Airedale *W Yorks* **48 C4**
Aird of Sleat *Skye* **79 D7**
Airdrie *S'clyde* **65 E 2**
Aireborough *W Yorks* **49 E 4**
Airth *Cent* **72 C5**
Alcester *Warks* **27 E 2**
Alconbury *Cambs* **29 F 1**
Aldbourne *Wilts* **17 G4**
Aldbrough *Humber* **51 F 4**
Aldeburgh *Suff* **31 H3**
Alderley Edge *Ches* **42 D3**
Aldermaston *Berks* **18 B5**
Alderney, I *Channel Is* **3 G4**
Aldershot *Hants* **18 C6**
Alderton *Suff* **31 G4**
Aldford *Ches* **42 A5**
Aldridge-Brownhills *Staffs* **35 F 4**
Alexandra Park *London* **19 G3**
Alexandria *S'clyde* **64 B1**
Alfold *Surrey* **11 F 2**
Alford *Gramp* **83 E 5**
Alford *Lincs* **45 H4**
Alfreton *Derby* **43 H5**
Alfriston *E Sussex* **12 B6**
All Stretton *Salop* **34 B4**
Allendale Town *N'land* **60 D5**
Allenheads *N'land* **53 G1**
Allerston *N Yorks* **55 G6**
Allerton *W Yorks* **48 D4**
Alloa *Cent* **72 C5**
Allonby *Cumb* **59 F 6**
Alloway *S'clyde* **56 D2**
Allt na Caillich, waterfall *H'land* **84 E 3**
Alness *H'land* **81 F 1**
Alnmouth *N'land* **61 G1**
Alnwick *N'land* **61 F 1**
Alrewas *Staffs* **35 G3**
Alsager *Ches* **42 D5**
Alston *Cumb* **53 F 1**
Altguish *H'land* **85 D8**
Altnacealgach *H'land* **85 C6**
Altnaharra *H'land* **84 F 4**
Alton *Hants* **10 D1**
Altrincham *Gtr Man* **42 D3**
Alva *Cent* **72 C5**
Alvechurch *Heref/Worcs* **27 E 1**
Alwinton *N'land* **60 E 1**
Alyth *Tay* **76 C6**
Amberley *W Sussex* **11 F 4**
Amble *N'land* **61 G2**
Ambleside *Cumb* **52 D4**
Amersham *Bucks* **18 D2**
Amesbury *Wilts* **9 H1**
Amlwch *Gwyn* **40 B2**
Ammanford *Dyfed* **14 C1**
Ampleforth *N Yorks* **50 B1**
Ampthill *Beds* **29 E 4**
Amulree *Tay* **72 C1**
Ancaster *Lincs* **44 D6**
Ancrum *Borders* **66 D6**
Andover *Hants* **10 B1**
Angle *Dyfed* **22 B5**
Angmering-on-Sea *W Sussex* **11 G5**
Annan *Dumf/Gal* **59 G4**
Annfield Plain *Durham* **61 F 6**
Anstruther *Fife* **73 H4**
Apperley *Glos* **26 D4**
Appersett *N Yorks* **53 G5**
Appleby *Cumb* **53 F 3**
Applecross *H'land* **78 E 4**
Appledore *Devon,* **6 C2**
Appledore *Kent* **13 E 4**
Arborfield Cross *Berks* **18 C4**
Arbroath *Tay* **73 H1**
Archiestown *Gramp* **82 B3**
Ardeonaig *Cent* **72 B2**
Ardersier *H'land* **81 G2**
Ardessie, waterfall *H'land* **85 A7**
Ardgay *H'land* **85 F 7**
Ardgour *H'land* **74 B5**
Ardleigh *Essex* **31 E 5**
Ardlui *S'clyde* **71 E 3**
Ardnamurchan *H'land* **68 C3**
Ardrishaig *S'clyde* **70 A6**
Ardrossan *S'clyde* **64 A4**
Ardsley *S Yorks* **43 H1**
Ardvasar *Skye* **79 E 7**
Arisaig *H'land* **68 E 1**
Arkaig, Loch *H'land* **74 B2**
Arksey *S Yorks* **44 B1**
Arlingham *Glos* **16 C1**
Armadale *H'land* **86 A2**
Armadale *Loth* **65 F 2**
Arnisdale *H'land* **79 F 7**
Arnold *Notts* **44 B6**
Arnside *Cumb* **47 F 1**
Arran, I *S'clyde* **63 F 4**
Arrochar *S'clyde* **71 E 4**
Arthur's Seat, hill *Loth* **65 H2**
Arundel *W Sussex* **11 F 4**
Ascog *Bute* **63 G2**
Ascot *Berks* **18 D4**
Ashbourne *Derby* **43 F 6**
Ashburton *Devon* **4 D4**
Ashbury *Berks* **17 G3**
Ashby-de-la-Zouch *Leics* **35 H3**
Ashby Woulds *Leics* **35 H3**
Ashdale Falls *Bute* **63 G5**
Ashdown Forest *E Sussex* **12 B4**
Ashford *Kent* **13 F 3**
Ashford *Surrey* **19 E 4**
Ashington *N'land* **61 G3**
Ashkirk *Borders* **66 C6**
Ashley *Staffs* **34 D1**
Ashover *Derby* **43 H4**
Ashtead *Surrey* **19 F 5**
Ashton-in-Makerfield *Gtr Man* **42 B2**
Ashton-under-Lyne *Gtr Man* **43 E 2**
Askam *Lancs* **46 D1**
Askrigg *N Yorks* **53 H5**
Aspatria *Cumb* **52 B1**
Aspull *Lancs* **42 B1**
Assynt, Loch *H'land* **85 C5**
Aston Cross *Glos* **26 D4**
Atherstone *Warks* **35 H4**
Atherton *Gtr Man* **42 C1**
Attleborough *Norf* **39 E 5**
Attlebridge *Norf* **39 F 3**
Auchenblae *Gramp* **77 G3**
Auchinleck *S'clyde* **64 C6**
Auchmithie *Tay* **77 F 6**
Auchterarder *Tay* **72 C3**
Auchterderran *Fife* **73 E 5**
Auchtermuchty *Fife* **73 E 3**
Audenshaw *Lancs* **42 D2**
Audlem *Ches* **34 D1**
Audley End *Essex* **30 A4**
Auldearn *H'land* **81 H2**
Aultbea *H'land* **78 F 1**
Aultguish, waterfall *H'land* **80 D6**
Aust *Glos* **16 B3**
Avebury *Wilts* **17 E 4**
Avening *Glos* **16 D2**
Aveton Gifford *Devon* **4 D5**
Aviemore *H'land* **81 H6**
Avoch *H'land* **81 F 2**
Avon, co **16 B4**
Avonmouth *Avon* **16 A4**
Awbridge *Hants* **10 A2**
Awe, Loch *S'clyde* **70 B4**
Axbridge *Som* **15 H5**
Axe Edge *Derby-Staffs* **43 E 4**
Axminster *Devon* **5 H1**
Aycliffe *Durham* **54 C3**
Aylesbury *Bucks* **18 C1**
Aylesford *Kent* **12 D1**
Aylsham *Norf* **39 F 2**
Aymestrey *Heref/Worcs* **25 H1**
Ayr *S'clyde* **56 D2**
Aysgarth *N Yorks* **53 H5**
Aysgarth Force, waterfall *N Yorks* **54 A5**
Ayton *Borders* **67 F 3**
Babbacombe *Devon* **5 E 4**
Bacup *Lancs* **47 H5**
Badachro *H'land* **78 E 2**
Badcall *H'land* **84 B3**
Bagillt *Clwyd* **41 H4**
Baginton *Warks* **35 H6**
Bagshot *Surrey* **18 D5**
Baildon *W Yorks* **48 D4**
Baillieston *S'clyde* **64 D3**
Bainbridge *N Yorks* **53 H5**
Bakewell *Derby* **43 G4**
Bala *Gwyn* **33 F 1**
Balallan *Lewis* **88 B2**
Balby *S Yorks* **44 B1**
Baldock *Herts* **29 F 4**
Baldwin *I of Man* **46 B5**
Balerno *Loth* **65 H2**
Balfron *Cent* **64 C1**
Balintore *H'land* **81 G1**
Ballachulish *H'land* **74 C5**
Ballagan, Spout of, waterfall *Cent* **64 C1**
Ballantrae *S'clyde* **57 B5**
Ballasalla *I of Man* **46 B6**
Ballater *Gramp* **76 D2**
Ballaugh *I of Man* **46 B4**
Ballindalloch Castle *Gramp* **82 B3**
Ballinluig *Tay* **76 A5**
Balloch *S'clyde* **64 B1**
Balmacara *H'land* **79 F 5**
Balmaclellan *Dumf/Gal* **58 F 3**
Balmoral Castle *Gramp* **76 C2**
Balquhidder *Cent* **71 F 3**
Balsham *Cambs* **30 B3**
Bamber Bridge *Lancs* **47 F 5**
Bamburgh *N'land* **67 H5**
Bampton *Devon* **7 G3**
Bampton *Oxon* **17 G2**
Banavie *H'land* **74 C4**
Banbury *Oxon* **27 H3**
Banchory *Gramp* **77 F 2**
Banff *Gramp* **83 E 1**
Bangor *Gwyn* **40 C4**
Bankend *Dumf/Gal* **59 E 4**
Bankfoot *Tay* **72 D2**
Bannockburn *Cent* **72 C5**
Banstead *Surrey* **19 F 5**
Bardney *Lincs* **45 E 4**
Bardon Mill *N'land* **60 D5**
Bardsea *Lancs* **46 D1**
Bardsey, I *Gwyn* **32 A3**
Barford *Warks* **27 G2**
Barking *London* **19 H3**
Barlborough *Derby* **44 A3**
Barmouth *Gwyn* **32 D3**
Barnard Castle *Durham* **54 A3**
Barnby Moor *Notts* **44 B3**
Barnet *London* **19 F 2**
Barnoldswick *Lancs* **47 H3**
Barnsley *S Yorks* **43 G1**
Barnstaple *Devon* **6 D2**
Barr *S'clyde* **56 C4**
Barra, I *W Isles* **88 D3**
Barrhead *S'clyde* **64 C3**
Barrhill *S'clyde* **57 C5**
Barrow-in-Furness *Cumb* **46 D2**
Barrowford *Lancs* **47 H4**
Barry *Tay* **73 G1**
Barry *S Glam* **15 F 4**
Barton-in-the-Clay *Beds* **29 E 4**
Barton-upon-Humber *Humber* **51 E 5**
Barton-under-Needwood *Staffs* **35 G3**
Baschurch *Salop* **34 B2**
Basildon *Essex* **20 D3**
Basingstoke *Hants* **18 B6**
Baslow *Derby* **43 G4**
Bass Rock I. *Loth* **73 H5**
Bassenthwaite *Cumb* **52 C2**
Bassingbourn *Cambs* **29 G3**
Bath *Avon* **16 C5**
Bathgate *Loth* **65 F 2**
Batley *W Yorks* **49 E 5**
Battle *E Sussex* **12 D5**
Battlesbridge *Essex* **20 D2**
Bawdeswell *Norf* **39 E 3**
Bawdsey *Suff* **31 G4**
Bawtry *S Yorks* **44 B2**
Baycliff *Lancs* **46 D1**
Baythorn End *Essex* **30 C4**
Beachley *Glos* **16 B3**
Beachy Head *Sussex* **12 C6**
Beaconsfield *Bucks* **18 D3**
Beaminster *Dorset* **8 C4**
Bearsden *S'clyde* **64 C2**
Beattock *Dumf/Gall* **59 F 2**
Beaulieu *Hants* **10 B4**
Beauly *H'land* **81 E 3**
Beaumaris *Gwyn* **40 C4**
Bebington *Ches* **41 H3**
Beccles *Suff* **39 H5**
Beckenham *London* **19 G4**
Beckingham *Notts* **44 C2**
Beckington *Som* **16 C6**
Bedale *N Yorks* **54 B5**
Beddgelert *Gwyn* **40 C6**
Bedford *Beds* **29 E 3**
Bedfordshire, co **29 E 3**
Bedgebury *Kent* **12 D3**
Bedlington *N'land* **61 G3**
Bedwas *Gwent* **15 G3**
Bedwelty *Gwent* **15 G2**
Bedworth *Warks* **36 A5**
Beeley *Derby* **43 G4**
Beer *Devon* **5 G2**
Beeston *Notts* **36 B1**
Beeston *W Yorks* **49 E 5**
Begelly *Dyfed* **22 D5**
Beinn Dearg, mt *Tay* **75 H3**
Beith *S'clyde* **64 B3**
Belford *N'land* **67 G5**
Bellingham *N'land* **60 D3**
Belper *Derby* **43 H6**
Belsay *N'land* **61 F 4**
Belvoir *Leics* **36 D1**
Bembridge *I of Wight* **10 D5**
Ben Alder, mt *H'land* **75 F 4**
Ben Cruachan, mt *S'clyde* **70 C2**
Ben Hope, mt *H'land* **84 E 3**
Ben Lawers, mt *Tay* **71 G1**
Ben Lomond, mt *Cent* **71 E 4**
Ben Macdui, mt *Gramp* **76 A2**
Ben More, mt *Mull* **69 D5**
Ben More, mt *Cent* **71 F 3**
Ben More Assynt, mt *H'land* **85 D5**
Ben Nevis, mt *H'land* **74 C4**
Ben Vorlich, mt *S'clyde* **71 E 4**

INDEX